Jan-Peter Herbst & Jonas Menze

Gear Acquisition Syndrome

Consumption of Instruments and Technology in Popular Music

Published by University of Huddersfield Press

University of Huddersfield Press
The University of Huddersfield
Queensgate
Huddersfield HD1 3DH

Email enquiries university.press@hud.ac.uk

First published 2021

Every effort has been made to locate copyright holders of materials included and to obtain permission for their publication.

The publisher is not responsible for the continued existence and accuracy of websites referenced in the text.

A CIP catalogue record for this book is available from the British Library.

ISBN: 978-1-86218-184-7
e-ISBN: 978-1-86218-185-4

Cover design by Erika Herbst

Foreword

A few months ago, I was struck by a strong urge to buy a new electric guitar. I already owned several. Some—a lovely purple Ibanez, a cheap red Hamer—lay in various states of disrepair. I had retired a red Gibson Les Paul Studio guitar several years ago, which now sits neglected, rarely taken out of its case. The guitar with which I had replaced it, a brown sunburst Gibson Les Paul Signature "T," is my favorite guitar in terms of sound and playability, but as my aging body has become more subject to back and shoulder pain, it has become too heavy to play comfortably. So, too, has my far less expensive but still very fine 'Made in Mexico' Fender Stratocaster. I bought a lighter guitar, a Guild Bluesbird, that has mostly served me well in recent years, but has sometimes been unreliable. My goal, then, was to purchase another lightweight solid-body electric guitar that would prove to be sturdy while having great sound, good feel, and a nice aesthetic design. It did not take long for me to set my sights on a Gibson SG, a guitar I had long coveted and almost bought in the past. But then several other questions arose: which model of SG, or year? Did I want a brand new instrument or a used one? Was I willing to pay a high price for a 'vintage' SG or would a more recent model suffice? I spent the better part of a month exploring my various options, reading online reviews of different SG models and years, before finally settling on a used SG '61 Reissue model made in 2006 that I found for a reasonable price on the online musical instrument and gear mega-site Reverb.com. I have played the new guitar nearly every day since my purchase and remain pleased with my choice. For now, my guitar collection feels sufficient to suit my needs. However, the purchase of a new amp may not be too far in the future…

Do I suffer from GAS, or Gear Acquisition Syndrome, the phenomenon that gives this book by Jan Herbst and Jonas Menze its title? I have never considered myself to have anything like an excessive interest in buying guitars and related gear. The guitars that I own have been accumulated over decades, although I have admittedly purchased more in the last ten years—three—than at any previous time. Yet that can be explained by different factors: my increased disposable income as I have advanced in my academic career; the fact that I joined a band at the age of 48; and as alluded to above, my aging body which has entailed searching for a guitar that is comfortable to play. I own three amplifiers, each with a distinct purpose: one is my full-time amp that I play at home and when I gig; one stays in my office on campus; and one resides in the space where I rehearse with my band. My pedal collection is notably small, and many of the pedals that I own I acquired more than twenty years ago, such as an early generation Boss DD-2 digital delay dating from the mid-1980s. The only significant recent addition is an MXR Super Badass distortion pedal, which I use all the time to feed into my Traynor tube amp. Otherwise, I mostly prefer the straightforward signal that exists between my guitar and amplifier, something that sets me apart from so many contemporary players whose well-stocked pedal boards are a key to their expressiveness.

My moderation might make me an unlikely victim of GAS. The popular image of GAS is one of excessive, extreme behavior, of unregulated desire for that next object, the purchase of which only leads to temporary satisfaction before the quest begins again with a new target. While some have treated GAS as though it merits serious consideration as a psychological disorder, more common is the tendency to present it with humor, as Jay Wright does in what has been to date the only book-length treatment of the subject. In a passage quoted by Herbst and Menze, Wright (2006: 22) observes:

> GAS can strike you at any time, but onset normally occurs upon seeing, hearing, or touching a particular axe. The attack itself can range from mild to severe... You drool, you stare, you drool some more... Your mind races, as you imagine the rest of your life with this baby in it—how much more skilled, happy, and fulfilled you would be... You're faced with two immediate problems: 1) how to find relief from this powerful force, and 2) how to manage a transfer of ownership. That, my friend, is a GAS attack.

I am tempted to say that Herbst and Menze address the topic with more seriousness, but that does not tell you very much. More to the point, they address GAS with far more nuance than available commentaries have typically done. In their analysis, GAS is comprised of a complex set of motivations, some eminently practical and some thoroughly driven by emotion. Rather than draw a strict line between those impulses that may be deemed 'healthy' and those that may appear 'unhealthy,' they view the phenomenon as existing along a continuum wherein the pragmatic drive for improvement and a more basic sort of wish-fulfillment are always vying with each other for supremacy. From their perspective, GAS is a particular manifestation of the wider field of desires and practices that arise from living in a society and an economy that are organized to a large degree through acts of consumption.

In his groundbreaking study of digital music technologies, Paul Théberge emphasized the degree to which consumerism had become central to what musicians do *as* musicians. With the advent of affordable digital synthesizers in the 1980s, electronic keyboard instruments were equipped with an expanding range of pre-set sounds that the practicing musician could select at the touch of a few buttons. Addressing this new availability of ready-made electronic sounds that were designed to emulate everything from a violin to a snare drum to a digeridoo, Théberge (1997: 200) asserted:

> In effect, musical production has become closely allied to a form of *consumer* practice, where the process of selecting the 'right' pre-fabricated sounds and effects for a given musical context has become as important as 'making' music in the first place. Musicians are not simply consumers of new technologies, rather their entire

approach to music-making has been transformed so that consumption...has become implicated in their musical practices at the most fundamental level.

GAS might be seen as an outgrowth of this development. As Herbst and Menze demonstrate, many musicians spend as much or more time shopping for new gear—whether instruments, effect pedals, amplifiers, or for horn players, new mouthpieces—as they do playing their instruments. They do so out of a hope or conviction that a new piece of equipment will reinvigorate their playing or expand their stylistic range by giving them new sounds or techniques to apply. In this way, and following from the insights of Théberge, the act of purchasing new equipment is not only incidental to their musical lives and identities but is essential and inextricable from the self-definition of contemporary musicians.

Study of these aspects of modern music culture has remained limited in the more than two decades since Théberge's work appeared. When music consumption is treated by scholars, it is nearly always the consumption of recordings that is at issue. While musical instruments have begun to receive more dedicated analysis in recent years, the 'new organology' as it has sometimes been called has not typically placed consumption at the forefront of concern. Herbst and Menze's study of Gear Acquisition Syndrome therefore constitutes the most concerted and substantial effort to address the drives and processes through which musicians acquire the tools of their trade to appear in many years, and this book makes plain why the subject deserves attention and how much we have left to learn about it.

Central to the book's success is the authors' deft balance between theoretical and empirical considerations. Theoretically, they employ concepts such as Robert Stebbins' notion of 'serious leisure' and Russell Belk's idea of the way that consumer items contribute to the formation of an 'extended self' to explain why the purchase of instruments and associated gear has such consequence for understanding how musicians think of themselves and what they do. Empirically, they combine the results of extensive survey research with close reading of online message boards to bring us inside the world of practicing musicians and their ways of talking about their gear to an unusual degree. Doing so, they examine such factors as how musical genre affects decisions about gear, whether or not players think of themselves as 'collectors,' how much influence the gear choices of well-known musicians have upon the preferences of amateur players, and how gender informs participation in networks of gear consumption, among several other issues. Their findings are sometimes surprising and always illuminating, not least in the discovery that GAS is not only found among guitarists—who have been most commonly associated with the phenomenon—but is to a significant degree shared among players of diverse musical instruments.

To return to the question I asked above: do I suffer from GAS? I would have resolutely said no before reading this book. Now, I am not so sure. Yet I think a yes or no answer is not the point. Reading the insights of Herbst and Menze prompted me to reflect on my own relationship to the musical equipment I possess in a new light. I may not feel compelled to regularly update my gear collection at every turn, but I absolutely view the amps, pedals, and especially the guitars that I own as a major part of my 'extended self,' every bit as much as my collection of vinyl and compact discs, or the shelves of books that fill my house and campus office. Anyone who plays an instrument in a more than casual way will likely see themselves in some facet of this book, and will come to a new understanding of how the gear they own and use is both personally and socially meaningful.

Steve Waksman

Sylvia Dlugasch Bauman Professor of American Studies and
Professor of Music, Smith College

Northampton, Massachusetts, USA, January 2021

Preface

Many musicians know the nagging feeling of incompleteness when it comes to their rig. There is always a new instrument, another amplifier or accessory that would improve one's tone and help one progress as a player, or that would just be 'cool to have'. Discovering a new band, watching a video or learning a song might be enough to plant the seed that there may be ways to further improve one's setup. This phenomenon, which comes in many different forms, has a name: 'Gear Acquisition Syndrome' or 'GAS', as it is usually known. Initially, the term stood for the 'Guitar Acquisition Syndrome', pointing to a musical background. However, as it was coined in 1996 by Steely Dan guitarist Walter Becker, the term has also been applied to other instruments and eventually spread to leisure activities outside music.

It was at the end of 2016 that we sat in the Gownsmen's pub at Paderborn University, Germany, and contemplated the fun we could have from studying GAS. After a proper literature review, we were surprised by how little attention GAS had received in popular music studies and music technology. Perhaps a bit naive, we decided to develop a theory and test our hypotheses with a comprehensive international survey of musicians, based on the few available studies and relevant blogs, and supported by face-to-face interviews conducted in a music store.

The results confirmed some of our assumptions but left more questions open than were answered, and we realised that a complex cultural phenomenon such as GAS required and deserved a more large-scale investigation. Since the gathered material had meanwhile become too extensive for a research article, we planned to write a short book. Gradually, we saw that it neither worked and that only a full-fledged book might answer our research interest satisfactorily. The outcome is a substantial book examining GAS from various disciplines, bringing together selected theories and empirical studies from the fields of popular music studies and music technology, cultural and leisure studies, sociology, psychology, psychiatry and consumption research.

GAS turned out to be a complex cultural practice, so we are wary of proposing a 'definite theory of GAS'. Instead, we regard our work as a starting point for future investigations and hope that it will be useful for other researchers. Although we concentrate on popular music and a few selected instruments—guitar, bass, drums, keyboards, saxophone, trumpet—conversations with colleagues and fellow musicians suggest that the principles are similarly applicable to classical music or, in fact, any music. Likewise, we see many similarities between music performance and record production. Just as musicians tend to upgrade and expand their rig, recording engineers invest in their microphone collection, and producers extend their (digital) tools. The same formula applies: Guitar or Gear Acquisition Syndrome could well be Plugin or Microphone Acquisition Syndrome. That is why the results of our work may be valuable for the relatively new academic field of the 'art of record production' and many others. The practice of collecting appears to be another understudied area of popular music, cultural and leisure studies, so our work offers a new perspective in addition to the small body of work on record collecting. We also came to realise that GAS is most probably related to developmental processes and musical expertise, which would allow researchers in music education, psychology and sociology to benefit from our findings.

In evaluating theories and adapting them to GAS, we drew on our own experience as musicians and academics. To make our interpretations more transparent, we would like to give some personal background information. Jan has studied concert and electric guitar and took drum and piano lessons. Throughout his career, he came to enjoy playing the electric bass guitar. Although not considering himself a keyboard player, his day-to-day teaching involves keyboard-related technologies such as sound synthesis. Jan has experienced GAS to different degrees on the guitar, but curiously more so on amplifiers than on the actual instrument. In the last years, his creative work has shifted towards music production, accompanied by the respective GAS tendencies. Today, these mainly concern recording gear and production software, a highly tempting field for GAS-related behaviour, given the immense amount of audio plugins that are vividly debated on message boards and in social media. Moreover, discounts promising huge savings are presented almost daily by emails. Such offers are highly tempting for customers susceptible to GAS. Jonas enjoyed piano lessons as a kid and has been playing the electric guitar for about twenty-five years as a hobby. He also enjoys casual drumming and digital home-recording. His propensity for GAS has never been too pronounced since the lack of space in his living environment has led him to limit his activities to the reconfiguration of two distinct electric guitar setups—including appropriate backups for gigging—which enable him to meet a wide range of sound requirements. He manages to balance his buying and selling of equipment.

Acknowledgements

We are grateful for the generous support of the University of Huddersfield's subject area 'Music and Music Technology', which makes it possible to release this book not only in print but also as an electronic open-access publication. Likewise, our thanks go to The University of Huddersfield Press, especially Dawn Cockroft, for the pleasant collaboration. We would further like to express our gratitude to all reviewers and colleagues who provided constructive feedback during our planning phase and on the final manuscript. Furthermore, we would like to thank Erika Herbst for her careful proofreading and the cover design. Last but not least, we would like to thank the many musicians who took the time to give us insights into their views on equipment and their buying behaviour in interviews, filled in our questionnaire and who made great efforts to share their experiences with us in detailed comments and descriptions.

Jan Herbst & Jonas Menze

Huddersfield (United Kingdom) & Münster (Germany), February 2021

Contents

List of Figures

List of Tables

1   Introduction

> You're sweating, you haven't slept properly in days, and you're pretty sure that you've been talking to yourself. Your search history is an endless stream of forums and reviews, and you've discovered that against all odds you're able to carry multiple completely opposing opinions in your head at the same time. You're pretty sure that you're about to lose it completely, possibly in a public place. You're scared. (Power & Parker 2015)

This phenomenon has a name: 'GAS'. The abbreviation stands for 'Gear Acquisition Syndrome', a term that goes back to Steely Dan's guitar player Walter Becker, who wrote an editorial for the American *Guitar Player* magazine in 1996. Becker first contemplated the '*Guitar* Acquisition Syndrome', a phenomenon he observed in the Los Angeles music scene and suspected many of the magazine's readers also to have:

> I have decided to break my long standing editorial silence to draw the attention of the musical community at large and guitar players and guitar owners in particular to a grave situation whose tragic dimension is constantly expanding and is in fact threatening to engulf us all. Picture this: ... I'm working at a studio in town with another well known session cat who has had roughly the same readily identifiable and winning sound for the last twelve years or so—but I've noticed that he never shows up for a call with the same guitar twice—true, they all sound about the same but for some reason these excellent sounding (and looking) axes are constantly falling out of favor and being replaced by sonically indistinguishable ones—and further probing reveals that each one of these guitars has been extensively modified and remodified using the latest space age ... materials and techniques ..., only to be rejected and discarded AFTER TWO WEEKS OR LESS—What's up with these guys? It's called G.A.S.—Guitar Acquisition Syndrome. You undoubtedly know someone who has it. Reading this rag, you probably have it yourself. Or will have it someday soon or would like to have it. ... How many Strats [Stratocaster guitars] do you need to be happy? How many Strat copies, each extensively modified to be able to produce the variations in tone that once would have required maybe four different guitars? How many knobs and switches does that Strat need? ... The horror stories could fill this whole magazine (not a bad idea). (Becker 1996)

Becker expresses his unease with the scene's common practice of changing and modifying instruments unnecessarily with a wink. His intention for the editorial was to raise awareness of this practice being a widespread issue amongst musicians. GAS became a familiar acronym and eventually changed from '*Guitar* Acquisition Syndrome' to '*Gear* Acquisition Syndrome' because other musicians showed similar tendencies to guitar players.

Although acquiring musical instruments can indeed become an addiction, like any other form of compulsive collecting, GAS is usually not a 'clinical condition'.

It is rather a cultural phenomenon which leads those affected to joke about themselves. In their view, GAS describes the unrelenting but harmless urge, triggered by the endless search for the 'magic tone', to buy and own gear as an anticipated catalyst of creative energy and bringer of happiness (Diiorio 2016). Humorous illustrations and discussions in musicians' boards can be found everywhere on the Internet, and GAS merchandise is sold online and in music stores. Video platforms showcase musicians' precious instrument collections, and the website www.guitaracquisitionsyndrome.com presents documentary films of most 'serious' cases. Although not directly related to GAS, it is worth mentioning that the German music instrument retailer Thomann (2019) hosts an annual summer camp as part of its 'Gearhead University'. YouTubers get the opportunity to review each piece of equipment in Thomann's warehouse in a small village in southern Germany, document their experiences on video and share them online with fellow musicians. This marketing strategy celebrates music gear for its own sake and takes the opportunity to influence the large community of subscribers to these video channels in their purchasing decisions. Furthermore, numerous blogs, online articles (Kwisses 2015; Leonhardt 2015; Power & Parker 2015; Robair 2015) and even a video documentary (Diiorio 2016) are dedicated to GAS. Contrary to its omnipresence on the Internet, only a few print media discuss GAS. With Jay Wright's (2006) *GAS: Living with Guitar Acquisition Syndrome,* there is only one book on this topic. Even though being of journalistic nature, the book nevertheless provides rich qualitative data from interviews with 200 guitarists from 23 countries aged between 18 and 68 years.

The *Merriam Webster* (2019) dictionary defines a syndrome either as a 'group of signs and symptoms that occur together and characterize a particular abnormality or condition' or as a 'set of concurrent things (such as emotions or actions) that usually form an identifiable pattern'. In this book, the Gear Acquisition Syndrome will *not* be studied primarily as a compulsive disorder or addiction in the pathological sense. We instead understand it as a pronounced interest in music equipment, combined with a salient desire to acquire and possess certain items of gear. For those affected, the urge to make new purchases can be emotional. Sometimes, when triggered by watching a music video or reading a music magazine, it is short-lived and disappears within hours. At other times, the urge is longstanding, causing actions such as researching music equipment, testing gear in music stores and selling currently owned instruments or other possessions to finance a new purchase. In this study, we focus on the longstanding or recurrent disposition of the syndrome since the short-lived urge seems less significant. As Becker's (1996) editorial suggests, few musicians reach a point in their amateur or professional careers where they are entirely and indefinitely satisfied with their setup. Some musicians sell or trade instruments to make room for new ones, but others do accumulate equipment. There are rumours about impressive instrument collections like the ones of Scorpions guitarist Matthias Jabs with about 400 guitars, Aerosmith's Joe Perry with 600 guitars and the Rolling Stones' Keith Richards with allegedly about 3,000 guitars (Backhaus 2015; Legge 2011). Given the variety of forms that GAS can take, we expect it to involve diverse cultural practices. Those could vary due to various levels of professionalism, age and capital, gender, the type of musical instrument played, band membership and engagement with social media and other online platforms. These different practices and social contexts potentially spark, increase and maintain interest in music gear.

At first glance, GAS appears to be particularly pronounced among musicians of instruments whose sound production is technologically influenced, which we take as a starting point for further considerations. Reassuring is that popular music scholars have emphasised the central role of technology for popular music cultures. As Théberge (2001: 3) rightly claims, '[a]ny discussion of the role of technology in popular music should begin with a simple premise: without electronic technology, popular music in the twenty-first century is unthinkable'. However, a closer look at the body of research reveals that most attention regarding music-related technologies has been paid to music production and the reception of records or other media. Since the late 1960s, researchers have advocated the recognition of the record as *the* primary medium of popular music (Belz 1969; Clarke 1983; Gracyk 1996; Zak 2001) and provided historical accounts of the development of recording technology and its creative use (Cunningham 1996; Moorefield 2010; Schmidt-Horning 2013; Warner 2003). This emphasis on recording and production technologies and related practices is understandable, given the acknowledged importance of technology for popular music genres. Yet when focusing on commercial records, attention inevitably turns to renowned artists and the work of audio engineers and producers. That leaves behind the majority of amateur, semi-professional and professional musicians who are not in the international spotlight. Furthermore, while the study of production involves the analysis of technology, it favours recording and processing technology such as microphones, mixing consoles and signal processing effects over source technology: the musical instruments where sound and expression begin. In light of the pivotal role of musical instruments in the creation of music, it is surprising that they are still a relatively unresearched field in popular music.

> Given the vast complexity of musical instruments as cultural artifacts, and their fundamental importance to the making of music, it is worth pondering why they have been given relatively little attention in the study of music, and of popular music in particular … For all too many popular music scholars, musical activity does not exist for all intents and purposes before the moment of recording. Such an assumption, whether explicit or unspoken, leaves scholars to concentrate upon a range of issues that, while of key importance, tend to exclude the ways in which instruments figure into musical practice and production. (Waksman 2003: 252)

This statement in no way suggests that research on musical instruments in popular music does not exist. There are numerous examples of authors who have written about the electric guitar. Waksman (1999) explores the historical and cultural significance of the electric guitar by focusing on how influential performers have shaped the instrument's use and meaning. Herbst (2016) analyses the musical and cultural significance of guitar distortion for rock and metal music, and Uimonen (2016) discusses celebrity guitars as luxury items. Théberge (1997) deals with the increasing commodification of music-making and examines democratisation processes through advances in digital keyboard technology. From practitioners' perspectives, Bruford (2018) analyses how expert drummers experience creativity in performance. Recently, Brennan (2020) provided a long-overdue social history of the drum kit. There are also handbooks on popular music instruments (Bacon 1996), histories of manufacturers and inventors (Maloof 2004) and lists of the 'greatest players' of certain instruments, which often include information about their equipment and its influence on playing and sound (Kitts & Tolinski 2002). Magazines such as *Premier Guitar*, *Modern Drummer* or *Keyboard Magazine* regularly feature so-called 'rig rundowns' that give insights into the secrets of renowned players' distinct tones. Gear reviews also take up large parts of these magazines. Academic, journalistic and educational resources focus on a range of topics, including various histories, inventions, star performers, vintage gear and the latest technology. In these discourses, the focus is mainly on musical and aesthetic issues but less so on the cultural significance and social relevance of musical instruments. Yet such a view is too limited and does not consider the multitude of meanings:

> 'Reading the instrument' … involves acknowledging the complex relationship between musical and extramusical factors in the cultural life of musical instruments. This pursuit, in turn, involves thinking through the ways in which a musical instrument becomes embedded in a given cultural setting, or alternately in a web of discursive meanings that coats the materiality of the instrument with a residue of symbolic import. (Waksman 2003: 252)

Musical instruments are deeply intertwined with cultural practices rooted in society. In the more direct sense, playing an instrument requires consideration of genre conventions and aesthetics. That may involve selecting the right instrument model, combining it with suitable effects and amplifiers, and fine-tuning the resulting sound within the arrangement of a larger ensemble. All these decisions, explicit or implicit, are based on musical traditions that shape the actions. Players must give thought to conventions they wish to follow and the importance of having an original sound. It is not only a question of tone; gear choice also affects playing feel, and thus, how emotions are expressed musically. Therefore, lack of access to the right equipment can hold performers back and prevent them from reaching their full potential. At least, this is what discussions in online message boards, musicians' magazines and equipment-related videos often suggest.

With the availability of a wide range of music magazines, blogs, social media communities and message boards, musicians can easily keep up with the latest trends, which increases the likelihood that they will reflect on their musical setup and compare it to that of their fellow musicians. These media have become part of everyday life and tempt players more than ever to focus on their hobby's material side. According to Théberge (1997: 245), modern musicians do not necessarily consume more equipment than older generations of musicians, but 'consumption has become an integral aspect of their musical production practice'. Dealing with gear is part of modern musical practice, and its implications go beyond the mere activity of music-making.

> Instruments are commodities, the sale of which represents an often unrecognized aspect of the business of music. They are material objects subject to variations in design, and often tied to broader shifts in the technological basis of music making ... Musical instruments are sources of knowledge, the material embodiment of musical theory and technique. They are cultural resources that can be used to transmit long-held traditions or to enact far-flung innovations. (Waksman 2003: 252)

The primary intentions for using instruments are music-related and require respective deliberations, decisions and actions. However, we argue that there are deeper cultural, social and psychological motives at work. Dealing with instruments necessarily involves broader attitudes, such as openness to innovation versus tradition-consciousness, which are part of a player's identity. Empirical research has even indicated that personality characteristics differ between musicians of various instruments (Bell & Cresswell 1984; Cameron et al. 2015; see also Rötter & Steinberg 2018). Although such research has focused mainly on personality traits like extraversion, everyday experience suggests that keyboard players, for example, would appreciate technological innovation more than guitarists who are more likely to use vintage guitars and analogue valve amplifiers (Herbst 2019b).

Consumption and collecting are two important practices associated with the broader socio-cultural networks linked to music-making. Both have been widely discussed in social sciences and cultural studies research focused on leisure, demonstrating how recreational activities such as making music are relevant to a person's identity (Stebbins 2009). Playing an instrument and acquiring gear touches on phenomena such as nostalgia and the 'extended self' (Belk 1988), which are influenced by sociodemographic factors like gender, age, relationship status and living situation (Belk 1995a). Less often discussed in the field of popular music technology are consumer research, marketing and business studies, all of which can provide a different perspective on the social context of consumption around making music. Such research offers theoretical approaches to understanding how 'desire' and 'necessity' (Braun et al. 2016), 'fetish' (Fernandez & Lastovicka 2011), 'taste' (Arsel & Bean

2013), 'facilitation' (Hartmann 2016) and 'use-value' (Cole 2018) can nourish a musician's urge to invest in equipment. This economic view is one way of understanding buying behaviour in a broader socio-cultural context. It draws connections between musical practice and concepts such as 'craft consumption' (Campbell 2005), which describe the players' modification and customisation of stock items as a strategy for re-appropriating standard goods to shape their creative identity and obtain unique tools for musical expression.

The last fact worth mentioning is that the phenomenon is not limited to music. GAS occurs in many areas of everyday life. In music, it can be observed in hi-fi audio culture (Schröter & Volmar 2016), record collecting (Shuker 2010), home recording (Strong 2012) and jingle composition (Fisher 1997). Outside music, GAS occurs amongst photographers (Arias 2013; Kim 2012; Sarinana 2013), aquarium hobbyists (Wolfenden 2016), amateur astronomists (Chen & Chen 2017), cyclists (Peters 2013) and eBayers (Zalot 2013). Despite its high prevalence in contemporary culture, the phenomenon has hardly been researched. This book's overarching aim is to explore GAS in popular music from various perspectives, such as music technology, social, leisure and cultural studies, as well as consumption research, and to develop a theoretical understanding of this phenomenon (chapters 2 to 5). With original quantitative and qualitative empirical research, this working theory will be tested and refined (chapters 6 and 7). Some of the guiding questions are:

- Which sociodemographic variables and other personal, social and musical motives play a role in instrument consumption?

- Do players of various instrument types differ in their buying and collecting behaviour? Do musicians of electric or electronic instruments show a greater tendency towards GAS than those of acoustic instruments?

- What are the mental processes musicians are going through when the desire for music equipment develops?

- How do offline and online practices contribute to a pronounced interest in musical gear and the urge to buy?

The findings will provide insights into socio-cultural practices of how musicians deal with gear and what attitudes they have towards equipment. That will set the foundation for an interdisciplinary theory of the Gear Acquisition Syndrome grounded in empirical data. Lastly, it will be discussed how the psychological urge to acquire gear, consumption as part of music-making, and collecting are related.

GAS is assumed to occur in all musical genres, classical and popular, and concerns all instruments. It is not only common among players of traditional instruments but also widespread in modern, digital production-based forms of music-making, whose creators are tempted to invest in microphones, controllers and virtual plugins

(Bourbon 2019; Carvalho 2012; Cole 2011; O'Grady 2019). Given the significant differences between all these groups and the respective activities, it is necessary to limit the research scope. While the theoretical chapters (2 to 5) can also be applied to classical musicians and music producers to some degree, we focus on players of popular music in the sample population of the empirical studies (chapters 6 and 7). More specifically, we will focus on the traditional core instruments of popular music genres that still rely on band instruments: guitar, bass, drums, keyboards, as well as saxophone (woodwind) and trumpet (brass), as exemplarily selected wind instruments.

Book Structure

Chapter 2: Gear Acquisition Syndrome
The Gear Acquisition Syndrome is a phenomenon with which musicians are commonly confronted. This chapter examines musicians' different attitudes to identify the reasons as to why many of them feel the urge to acquire new equipment. First, it gives an account of the so-called 'GAS attack', which is frequently described in blogs and other journalistic media. What triggers the musicians' ceaseless quest to improve their setup and drives them to acquire gear is discussed. The chapter finishes with the differentiation between various subgroups of musicians such as players, collectors, gear heads, purists and crafters. These groups are believed to have different attitudes towards equipment and diverging consumption patterns and manifestations of GAS.

Chapter 3: Role and Context of Technology for Music-Making
Here, the role of technology for popular music in general and in relation to the different attitudes and practices of players of various instruments is explored. Vintage instruments are another subject of investigation. What are the reasons for their popularity, and is innovation in music instrument technology important? If so, what are the consequences for the music industry? By analysing special-interest books, we examine which topics industry and media consider relevant, and what role equipment and sound quality play for popular music instruments. The chapter ends with a discussion of gendered practices in music-making. We have come to conclude that the musical instruments industry has historically tended to consider female musicians less relevant as consumers of gear because they were generally regarded as relatively inexperienced in the use of music technology. Although there are signs of change, our investigation into manufacturers' practices suggests that relatively few female musicians receive prestigious signature instruments and that they are often overlooked in endorsement deals.

Chapter 4: Collecting
Little is known about how collecting relates to GAS, as it is a largely unexplored area of popular music research. By drawing on theories and empirical studies from various disciplines such as sociology, consumption research, psychology and psychiatry, this chapter offers a multidisciplinary perspective to evaluate the blurry relationship between GAS and collecting. As a starting point, collecting is established as a widespread practice in Western societies, and its benefits to identity construction are considered. Collecting is understood as a social practice marked by social hierarchies that are formed by individuals who seek to distinguish themselves through their prestigious collections and valuable items. The psychological and social processes and circumstances of collecting are examined in its entire range from the harmless pastime to obsessive acquisition and hoarding.

Chapter 5: Consumption
Consumption, by definition, is at the heart of the Gear Acquisition Syndrome. Based on the large variety of empirically derived theories within the multidisciplinary field of consumption research, this chapter focuses on musicians' relationships to their possessions to determine how these become the 'extended self' of their identity. Leisure studies provide a useful lens for understanding the strong motivations that drive musicians in their amateur and semi-professional endeavours. Key terms for GAS, 'desire' and 'necessity', are theorised, attempting to explain why musicians like to be seduced by gear and why they do not even mind participating in the marketing efforts of music industries. Two other relevant concepts, 'prosumption' and 'craft consumption', are explored. The discussion includes fabrication, modification and combination of music equipment as standard DIY practices. We found two effective facilitators of desire and the impulse to buy new gear in the online phenomena 'eBaying' and the exchange on message boards.

Chapter 6: Interviews and Survey of Musicians
GAS has not yet been studied academically. This chapter deepens and tests the theoretical deliberations developed in the previous chapters. It begins with an explorative study of musicians interviewed in a music store. What follows is a standardised online survey taking stock of musicians' gear collections, their attitudes and practices towards gear, their criteria for choosing an instrument and other personal, social and musical motives that affect their dealing with equipment. A large number of open comments help explain the survey results and reveal further practices not covered in academic and journalistic writing on GAS.

Chapter 7: Online Message Boards

Musicians have always 'talked gear', but with the Internet, discussions have proliferated. Social media and special-interest message boards bring together people around the world who share the same interests. Building on the concept of 'communities of practice', we analyse how GAS is discussed in fifteen selected message boards. It is a common theme shaping community life. As a learned and expected behaviour, GAS is structurally reflected in recurring threads across all message boards. One of the main forms it takes is 'flipping', the selling of gear to buy other used equipment. Major GAS facilitators are eBay and other gear-related websites, besides the globally online operating musical instruments industry. The discourse focuses on the relationship between playing and interest in gear. Individual circumstances and personal motives explain varying interests in music equipment. Experimenting with gear is considered a natural part of learning and musical development. However, for various reasons, a musician might show more interest in gear than actually playing it: limited time, better compatibility with other responsibilities and family life, stagnation in musical development, lack of meaningful projects or artistic directions or plain boredom. Online discussions occasionally hint at impulsive and compulsive behaviour, suggesting that interest in gear is not always harmless. Speculations have it that GAS is a symptom of an underlying problem, so many discussions in the community revolve around how to counteract it. While there is general agreement that GAS is 'incurable', the discussions suggest several mitigating circumstances, strategies and principles that turn it into a harmless interest inseparable from music-making, with the potential to contribute to a musician's development.

Chapter 8: Conclusion: Towards a Theory of GAS

This concluding chapter takes stock of the theoretical and empirical insights into GAS. Even though the term emerged as 'Guitar Acquisition Syndrome', and special-interest books easily create the impression that electric guitarists are most gear-centric and thus susceptible to GAS, this perception is not entirely accurate, as our findings show. The discrepancy between the thematic focus on gear in books about the electric guitar and the shared interest in equipment amongst *all* instrumentalists suggests that authors and publishers, perhaps even parts of the wider musical instruments industry, may have a distorted image. The chapter goes on evaluating the role of the Internet concerning the musicians' interest in gear and its temptation for GAS. It concludes that easy access to information, social exchange in special-interest communities and the large market for used instruments made available through auction and other selling websites are crucial factors for the prevalence of GAS in musicians' communities. GAS is a learned behaviour and expected in communities of practice. Fundamental to the urge to acquire gear is the indefinite quest to improve one's rig. GAS rarely disappears completely; it can strike in times of doubt, stagnation or other situations preventing musicians from playing or pursuing their projects. Like an umbrella, the term encompasses various practices related to the way musicians think about and deal with equipment. There is no single form of GAS; instead, the term summarises a spectrum of cultural practices related to and part of music-making. Since GAS accompanies musical learning processes, exploring the gear's affordances should be considered a contributing and reflecting part of musical expertise, at least in popular music. GAS is usually not the 'disease' often described. As a constant companion of musicians, it is possibly a sign that engagement in music has not lost its importance for the individual.

2   Gear Acquisition Syndrome

This chapter introduces the Gear Acquisition Syndrome in more detail and gives an overview of views and related issues surrounding the phenomenon. Most of the content will be discussed further in the following chapters from perspectives of various disciplines and with stronger links to theoretical discourses and empirical research.

2.1   The 'GAS Attack'

GAS is a much-discussed phenomenon in online communities for musicians. Several blogs (Kwisses 2015; Leonhardt 2015; Power & Parker 2015; Robair 2015) demonstrate the range of views from joking acknowledgement to serious warnings. Leonhardt (2015), for example, takes a serious stance on his blog:

> Most of us guitarists suffer from an affliction called GAS—Gear Acquisition Syndrome. That means we are buying gear nearly compulsively—more and more often than we really need … We often spend more time shopping and searching for gear than playing guitar—it's like an addiction: difficult to stop and expensive.

This behaviour is characteristic of those affected by GAS. Thinking about gear and finding strategies to improve one's rig can take precedence over practising and playing, to a point when dealing with equipment becomes more important than making music. Much of a day's recreational time will then be spent researching equipment. One of the guitarists Wright (2006: 35) interviewed depicts how this compulsive urge to contemplate gear can become overwhelming: 'When my GAS kicks in, there is only one solution and that is to buy the gear that preoccupies my every waking moment. Scouring the internet, searching eBay, trolling for that special instrument, when will it end?'. The Internet seems to play a central role in sparking GAS because musicians quickly find information about new instruments or sales. Musicians who have an affinity for gear may not want to miss out on exclusive deals or limited instrument editions, hoping that new gear will improve their playing or at least allow them to get hold of rare equipment that few other musicians have.

Less serious than Leonhardt's (2015) statement is a blog post by Power and Parker (2015), which proposes a seven-phase model for the temporal development of a 'GAS attack'. 1) The players are *dissatisfied* with their instruments and believe that other musicians play better gear. 2) The subsequent search leads to the discovery of new instruments that arouse *desire* because they are believed to bring happiness. 3) The next step is *research*, a challenging task given the large number and diversity of opinions on the Internet, in print magazines and amongst local musicians. 4) Once an overview of the stocks within commuting distance has been obtained, the instruments are *tried out* in music stores, possibly followed by confirmation that the purchase meets the requirements. 5) After the relief that the new owner experiences from this achievement, they will probably feel *guilty*. 'For the next week, the guilt ruins your enjoyment of the lovely new guitar. You can barely even look at it for the shame'. 6) Finally, the guilt subsides, and the owner can *enjoy* their dream instrument. 7) When some time has passed, the musician affected by GAS *relapses*. The less money was spent on the last purchase, the sooner the urge to buy new gear will creep in again. It is not difficult to imagine that several of these cycles are taking place in close succession or even at the same time. Musicians know exactly when they last invested in a new instrument, amplifier, effect or other accessories. Once an instrument has been bought, the player may believe that a new and better-suited amplifier matching the piece of gear just bought will take their playing to the next level. This belief can trigger continuous investment in effects and other accessories. The budget determines how many cycles for instruments, amplifiers and other gadgets are taking place, and each one is potentially affecting another, which can lead to a complex psychological state in the form of an intense craving for one or more pieces of equipment at the same time.

Like Power and Parker (2015), Wright (2006: 22) describes the 'GAS attack' in a humorous way:

> GAS can strike you at any time, but onset normally occurs upon seeing, hearing, or touching a particular axe. The attack itself can range from mild to severe. Your eyes open wider as the pupils dilate; your breathing becomes more noticeable as your heart rate increases. You drool, you stare, you drool some more … Your mind races, as you imagine the rest of your life with this baby in it—how much more skilled, happy, and fulfilled you would be. Then you begin to imagine how incomplete and unfulfilled the rest of your life would be without it. A battle erupts inside you: heart vs. head. You're faced with two immediate problems: 1) how to find relief from this powerful force, and 2) how to manage a transfer of ownership. That, my friend, is a GAS attack.

This quote indicates that different stimuli trigger the desire for a new instrument, for example, by seeing someone play it live or in a video, listening to it on a record, or playing it at a music store, rehearsal room or friend's house (see also Hartmann 2016). Such experiences stimulate the imagination that the purchase will benefit musical development and bring happiness. Wright (2006: 50–59) does not divide the 'GAS attack' into discrete stages but identifies more than forty 'strains of GAS' based on interview statements from afflicted guitar players. He concludes that the 'GAS attack' can be of varying intensity and develop differently over time. A *continuous* GAS 'sufferer' is likely to spend a great deal of time contemplating their equipment, which triggers the urge to invest. Less drastic is the *episodic* type, which is occasionally triggered by the syndrome but repeatedly occurs due to various tempting stimuli. The least severe form of GAS is *single episodic*, as it allows partial or even full 'remission'. Similar to Power and Parker's (2015) model, Wright considers GAS to be cyclical. Hence it would not be a one-off phenomenon in most cases but a longstanding and recurrent disposition that varies in its 'severity' throughout a musician's life due to changing musical interests, family responsibilities, social situation, professional career stages and available budgets.

The strong urge to acquire is not limited to musical equipment but also occurs in other collecting forms. Shuker (2010: 111), in his study of record collectors, observes that often 'the acquisition of the desired item will be immediately followed by the creation of a new "need" and a return to the chase, in an ongoing cycle of desire-success-stasis-renewed desire, a related pattern of repetition'. Stebbins (2009: 21) explains this behaviour with *thrills*. Purchasing a leisure item such as a musical instrument or record is an exciting moment that serves as a personal reward and shows commitment to a hobby or profession. Since these are memorable events that evoke the hope of reliving them all over again, the musician feels urged to acquire new gear, possibly without actual need. All these concepts and theories highlight the probable gap between musical necessity and the psychological world, both of which contribute to the gradually growing desire to buy new equipment.

Of the few texts available, many reflect on strategies to mitigate or prevent GAS and therefore centre around the psychology of necessity. From a guitarist's perspective, Kwisses (2015) argues that the beliefs players have about their setup must change if they wished to stop unnecessary buying habits. While he does not deny that some acquisitions are sensible, he stresses that a player's circumstance and intention must be considered. Not the purchase and possession of gear should guide the music played, but the music should dictate what equipment is required. Based on this reasoning, he advocates a smaller gear collection because it improves tone quality. Technically, fewer devices in a signal chain would cause less signal degradation, noise and other unexpected problems, especially in a live situation where multiple sources of error could be potentially catastrophic to the show. Musically and stylistically, limited gear would encourage experimentation and thus mastery of every nuance it had to offer in terms of tone and playability. Having more equipment than necessary would lead to a 'strong tendency to jump from one piece of gear to another which results in an average tone from gear to gear (and what guitar player wants and [sic!] average tone?)'.

In his editorial introduction to GAS, Walter Becker (1996) already proposed several strategies to counter a 'GAS attack', some of them concurring with Kwisses' suggestions. Surely tongue-in-cheek, Becker recommends: 'Consider for a moment the karmic implications of owning all those guitars. Picture yourself dragging your ass through eternity with all those guitars strapped to your back. In hardshell cases, not gig bags'. He further advises:

> Imagine that you are in whatever vintage guitar shop you visit frequently and are dealing with the owner of the shop. He is of course severely stricken with G.A.S. Now imagine that you are taking on his personality, with each new purchase you become more and more like him. This one exercise, done

properly, will do more to stem the tide of new G.A.S. sufferers than anything else I can think of right now. (Becker 1996)

Becker is also concerned about the effort it takes tuning the guitar strings on all instruments. However, he admits it might not pose a problem for those not keeping the instrument long enough to change the strings once while owning it. Other strategies seem to be related to social perceptions. Becker advises GAS-afflicted musicians to ask themselves whether they would rather be remembered as guitar players or guitar owners. He also warns about problems potentially arising when the musician's partner finds out how big the instrument collection truly is.[1] This concern accords with Wright's (2006: 102ff, 174) conclusion that although GAS was usually incurable, the only counterbalance was having a family or living with a partner.

2.2   The Indefinite Quest to Improve the Musical Setup

Besides Wright's (2006) substantial collection of interview statements from musicians, numerous blogs and a limited body of research on music technology provide a good starting point for exploring possible reasons as to why musicians feel compelled to invest in equipment. Referring to studio technology, Johnston (1987 as cited in Jones 1992: 91) notes:

> There [is] a desire always to get better equipment, but it's predicated on what you can really afford and what's absolutely necessary. As you get more and more into refining your system you want to make it better and better and as you use it you discover things about it that you're not totally satisfied with. A lot of this stuff does become obsolete.

Since the advent of recording technology in the late nineteenth century, technological development has had a major impact on music production practices (Cunningham 1996; Schmidt-Horning 2013). As per Johnston, recording equipment becomes obsolete sooner or later. Therefore, regular updating is a logical consequence or even an economic necessity for professional studios. Similar forces characterise the hi-fi sector. Analysing manuals and the wider discourse, Schröter and Volmar (2016) find that the search for the perfect audio system is endless for serious hi-fi enthusiasts. The status quo is apologetically 'justified' by the current budget, accompanied by an assurance of improving the system in the future. Constant investment is thus necessary for aspiring hi-fi audio connoisseurs. But unlike the recording sector, where gear can become obsolete when, for example, distribution formats change, or more modern digital units outperform older devices, hi-fi enthusiasts are driven by another

---

[1] Becker's editorial is written from a male perspective. He does not acknowledge the possibility that female musicians may also be affected by GAS. Therefore, he mentions the 'wife' as a factor limiting GAS, not just any partner. Wright (1996: 26) concurs with this view, believing that GAS is an exclusively male phenomenon.

motivation. They generally prefer older analogue technology, so enhancing their system is about nuances of sound quality, with small improvements already requiring substantial investment.

Musicians affected by GAS are akin to music producers and hi-fi audio enthusiasts. Musical setups of all kinds of instruments can *always* be improved, if only for flexibility, made possible by a larger collection of instruments, amplifiers or other accessories. As Théberge (1997: 244) argues:

> musicians have found themselves increasingly drawn towards a particular mode of consumption in order to supply themselves with not only instruments and recording devices but with the very sounds they need to produce music ... there has been an expansion in the range of technology deemed necessary for contemporary amateur and semi-professional practice. Many musicians no longer find it adequate to simply own a guitar or a keyboard and an amplifier.

Setups have become increasingly complex. Guitar and bass players may have a pedalboard, with some devices being routed into the amplifier's input and others into the effect's loop circuit—usually time-based effects that sound clearer after the pre-amplifier. The signal may further be routed to two cabinets for stereo effects or split to blend tones of different amplifiers. Some keyboard players stack a fortress of instruments on top of each other to blend various sounds by different synthesis and sampling technologies. Drummers also have numerous options to extend their basic kit: additional snares, toms and kick drums, an array of cymbals and percussion instruments from cowbells to triggers for blending in electronic sounds, or even trigger pads to replace the acoustic sound.

Apart from modifications and extensions of instrument setups, collections seem to have grown over time (Théberge 1997: 244). At present, little is known about the average size of gear collections for different types of instruments. Data is only available for electric guitar players. Wright (2006: 47) asked 200 guitarists about the ideal size of their instrument collection. The largest group (30%) stated 4 to 6 pieces, followed by the groups with 7–10 (21%), 11–15 (11%) and 16–20 (12%) instruments. The range between 21 and 50 pieces was less popular (12%), but 13% stated liking to possess more than 50 instruments. Only 5% were content with a small collection of 1 to 3 guitars. Hence more than half of the sample considered 4 to 10 guitars as the ideal size of an instrument collection. This result is consistent with an explorative study with 418 electric guitar players (Herbst 2017a), finding that guitarists own five instruments plus three amplifiers on average.

2.3   Reasons for Gear Acquisition

Musicians have many reasons to invest in equipment. In popular music, as in classical music, a performer's unique tone is what counts. Yet contrary to classical music, many popular music instruments such as electric guitar, bass, keyboards, synthesisers and electronic drums rely on numerous tone-shaping devices. The consequence is the widespread belief that the acquisition of new equipment helps performers reach new levels of expressiveness, improve their stylistic versatility and play other genres (Kwisses 2015; Leonhardt 2015). There is some merit in this belief. Musical genres have standard equipment, and the more one wishes to conform to genre-specific aesthetics, the more genre-specific gear may be necessary. Choosing the right instrument may even require separate equipment for individual songs. As Wright (2006: 158) suggests: 'Different guitars and basses have their very distinctive characteristics, and in choosing which guitar or bass to use to play a certain song, we have to choose the one that matches the song best in order to bring out the best feel of the song'. Various instrument models and types have distinct and sometimes more suitable characteristics for a song than others. Furthermore, some instruments afford specific playing styles; for example, a twangy Telecaster guitar may encourage country-inspired licks and riffs. The suitability of the equipment for certain genres or styles is usually noticeable to the performer but less so to the audience. That is the case when it comes to recognising an instrument's playability or how an amplifier reacts to phrasing. Such variations in gear may be subtle but have a considerable impact on the performer's playing feel. Every instrument, even if mass-produced, will be slightly different in playing and tone. Musicians likely perceive these small details differently, and some might purchase a similar or the same instrument model exactly for these differences. Not all musicians give thought to how observable musical details are to an audience. They are driven by the hope of becoming a better player through upgrading or expanding their gear. Another wish is to improve their tone as best as possible by reproducing phrasing truthfully or concealing flaws in their playing technique, which often is done by guitarists who rely on the facilitating effects of distortion (Herbst 2017c). What is more, buying new gear is a motivating factor that encourages musicians to practise, which in turn might add to their long-term development.

According to Wright (2006: 30f), musicians buy an instrument mainly for two qualities – special timbre and uniqueness. That particularly applies to gear in the middle and upper price ranges, where instruments are expected to be hand-crafted or their material carefully selected. Hence instruments of the same model can sound substantially different to the trained ear. They also vary in weight, which is a practical consideration for touring musicians. Those are likely to own more than one instrument of the same model, although this may vary between instrumentalists. What is sensible for a guitar player may not be so for a drummer or keyboardist. Also, instruments are probably different from other devices such as amplifiers and effects because their natural components, especially wood, vary in tone more than electronic and digital devices do. Nevertheless, each item offers the prospect of adding a new timbre to the instrument collection (Wright 2006: 29). It is up to the individual to decide how many different tonal colours they wish. Hence one's perception of an instrument collection size varies considerably, as is evident in a guitar player's statement: 'My collection really isn't big, somewhere around eighteen' (Wright 2006: 31). Other musicians would consider anything between one and five guitars sufficient for any purpose, as the previous discussion has indicated.

Where the instrument is played may also be decisive for buying a similar model or an exact copy. A guitar player justifies 'duplicate GAS purchases' by preserving an instrument's quality by playing it only at home, while the duplicate could be 'take[n] out to play in the clubs' (Wright 2006: 40). Moreover, buying cheaper instruments for the road might lessen the worry of theft, as another player explains (Wright 2006: 31).

From an aesthetic point of view, musical instruments are appealing for their tonal or visual attributes. Such attractiveness can spark GAS in the words of a guitar player: 'When I get GAS, I have an urge to taste a flavour that I've wanted to try, but haven't. It's because of a tonal, visual, or other aesthetic / artistic attraction' (Wright 2006: 31). An instrument's shape, colour or even wider associations with a genre or a revered player can have alluring qualities. Another guitarist highlights that he would not buy an instrument for its tonal quality if he were not visually drawn to it (Wright 2006: 28). There are even statements admitting that visual attraction could go as far as reaching a romantic or sexual level:

> It is a surreal feeling when GAS hits me. I get very focused on that instrument. Everything else turns black, and I develop tunnel vision. I can use the analogy of seeing a very attractive woman... my instinct is to take her, hold her, then look her over good and listen to her, get to know her, feel her weight, then give us some time together to check if there is compatibility. As with a female, the first attraction is physical, but after we're introduced, the next step is to see if love is really there. (Wright 2006: 36)

This quote indicates an intimate relationship between the instrument and its potential buyer, suggesting that GAS is like falling in love. It even may cause the same symptoms, such as 'butterflies' and 'ultimate craving' (Wright 2006: 36). What differentiates GAS from interpersonal, human relationships is that new equipment can be bought at any time and that several valued pieces can co-exist without having to choose one over the other.

In her ethnographic study of Liverpool's rock scene, Cohen (1991: 135) discovered that instruments are sometimes appreciated primarily for their visual qualities in the context of broader associations and the image a band wishes to convey. It can take different forms for different instruments. To match a genre aesthetic, drummers can, for example, adjust the size of their kit. A rock or metal drummer usually has more shells, cymbals and kick drums than a jazz or soul drummer. Similarly, a metal guitarist may prefer a wall of amplifiers over a small combo amplifier for tonal and visual reasons. Appearance can be part of a band concept, so guitar and bass players may wish to match their instruments' colours for a coherent impression. Aesthetic conventions also extend to instrument shapes, which can even differ between substyles within a genre. For example, a black metal guitarist might appreciate a spiky model such as a BC Rich Beast. In contrast, a progressive metal player might prefer the characteristic shape of a Strandberg Boden model that supports virtuoso solo performances due to the better accessibility of higher frets.

Motivations to buy and keep instruments for their visual qualities take different forms, some not even influenced by musical motives. For their study on the guitar's role for the baby boom generation in the USA, Ryan and Peterson (2001: 109) interviewed middle-aged people who, although not playing the guitar regularly anymore, 'just like having that Les Paul sitting in the corner. It's beautiful to look at, wonderful to hold, and *means* something'. The look of instruments seems to be motivation enough to keep them or buy new ones for home decoration.

A musician's financial situation dictates how much money can readily be spent on equipment. How they handle their budget determines their relationship with GAS. If the urge to buy new equipment exceeds their budget, the condition may become problematic if not clinical. People who intend to stay within their budget when upgrading their rig may need to sell or trade some gear. According to common sense, an instrument's price must match the value of the material, mechanical and electrical parts and craftsmanship. However, musical instruments are also valued for historical, symbolical, cultural and social reasons. Owning the same type as a revered role model can have ideological value for potential buyers, which prompts them to spend more money than the instrument's parts and craftsmanship are worth. Signature models of artists are a good example, as they are often modified versions of stock models that cost more. Another possibly related phenomenon is vintage gear. The price of an old instrument may well be a multitude of a new one, even if the specifications are identical. Recent trends go towards authentic replicas as well as heritage and relic models. These unique models are strategies utilised by the industry—possibly in response to popular demand—to satisfy the desire of many musicians for authentic instruments played by renowned musicians on records and at famous concerts in music history. A notable example is Jimi Hendrix's 1968 Olympic White Fender Stratocaster guitar with characteristic cigarette burns on which he played 'The Star-Spangled Banner' at Woodstock. It was sold in the 1990s for $198,000 (Marten 2008). Replicas of adored instruments are often artificially aged and show visible signs of wear, such as worn lacquer and oxidised metal parts. Acquiring such gear may be motivated by the romantic notion of reliving music history and being closer to revered musicians. Of course, there could also be musical reasons for buying vintage models because they may provide a different playing feel and sound. Aged wood, for example, has a different resonance behaviour affecting the tone of an instrument. What is more, if the lacquer on the back of a guitar's neck is sticky, removing it makes it easier to move fast on the fretboard.

Fandom is another strong incentive to buy gear. Many guitar players' statements point to it, for example: 'If I see a hot guitar player on TV ripping on a Tele, I start GASing for one' (Wright 2006: 41). Research in the field of music education emphasises the relevance of role models. Beginners learn an instrument by covering songs of their favoured artists and imitating their way of playing (Green 2002). As the previous quotes demonstrate, this influence of role models spreads to gear, which can be a powerful trigger for GAS. Revered artists sometimes change their equipment throughout their career, which can inspire their fans to follow suit. As a consequence of developing musical preferences and growing expertise on the instrument, aspiring musicians often find new role models. Therefore, both long-term changes in musical preferences and short-term moods influence the desired musical setup, encouraging musicians to adjust their gear or expanding their collection.

There is reason to believe that learning an instrument goes hand in hand with gaining experience in music equipment and finding the right rig that fits a musician's playing. One finding of Gay's (1998: 84f) ethnographic study of New York rock musicians is that a 'musician's rig—the assembled musical equipment—and the ability to make music with it … begins with listening to and imitating rock recordings, acquiring an initial repertory and a sense of what constitutes a good rock sound'. Pinch and Reinecke (2009: 158ff) studied the development of a rock guitarist who bought an instrument early on in his musical journey without much knowledge of equipment. As it turned out, the purchased guitar did not match his musical preferences, and a more experienced musician advised him on what he needed. The important role of mentoring by a more experienced peer is reflected in the reaction of the aspiring player: 'I was a little bit wary, but Johnny Dowd [one of the major rockers of the Ithaca scene] was like a hero to me, he was like real … the real deal. And if he said I should trade my guitar in then I should trade my guitar in' (Pinch & Reinecke 2009: 159). When he exchanged the Les Paul for a Stratocaster, the novice guitarist had to rely on the experience of his local icon: 'I knew like that Johnny knew what a guitar should sound like. Me myself couldn't really rig it up; like if I had to stand there and say "This is the good sound and this is the bad sound" it would be dicey, like I wouldn't really know' (Pinch & Reinecke 2009: 159f). By gaining more experience as a guitar player, the musician eventually learned how to recognise a 'good sound'. This case study highlights technology as part of musical development that benefits from mentoring by a more experienced musician or teacher.

Another effect of musical development regards physical strength and flexibility through regular practice, which influences what instrument models can or should ideally be played. For example, smaller necks are handier for novices of guitar and bass, but a wider range of musical instruments becomes available with more practice. The same is true for keyboards and drums, for which the number of keys, drums and cymbals that can be reached is initially determined by the size and capabilities of a player.

Affordability is an important factor when acquiring gear. It cannot be measured objectively but is determined by sociodemographic factors such as age, gender, employment status and geographical location. The price of instruments also varies significantly, both within and between instrument groups. An analogue synthesiser can cost more than a grand piano and an electronic keyboard less than a drum cymbal. Little is known about how much money musicians are willing to spend on their instruments. For most of the guitar players interviewed by Wright (2006: 46f), the price was not decisive if the quality was right. Asked about the maximum amount they were ready to pay for the instrument of their dreams, the largest group (41%) chose the highest category of more than $3,000, followed by $1,000 to $2,000 (34%) and $2,000 to $3,000 (18%). Only 6% were not willing to spend more than $1,000. This finding indicates that many musicians are prepared to invest a significant amount of money if the instrument's specifications match their requirements. At the other end of the spectrum are special offers, promotions or sales that entice musicians to buy an instrument because it is temporarily sold below the regular street price: 'Price is always a deciding factor, because, if it's cheap enough, I can justify it as a great deal I just couldn't pass up. If it's too expensive for my budget, I can walk away' (Wright 2006: 40). The motives for buying are manifold and range from satisfying GAS out of pure acquisition interest, musical reasons such as expanding the collection with an instrument that was previously unavailable, to the intention of selling or trading for profit. The latter is nowhere as pronounced as in auction formats. Interviewed guitarists describe the process as 'hunting for prey', accompanied by an emotional state of 'suspense' (Wright 2006: 31, 39).

Besides the price, longevity is a factor in the purchase decision, which can take various forms. In the most direct sense, it concerns the physical durability of an instrument and its wearing parts. A sensible decision might be to spend more money on drumheads or bass strings if they sound fresh longer and are less likely to break soon. Instruments normally do not break easily, but individual parts can wear out. On a guitar, for example, the potentiometers begin to make noise or stop functioning, and the tuners loosen string tension, affecting pitch stability. In a wider sense, longevity can refer to aesthetic issues. This is neither a big problem for drummers nor for bassists and guitarists, who tend to have a tradition-conscious mentality that values vintage qualities (Herbst 2019b). Keyboards, on the other hand, rely on computing power and processing algorithms, and therefore newer devices offer their players improved functionality and powerful sounds that are better suited for contemporary music genres. Instrument sounds become obsolete, and those relying on preset libraries are the most affected (Théberge 1997: 245). Synthesisers that require manual patching or analogue programming are generally less impacted than other electronic keyboard instruments that rely on stock sounds. For the latter, Théberge (1997: 245) predicted that the top products would 'become obsolete within one or two brief product cycles', which would take less than five years. His reasoning still holds because it requires frequent and considerable investment to stay up to date with the latest keyboard technology. In contrast, purchases for other instrumentalists may have other motivations.

The purchase of an instrument can be justified as an investment or for reasons of prestige. Just as in the field of classical music, where a Stradivari violin is one of the most sought-after and valuable instruments, similar trophies exist in popular music. Such could be instruments produced during a specific time because they are believed to be of a better manufacture quality. For example, the Fender guitar models produced before CBS bought the company in 1965 are considered the 'holy grail' by many guitarists (Gilmer 2017). Sometimes it is the rarity that determines the value. That is the case with the Gibson Flying V of which only 98 were manufactured between 1958 and 1959. Production was then stopped because the guitars were considered too modern for the time. In 1967 production continued, but it is the rare early models that today have a high estimated market value of $200,000 to $250,000 (Greenwood & Hembree 2011). Yet other times, it is a combination of various elements. For example, Gibson's Les Paul Standard, produced between 1958 and 1960, is revered for the quality, rarity and symbolic value that iconic players like Eric Clapton or Jimmy Page have lent them (Gay 1998). These models are now worth about $225,000 to $375,000 (see also Dawe 2010: 28). Finally, there are specific instruments that were owned and played by famous players, which makes them much more valuable than the 'normal' versions that were produced at the same time and place. For example, Eric Clapton's 'Brownie Stratocaster' is estimated at $450,000, his 'Blackie Stratocaster' at $959,000 and Jimi Hendrix's Woodstock Stratocaster from 1968 at up to two million US dollars (GAKMusicBlog 2016). Within less than twenty years, the value of Hendrix's guitar increased tenfold.

Prestige is not limited to such expensive and selected instruments. Cohen (1991: 50) observed that for some rock musicians, the accumulation of gear was synonymous with status or success, which indicates that the size of one's instrument collection can also be a source of prestige. Moreover, the rarity of an otherwise non-expensive piece of equipment can be prestigious. GAS is sometimes triggered without any reason related to an instrument's characteristics, which is apparent in statements such as 'I'm in a constant state of "gear envy"' (Wright 2006: 41). The mere fact that a fellow musician owns another instrument is reason enough to buy that model as well, or something else may be acquired to satisfy gear envy.

The acoustic properties of venues where musicians with busy touring schedules perform could also justify extensive collections. Musicians interviewed by Bennett (2017: 175ff) emphasise the impact of room acoustics on their sound. Specific equipment choices are neither considered by the musicians nor Bennett, though a small bar or club gig will benefit from other gear than what is played outdoors or in large arenas. In this context, the sound system plays a considerable role because it can compensate for deficiencies in musicians' gear to some extent. Still, either of the unplugged and amplified show requires completely different equipment.

Finally, since music-making is a form of leisure activity for many musicians, buying gear can be motivated by the gratifying experience it promises. A guitarist interviewed by Wright (2006: 29) expressed to buy gear as a way of dealing with stress, but it may as well be a reward for accomplishments such as passing an exam or special efforts at work. Acquiring something unique or rare particularly strengthens the feeling of gratification.

2.4   Interest Groups

In his influential text, Becker (1996) encourages musicians to ask themselves whether they want to be remembered as 'guitar players' or 'guitar owners'. This is an important distinction that highlights the likelihood of different interest groups amongst musicians. Wright (2006: 63) comes to a similar conclusion. He considers the kind of motivation distinguishing a player from an owner. For a player, selling or trading gear would be provoked by the necessity to make space in the collection for new equipment. The motivation is likely of musical nature. Musicians change their preferences and role models over time; they develop as performers, and their equipment must reflect this development (Pinch & Reinecke 2009). Owners or collectors, on the other hand, would immediately ask themselves how the instrument could be financed. While they find many reasons for purchase—to complete their collection, get hold of a rare piece or a special edition, or buy as an investment— hardly any is musically motivated. Wright's (2006: 63) investigation suggests that most players prefer a smaller instrument collection, even if they could comfortably afford more items, and that they like to have just as many as they can regularly play. For collectors, the number of instruments is often a defining feature of their leisure identity.

A third group not addressed by Becker and Wright is the so-called 'gear head'. Collectors may also be players, but other motivations probably drive them. Gear heads are situated between players and collectors because they are active players with a keen interest in musical gear. They fit best with Théberge's (1997) theory about the commodification of music-making because their musical practice is over-commodified, possibly to the point of pathology. Cole (2018: 1061ff) gives an example in his analysis of consumption within virtual communities:

> I have more than enough pedals to do whatever I want to do. I have variations on all types of sounds/combinations. I have old, I have new—I have cheap, I have boutique. Whenever I think I am satisfied—another shiny box is produced, and I want to try it. I have so many options—it's kind of overwhelming. Amps and guitars and pedals and combinations … I have reached tone chasing fatigue.

This GAS-afflicted guitar player resembles a collector, but the motives for buying items lie elsewhere. While a collector usually tries to acquire rare (historical) instruments that systematically fit into a collecting system, the 'gear head', irrespective of a particular need or system, is mainly after the latest product or any item momentarily desired. Falk (1994) describes such behaviour as 'neophilia', the fetish of constantly striving for or desiring something new. 'Here the collection is not the mark of an order but of an unending unease, and the revealing moment is not that in which the newly-acquired object takes its place within an intelligible series but, rather, the immediately subsequent moment in which desperate desire is born again' (Straw 2000: 166). This urge seems to dominate the joy of playing and developing as a performer, as is evident in the explanation of the message board user quoted above. It is the fascination with gear that takes precedence, as another statement by a guitar player underlines: 'Since I've been around guitars for so long I own all I will ever need in terms of playing. I will never encounter a piece of music that requires a guitar I don't have' (Wright 2006: 33). Although it is not necessary to buy another piece of gear, the player admits that he would continue buying out of 'pure admiration and a strong urge to own'.

Yet another group of musicians is focused on modifying or crafting instruments. These could be called 'crafters' and overlap with any group but collectors, who do not usually modify their instruments because it would reduce the value. For the other groups, modifying or crafting instruments is motivated differently, namely by the wish to support playing, to renew parts of the instrument collection at little cost, or to have individual gear nobody else has.

> The musical adoption of technologies rarely occurs as straightforwardly as manufacturers intend. Musicians routinely transform or circumvent the original design of an instrument or component to suit needs or preferred concepts of sound. Hotwired Marshall amps allow highly distorted guitar sound at lower volumes, something not envisioned by the manufacturer, but effective musically. (Gay 1998: 85)

Music history has a long tradition of players modifying their instruments to create unique gear that supports their playing or sets them apart from others. Edward Van Halen's *Frankenstrat*, a combination of Les Paul and Stratocaster guitars, is a famous example of modification (Waksman 2004). In his editorial, Walter Becker (1996) sees the 'Guitar *Modification* Syndrome' as a 'dangerous complication to the original syndrome, that seems in more advanced cases to be doing most of the damage', highlighting the afflicted person's (irrational) reaction to 'the latest space age … materials and techniques'. Regardless of whether such modifications make sense, cursory glances at musicians' boards suggest that some users are more preoccupied with modifying their instruments than playing them. There are many variations of this practice, ranging from minor adjustments such as exchanging pickups on a guitar to building an instrument from scratch. The growing market of replacement parts and the increasing number of assembly kits for stomp box effects pedals, instruments, speaker cabinets and amplifiers have made craft consumption more accessible because of the reduced handcraft skills required. This development has created the potential to customise a performer's equipment and to provide access to replicas of historical gear, but this may again tempt musicians to focus more on the materiality of music-making than on playing.

A final group that directly opposes the 'gear head' are purists. These 'claim that optimal tone, the elusive timbre players desire, is "in the hands" rather than in the gear' (Cole 2018: 1056f). At first glance, one might believe that purists are less interested in musical equipment than gear heads, but what distinguishes them is mainly the amount of gear used. Gear heads enjoy changing their setup by adding more pieces and varying them frequently, while purists keep it as simple as possible. It does not imply that purists are less affected by GAS because the less gear they own, the better the quality of each piece must be. In contrast to gear heads that evolve artistically by changing their equipment more often with potentially cheaper items, purists would likely acquire fewer but more expensive gear that they expect to improve their musical expression best possible. This belief is evident in a statement by a rock guitarist: 'too many knobs between the guitar and the amp's speaker ... every electronic thing adds some muck to the sound and deteriorates the fidelity, hindering the directness of the "feel" of the guitar' (Gay 1998: 82). Purists consider playing with a simple rig more expressive because they believe that technology disconnects musicians from their instrument. Besides, less processing creates a more direct and potentially 'real' communication between musician and audience because the feeling is transmitted more authentically due to the shorter conduit (Gay 1998: 82, 85). Overall, purists potentially overlap with crafters, both convinced that customisation enhances playing, unlike stock gear designed for a wide range of players and purposes.

3 Role and Context of Technology for Music-Making

The previous chapter has introduced various facets of the Gear Acquisition Syndrome phenomenon and discussed psychological, social and musical reasons why musicians spend money on their equipment. It also suggested the existence of different overlapping subgroups: players, collectors, gear heads, purists and crafters. The purpose of this chapter is to develop a deeper understanding of equipment in the context of music-making. Against theoretical and empirical backdrops, we analyse why musicians invest in gear and how the musical instruments industry and other factors influence the intention to buy.

3.1 Music Technology and Popular Music

Academically, the popular music discourse generally recognises the significance of music technology: 'Without technology, popular music would not exist in its present form … popular music is, at every critical juncture of its history, determined by the technology musicians use to realize their ideas' (Jones 1992: 1). Each step of the process requires technology, be it in the rehearsal room, on the live stage or in the studio. Despite the crucial importance of recording and production technology for the mediatised manifestations of music we consume in everyday life, 'it is at the level of composition and realization that one should begin to analyse the relationship of technology and popular music, for it is at that level that popular music is formed' (Jones 1992: 7). Music takes shape through musicians playing their instruments, which is what the media-focused study of popular music sometimes overlooks. We begin our investigation at the source of musical creation by considering musicians' intentions when selecting gear and configuring setups, choices that will influence their artistic expression in the long term.

A decisive factor in the discussion of technology and sound is the music genre. Genres are characterised by various styles, such as playing styles of different instruments, personal styles of individual performers, and recording and production styles.

> Musical style is analogous to spoken language. Just as the sounds that make up a word mean different things in different languages (or, at least, potentially do so), so the sounds that make up music have different significances depending on the style. This is a tricky idea since, although we know implicitly the difference of sound between the blues and gospel, between swing and country, between rock and metal, those differences cannot be defined exclusively. (Moore 2012: 13)

On a holistic level, every style of music has sounds that define it in some way. Such defining sounds can be as general as the use of a particular tone, as per Walser's (1993: 41) often cited definition of metal music: the 'most important aural sign of heavy metal is the sound of an extremely distorted electric guitar. Anytime this sound is musically dominant, the song is arguably either metal or hard rock; any performance that lacks it cannot be included in the genre'. Sometimes much smaller differences between sounds of individual instruments are accountable for the distinction between genres. The sound of a kick drum fundamentally differs within the subgenres of electronic dance music (Zeiner-Henriksen 2006), as much as it does between rock and metal genres (Mynett 2011). Consequently, musicians must consider their choice of gear. In their musical development, they learn what equipment is expected or works best in a particular style. This expertise is accumulated through playing experience, experimenting with gear, and discussing it with fellow musicians, reading magazines, visiting websites, and watching video tutorials. Some instrument guides advise on purchasing and modifying equipment to suit musical styles (Balmer 2018; Brewster 2003; Chappell 2010; Kovarsky 2013; Sidwell & Dickinson 2011; Smith 2017), but such traditional teaching texts today play only a minor role compared to the diverse educational resources on the Internet (Menze & Gembris 2018, 2019), many of which are freely available. Sometimes retailers classify instruments stylistically, hence setting a normative reference point. Thomann, for example, lists 'Heavy Basses' and 'Heavy Guitars' in addition to classic shapes like Stratocaster and Telecaster, thus separating instruments models by genre.[2] 'Heavy' is not a genre, but even novice musicians will understand that this gear is intended for 'heavy metal' and the more extreme subgenres within metal music. Interestingly, this stylistic classification is only made for selected instruments such as the guitar, indicating a higher level of genre-specific specialisation for this instrument. For other instruments, a distinction is made between acoustic and electronic (drums), the kind of sound generation (keyboard instruments) or the tuning and pitch range (brass and wind instruments). The primary criterion for distinguishing 'heavy' guitars and basses seems to be visual because most of them have more extravagant shapes and finishes. The technical differences concern both pickups, which are more suited for high distortion levels, and vibrato systems like Floyd Rose, allowing more extreme modulation techniques such as 'pitch bombs' common in metal music. Apart from Thomann, several larger retailers distinguish between 'regular' and 'heavy' instruments. Music Store, for example, has a dedicated 'Heavy Metal Shop'[3] for guitars, guitar amplifiers, guitar effects and guitar accessories like leather and rivet straps, but nothing comparable for any other instrument.

Little research exists on musical instruments typically played in the diverse genres. Considerably more has been written about recording and production, at least if practice-oriented manuals are considered (Felton 2016; Langford 2011; Morton 2000; Mynett 2011, 2017; Snoman 2009). Herbst's (2016, 2019b) study is one of the

---

[2] The only other 'exoticised' genre is jazz.

[3] The British version of the online store, operated by DV247, labels the subsection as 'Heavy Metal Shop', whereas the original German version lists it as 'Heavy Shop'.

few investigating how genre preferences relate to guitar players' favourite gear. As was to be expected, musicians of less distortion-intensive genres such as jazz, soul, funk and reggae prefer guitars with single-coil pickups (Stratocaster and Telecaster) and semi or hollow-body models, amplified by combined head and cabinet devices ('combos') with less than 30 watts of power. As a traditional setup, it is best suited to produce undistorted and slightly overdriven sounds and offers a wide range of tones. Players of blues, classic rock and hard rock prefer the Les Paul shape with humbucker pickups played through larger amplifier stacks (separate head and cabinet) with various power specifications; such a setup works effectively for these genres because it is characterised by moderately distorted sounds that can be 'cleaned up' if necessary. Most metal guitarists prefer 'Superstrat' models (Stratocaster shape with humbucker pickups) combined with high power amplifier stacks. This setup allows for producing low frequencies and significant distortion with relatively little noise. In terms of preferences for technology (valve, transistor, hybrid, simulation), players of the various genres differ in many respects, especially their use of additional pedals or specific rigs.

Similar differences between genres also exist for other instruments. Bass players, just like guitarists, can choose from a range of physical shapes and pickup configurations that affect the sound to better suit 'cleaner' or 'grungier' genres. They also need to find the right amplifier technology, for example, transistor, valve or hybrid, and a suitable speaker cabinet. Smaller 10-inch speakers support more percussive styles like funk, while larger 15-inch speakers reproduce lower frequencies suitable for modern metal or reggae. For drummers, shell sizes determine the overall tone and suitability for different genres. 'Lighter' genres tend to use smaller shells like 16 or 18-inch kick drum and 8 to 14-inch toms. In comparison, the demand for sonic weight motivates many rock and metal drummers to use 20 to 24-inch kick drums and 12 to 18-inch toms (Mynett 2017). In metal music, shells are also increasingly triggered and sample-reinforced, even in the rehearsal room, so that the acoustic sound of the natural kit is gradually replaced by a studio-produced aesthetic (D. Williams 2015). The cymbal preference is also likely to vary between genres. There are no set rules, but more 'funky' styles can benefit from splash cymbals—smaller crash cymbals with a shorter decay time—while drummers of 'harder' genres tend to make frequent use of china cymbals, which are a more penetrating version of crash cymbals. Similarly, metal drummers might choose a heavier ride cymbal with a clearly defined short 'ping' that remains transparent in a dense arrangement. Jazz drummers probably prefer a light and 'washy' ride that fills out space in a trio ensemble. Keyboard players must decide whether they wish to have many sounds in one instrument, for example, analogue synthesisers, electric organs and stage pianos, or prefer specialised gear for specific sounds. Also, an instrument's playing feel depends on the kind of keys: they may be unweighted in synth-style or (semi-)weighted, reproducing the feel of playing the piano. While weighted piano-style keys have a more differentiated touch response and may support the feel of a pop ballad, synth-style keys allow faster funky licks and slides. Hence, the need for certain sounds and the amount of equipment can vary depending on genre.

Over the last decades, many popular music genres have developed various sub-genres and sub-subgenres, which brought about diversification and specialisation of gear. 1950s rock & roll had a more defined band configuration of the drum kit, up-right bass, piano, saxophone and vocals, and performers could choose from a limited number of available instrument models. Seventy years on, a djent metal band[4] has a rock setup added with electronics (Marrington 2017), and the band members can pick from a multitude of different electric and bass guitars, amplifiers, effects, drum kit configurations and vocal microphones. Equipment that works for djent, for example extended-range guitars with seven or eight strings (Gil 2014), may not fit other genres of rock and subgenres of metal. Therefore, musicians playing different substyles of a genre may need to invest in different equipment suitable for each style. If musicians play various genres of a fundamentally different aesthetic, the need may be amplified. Stylistic flexibility is an interesting element concerning GAS; musicians, who want to realise their full potential in a genre, will most probably expand their instrument collection. However, it could also be tempting to buy more gear to avoid the effort of getting the most out of the current setup.

The discussion of genre conventions in terms of aesthetics and gear touches on another essential variable, the question of uniqueness and individual sound. As Théberge (1997: 191) states:

> musicians today (as well as critics and audiences) often speak of having a unique and personal 'sound' in the same manner in which another generation of musicians might have spoken of having developed a particular 'style' of playing or composing. The term 'sound' has taken on a peculiar material character that cannot be separated either from the 'music'.

Besides the two main elements of making music before a recording can take place, performance and composition, sound quality has become increasingly important. As the mediating element, the sound transports the performed composition to its audience (Gay 1998). Théberge (1997: 186) goes on saying that 'a concentration on the "right" sounds for a given musical context can shift the musician's attention away from other, more familiar levels of musical form, such as melody, rhythm, and harmony'. Consequently, the material need for good tone in the form of gear has gradually gained importance, a trend unbroken since Théberge's writing more than twenty years ago. Just as a singer's timbre can be their main appeal, an instrumentalist's unique sound can attract an audience. To give one example: Tom Morello's

---

[4] Djent is a progressive subgenre of metal, defined by its 'virtuosity and complex rhythms' and a 'characteristic guitar timbre' (Marrington 2017: 260). It was named after an onomatopoeia based on the highly distorted, low-tuned and palm-muted guitar sound.

creative use of guitar tones and effects demonstrates a less conventional kind of expressiveness that has made him popular amongst guitarists, some even seeing him as the greatest revolutionary since Eddie Van Halen (Rensen & Stösser 2011: 217ff). However, the distinctiveness of sound is not as easily perceptible as that of the voice. If musicians in the audience play the same instrument as the performer, they will probably be more aware of the sound's uniqueness than players of other instruments or an audience of non-musicians.

The demand for a unique and personal sound is conflictual. On the one hand, genres have an expected aesthetic with varying tolerance for disregarding it. To match acoustic requirements, genre-specific instruments and sounds have become established (Herbst 2019b). On the other hand, artists are expected to be original and have a unique sonic signature, which is perceived as a mark of quality (Zagorski-Thomas 2014: 66ff). There are diverse ways to fine-tune sounds of the instruments used in popular music. Electric guitar and bass tones can be shaped by carefully combining the instrument with selected amplifier(s) and effects devices. Acoustic drum sounds can be varied by changing drumheads, adding cymbals and percussion pieces, and electrifying the whole kit or parts of it. Keyboard and synthesiser sounds can be designed from scratch and modulated for artistic effect. Moreover, it has become possible to create or refine the sounds of all the discussed instruments on a computer. Software such as Native Instruments' Guitar Rig provides access to numerous amplifiers and effects that can be combined in multiple ways with high control over signal routing. Although the name of the software implies the guitar as the target instrument, it can also be used for basses, keyboards and other application, including music production. For keyboards, some bundles authentically emulate vintage synthesisers, organs and pianos, such as Arturia's V-Collection. Furthermore, innovative software synthesisers like Xfer Record's Serum or Native Instruments' Massive define the sound of modern electronic music. These instruments are either controlled with a MIDI keyboard or programmed with a mouse. Electronic drums can be based on hardware sampler engines or software, and acoustic drums can be extended by electronic sounds with special pads or by using trigger devices. In the 1980s and 1990s, powerful computer processors brought about keyboard synthesisers and drum machines. More recently, hybrid analogue and digital systems and digital signal processing have opened up vast opportunities for tone shaping, making it possible to create individual sounds for all instruments used in popular music. Bennett (2017: 54) already observed in the 1980s the common 'religious quest' of musicians to combine the right equipment to meet their expectations and needs. Now, forty years later, the fine-tuning and specialisation of gear has become considerably more fine-grained due to greater control over sound settings and the vast range of consumer goods available.

As has been argued, musicians have benefitted from an increased range of instruments and options of customising and combining gear. To what extent musicians customise their equipment in practice is unclear. Théberge (1993: 248) believes that there are two types of keyboard players. One group appreciates the improved functionality of synthesisers, while the other group feels overwhelmed and looks for preset sounds that work right away. The latter can be referred to as 'push-and-play-people', a market term by manufacturers to describe 'people who do not want to get very involved in the technical aspect of recording and music-making, but who do want to perform or create music' (Jones 1992: 85). According to Jones, 90% of musicians belong to this group. Yet, equating 'push-and-pull' musicians with amateurs is too simplistic (Jones 1992: 86); they are represented in all status groups, from beginners to professionals. Some musicians do not have the time to experiment with equipment or do not want to invest in it:

> When I look at a synthesizer, I go for the presets. If the presets aren't happening, I don't want it. I don't have time to be fooling around. I just want to punch through some stuff, hit a sound, and say, 'Oh yeah. This is it.' I mean, people get paid at the factory to put programs in it … I'm not getting paid to get sounds out of a machine. I'm paid to make a record. (Jam as cited in Doerschuk 1987: 80)

This statement comes from Jimmy Jam, producer of internationally successful artists such as Janet Jackson, Mariah Carey and Chaka Khan. Since stock presets are usually created by highly skilled professionals, they are unlikely to be inferior to customised settings. As Jones (1992: 87) points out, 'push and play' does not prevent musicians from producing innovative sounds. One way to use presets is to blend standard sounds unconventionally. Yet, the main reason why Jimmy Jam relies on presets is the workflow in the studio. Efficient working habits contribute to creativity and low costs (Herbst 2021). Musicians who are not under time pressure can choose to spend more time optimising their sound, either as a long-term 'investment' or for experimentation. How this situation has changed over the past twenty years is not clear. It may well be that musicians have increasingly adopted customisation of sounds and instruments so that it has become standard practice in music-making. Yet few signs point to it. Inventor Christoph Kemper reveals (Herbst 2019a) that guitar players rarely use the powerful sound shaping functions of profiling amplifiers, a relatively recent technology that sits between valve amplifiers and emulation. In chapter 3.2, we will discuss whether this reluctance of guitar players to explore drastically different sounds is possibly due to a deeper, instrument-specific ideology.

So far, we have mainly been concerned with the aesthetical motivations for the choice of gear. Playability is another reason for selecting an instrument. Its physical properties are the main determinants of playability, accompanied by secondary aspects such as functionality. Often overlooked is the influence tonal quality has on playability and expressiveness (Herbst 2016), which can differ between instruments and take various forms too. Sounds require a reaction and therefore affect the choice of notes, as keyboardist Starr Parodi emphasises:

> Sounds really make you play a certain way. If you have a little, dry, ticky-type sound, you might not take the soaring solo that you would with a different sound … I really think that sounds inspire you … If you get a keyboard that has an interesting sound, you don't have to play a lot of notes on it. The sound takes over. (Parodi as cited in Théberge 1993: 264)

During improvisation, reaction to sound is strongest. But even if musicians have a composed lead line or solo, the sound can be set up in advance to best support musical intention. It may require adding effects or changing sounds fundamentally during a solo.

The guitar is another instrument where the choice of model and tonal subtleties significantly impacts expression. According to Dire Straits guitarist Mark Knopfler:

> If you take your song and change the key or the instrument that you play it on, or you pick up something else and do it a different way, very often the instrument will dictate something new to you. It's the difference between sitting down with a piano and sitting down with a guitar, or sitting down with a Spanish guitar as opposed to an electric. I often find that what I've written can yield something else. Even a different string gauge can create something completely different. Very often I've found that if I'm playing something with very heavy strings, I'm not bending them, and it leaves room for something else to happen. (Knopfler as cited in Blackett 2019)

Knopfler stresses the effect a sound can have on composition and arrangement, but he also hints at consequences for playability. The guitar's natural characteristic is staccato (Weissberg 2010: 99f); notes cannot be sustained as easily as on a piano, nor can they be connected as fluently as on a bowed string instrument. Adding distortion increases the guitar's sustain and allows the performer to modulate it like a voice (Jauk 2009: 268f) or a violin (Middleton 1990: 30ff; Walser 1993: 63ff). It smoothens the sound through compression and masks lacking synchronisation between the fretting and picking hand, which makes it easier to perform fast solo lines (Herbst 2017c). Distortion further brings out characteristics of distinct playing techniques like artificial harmonics. It enables, for example, responding to playback feedback, which is not possible on an acoustic guitar. Sound quality can be inspiring, both in melodic phrasing and in songwriting. Mark Knopfler points out that compositions written on the piano differ from those written on a guitar. Choosing different instruments for composing affects harmony, especially with keyboard instruments allowing for more sophisticated voice leading and complex chords. But even the different sound qualities of a single instrument influence creative choices, as Billy Gould, guitarist of Faith No More, explains:

> Every amp has its own strengths and weaknesses and you learn how to play to these amps … And what you can do, is you can start writing and using the strengths of the amplifier, where it sounds better on certain chords than on other amps. When I

write now, I write using those characteristics, the character. (Gould as cited in Herbst 2021)

Compared to the electric guitar, an acoustic drum kit's sound impacts performance behaviour less. Using microphones or trigger clips to amplify or extend the sound still contributes to a better playing feel. For example, compression can compensate for volume irregularities or produce powerful volumes in fast sections. This dynamic range reduction is crucial for the fast double-kick playing common in modern metal genres (Mynett 2017). But even today, rhythmic quality cannot be manipulated and controlled in a live performance the same way as in the studio, where there are multiple post-processing possibilities.

All these previous discussions highlight the strong connection between genre aesthetics, the performer's individuality and a setup's playability. The material component of music-making has become ever more important, requiring musicians to possess more gear and to become masters of its sonic potential. Hence the understanding of playing and the definition of playing skills have changed because both must include technical efficiency more than ever before. As Théberge (1993: 190) argues, innovations in musical technology and the specialisation of musical genres have led to a 'general blurring of distinctions between musician and technician, amateur and professional'. A musician's role more and more entails the role of a technician or technologist because they are increasingly expected to engineer their sound on stage and recordings. Moreover, musicians might wish greater control over their sound as they progress in their careers (Herbst 2021; Herbst & Albrecht 2018).

Until now, we have concentrated on matters related to playability and wider conventions associated with genre or music history. There is also the social component which is easily overlooked. The discussed relevance of an individual sound and originality touch on social aspects, as they situate the performer in a broader context. Nowadays, the virtual community of musicians on online and video platforms can put pressure on a musician to live up to expectations (see Herbst & Vallejo 2021). The immediate social environment—local music scenes and bands to which the musicians belong—can also influence how a musician deals with gear (Bennett 2017). Little research has concentrated on the gear-related effects of social units like a band. From a holistic viewpoint, the best musical result will be achieved when all band members jointly decide on what gear to use. Acoustically, instruments must complement and support each other to create an intelligible and expressive ensemble sound. Aesthetically, equipment choice is inseparably linked to an artistic concept and therefore decisive for the overall effect. However, this whole concept is sometimes difficult to achieve if band members have different musical preferences or do not understand acoustic principles. Ambitious bands with technologically minded members carefully select their instruments for certain songs and adjust amplifier and effects settings to support their artistic message. Depending on the ensemble's stylistic breadth, matching requirements of certain songs with optimal gear may require an extensive gear collection across the band. That is why purchases within the ensemble should best be strategically discussed to work towards a more effective collective sound. From a GAS point of view, purchases by one band member may trigger fellow musicians to follow suit. Such a process can be musically motivated, for example, to better complement the sound of new gear, or psychologically motivated. A bandmate's purchases could be envied and encourage experimentation with new equipment.

3.2   Vintage, Nostalgia and Innovation

The previous discussion highlighted the relevance of specialist music equipment from a musician's perspective and presented examples of why musicians wish to invest in equipment. Some of the reasons found were conforming to genre conventions, creating a unique personal sound and improving the playability of one's setup. But as has already been indicated, the choice and handling of gear are not only determined by musical reasons; musical instruments are a rich symbolic terrain (Frith 1986; Théberge 1997; Waksman 2003).

Before, we have discussed musical reasons why musicians choose older instruments or artificially aged gear. Our elaborations on vintage musical equipment indicate that its popularity has been maintained for a long time, and there is no reason to believe this will change anytime soon. Influential musicians like Eric Clapton, Jimmy Page, Tony Iommi and Geezer Butler played some of the most popular guitar and bass models manufactured by Fender and Gibson in the 1950s and 1960s. Subsequent generations of artists such as Saul 'Slash' Hudson, John Sykes and Doug Aldrich were inspired to play the same models and, if available, from the early years of manufacture. Other players in the late 1970s and 1980s, such as Eddie Van Halen, George Lynch and Gary Moore, experimented with amplifiers and guitars, contributing to the development of new instrument technologies used in modern forms of rock and popular music. In the late 1980s and early 1990s, two interest groups became more common than they were in previous decades: one valuing innovation and one vintage gear. Towards the end of the 1980s, specialist magazines for vintage equipment emerged. In 1986 the North American *Vintage Guitar* magazine was launched, dedicated to vintage fretted instruments (guitar and bass), amplifiers, effects and other accessories. It included stories about established players, interviews with classic gear manufacturers and workshops by luthiers on refurbishing ageing instruments. Two years later, in 1988, the first vintage drum magazine, *Not So Modern Drummer*, entered the American market. It pitched itself as a 'treasure trove of information about vintage drums, custom drums & legendary drummers'[5] similar to

---

[5] www.notsomoderndrummer.com; accessed 16 September 2019.

Vintage Guitar. Another magazine was *Vintage Drummer* (2001–2005), which was renamed *Classic Drummer* in 2005 to shift the focus of vintage drum and gear to 'artists of any era who played in a feel-based classic style'.[6] There was no equivalent magazine for keyboard instruments with a vintage focus. *Keyboard* magazine (since 1975) occasionally covered old instruments. Still, it was not until 1993 that it published a dedicated book on vintage instruments—*Vintage Synthesizers: Groundbreaking Instruments and Pioneering Designers of Electronic Music Synthesizers* (Vail 1993). This book finally dealt with renowned analogue synthesisers from 1962 on, developed by pioneering manufacturers such as Moog, Buchla, EMS and ARP. It included interviews with artists such as Keith Emerson and Wendy Carlos. However, most print keyboard magazines were mainly interested in the latest technologies, and discussions about vintage gear took mostly place in online forums that emerged in the 1990s. At this time, other vintage instruments like the Rhodes piano also began to arouse interest.[7] But still, a long time passed until an 'analogue revival' began to shape the keyboard world more generally by the turn of the 2000s (Pinch & Trocco 2002: 317ff). Overall, the continuing popularity of replicas of older instruments, not only for guitars, drums and basses but also for synthesisers, indicates that vintage gear is not a short-lived trend but rather reflects the desires of many musicians of various instruments for more than two decades by now – similar to the general interest in older popular music from the 1960s to the 1990s (Reynolds 2012). Indeed, Bennett (2017: 55f) observes that musicians in the early 1970s were most interested in instruments from the early 1950s because they believed in the better quality of older fabrications. The appreciation of older devices seems to be a widespread phenomenon among musicians that occurs independently of specific instruments or generations.

In Western societies, novelty and, as a result, technological progress, are generally regarded as beneficial to creative practices (Niu & Sternberg 2006). Any technological innovation is viewed positively. Taylor (2001: 1) considers the advent of digital music technology the 'most fundamental change in the history of Western music since the invention of music notation in the ninth century'. In a similar vein, Jones (2006: 19f) asks how anyone could be 'against' technology in the face of its 'unprecedented and ubiquitous force' and universal impact. Those rejecting novel technologies like the 'neo-Luddites' do so as a conscious symbolic act. How this can

---

[6] www.classicdrummer.com/contact; accessed 16 September 2019.

[7] There is little research on the interest in vintage keyboard equipment in popular music. Our perception is based on a cursory analysis of keyboard magazines like *Keyboard* and *Keys*. The impression we got was confirmed by keyboard expert Immanuel Brockhaus. He is investigating cult sounds in popular music in an ongoing research project. Results are available on the project website (http://www.cult-sounds.com) and published in a monograph (Brockhaus 2017).

take form becomes evident in the practices around vintage instruments. In the field of record production, several studies have discussed the oversimplified view of technological development as progress. Barlindhaug (2007: 75) points out that new production technology, despite its increased functionality, does not just replace older gear. Likewise, Bennett (2012) argues that analogue recording equipment has tangible advantages over digital tools beyond their mere iconic value, mythology and romance, for example, easier maintenance and more ergonomic workflow. In music production and music technology more generally, including musical instruments, both tradition and innovation have their place, and both can coexist and fulfil distinct functions (Negus & Pickering 2004: 91).

Discussion of affordances and attitudes towards analogue and digital equipment for various instruments requires a theoretical understanding of innovation. From a sociological perspective, Braun-Thürmann (2005: 6; our translation) understands innovations as 'material or symbolic artefacts that observers perceive as novel and experience as an improvement over the existing'. Innovations do not come from nowhere. They are usually based on the application of a new idea to an existing product. Thus, even when innovations are advertised as a novelty, they build on existing technology but add quality or extended functionality (Taylor 2001: 7f). Just like music technology, innovations are always integrated into a social system. As an *interactive* product, innovations only become real when a second party experiences the product as innovative and bases its actions on it (Braun-Thürmann 2005: 6). In his influential work *Diffusion of Innovation*, Rogers (2003) points out the high degree of uncertainty for the individual that must be overcome before an artefact is evaluated as an improvement and finally adopted. To convince an individual, an innovation must fulfil five criteria in Rogers's theory (2003: 15f). The most fundamental one is the 'relative advantage' that new technology must provide. Taking the keyboard as an example, more advanced electronic circuits and increased memory and hard drive space allow more realistic sounds and larger sound libraries. Another core criterion is 'compatibility' with existing values and past experiences. For musicians whose convictions are fundamentally opposed to digital technologies, their 'relative advantage' over analogue gear must be significant to make them adopt a digital device. A third core criterion is 'complexity', the ease of use. The final two criteria are secondary for an innovation to be adopted. 'Triability' is the opportunity of trying out, and 'observability' concerns the degree to which its use is visible to others.

Players of different types of popular music instruments vary significantly in their views on analogue and digital equipment and their preferences for either vintage or cutting-edge musical gear. Distinguishing analogue from digital and innovation from tradition is rarely black and white. Théberge (1993: 278) emphasises the role of digital signal processing power and falls into the trap of equating guitar players with keyboardists:

'effects' such as delays, flangers, reverbs, and the like, have come to be thought of as inherent properties of a sound (and this is as true for guitar players, who process their guitar sounds through an array of footpedals and special effects devices, as it is for synthesizer players) and virtually all contemporary keyboards now contain sophisticated digital effects units built directly into the instrument.

He makes no distinction between keyboards, synthesisers and guitars regarding effects, claiming that all benefit from technological advances. Since most keyboard instruments are digital, better processing power allows more oscillators or other sound generators such as wavetables, higher sampling rates and bit depths, besides a more complex rendering of reverb and modulation effects. Consequently, advances in computing power and technologies that extend the functionality, such as synthesis and sampling, improve keyboard instruments. With synthesisers, it may be the same but not necessarily so. Technological advances in *digital* synthesis since the advent of early models such as Yamaha's frequency modulation synthesiser DX7 (1983), with its cumbersome interface, have improved parameter control. Better computer memory (RAM) has increased the complexity of early wavetable synthesisers like PPG's Wave (1981) by a higher number of wavelets, improving the general audio quality. Similar improvements ensuring better quality and controllability apply to early vector synthesisers like Sequential Circuits Prophet VS (1986). Newer forms of synthesis, such as the processing-intensive physical modelling synthesis at the heart of popular instruments like the Nord Lead keyboard (1994), would not have been possible without enhanced computational power. All these technological advances have provided a variety of positive effects. They increased the instruments' audio quality, functionality and number of oscillators, filters and polyphonic voices without any disadvantages. According to Rogers's (2003) theory, these improvements are all 'relative advantages' because they improve an instrument's sound, adjustability and usability.

Analogue synthesisers have benefitted differently from technological advances. Buchla and Moog's early synthesisers were purely monophonic, which frustrated keyboard players used to polyphonic instruments such as organ and piano (Théberge 1997: 52). Introducing polyphony and increasing the number of voices on synthesisers during the 1970s improved the instrument's functionality, sound design options and playability. Other enhancements include the portability and handling of new devices like the Minimoog (Théberge 1997: 52), modular designs affording more detailed sound design, and the introduction of a pattern sequencer as in the case of Buchla's Music Box Series 100 (Pejrolo & Metcalfe 2017: 13). Compared to digital keyboard instruments, these analogue synthesisers are valued for their tactile controls (Pinch & Reinecke 2009: 156f). All parameters are accessible in the form of knobs and sliders, making it easy for musicians to manipulate sound while playing (Pinch & Trocco 2002: 224). From the beginning, live sound manipulation was an essential part of the performative expression of synthesisers (Barlindhaug 2007: 81), which was lost with digital keyboards that allowed quick switching between fundamentally different sounds at the touch of a button. According to composer Brian Eno, 'muscular activity' was replaced by 'mental activity' during the transition from analogue to digital keyboard instruments. Others like Taylor (2001: 97) see the main difference in 'agency', arguing that analogue gear allows greater control. However, digital keyboard instruments offer similar means of control over sound parameters that go beyond analogue gear, even if they are less intuitive and therefore possibly less attractive to musicians, according to Rogers's criterion of 'complexity' for adopting an innovation.

The introduction of digital synthesisers was, above all, a fundamental split in sound aesthetics and conception: analogue synthesisers offered more organic and individual sounds, digital keyboard instruments better functionality (Pinch & Trocco 2002: 318f). Analogue synthesisers were valued for their warmth and transparency of signal flow (Théberge 1997: 119), so further technological development was considered not as crucial as for their digital counterpart. Therefore, affordable remakes of classic analogue synthesisers tend to be more popular than newly introduced synthesisers with innovative features (Pinch & Reinecke 2009: 156f). This situation is similar for guitar players, who Théberge also included in his assertion about advances in effects technology. He is right in saying that for *some* players, effects are a relevant or even crucial part of their sound. However, guitarists throughout history have been divided over digital technology. Digital effects were popular when they were new in the 1980s, with guitar players exploring modern rack setups with hybrid amplification using valve and transistor technology (Maloof 2004). Yet in the 1990s, most guitarists returned to simple, traditional setups that consisted of an amplifier (combo or stack) and pedalboard, commonly all analogue (Herbst 2019b). Indeed, musicians' growing interest in low output valve amplifiers and the rise of such offers indicates an increasing preference for classical sounds of the 1960s and 1970s (see also Reynolds 2012). A small group of guitar players tolerant of change showed considerable interest in advanced modelling, simulation and profiling technology for amplifiers and effects (Herbst 2021). Nevertheless, progress in guitar technology has not yet been widely appreciated, especially when it comes to digital systems (Herbst 2019a; Herbst et al. 2018). Even for players open to digital equipment, amplifier simulations are often out of the question (Pinch & Reinecke 2009: 163). Gay (1998: 87), in agreement with Taylor (2001: 97), argues that less complex analogue gear gives guitar players a sense of agency, while Pinch and Reinecke (2009: 163) observe that digital guitar amplifiers make it challenging to find the sweet spot and that they lack individuality. According to the beliefs of the interviewed guitar players, it is the

> imprecision and parts that don't quite work properly which give these old instruments and equipment their special value … In a way, this is reminiscent of the value placed upon instruments before the age of mass production and electronics,

when each individually crafted instrument with its own idiosyncrasies of sound and action were what people valued. (Pinch & Reinecke 2009: 163)

Given the high degree of control over sound parameters and the sonic authenticity of modern digital amplifier simulations, these views and reasons say more about the cultural values players associate with technology than about its musical suitability. Crowdy (2013) suggests that musicians tend to make claims about equipment based on their attitudes and beliefs rather than on facts or the listening impression. Often,

the aural differences are so subtle that most people are unable to actually hear them. Here we have sound aesthetics effectively acting as a proxy for other areas of opinion and value. These may include appearance, usability, brand loyalty, peer pressure and justification of expense. (Crowdy 2013: 152)

There seems to be an implicit understanding amongst guitar players that analogue gear is more suitable for the skilled player (Herbst 2019b). Interviews with guitarists conducted by Pinch and Reinecke (2009: 158) indicate a widespread practice of amateurs familiarising themselves with vintage gear through listening and practical experimentation, often under the guidance of more experienced players. Individual preferences for non-mainstream technologies and instruments are difficult to maintain due to the strong influence of social expectations within the guitar scene.

With a drum set, the distinction between the traditional acoustic kit and the modern electronic set is less clear. Electronic drums are becoming increasingly common for reasons of affordability, lower volume, smaller size, various selectable sounds and the fact that they require neither tuning nor maintenance (Bache n.d.). But generally, they are not regarded as an improvement or even an adequate replacement of an acoustic kit; they serve different purposes, be it for live or studio work, for practising or touring, or as a primary or additional instrument (Andertons n.d.; Bache n.d.). For musical reasons, most drum guides still present the acoustic kit as the 'real deal' and recommend an electronic set to drummers interested in electronic genres. That points to acoustic drummers not benefitting from technological innovation to the same degree. In contrast, electronic drummers do so from better audio quality such as high-resolution samples, improved accuracy and velocity in terms of dynamics, and generally from larger instrument libraries.

While keyboards and digital synthesisers are prone to becoming outdated, Théberge (1993: 178) reasons that 'the discourse of "vintage" instruments is a strategic one: it helps to counteract the fear among many consumers of new technology that their purchases will become obsolete and worthless'. This concern is likely to be specific to digital keyboard instruments, guitar amplifier simulations, effects units and potentially electronic drum kits, as limited computational power and hard drive space negatively affect sound quality. With analogue equipment as guitar amplifiers or subtractive synthesisers, sound quality is negatively affected by a complex signal path; from a technical viewpoint, the quality of a simple signal path is superior (Gay

1998). Innovation rather concerns the adjustability of sounds, such as expanding the amplifier's filter section with resonance and presence controls, which were increasingly added to devices in the 1970s (Herbst 2016: 36).

Little empirical research has focused on the attitudes of players of different instruments towards their gear. Electric guitarists have been researched the most. Herbst's (2016, 2019b) study demonstrates that guitarists commonly appreciate traditional equipment and that players of more modern or 'extreme' genres such as metalcore or nu metal tend to deviate from this general pattern. The study also finds that guitarists have only little interest in experimenting with equipment, for example, by comparing guitars, amplifiers and effects pedals. An innovative sound was generally not overly relevant, although the sound quality was of the highest importance. This finding supports the notion that guitar players tend to care much about their sound, but that originality, as Théberge (1997: 191) suggests, is not the top of their priority list. The answers regarding attitudes and preferred equipment instead suggest that many guitarists intend to conform to genre aesthetics, and apart from some modern or experimental genres, most genres rely on classic instruments, amplifier models and pedals. In summary, we can safely assume that most guitarists are tradition-conscious, consistent with the popularity of vintage equipment among them.

In their study of the guitar as an artefact and icon, Ryan and Peterson (2001: 104f) identify three types of vintage buyers. The first type is the successful professional musician who has the money to purchase expensive equipment and the skills to use it. The authors do not explain what specific skills are required to 'operate' vintage instruments. One can guess that for keyboard instruments, the ability to handle complex routings of modular synthesisers is required. Guitar skills are likely the mastery of accurately responding to the tone produced by a low-output pickup in combination with a low-gain amplifier because such a tone does not mask a weak playing technique (Herbst 2017c). The playability of drums and basses seems to be less affected by the vintage quality of instruments, apart from the consequences for maintenance. The second type of vintage buyer are collectors who either wish to systematically complement a collection or see the purchase as an investment, speculating that the instrument will eventually increase in value. The third type is the non-professional player; most vintage buyers belong to this group. Their motivations range from owning a high-quality instrument with aged material to speculative investment. In discussing vintage guitars, Ryan and Peterson (2001: 110) claim them to be less popular with younger generations. Contesting the idea that vintage instruments are of better quality per se, younger players stress these may be noisy and subject to unpredictable production standards. They also argue that inflated prices deter younger musicians. Besides, some of them might be less excited about old instruments when their idols play more modern gear to achieve a contemporary sound. This theory accords with Shuker's (2010: 102) claim that vintage guitars are aimed at an age group over thirty.

Nostalgia is another potential motivation for buying and honouring vintage gear. Boym (2001) distinguishes two forms of nostalgia that are useful for understanding the popularity of vintage instruments: *restorative nostalgia* and *reflective nostalgia*. Reflective nostalgia is about a person's biography, while restorative nostalgia is concerned with the past more generally. Drawing on Hobsbawm and Ranger's (1983) theory of 'invented traditions', restorative nostalgia is about preserving 'truth' and 'tradition'. It comprises the genuine restoration and preservation of history and origin, and it further involves a longing for temporal distance, which it satisfies by an 'intimate experience and the availability of a desired object' (Boym 2001: 44).

In the practices relating to vintage instruments, there are several forms of restorative nostalgia. For the individual musician, authentic vintage gear or authentic replicas are a direct link through a physical object to a previous time in music history that can be valued for multiple reasons. According to Théberge (1993: 178), '"vintage" instruments are understood to give the player a form of direct sonic (and sometimes iconic) access to the past and, thereby, an almost magical ability to evoke the power of some past music'. This nostalgic longing seems to be a reason why guitar and bass players appreciate instruments from the 1960s and 1970s. Feature stories in magazines indicate that many regard this period as the heyday of rock music, in which innovative players like Jimi Hendrix, Jimmy Page, Eric Clapton and Geezer Butler became role models for future generations of musicians (see also Reynolds 2012). This phenomenon is not bounded to modern players. For example, Aerosmith's Joe Perry bought a Les Paul guitar because Jeff Beck played one, and Rolling Stones' Ron Wood chose a Gibson guitar because of Elvis Presley (Ryan & Peterson 2001: 99). A guitarist in Pinch and Reinecke's (2009: 164) study has a shelf of books about the history of instruments in his studio so that he can feel a 'connection to the past playing a real instrument from the past, I can imagine the people who might have played it before me'. At all times, musicians have been attracted to older instruments played by esteemed musicians to connect with them and to feel part of a culturally meaningful community.

For more recent musicians, the appreciation of early rock music harbours romantic notions of authenticity because the setups of that time were simple, all analogue, rarely amplified by a PA system, pure and thus 'good' in the ears of musicians who value vintage instruments. Hence vintage gear fulfils the romantic promise of the good old times in history. Music was 'authentic' because it was handmade, skilled, serious and as little mediated as possible. In contrast, pop music since the 1980s embraces a modernist ideology that celebrates the affordances of newer technology to shape music drastically beyond human performances (Keightley 2001). Characterised by an imagined 'golden age' that may have never existed (McCracken 1986), early rock music is still idealised. Furthermore, the playing skills of renowned musicians such as Jimi Hendrix are celebrated to the present day (Herbst & Vallejo 2021). Playing an authentic vintage instrument of that time or a relic model is linked with the hope that part of the power is in the device itself and flows straight into its player (Lévi-Strauss 1963). Such superstition becomes evident from a statement by Joey, a successful guitarist in the 1970s and 1980s, interviewed for Fernandez and Lastovicka's (2011: 292f) study on fetishes in contemporary consumption:

> I pick up the '54 Strat[ocaster] and I'm channeling Buddy Holly because that's [just like] the exact guitar he played, same year, same everything, same finish. So in a way it becomes the soul of the [original] guitar in my mind, I don't know where this guitar has been, obviously it's not Buddy's.

The mere thought that the instrument could be a 'sibling' of Buddy Holly's original guitar has symbolical value for its player. Guitarist Joey is aware that the 'magic' is only imaginary, while from other interviews, it is less certain to what extent players believe in the magic of an instrument. When asked about his dream guitar, Artie, another player who participated in the study, replied: 'the one Billy Corgan [lead guitarist of the Smashing Pumpkins] played... maybe his genes rubbed off on the fingerboard [of the guitar] and I might pick them up a bit? ... I don't know, just because it was his'. Fernandez and Lastovicka (2011: 282) argue that Artie genuinely believes that the original guitar Billy Corgan played would improve his performance due to 'contagious magic'. Drawing on Belk's theory of fetishes as 'magical objects' (1991: 28) with 'magical power' (2001a: 61) and 'magical aura' (1996: 81), Fernandez and Lastovicka (2011: 279) argue that this effect is not limited to instruments owned and played by the esteemed artist but also occurs in mass-produced replicas.

A strong motivator for restorative nostalgia is the prospect of reliving a musical time of the romanticised past that players may not even have experienced themselves. On the early stereo records between 1965 and 1972, mixes were often not yet symmetrical (Moore & Dockwray 2010), so their listeners can switch off the instruments that are just on the left or right channel. That allows hobby musicians to play the muted instrument part along with the original band. The nostalgic reliving of the experience and the feeling of being part of the ensemble become even more authentic when a similar setup to the original is played. The emotional impact of such an experience is demonstrated by guitar player Jack: 'wow ... I sound just like him! And I tell you, it's quite a magical feeling. You know, to blend in with this group whose music you love so much and you hold them in such high-esteem. You know, to be part of it' (Fernandez & Lastovicka 2011: 286). Playing along to a record with an authentic vintage instrument increases the authenticity of the arbitrary situation whereby the nostalgic experience reaches a new level as the player takes the position of a band member (Fernandez & Lastovicka 2011: 286f).

Restorative nostalgia is based on a collective appreciation of influential musicians, the instruments they played, references to specific years of their production as well as reissues. Joey, the guitarist with an international career mentioned before, is an excellent example of this:

This is my 1969 [Gibson] Les Paul Gold Top—the first really good guitar I ever had it's taken me around the world. I bought 'Goldie' brand new at Guitar Heaven [after I] scrimped and saved money from gigs and went down there with $450 … and picked this one out and it was like the kind of guitar that you put it in your hands and it plays itself. I just knew it was the right one … I [had] looked at my Rolling Stone books and saw that a 1959 [Les Paul] Gibson is what Keith Richards played a lot. Those 1959 Les Paul guitars are like the Holy Grail! … I just knew it was the right guitar for me [because it is] pretty much a really good reproduction of the way the Les Pauls were in the 50s and this was the first time they reissued them … So it represented success, you know, real musicians. This was the unattainable, what you reached for … the star power it represented … It's a very special guitar and whenever I bring it out onstage now I feel like I'm nineteen again, suddenly I'm the kid … onstage opening up for Led Zeppelin with this guitar. (Fernandez & Lastovicka 2011: 285)

This quote sheds light on several motivations. It shows the glorification of a guitar model from a particular year that is considered the 'holy grail', and it is linked to a personal icon. From his perception, the models from 1969 equal those of 1959, which may or may not be the case. More importantly, Joey's perception of some 'magic' or 'aura' results from symbolic links. The belief in these symbolic links is meaningful even for a successful artist like Joey who trusts that the aura benefits his performance.

The strong symbolic power and value that restorative nostalgia lends to vintage instruments make it convenient for the musical instruments industry to capitalise on tradition-conscious musicians. According to Uimonen (2016: 121), vintage instruments are 'perfect examples of the past which needs to remain untouched, pristine, and uncontaminated not only for collectors but also for the guitar manufacturers who curate their history and recycle their designs for contemporary production'. Precious items are not only authentic vintage instruments from a particular time but also relic or heritage models besides accessories and signature instruments, even those of deceased musicians who received them post-mortem. Such instruments seem to attract musicians, although most players understand that the 'magic dust' is just imagined.

The second form of nostalgia in Boym's (2001: 49f) framework is *reflective nostalgia*, which focuses on a person's biography. Memories are preserved as 'perfect snapshots' of cherished experiences. Reflective nostalgia is not concerned with 'truth' and 'tradition'; its narrative is 'ironic, inconclusive and fragmentary' and often humorous. Amongst musicians, it may take the form of holding on to the first instrument one owned or trying to reacquire the model once sold because positive memories are associated with it. This kind of nostalgia is reflected in a statement of Joey when talking about 'Goldie', the guitar he played on some of his big hit records in the 1970s and 1980s:

> When I'm up on stage, when I take out Goldie on stage I become that guy when I was 19, I play *different*! Lenny [a long-time collaborator] says, 'you play different on that guitar'—I say, 'I know!' because I'm channeling back to that era when I recorded 'My International Hit'—I'm suddenly transported to that year. (Fernandez & Lastovicka 2011: 292)

This guitar holds special memories of Joey's most successful time as a musician, and he associates his success with the guitar because it is the instrument on which he wrote his hits (Fernandez & Lastovicka 2011: 293f). Such longstanding and influential nostalgic feeling prompted Joey to create a web page for his guitar. It attracts a broad international audience, suggesting that other people receive this personal nostalgic object well. Maybe they see in 'Goldie' a connection to Joey's artist persona and his fame. Or maybe 'Goldie' sparks the hope that a special guitar will allow them too to write a hit one day, as it did for Joey.

Restorative and reflective nostalgia manifest themselves in numerous ways and influence certain groups of people. Restorative nostalgia is likely to affect all musicians, regardless of age and experience. Shuker (2010: 28) argues that young music collectors consume formats such as vinyl that are older than they are, just for the sake of 'musical authenticity' and 'romance of a nostalgic past'. The same is true for musicians who listen to music and artists older than themselves. This can awaken their interest in old musical equipment, genuine vintage instruments or gear based on them. Reflective nostalgia takes a different form. Due to the biographical component, it tends to occur among more experienced players, as Joey's example suggests.

Concerning GAS, it should be noted that '[n]ostalgia is not always about the past; it can be retrospective but also prospective. Fantasies of the past determined by needs of the present have a direct impact on realities of the future' (Boym 2001: xvi). Nostalgia can strike at any time and tempt a musician to acquire 'new' old gear. It triggers a process of improving the setup that may not end with only buying the instrument because a vintage guitar, for example, may require the right (vintage) amplifier and other accessories to guarantee the authenticity of the whole setup.

To conclude the discussion about tradition and innovation, it is crucial to explain the popularity of vintage instruments and the analogue revival not only as a consequence of dissatisfaction with the present but also as a nostalgic longing for an idealised past (see Reynolds 2012). Pinch and Trocco (2002: 318f), focusing on the synthesiser, see nostalgic longing more as a criticism of how this instrument has evolved, from complete control over the tone to sound charts and finally presets, bringing about reproducibility and creation of the same sounds. However, their 'technostalgia' for vintage gear should not be equated with a longing for past musical expression. Instead, it is a 'movement toward both new sounds and new interactions, whether aural, social, or physical, made concrete through combinations of the past and present' (Pinch & Reinecke 2009: 166). Technostalgia thus reflects the desire to make new and modern music with 'real' instruments. For many musicians, regardless of what instrument they play, better sound quality and easier playability are the beneficial features making them prefer analogue over digital devices rather than the romantic notions of the past. As per Rogers's (2003) theory of innovation, for those musicians who opt for analogue gear, digital equipment does not sufficiently meet the three most essential criteria of 'relative advantage', 'compatibility' with values and 'ease of use'.

3.3   Special-Interest Books for Musical Instruments

To understand why specific instruments are more strongly associated with gear-related practices in common perception, we analysed special-interest books for the instruments included in this study. A search on Amazon UK with the term 'music gear' resulted in a list of more than 900 books. The most relevant ones to the search were on the electric guitar and, in much fewer numbers, recording equipment and practices. This search result is consistent with Becker (1996) and Wright (2006), who present electric guitarists as the instrumentalists most likely to show a pronounced interest in gear. After this exploratory search, we browsed through Amazon's product offer of books on the respective instruments to get an overview of the educational and special-interest material available, reflecting the authors' and publishers' perceptions of which topics and practices are relevant to the respective instrumentalists. Studying the book titles and blurbs suggests different topics and varying relevance of gear for various instruments.

It met our expectations that of all instruments, books on the electric guitar focus on gear the most. With the acoustic guitar, this is less the case. In many instructional books, guides and manuals about the electric guitar, gear is omnipresent. It is usually mentioned in the blurb, if not in the title. The book *Beginners Guide to Electric Guitar: Gear, Technique, and Tons of Riffs* (Speed 2010) pitches itself by teaching 'all about the different types of electric guitars, amplifiers, and effects', followed by a list of renowned rock bands whose songs can be played once the right guitar sound is achieved. Carter's (2016) *Electric Guitar Gear: A Complete Beginner's Guide to Understanding Guitar Effects and the Gear Used for Electric Guitar Playing & How to Master Your Tone on Guitar* is even more gear focused. Considering that the book is intended to introduce beginners to the instrument, the blurb begins by pointing out how 'daunting' sound manipulation and 'all the different gear' is. The book undertakes to assist players in finding the right gear for their playing, control it and add effects to make them sound 'more expressive and unique'. Holland's (2013) *Guitar Gear FAQ* similarly intends to help less experienced musicians to 'improve their tone, make better purchase decisions, and avoid many of the costly mistakes that are commonly made'. Even more revealing are two guides to worship music, one for the guitar and one for the bass. While the book for the bass—*The Worship Bass Book:*

Bass, Espresso, and the Art of Groove (Stockton 2014)—focuses on groove in the title, the book for the guitar—*The Worship Guitar Book: The Goods, the Gear and the Gifting for the Worship Guitarist* (Doppler 2013)—emphasises gear.

In addition to instructional guitar books, there are several other books dedicated exclusively to gear and setup. Some of them promise rare insights into the sound secrets of renowned guitarists. Fornandley's (2015) *Tone Wizards: Interviews With Top Guitarists and Gear Gurus On the Quest For The Ultimate Sound* contains a 'series of interviews that strives to dig deep into the various aspects of electric guitar tone and style' to unravel the elements of the signature sounds of 'some of the world's top guitar players', such as Joe Bonamassa, Peter Frampton, Eric Johnson, Joe Satriani and Steve Vai. Similarly, Bruck's (2005) *Guitar World Presents Guitar Gear 411: Guitar Tech to the Stars Answers Your Gear Questions* gives rare insights into the sound of renowned players based on statements from their guitar technicians.

Another strand of guitar books equates mastery of gear with the dedication and commitment of a player. This equation becomes clear from the title of Hurwitz's (2013) book *The Serious Guitarist. Essential Book of Gear: A Comprehensive Guide to Guitars, Amps, and Effects for the Dedicated Guitarist*. It includes 'tons of photographs and illustrations, real-world explanations on how to achieve signature tones in a variety of genres, helpful tips on gear maintenance, and an in-depth overview of the landmark innovations in guitars and guitar-related technology from the 1930s to the present'. The deep understanding gained from Hurwitz's book should enable serious guitarists to 'unlock a signature sound that will set you apart from the crowd'.

The books presented here represent only a fraction of the books offered by major vendors such as Amazon. Nevertheless, our examples give indications that guitarists are viewed as technologically determined. The authors suggest that the guitarist's status, dedication and expressiveness depend primarily on their gear and how they tweak it for their individual use. Comparing the books about the guitar with those for other instruments makes this even more evident.

For the bass, several books contain transcriptions of signature grooves like that of the Red Hot Chili Peppers' Flea (Johnson 2004). It is different with the guitar because books tend to focus on both gear and playing, for instance, signature solo licks. Other books about the bass concentrate on rhythm sections, such as Slutsky and Silverman's (1997) *Funkmasters: The Great James Brown Rhythm Sections, 1960–73*. Yet the largest number of books focus on bass lines, grooves, playing techniques and harmony. Only one book explicitly includes gear, if only as a small part of various elements, Gordon's (2018) *Bass Player Q&A: Questions and Answers about Listening, Practicing, Teaching, Studying, Gear, Recording, Music Theory, and More*. The blurb describes the book as a guide to 'various music-related questions' and a comprehensive manual for hobbyists. It does not deal with signature sounds that are the focus of many guitar books. Although guitar and bass are related instruments with similar equipment, the books as a whole concentrate on completely different areas: guitars on gear and basses on the groove.

Keyboard instruments must be classified as either electronic keyboards or synthesisers, and their books differ considerably. With a focus on sound design, the synthesiser books are much closer to guitar manuals. In comparison, keyboard and bass books concentrate on songs and playing. Most books for synthesiser players concentrate entirely on sound design and consider playing even less than guitar books. The book titles already make this clear: *Becoming a Synthesizer Wizard: From Presets to Power User* (Cann 2009), *Synthesizer Explained: The Essential Basics of Synthesis You Must Know as a Digital Music Producer* (Cep 2020), *Refining Sound: A Practical Guide to Synthesis and Synthesizers* (Shepherd 2013) and *Creating Sounds from Scratch* (Pejrolo & Metcalfe 2017), amongst others (McGuire & Van Der Rest 2015; Russ 2008). These books have in common the introduction of traditional (subtractive, additive, modulation) and more modern (granular, physical modelling) synthesis methods, sequencing and signal control. Even if explicitly addressing 'performance', it is limited to technological aspects such as sound control (for example, Vail 2014). Many of these books cover historical synthesiser instruments in passing; some put greater emphasis on historical developments (for example, Jenkins 2007). Books about synthesiser players are rare, consistent with the relatively low relevance of performance in most literature. A publication from the circles of the *Keyboard* magazine focuses on the *Best of the 80s: The Artists, Instruments, and Techniques of an Era* (Rideout et al. 2008). This book pays tribute to the synthesiser sound of the 1980s that every 'serious player' must know. Its blurb reads: 'how technological developments in keyboards helped artists such as Erasure, Human League, Peter Gabriel, Kraftwerk, Bruce Hornsby, Frank Zappa, and Jam and Lewis create entirely new sounds and how their production tricks can help you make great music today'. This book suggests that copying great sounds from the 1980s with instruments from the past is still the foundation for modern music (see also Reynolds 2012). Unlike books about most other instruments focusing on just one player, very few synthesiser books are dedicated to only a single keyboardist. One of the few is Jordan Rudess's (2009) *Dream Theater Keyboard Experience: Featuring Jordan Rudess.* It includes two topics: 'Note-for-note keyboard transcriptions of nine keyboard-intense Dream Theater songs from 1992-2007' and a 'conversation with Jordan Rudess' in which he reveals details of his playing style and 'special "exercise" pieces to precede each song, each focusing on a challenging playing technique'. In this rare example, playing is emphasised as opposed to synthesis techniques and the respective gear.

Keyboard literature is quite different from that of synthesisers. Most of it focuses on learning the instrument, like for the piano. The books range from songbooks and transcriptions of chart hits to introductions to specific styles, decades, players and bands. Gear plays only an insignificant role, if one at all.

The drum books show a wide variety of topics. Next to general educational books, there are books with varying focuses: drum grooves (Riley 2015; Süer & Alexander 2017), solos (Karas 2014), fills (Toscano 2019), warm-ups (O'Shea 2017) and particular bands that are covered with transcriptions of grooves and play-along CDs (Holliday & Weeks 2007). Several books are dedicated to 'rudiments'; technical exercises usually practised on a snare drum or a silent practice pad. Such practising differs from all other instruments considered in this study because it is detached from any equipment and tonal considerations. Similarly, books on some genres focus on grooves and tend to ignore gear requirements (Lewitt 2015; Zubraski & Jenner 2001). A few books are dedicated to influential drummers such as Vinnie Colaiuta (Atkinson 2003), John Bonham (Bergamini 2005) or Neil Peart (Wheeler 2000), and they primarily contain transcriptions and some information about their playing technique. Very few books like Nicholls' (2008) *The Drum Book: A History of the Rock Drum Kit* deal with equipment and development of drum instruments concerning renowned drummers. Books about drum manufacturers and their most famous players are rare (Falzerano 2008). In contrast, a moderate number of books on drum gear and related practices exists. Balmer's (2018) *Drum Kit Manual* deals with the purchase and maintenance of drums, and Nicholls and Nicholls' (2004) *Drum Handbook* provides advice on buying, setup and maintenance. Schroedl's (2003) *Drum Tuning* covers drum setup from the basics of construction and head properties to tuning drums for different genres. Most drum books deal with traditional acoustic kits, but a limited number concentrates on electronic drums (Graham 2019; Ledermann 2015), offering playing advice and stressing the historical significance of electronic drum systems.

We include the saxophone and trumpet as control instruments in our investigation, assuming that gear would not be as psychologically important for these players as for the other musicians under consideration. The special-interest books on the two wind instruments do not indicate a strong focus on equipment. Most books centre on studies, playing technique, scales, fingering charts and drills instead of gear. Neither does gear play a significant role in the numerous songbooks and 'omnibooks' for specific genres, players and composers.

Overall, the electric guitar and synthesiser seem to be the two instruments where gear and sound design play the most significant role in musical practice. This finding is consistent with the academic literature on music technology and the journalistic texts on GAS.

3.4   The Musical Instruments Industry

The musical instruments industry cannot be ignored in any discussion of GAS. The already addressed role of technological innovation for the personalisation of sounds and the growing market for vintage and relic instruments are just two examples illustrating the industry's commercial strategies.

Consumption has always been an inevitable part of music-making, not only on a larger scale such as concerts or media formats but also at the level of instruments required for the performance of popular music genres. For Bennett (1983: 231), the 1950s and 1960s were a crucial period in musical practice. During these decades, popular music was increasingly recorded and sold as a studio-produced commodity. At the same time, live shows became more professional and bigger, and as a result, instruments were amplified by a sound system. Sound quality was improved by a front of house engineer able to process the instruments much more extensively than is possible with just an instrument and amplifier. Both the live show and studio product, created with increasingly sophisticated recording and mixing approaches, changed audiences' expectations of how individual instruments and their collective sound were supposed to be. Comparing the less refined sound produced at home or in a rehearsal room with a professional recording or live show stirred musicians' desires for better quality. Players' rising frustration let the musical instruments' manufacturers recognise economic opportunities with a market to be exploited, so they began extending their range of models to include specialised instruments for various purposes. According to Jones (1992: 92), rock music's economic value brought about equipment that was created just for this genre. As a consequence of popular music genres diversifying, more specialist equipment was gradually designed and advertised for particular genres and subgenres, such as special 'metal axes' from guitar manufacturers like BC Rich. As per Jones (1992: 84), this specialisation strategy though bears economic risks: 'Manufacturers are in some ways caught in a bind, because though designers want to create equipment that is flexible and does not restrict music making, they must also meet the demands of the market'. The high degree of specialisation attracts musicians with a narrow stylistic range or players with large instrument collections inclined to use the optimal gear for specific genres. However, such specialised equipment might prove inflexible and be a reason for musicians to choose a single all-round instrument instead of several niche models.

Focusing on keyboard instruments and digital technologies like samplers, Théberge (1993: 159ff) argues that the emergence of special-interest print magazines such as *Music Technology*, *Electronic Musician*, *Home & Studio Recording* and *Music, Computers & Software* went hand in hand with the developing musical instruments manufacturing industry for the sake of promotion. The specialised nature of these magazines made it possible to target audiences effectively. The degree of specialisation increased and reached its first peak in the mid-1980s. As we noted earlier, this was also when the first magazines emerged dedicated to vintage instruments. Furthermore, endorsing artists and showcasing instruments in music videos were strategies that came up in the 1980s (Théberge 1993: 164). This move helped the wider audience understand who the leading players of the time were and what equipment they were playing. Linked together, this created a strong connection between gear, musical quality and non-musical associations such as lifestyle and success. According to Théberge (1993: 326), it was only a natural consequence that in the 1980s, consumption became a fundamental part of music-making.

> musicians have not simply become consumers of new technologies but their entire approach to music-making has been transformed into one where consumption— the exercise of taste and choice—has become implicated in their musical practices at the most fundamental level. (Théberge 1993: 267)

Music-related purchases have become more frequent and plentiful due to the diversification of gear and the shorter lifespan of electronic and digital instruments, which become obsolete more quickly.

In the musical instruments industry, there are many competing interests related to the various attitudes of musicians and players of different instruments. Most devices based on digital technology benefit from advances in technology, making it easy for manufacturers to promote new instrument models because of their improved processing power, larger sound libraries and better connectivity to external devices such as computers (Bennett 2009, 2012). Manufacturers may be motivated by the prospect of being a leader in innovation. Alternatively, they may be tempted to offer just small updates with subtle changes to sell consistently (Frith 1986: 272). Rather than introducing ground-breaking instruments every few years with the prospect of high sales and profits from patents, they would take the more predictable and conservative approach of gradually releasing slightly modified and updated instruments every year. Hence, genuine innovation is not the primary goal for many manufacturers; instead, they prefer to moderately adjust established instruments because minor changes are unlikely to irritate musicians and are still new enough to sell. The introduction of 'improvements' bears risks. For example, in 2015, guitar manufacturer Gibson updated the manual tuning system in favour of the G-Force. With this automated tuning system, strings are prevented from going out of tune during a performance, eliminating the need to break in new strings and making it easier to switch between tunings. Despite these apparent advantages, most of the tradition-conscious Gibson community did not accept this 'upgrade', prompting the manufacturer to return to traditional tuners (Corfield n.d.).

In the formative years of rock music, instrument technology has developed rapidly through close cooperation between renowned musicians and manufacturers. Taking the guitar as an example (see also Herbst 2016), the British company VOX released the AC15 in 1958, the first amplifier specifically designed for the electric guitar. Shadows' guitarist Hank Marvin requested VOX to increase the output from 15 to 30 watts the following year. In 1962, the Marshall JTM45, a modification of the American Fender Bassman, was invented by the British developer Jim Marshall in collaboration with The Who's Pete Townshend. Soon after, the equalisation section was extended to include controls for treble, middle and bass frequencies as well as presence and resonance shaping, allowing players to customise their sounds. In the 1970s, guitar amplifier innovators such as Jim Marshall and Randall Smith added a pre-amplifier stage that allowed players to switch between clean and overdriven sounds at selectable volumes. The 1980s saw a development of nuanced control through sophisticated rack designs requested by famous shred guitarists. During the 1990s, hybrid and transistor technology became more widely accepted due to the popularity of nu metal, but since then, hardly any aesthetically novel technologies have gained acceptance. Profiling and simulation amplifiers are becoming increasingly popular because they come closer to a valve amplifier's sound than ever before. Producer and engineer Alex Silva at Hansa Studio notes, 'I think companies like Kemper are on the cutting edge of being able to provide musicians with the quality that they need without feeling that they're kind of losing connection to the past of guitar playing ... I don't think one thing suddenly replaces the other' (Herbst 2021). However, digital guitar technology does not intend to establish a new aesthetic; its acceptance in the community relies on delivering a variety of analogue valve tones at the touch of a button (Herbst 2019a). The development described for the guitar is similar for bass and drums, with most players appreciating old equipment, technologies and sounds. From an economic perspective, this stagnation causes problems, as Will Straw (2000: 156) points out:

> The market for individual cultural commodities is perpetually marked by the probability of saturation of a pool of potential consumers. Sales of an individual title may neither follow an irreversible upward movement nor stabilize at a permanent level; rather, any growth in the sales of a cultural commodity will bring it closer to the point at which its sales potential is likely to be exhausted. As a result of these conditions, the fate of a cultural commodity is more likely than that of other commodities to be imagined in temporal terms, as a life cycle. This lifecycle will unfold in a series of stages between the moment of its release and the point at which the probable upper limit on its sales has been reached.

Straw (2000: 156f) goes on to argue that the use-value is hardly relevant in this respect, stating that a 'record or book bought once need not be bought again, however stable and solid the use-value which it provides'. The general principle applies to musical instruments as cultural commodities, but we do not see the same pattern. It is not uncommon for musicians to own the same instrument model more than once. On the one hand, live gigs and touring may require the acquisition of more than one instrument of the same type. Most musicians will feel more comfortable having backup gear to limit the impact of broken strings or valves during a live performance.

On the other hand, unlike a book or record[8], musical instruments are rarely entirely identical; even the same model built in the same year and factory may sound slightly different due to production irregularities and natural variations in the organic parts. Furthermore, the colours could differ, either deliberately by design or by coincidence. This higher degree of variation distinguishes musical instruments from many other cultural commodities. It allows the industry to reap multiple benefits from selling the same product and allures GAS-affected musicians to purchase additional gear. This business strategy is noteworthy, given the many players who prefer traditional instrument models over modern interpretations. Notions of 'progress and change', as Théberge (1993: 166) claims, seem to be relatively unimportant for most players of popular music, apart from specialist groups such as future-minded keyboard players. For most others, the musical instruments industry needs to provide more convincing reasons to invest frequently in gear that is not substantially different from that already owned.

3.5   Gender

Any discussion of music technology and GAS must consider gender. Previous studies on music technology in general (Comber et al. 1993), music production (Hepworth-Sawyer 2020), hi-fi audio (Jansson 2010; Schröter & Volmar 2016), the musical instruments industry (PRS Foundation 2017) and gear collection (Wright 2006) have provided ample evidence of gender inequality and discrimination. Wright's (2006) claim that GAS is an all-male phenomenon either reflects common discriminatory practices or merely a superficial statement. The little research available strongly supports the first option: discrimination. The ratio of female participants in quantitative studies on music gear has rarely reached over 5% (Herbst 2017a), and qualitative studies on guitar players often do not include a single female musician (Fernandez & Lastovicka 2011) let alone players of non-binary gender. In the following, we understand gender as a 'system of social practices within society that constitutes distinct, differentiated sex categories, sorts people into these categories, and organizes relations between people on the basis of the differences defined by their sex category' (Ridgeway 2011: 9). In music technology and musical practices, this distinction is usually binary between male and female, but it is commonly implicit, as female presence is often not existent.

    In music education and psychology, a large body of research has confirmed that instrument choice is gender-specific from early childhood. In Western cultures, instruments are traditionally divided between female—harp, flute, piccolo, clarinet, oboe, violin and voice—and male—electric guitar, bass guitar, tuba, drum kit, table

---

[8] Music albums differ from books in that collectors or fans of a band can purchase the same music in different formats, and special editions can justify buying the same album more than once (Shuker 2010: 57ff).

and trombone (Clawson 1999a; Hallam et al. 2008: 7; Sheldon & Price 2005; Wych 2012). Some instruments are considered more neutral, such as African drums, cornet, French horn, saxophone and tenor horn (Hallam et al. 2008: 7). The reasons for this gendered distinction range from the physical shape and attractiveness of instruments to their pitch range, sound quality and specific playing requirements like physical endurance (Hallam et al. 2008: 7ff). Social factors such as parents' instrument preferences also play a role (Delzell & Leppla 1992; Griswold & Chroback 1981). Some research has found primary schools to have the most significant impact, and consequently, children and adolescents would tend to adhere to such learned and stereotypical instrument choices throughout secondary school (Zervoudakes & Tanur 1994). However, other research has suggested that young female musicians in later phases of their education increasingly decide to learn more male-associated instruments such as the drum kit and the electric guitar (Hallam et al. 2008: 15). Overcoming traditional stereotypes thus seems possible with developing identity through maturation, role models, emancipation from parental influences and changing musical preferences.

Studies of the rock music scene suggest that the 'social prestige' of an instrument determines who is to play it. According to Berkers and Schaap (2018: 69), status and prestige are determined by the two factors of being a member of a band and having a particular role in it. In addition to 'social barriers' (Bennett 2017: 26) to joining a band arising from the tendency towards homosocial solidarities and the potentially disturbing 'threat' of sexual tension (Clawson 1999a), Berkers and Schaap (2018: 70f) cite two other reasons that often determine the role of female musicians in a band. According to the 'queuing theory' (Reskin & Roos 1990), women can gain access to a field if they take on roles that men have begun to abandon. Similarly, the 'empty-field theory' (Tuchman & Fortin 1984) suggests that women are more likely to take on roles with lower skill requirements and hence less prestige. In the rock context, the bass has traditionally been the instrument that made an otherwise purely male band most accessible to women (Carson et al. 2004: 4; Gay 1998: 88ff) because, despite its fundamental musical role, the bassist is receiving less attention on stage and is less audible on the record. For the same reason are keyboard, string and wind instruments regarded as 'feminine' in a rock context (Gay 1998; Berkers & Schaap 2018). However, depending on the reputation these instruments enjoy in other genres, the opposite could be the case. Many gender-specific rules involved in a band context go far beyond musical reasons (Berkers & Schaap 2018: 52ff). The supporting role, as opposed to the leading, is what allows female instrumentalists to join a band. In contrast, it is no problem when women are in the spotlight as singers (Clawson 1999b; Gay 1998). Although research would allow the conclusion that women have been suppressed and reduced to an unattractive role or accepted as a 'band ornament' (Gay 1998: 88) or 'token' (Berkers & Schaap 2018: 82ff), Gay (1998: 90) suggests that female bass players have found ways to create 'new configurations of meanings and relationships' and to 'exploit, adapt, and transform the technology and its cultural meaning', thereby undermining discriminatory practices from within the scene and social context of a band.

Another common explanation for gender differences in instruments, especially when it comes to genres like rock music or electronic dance music (EDM), regards technology. As the argument goes, boys are interested in technology, and this general interest extends to music. Boys are said to show interest in music that relies substantially on technology (Comber et al. 1993: 123; Hallam et al. 2017: 117). As a result, they enjoy playing electronic and digital instruments such as the electric guitar and bass, electronic drum kits and turntables. They further have an affinity with other computer-based music practices, thus constituting technical competence and respective musical activities as 'an integral part of masculine gender identity' (Gavanas & Reitsamer 2013: 56). In a recent meta-study of the metal genre (Berkers & Schaap 2018), women were found to mainly take on the roles of singer, keyboard player or acoustic guitarist but less that of the electric guitarist. As a key reason, Bayton (1997, 1998), who studied gender differences in rock music, identifies *technophobia* amongst women. An interviewed female electric guitar player expressed her opinion on this matter:

> I think there is a tendency for us still to be scared of equipment: the 'black-box-with-chrome-knobs' syndrome … I've obviously become very familiar with what I do but I still don't feel physically as at one with my equipment as I think most men do… It took me a year before I turned my volume up. Roger would see that my amp was turned up even if I turned it down, because I was still scared of it… of making a noise to that extent. I turned the knobs down on my guitar for a whole year. (Bayton 1997: 42)

The standard male behaviour was the opposite, as another female musician indicated in the same study:

> Men like twiddling about with their knobs and fiddling about with their electronics and what their equipment can do, and how many pedals they've got, and how many flashing lights they've got on it. Like they've got six strings on their bass instead of four. And what colour it is and what make it is. Whereas women just go, 'Oh, I've got an old drumkit, that'll do.' Women aren't specifically precious about their equipment, even though they'll try and get the best they can afford and get hold of. They won't be faffing about with knobs and spending three hours tuning up when you've only got three hours to practice in and you're trying to write a half-hour set or something … I think a lot of it is men trying to prove to each other that they've got bigger and better equipment. (Bayton 1998: 82)

Bayton (1998: 82) concludes that the interviewed female musicians commonly believe that women are less competitive in terms of equipment and instead focus on musical goals rather than on details of gear and tone. However, Bayton's findings may not be valid any longer since the interviews took place more than twenty years ago. With educational campaigns and a higher number of female role models, it could be assumed that today fewer women are affected by technophobia. However, recent research does not fully support this deliberation. Examining music technology education in Britain, Born and Devine (2015) find that although 55% of the general student body is female, the students enrolled in music technology courses are predominantly male (90%). As the authors demonstrate, this gender imbalance increases at higher education levels. Between the age of 6 and 16, almost half of the students choosing music technology as their primary instrument are female (Born & Devine 2015: 147). In the group over 16, the proportion of female music technologists drops to a quarter, followed by a drop to 18% for music technology A-levels, and finally to a low 10% for enrolment in university music technology courses. One of the possible reasons for the decline in female participation in higher music technology education regards historically derived notions of gender and technology. Referring to Blickenstaff (2005: 370), Born and Devine (2015: 147) note that 'women still display "lowered interest, negative attitudes, lowered performance, and ... anxiety" when it comes to computers and digital technology'. The same might be the case for musical instruments that rely on amplifiers and other electronic sound control devices, which would be consistent with Bayton's findings. This caution concerning music technology, Born and Devine (2015: 147ff) reason, stems in part from practices in music education that reinforce the distinction between boys and girls in terms of confidence in the use of technology (Citron 1993; Green 1997; Solie 1995) and the traditional gender-specific choice of instruments. They argue that

> Instruments can ... serve as key avenues through which larger musical formations such as genres are constructed as gendered communities of practice. In this sense, digitization in music education extends a tradition in which men have dominated electronic and electroacoustic composition and instrumental performance both in the classical avantgarde and in technologically oriented popular genres such as rock, hip hop, and various dance musics. (Born & Devine 2015: 149)

Born and Devine's meta-study suggests that female musicians still feel less confident than their male counterparts in using music technology, a disadvantage that is particularly noticeable in popular music genres.

Traditionally, the music industry has classified its customers by gender; women were perceived as passive fans and consumers, men as central actors and producers (Maalsen & McLean 2018). The readership of music magazines makes this divide clear. In the 1990s, the proportion of subscribers to *Vintage Guitars* was 99% male and 95% for *Acoustic Guitar* (Ryan & Peterson 2001: 105f). The *Keyboard* readership was 98% male (Théberge 1997: 122).[9] However, there are indications of this unequal distribution to be changing, as there is a rise in the proportion of female

---

[9] For comparison, Shuker (2010: 34) reports that small numbers between 5 and 18 per cent of readers of vinyl magazines are female.

musicians on formerly male-dominated instruments. In 2018, the renowned guitar and bass manufacturer Fender made headlines when it published a study showing that 50% of new guitar players were women (Duffy 2018). While many female guitarists stated moderate ambitions to play privately rather than contemplating becoming famous, 72% were motivated to gain a life skill and 42% considered the guitar part of their identity. However, the study's scientific quality, which the instrument manufacturer claims to have carried out with a brand strategy and innovation consultancy, must be questioned. We could not find a detailed description of the survey beyond a detailed press release (Fender Musical Instruments Corporation 2018), which is peppered with numerous references to Fender's own education platform Fender Play. Moreover, the postulated claim to representativeness appears doubtful against the study's methodological background, which is briefly outlined in the press release. While this study is primarily to be understood as an expression of the manufacturer's strategy to focus more on female musicians and thus expand its customer base, there are more tangible signs of change, for example, in guitar player magazines. A blog article on *Guitar Player*'s web presence (Molenda 2017) acknowledges that the community has been a 'boys club' since the magazine was founded in 1967 but stresses that male dominance has declined. There is a growing awareness of inappropriate sexist gear advertisement, which discredits women by depicting them in sexual positions, fetishizing women rather than expressing appreciation for their musical skills (Farrugia & Olszanowski 2017: 3, Théberge 1997: 123f). Although matters are improving, sexism is still not stopped altogether in guitarist Fabi Reyna's perception: 'It's always a woman holding a guitar half-naked or overtly sexualized, and it isn't matched with an article talking about her talent, or that she's a musician' (Berlatsky 2015).[10] For this reason, Reyna founded the guitar magazine *She Shreds*,

> the world's only print publication dedicated to women guitarists and bassists. We strive to change the way women guitarists and bassists are depicted and presented in the music industry and popular culture by creating a platform where people can listen, see and experience what it means to be a woman who shreds.[11]

This emancipation and the strong personal interest in guitar playing and technology are further confirmed by a Brainyard analysis of guitar search profiles, which shows that women made 49% of the web searches on guitar-related topics in 2017. Molenda (2017) on the *Guitar Player* blog concludes:

> These are rather earthshaking statistics, as they point out that women are, for the most part, equally active in seeking guitar data as are men. If the trend continues, the industry may need to adjust its perception of men as the movers and shakers and gear drivers, and look to women players as a viable and equivalent market for

---

[10] Another related phenomenon is the 'booth babes' at musical conventions like the NAMM, which have become less common in the last years (Gallier 2018).

[11] https://sheshredsmag.com/about; accessed 16 September 2019.

guitar products, guitar information, guitar marketing, and, well, pretty much all things guitar.

At present, however, we do not seem to be quite there yet, at least when considering the research from the last ten to twenty years. Berkers and Schaap (2018) confirm the widespread practice in music stores of regarding women as (girl)friends or family members of male musicians instead of recognising them as musicians in their own right (see also Carson et al. 2004: 18; Sargent 2009). A female interviewee describes the experience when buying her first drum kit: 'it's all guys there and they were surprised that I wanted to buy a drum set and that I wanted to buy drum things' (Berkers & Schaap 2018: 67f). Bayton (1998: 31) lists several similar experiences by female guitarists:

> Louise Hartley: I always think they're gonna laugh at me for some reason. I hate them... There's a massive guitar shop in Birmingham called Music Exchange and the guys who work in there just love themselves. They strut around. And if you walk in and try and buy something, they'll ignore you and you have to beg for your help … There's no women work there, either. It's all male guitarists with long hair and tight trousers.

> Aimee Stevens: I feel very intimidated. Especially going to ask—they're all stood behind the counter, these massive metal blokes. Well, that's what they look like, judging by their image. I go up and go, 'Can I have a top E string?' because I don't know the proper names or anything, so it's even worse. And they go, 'What gauge? What sort?' And I'm like, 'I don't know'. So I don't like going in and looking at guitars or anything in music shops … When you're trying they're just staring at you. If you don't know much as well—and then they pick it up and go (imitates complicated guitar playing) and you're going, 'Oh no, I'll just take that.'

> Fran: You go in and all the blokes are sitting in one corner talking about some riff that they came up last night, totally ignoring you. They are very patronizing. They see that you're a woman and they think, 'How you dare come in our music shop?'

These quotes demonstrate the uninviting atmosphere for women in music stores, where they are often treated with disrespect (see also Beaster-Jones 2016: 88f; Carson et al. 2004: 17ff; Gallier 2018). According to Sargent (2009: 665), the culture of music stores is 'driven by masculinist fantasies of the rock musician lifestyle'. Statements like 'all male guitarists with long hair and tight trousers' and 'massive metal blokes' confirm this theory. Besides the masculine rock star attitude, the relationship to technology plays a considerable role (Carson et al. 2004: 17ff). Habitus and knowledge of technical details serve as expressions of capital and power (Bourdieu 1991; Fiske 1992; Foucault 1990), allowing male employees and customers to defend their hierarchy and status within the store and the wider music community. Apart from the 'nerdy' verbal discourse, status is determined by practical skills in playing and using technology. Bayton (1997: 41) observes:

> boys tend to feel at home there [guitar stores]. In any of these shops you can observe
> the assertive way in which young men try out the equipment, playing the beginning
> of a few well-known songs time and again, loudly and confidently, and even
> through those few bars may encompass the sum total of their musical knowledge.
> In contrast, nearly every one of my interviewees said that guitar shops felt like alien
> territory … trying out the equipment was akin to being on trial.

The competitive character of guitar and musicians' stores contributes to the unwelcoming atmosphere for women, coding it as a male space and thus forming a social barrier (Bennett 2017: 26; Gavanas & Reitsamer 2013: 57) that may exclude especially young female musicians from contact with musical gear.

Gradually, stores are adapting to the higher number of female musicians playing instruments that were formerly seen as male-dominated. Increased employment of female store assistants and technicians is a strategy to create a more welcoming, non-sexist atmosphere for female customers (McMahon 2015; Sargent 2009: 666). Improving matters includes acknowledging different attitudes between the genders. General manager of Detroit Guitar, Charlie Lorenzi, explains:

> You have a guy coming in, and he has it in mind that he likes Martin guitars—he
> may never have played one before—and it's very unlikely you're going to talk him
> out of that. Women will take in information, keep an open mind and make a more-
> informed decision based on what's good for them, rather than what's trendy or
> what their grandparents bought. (Lorenzi as cited in McMahon 2015)

Other managers stress the importance of non-patronising, gender-neutral consultation to ensure that all customers are treated with the same high level of respect, with women being recognised as musicians and not exoticised as 'female musicians'.

Leaving aside the pressure from online music retailers, which forces music stores to improve their service, the attempt to be more inclusive could well be explained by the queuing theory (Reskin & Roos 1990) because rock music's relevance for popular music culture has declined continuously in recent years. Prestigious roles have shifted, leaving space for women to slowly enter the formerly male-dominated positions such as the drums or lead guitar. But also in other currently commercially more successful musical scenes, such as electronic dance music cultures and DJing with their strong focus on 'competence in the latest music production equipment and software' (Gavanas & Reitsamer 2013: 55), power structures are increasingly questioned, as recent publications demonstrate (for example, Farrugia 2012; Farrugia & Olszanowski 2017; Gavanas & Reitsamer 2013; Hancock 2017; Reitsamer 2012).

Farrugia (2012: 30) describes how record shops as the places of collecting and acquiring records supported power structures in the Foucauldian sense for a long time, thus supporting a gatekeeping process that excluded women from DJing:

> The organization of EDM in speciality record shops by subgenres and labels was
> more likely to mystify naïve consumers than to offer an inviting learning space,

especially for women. As EDM grew in popularity in the 1990s, these male-dominated spaces became central hubs where knowledge was shared and social networks developed between collectors, producers and DJs.

Male dominance in the scene may not have changed altogether, but over time, networks of female musicians have increasingly emerged, intending to break down these entry barriers. From a rare intersectional perspective, Hancock (2017: 74) uses the example of the lesbian Lick Club in Vancouver and its role in the regional electronic dance music scene to show that physical women-identified spaces can provide female, trans and non-binary musicians with access to mentors, female role models, equipment and performance opportunities and thus with access to former 'boys' club(s)': 'Being part of a localized network gives female DJs the opportunity to receive support from colleagues in invaluable ways, such as getting advice on skills and technology, and opportunities to play for an audience' (Hancock 2017: 80). Given the homosociality of male DJ networks (Farrugia 2012; Gavanas & Reitsamer 2013), these likely are safe spaces where women and non-binary musicians can gain experience in a supportive environment.

Unsurprisingly, similar approaches are also expanding into the digital realm. With a focus on the EDM scene, Reitsamer (2012) describes the translocal virtual network Female Pressure, founded in 1998, in which female DJs, music producers and club managers of all ages and different origins exchange and organise themselves in mailing lists and social media platforms. While a central concern of the network is the pursuit of a feminist agenda in the sense of third-wave feminism, it also enables the exchange of experiences on the practical aspects of DJing and thus represents a valuable resource for the acquisition of expertise as well as discussion of music technology by female DJs: 'Being part of a localized network gives female DJs the opportunity to receive support from colleagues in invaluable ways, such as getting advice on skills and technology, and opportunities to play for an audience' (Reitsamer 2012: 80). Networks such as Female Pressure, Pink Noises, Shejay or Rubina DJanes (Gavanas & Reitsamer 2013: 60) thus offer spaces for musicians who do not want to subordinate themselves to male hegemony. Nevertheless, they are not without controversy either. On the one hand, these networks are seen as a further means to democratise access to music technology and electronic dance culture. On the other hand, they find themselves 'confronted with the problem of possibly reinforcing hierarchical gender differences and as a result, the binary structure of male/female social network segregation, as well as self-presentation in terms of masculinity and femininity, is not altered' (Gavanas & Reitsamer 2013: 71).

Even if one leaves male spaces such as music shops aside, sexism plays a role in the structures of the musical instruments industry that should not be underestimated. A vivid example is the gear industry's failed marketing strategy of addressing its regular clientele by relying on sexist product names and graphics such as Steel

Panther's signature guitar pedal 'Pussy Melter' by TC Electronics, advertised as follows:

> Wanna make a physical impact on your audiences, with an epic delay tone? Then Satchel's got you covered! When we met up with Steel Panther's oh-so-humble guitarist, he had only one condition: that the tone be as wet as the ladies on the front row! With 'Pussy Melter' that's exactly what you get: a delay tone, which perfectly nails that heavy metal lead tone, while simultaneously ensuring that the janitor ain't going home early! So if glam rock guitar solos and wet floor signs are your idea of a good time, then 'Pussy Melter' for Flashback Delay is definitely the TonePrint for you! (Standell-Preston 2018)

The product was eventually removed on pressure from online petitions, but this recent example from 2018 highlights that the problem of sexism in connection with musical gear still exists.

A first sign that the musical instruments industry is opening up to female musicians is the recent increase in the number of instruments designed to adapt to their bodies. Nevertheless, until 2017, women-specific instruments were not produced and marketed to the extent that the media would have reacted to them. Pondering about the reasons, Cate Le Bon (2017), in a *Guardian* blog, speculates: 'I wonder why it has it taken so long for the anatomy of a woman to be considered when designing a guitar? Maybe it is the fear that it would immediately adopt the stigma of an inferior instrument, while suggesting its player's gender is a handicap'.[12]

Annie Clark of the American pop band St Vincent is considered to have designed the first electric guitar for women. She collaborated with manufacturer Ernie Ball and created her signature guitar, 'Music Man St Vincent' (released in 2017). It is based on Gibson's Explorer model but modified to avoid the curved shape of most conventional guitar models. On Twitter, she explains: 'I wanted to design a tool that would be ergonomic, lightweight, and sleek. There is room for a breast. Or two' (Scippa n.d.). With its smaller shape and lighter weight of about three kilograms, it is designed to be more comfortable for women and anyone of smaller stature to play. The extravagant design and unique specifications further underline the difference to traditional guitars and symbolically point to a modernist, future-looking mentality and the rejection of male-dominated vintage instruments. Another guitar for female players is the 'Glitterbomb' model, which has been manufactured since 2017 by Vance Guitars in collaboration with Glitoris guitarist Samantha Bennett. As the official website states, '[t]he principal requirement was to provide a lightweight guitar

---

[12] Originally, the guitar was a mainly female instrument, but as its popularity in jazz, country and big band music grew, men quickly adopted it. Changes in the guitar's physical shape, especially its increased size, are said to have made it more difficult for women to play it (Carson et al. 2004: 11).

designed for women players that wrapped around the body, didn't dig in and was a comfortable and slick player'.[13] Bennett explains the idea of the guitar as follows:

> One thing that's always pissed me off about guitars is how they are 100% designed for men. I practice and rehearse sitting down and there's this dimension—the point between your thigh/torso and chest where the guitar sits. My Bullet and Jaguar always crushes my right tit, so we worked on a more scooped out cutaway and a smoother, more angled cut out at the back of the guitar.[14]

Dimension may also be considered an issue by female musicians when it comes to the neck scale of bass guitars (Emiliani 2015; Wolfle 2013). As a reaction, manufacturers like Luna Guitars offer bass guitars with shorter necks for smaller musicians or musicians with small hands. The development of these instruments goes hand in hand with women entering the industry and the slow diversification of the manufacturer's recruitment policy (Gallier 2018). However, these observations seem to be limited to the guitar and bass. To our knowledge, there are no special designs optimised for the comfort of female drummers and keyboard players.

Another sign of change is the market for signature instruments that has long been dominated by male performers. In 1988, Bangles' Susanna Hoffs received a Rickenbacker signature guitar. Bonnie Raitt—winner of eleven Grammy awards and sixteen nominations—was the first female guitarist to obtain a signature model from the renowned manufacturer Fender in 1996 (Scapelitti 2016). Another woman honoured was Jennifer Batten, guitarist for Michael Jackson, receiving a Washburn signature guitar in 1998. But it took until the late 2010s that female guitar and bass players received signature models on a larger scale: Joan Jett's Gibson Melody Maker in 2010, Orianthi's PRS SE Orianthi in 2011, Sheryl Crow's and Avril Lavigne's Fender Stratocaster, Grace Potter's Gibson Flying V as well as Lita Ford's BC Rich Warlock in 2012, Lzzy Hale's Gibson Explorer and Nancy Wilson's Gibson Nighthawk in 2013, Eva Gardner's Fender signature bass in 2014. However, it is worth mentioning that several of these signatures are part of renowned manufacturers' budget series—for example, Squire endorsed by Fender—or of less reputable manufacturers. Nita Strauss, live guitarist for the Alice Cooper band, was the first woman to finally receive a signature model in 2018 from the popular manufacturer Ibanez.[15] She is one of only twenty-five selected musicians listed on the official website for the European market.[16] The increasing number of female musicians receiving signature models is a positive step forward, as they serve as influential role models

---

[13] http://vancecustomguitars.com/product/glitterbomb; accessed 16 July 2019.

[14] http://www.kitmonsters.com/blog/glitoris-making-the-glitterbomb-guitar; accessed 16 July 2019.

[15] https://www.ibanez.com/usa/artists/detail/568.html; accessed 16 July 2019.

[16] https://www.ibanez.com/eu/products/category/electric_guitars; accessed 16 July 2019.

for young musicians. Nonetheless, only the most distinguished female musicians re-ceive signature instruments in the same league as their male counterparts to this day. Many successful women players are still treated as second-class musicians, which reflects in endorsements. Manufacturers of drum accessories, for example, are will-ing to endorse female drummers with inexpensive signature drumsticks but hardly with full instruments. Of the 267 endorsed artists listed on the website of the drum kit manufacturer Mapex, only five (2%) are read as female.[17] Of the 184 Pearl artists in Europe, seven (4%) are female[18], and of those endorsed by Yamaha Europe, only one in 69 (1%) is a woman[19]. Apart from the meagre percentage of female drummers across all manufacturers, it is noteworthy that for those listed, mainly endorsements are offered but no signature models.[20] The small percentage of women is not limited to drums. Only one in 55 (2%) of guitar and bass players endorsed by Yamaha Eu-rope is female. The percentage amongst keyboard and synthesiser players endorsed by Yamaha Europe (2 out of 24; 8%), even if better, still is far from equal. Five of 153 (3%) players endorsed by Marshall amplifiers are women[21]. Bass manufacturer Warwick holds the negative record, with the eleven signature artists all being men, and only nine of 224 (4%) endorsers are women[22]. Like Yamaha, the popular Nord brand has a relatively high percentage of female keyboard players (32 of 350; 9%)[23]. However, although women often perform the role of keyboardists in bands, the rel-ative proportion of endorsements below 10% and the absence of signature models show a drastic underrepresentation of female musicians among the honoured profes-sionals, which indicates lacking recognition from the industry.

Wright (2006: 26) concludes his book on the Guitar Acquisition Syndrome with his impression that 'about 99+% of all GAS sufferers are male. It seems as though GAS is about as unlikely to strike a female as the art and craft of scrapbooking is to strike males'. The previous discussion has demonstrated the uninviting practice in physical spaces such as music stores, where historically, female musicians were seen as appendices to family and partners, rarely recognised as musicians. There are hints of change, but decade-long habits die slowly. Due to inappropriate behaviour,

---

[17] http://mapexdrums.com/international/artists.aspx; accessed 16 July 2019.

[18] http://www.pearleurope.com/artists/all-artists; accessed 16 July 2019.

[19] https://europe.yamaha.com/en/artists; accessed 16 July 2019.

[20] Endorsements usually mean that artists receive an instrument or piece of gear for free from the manufacturer with various conditions attached, such as the requirement to play only the sponsored equipment on stage. A signature deal is much more exclusive. It commonly in-volves the customisation of stock models or the creation of a unique model with the name of the associated performer. The honoured artist may receive a share of the profits made by the manufacturer.

[21] https://marshall.com/marshall-amps/endorsers; accessed 16 July 2019.

[22] http://www.warwickbass.com/en/Warwick---Artists--Artist.html; accessed 16 July 2019.

[23] https://www.nordkeyboards.com/artists; accessed 16 July 2019.

women likely feel insecure in such spaces and may refrain from openly showing their interest in musical equipment. With all its options for anonymity, the Internet seems more inviting, as the Brainyard analysis of web search data has shown (Molenda 2017). However, the increase of female musicians playing instruments such as the electric guitar, bass and drums is neither reflected in qualitative interview studies (Fernandez & Lastovicka 2011) nor anonymous quantitative studies advertised on message boards (Herbst 2017a). The lack of presence leaves room for speculation about whether many female musicians have low confidence in their (technological) abilities or whether they do not trust the respective research.

4 Collecting

From Wright's book (2006: 63), we assume that GAS and collecting gear should not be regarded as identical, although they are likely related. This chapter discusses collecting theories that provide a multidisciplinary perspective to unravel the relationship between the two phenomena further and find possible reasons why musicians feel compelled to acquire gear. It draws on a range of theories and empirical studies not related to music and Shuker's (2010) research on record collecting. Following Shuker, we reject the stereotypical image of collecting as a 'nerdy pastime' in favour of a broader understanding. In our interpretation, collecting is a behaviour that is both deeply personal and communal, which corresponds with general research on collecting and consumption. The purpose of this chapter is thus twofold: to gain a better understanding of the motives and patterns of collecting to draw clearer lines between GAS and collecting and to contribute to a developing theoretical framework for the following empirical investigations.

4.1 Definition and Theoretical Framework

Collecting is a practice that has received little attention in popular music studies, despite the discipline's cultural studies background, in which issues of consumption and the use and re-appropriation of goods in manners not intended by the manufacturer have been explored. One area of popular music studies where collecting is at least recognised is fandom. Traditionally, the industry has viewed fans as hyper-consumers and collectors who seek to buy and own anything released in connection with an esteemed artist or, in the case of music and videos, try to obtain them through unauthorised trading or bootlegging (Farrugia & Gobatto 2010). Fiske (1992: 47) sees 'a constant struggle between fans and the industry, in which the industry attempts to incorporate the tastes of the fans, and the fans to "excorporate" the products of the industry'. Regardless of the legal assessment of these practices, scholars of popular culture fandom agree that consumption is a crucial part of this practice and that it usually revolves around the act of collecting (Brown 1997; Duffett 2013a, 2013b; Hills 2002; Jenkins 1992; Sandvoss 2005). While such research inevitably takes consumption into account, often in contrast to a critical theory perspective in the tradition of Herbert Marcuse and Theodor Adorno (Sandvoss 2005), collecting is rarely explicitly examined (for example, Hills 2002). Shuker (2010: 4) observes in his review of research on collecting that 'general studies of music consumption, especially fandom, provide some insights, but more extended critical discussion is sparse'. In his chapter on fan practices in *Understanding Fandom*, Duffett (2013a) at least includes collecting alongside zines, blogging, fan videos, filking and cosplay as a performative fan practice, with the other two areas being connection and appropriation. For him, fans are more than ordinary customers; they are 'networkers, collectors, tourists, archivists, curators, producers and more' (Duffett 2013a: 21). The special issue on fandom in *Popular Music and Society* covers collecting neither in the introduction (Duffett 2015) nor any of its articles. Similarly, in Duffett's (2013b) edited collection *Popular Music Fandom. Identities, Roles and Practices*, Shuker's chapter 'Record Collecting and Fandom' is the only one addressing collecting as a fan practice. Given the lack of monographs, collected editions and special issues of journals, it seems that Shuker's *Wax Trash and Vinyl Treasures: Record Collecting as a Social Practice* (2010) is one of the very few major studies in popular music research devoted to collecting. Beyond the field of popular music studies, extensive literature on collecting exists, dealing with topics such as longing, desire, pleasure, ritual, passion, consumption, prestige and investment (Shuker 2010: 6; Shuker 2013: 346f). These topics overlap considerably with GAS.

Much of the research on collecting comes from the multidisciplinary field of consumption studies. Belk (1995a: 67) defines collecting as 'the process of actively, selectively, and passionately acquiring and possessing things removed from ordinary use and perceived as part of a set of non-identical objects or experiences'. Accordingly, it is a possessive and materialist pursuit that 'differs from most other types of consumption in the concern for a set of objects, the passion invested in obtaining and maintaining these objects, and the lack of ordinary uses to which these collected objects are put' (Belk 1995b: 479). In other words, while many regular purchases serve a specific, everyday purpose, the acquisition of objects for the sake of collecting is motivated by other sentimental or social objectives (McIntosh & Schmeichel 2004). This definition highlights two important points. Firstly, the hunt for 'unique useless objects' can be considered 'luxury consumption' (Belk 1995b: 479), and secondly, *acquisition* is the difference between simply owning a collection and being a collector (Belk 2001a: 66). As Shuker (2010: 8) points out, a record collection does not make a record collector. There is a fundamental difference between simply enjoying music and methodically acquiring it. Yet even amongst record collectors, there are those whose practice is motivated by their passion for music and those who are primarily interested in the size, rarity and economic value of their collection (Shuker 2010: 39). That points to a broad spectrum of motivations for collecting. Moreover, the purposefulness, energy and time spent on developing a collection, regardless of its forms and intentions, make a collection 'more a part of one's self than are isolated consumption items' (Belk 1988: 154). As these purchases and collections are not motivated by necessity, they must be understood as a form of distinction and self-definition. According to Muesterberger (1994: 165), such practice not only reflects individual motives and experiences but is determined by the 'prevailing culture pattern, the mood and values of the time'.

Given the relative lack of research on collecting in relation to music, record collecting seems a useful starting point to study other customs of collecting before drawing links to musical instruments. According to Shuker (2010: 3), record collecting has become a widespread practice that could only have developed due to social changes in the mid to late nineteenth century. Disposable income, the rise of consumerism, more leisure time and nostalgia made collecting a part of the social identity, at least of the new middle classes of Europe, Great Britain and the United States. Collecting became increasingly important for those who had sufficient economic resources so that today about 25% to 33% of the adult population in Western societies identify themselves as collectors across class and gender boundaries (Shuker 2010: 5). For such a development, the decisive prerequisite is that discretionary time and money are available to the general population and not just the wealthy elite (Mason 1981). Above all, monetary requirements, which are related to age, cannot be overlooked. In the case of record collectors, most develop this practice in young adulthood, not because they were not interested at an early age, but because they lacked the means (Shuker 2010: 53). Shuker (2010: 198) concludes from his study that the diversity of motives and practices allows for no standard definition of the record collector. He suggests instead acknowledging a range of types associated with specific collecting practices, such as 'the record collector as cultural preserver, as accumulator and hoarder, as music industry worker, as adventurous hunter, as connoisseur and as digital explorer'.

One of the main aims of Shuker's study is to break down the stereotype of the record collector as an obsessed middle-aged man who substitutes collecting for 'real' social relationships, ideally depicted in Nick Hornby's (1995) novel *High Fidelity*. His investigation suggests that despite the typical picture of the asocial collector, many collectors are part of a community characterised by diverse practices. While on the one hand, record collecting is the basis for lasting friendships and collegiality; on the other hand, the community is characterised by competition (Shuker 2010: 19). Without a social community, collecting could still fulfil some personal functions, such as the joy of acquiring a complete collection of an esteemed artist, which, however, would miss many of the social and cultural meanings that occur in sharing the practice. It is due to the considerable size of respective communities that collecting has gradually gained greater acceptance in society. Shuker (2010: 199) hence concludes that the term 'record collector', or more generally 'collector', is becoming less and less stigmatised and that collectors do not shy any longer to admit their pastime openly. Shuker's view of collecting as a social practice is consistent with research in social psychology, according to which the friendship and camaraderie of other collectors belong to the most rewarding aspects of collecting (Christ 1965; Formanek 1991; Sherif et al. 1961) with positive effects on wellbeing (Baumeister & Leary 1995) and self-esteem (Linville 1987).

Like in the previous discussion on music technology and popular music, research suggests a gendered way of collecting. The gender differences concern both the type and preference of collecting (Shuker 2010: 36f; Belk 2001a). Men are considered more prone to so-called *serious collecting* (Olmsted 1991; Webley et al. 2001), expressed in their ambitions of investment and competition (Shuker 2010: 5). Following Baekeland (1994: 207), they also differ from women in the kinds of objects they collect, from stamps and art to guns and cars, and unlike female collections, theirs are more public and often have a clear theme. Women feel less comfortable showing cultural capital in competition and more obliged to invest their money in domestic goods instead of male-connoted technology. Objects such as dresses, shoes, perfumes or porcelain are privately accumulated and rarely exhibited publicly in total, so that these are usually not perceived as 'collections', as per Baekeland (1994: 207). For Belk (2001a: 99), these different practices are consistent with fundamental gender stereotypes. Female collecting seems to be about preservation, creativity and nurturing, whereas male collecting represents competitiveness, aggressiveness and the desire to dominate a symbolic realm. Consequently, women may tend not to practise male forms of collecting for fear of appearing masculine. Although it is assumed that quantitatively comparable numbers, or even more women than men are collectors, their tendency to choose domestically related items is believed to make this practice less visible (Shuker 2010: 5). Regarding music, film and arts, it is not known whether there are fewer female collectors or whether they have not made their pastime public. A non-representative study by Bogle (1999) suggests that the proportion of male and female record collectors is equal, but that women play down the fact that they collect (Straw 1997: 4). Those female collectors who exercise their habit openly are faced with problems: 'There have been times I have had to "prove" to other collectors that I am not a girl who simply likes record collecting because their boyfriend got them into it... It is frustrating and sad' (Shuker 2010: 34f). This experience resembles those described before concerning the difficulties women face in rock bands and the discrimination in music stores. For the same reason, women were found to stay away from record fairs and other second-hand events (Shuker 2010: 38). As far as the collecting practice is concerned, women tend to collect records because of their 'use-value', while men pay more attention to collection size, rarity and value and thus owned more records on average (Shuker 2010: 38, 45). That illustrates the competitive intentions of male record collecting, either rational or as a fetishistic obsession, in contrast to women's more subjective and personal motivations (Shuker 2010: 35). The male dominance of collecting in a musical context is not limited to record collection but is similarly present in the related hi-fi culture (Jansson 2010; Schröter & Volmar 2016: 156).

McIntosh and Schmeichel (2004) provide a rare analysis of the collecting process from a social psychology perspective, which is remarkably similar to non-academic GAS cycles (Power & Parker 2015; Wright 2006). Their model of the collecting process consists of seven phases that overlap and repeat on completion. The first phase is *goal formation*. Collections begin for various reasons; sometimes they are a

deliberate project, sometimes a passionate, spontaneous act. What began as a reasoned pursuit can become highly emotional, and what started spontaneously can become extremely systematic (McIntosh & Schmeichel 2004: 88). The goal of collecting is formed, notwithstanding its initial motivation, and it is accompanied by both
the accretion and reduction of tension (Danet & Katriel 1989: 264). The goal serves
to create motivation for action and to provide satisfactory relief when it is achieved.
The second phase is *gathering information* because the collector must have sufficient
knowledge to achieve their goal. Becoming an 'expert' is essential, as it gains an
economic advantage and allows faster progress. Knowledge is acquired through observation of auctions, dealer catalogues and the Internet (McIntosh & Schmeichel
2004: 88f). The third phase is *planning and courtship*, whereby collectors, in their
anticipation of purchase, form an attachment to the desired object and imagine how
it would be like if they owned it. This phase of courtship is important for the positive
emotions attributed to the item. The collectables may increasingly appear as 'talis-
mans' and 'magical' objects (Belk 1991) to their future owners. The fourth phase is
characterised by the *hunt*. The collector can experience positive flow states
(Csikszentmihalyi 1990) by searching for deals, negotiating and completing the purchase (McIntosh & Schmeichel 2004: 91). For many collectors, the hunt is as exciting as the possession (Danet & Katriel 1989). The *acquisition* takes the collector
further towards their goal. The 'collector's actual "collecting self" is now one step
closer to congruence with his/her ideal "collecting self"' (McIntosh & Schmeichel
2004: 92). The *post-acquisition* phase is characterised by the evaluation of one's
position in a social group of collectors. Comparisons can strengthen or threaten the
collector's self-esteem (McIntosh & Schmeichel 2004: 93). The seventh phase consists of *manipulation*, *display* and *cataloguing*. It includes 'possession rituals'
(McCracken 1988) and cataloguing to keep track of the collection's goal (McIntosh
& Schmeichel 2004: 94). Since the collecting process is infinite, the collector either
concentrates on a new acquisition (phase 3) or revisits their goal (phase 1).

Several similarities exist between McIntosh and Schmeichel's model and
Shuker's study on record collecting. As Shuker (2010: 53ff) notes, record collecting
is a process that takes various forms and changes throughout a lifetime. Age, employment and income are key determinants for collecting. Increases or decreases in
income directly alter collection goals, means and strategies. Furthermore, Shuker
highlights domestic responsibilities that McIntosh and Schmeichel do not consider.
Record collecting is a social activity that can lead to the accumulation of social capital used in the wider community of collectors. Yet it can also serve personal nostalgia. Another aspect easily overlooked in a psychological consideration of collecting
is the expressive potential involved. As Campbell (2005: 34) points out, the collection is curated with great care and passion to create individual meanings. In this creative process, the collection is shared with other collectors. Not only the artefacts are

evaluated but also the collector's personality, which is expressed through the unique selection and combination of objects and how they are displayed.

This more 'human' perspective on collection is also reflected in the few classifications of collectors. According to Saari (1997, cited in McIntosh & Schmeichel 2004), there are four types of collectors. The first type is a *passionate collector*. Emotional, obsessive and irrational, they will do anything to acquire a desired object. The *inquisitive collector* sees the purchase as an investment, while the *hobbyist*, on the contrary, collects purely for enjoyment. For the fourth type, the *expressive collector*, items are intricately linked to their self-image. Pearce (1995: 32) presents a tripartite classification that defines the collector's relationship to the object. It can be a *souvenir*, a memorial item of a person's biography, possibly nostalgic. If it is *fetishistic*, it defines the collector's identity, and it can be *systematic*, motivated by a conscious, rational goal, often accompanied by an urge for completeness. In combining these classifications with McIntosh and Schmeichel's process model, we have a useful framework for associating the collector types and their relations to the desired objects with the psychological process of acquisition.

4.2 Prestige and Social Standing

The previous discussion has shown that although a collection is usually owned by a single person, this practice is embedded in a broader social context. It can be as simple as informing oneself about products—a crucial step in any collecting process (McIntosh & Schmeichel 2004)—or moving vinyl records from plastic boxes to shelves and shrines for domestic display (Shuker 2010: 131) to actively contributing to online communities where pictures and information of a collection are shared and compared (Shuker 2010: 199). To become an expert, collectors go through several stages, each of them increasingly public. For record collectors, this can take the form of writing for fanzines, music magazines or specialist collectors' magazines, disseminating and demonstrating their knowledge and tastes and possibly sharing pictures or other documentation of their collection (Shuker 2010: 134). The Internet has led to a proliferation of such practices, widening the community and making it easier than ever before to display collections. The more experienced a collector becomes, the greater their 'desire to share and display musical cultural capital' (Shuker 2010: 199).

Such cultural capital in the tradition of Bourdieu has been discussed in connection with musical instruments and music production equipment. All musical practices, such as record collecting, live music performance and record production, take place in a contested field where those involved compete for capital (Bourdieu 1990a, 1990b). The position in the field is determined by taste (Bourdieu 1986: 134f) and habitus (Bourdieu 1991: 77), a mixture of dispositions, values and practices. It is therefore likely that those who share a similar field or social position also share a taste for similar cultural objects, which makes taste a determinant of social position (Bourdieu 1984: 1f).

In music production, Bourdieu's sociological theories have been applied to analyse practices concerning the possession and collection of analogue and digital equipment. The increasingly widespread availability of relatively inexpensive but powerful digital music production equipment is generally regarded as a democratisation of recording technology (Leyshon 2009). However, as Alan Williams (2015) notes, this has not eliminated inequalities in music production. As production equipment became more affordable, access to valuable items, older analogue gear, remained unchanged and continue to be a means for social distinction: 'ownership of rarified technology bestows (or in the case of seasoned professionals, restores), a measure of elite status. For the rest of us, there's always software' (A. Williams 2015). This view coincides with that of Crowdy (2013: 158), for whom the revived appreciation of analogue gear with the spread of digital technology has strengthened the superior position of professionals for their access to old equipment, an opportunity that most amateurs and semi-professionals lack. Access to analogue hardware at a time when the same sound can be authentically emulated digitally with better functionality thus acts as a mark of social status and prestige (Kaiser 2017). Ownership of such vintage gear characterises social difference, as it shows how much the esteemed taste of equipment decisions is linked to the dominant class of recording professionals. The taste favouring these restricted and limited technologies is significant because it emphasises rare, expensive and inaccessible items that strategically build cultural capital (O'Grady 2019: 131). Hesmondhalgh (1998: 181) defines this 'unequal access to the means of production, distribution, ownership, control and consumption' as 'cultural imperialism'. This uneven standing refers to both social class and access shaped by geographical region. How this is taking shape has been analysed in online message board discussions on studio equipment and production practice (Carvalho 2012; Cole 2011). Foucault's (1980) discourse of power is also relevant in this context. Carvalho (2012) has shown how trade magazines and online message boards for audio recording and production define 'rules of conduct' with a set of rules, opinions and advice on buying, collecting and using recording technology. These rules include knowing the names of a large number and variety of gear, their functions and specifications. Similarly, Porcello (2004) finds that sound engineers must learn to talk about sound to position themselves as 'insiders', a prerequisite for raising their social standing within the recording community.

Bourdieu's capital theory and Foucault's concept of discourse of power are relevant concerning musicians' handling of gear. The common appreciation of vintage instruments, analogue amplifiers and keyboards is not only due to advantages in terms of playability, but also has a status component. Knowledge of the history, main players and technical characteristics of instruments, amplifiers and effects, as well as their possession or replicas if the originals are unaffordable, allow for social distinction and determine the owner's reputation in the community. The distinctive value of instruments, however, is not limited to vintage gear. Cohen (1991: 50) observes that some musicians regard the 'acquisition and accumulation of such gear as a means of achieving status or success ... Most band members showed great determination in acquiring their gear [and] employed considerable ingenuity in raising money to acquire what they wanted'. A gigging musician not only displays their musical talent on stage; the audience may see the equipment as another source of the appreciation of taste, knowledge and cultural capital. Consequently, collecting musical gear appears to be a multifaceted practice related to a variety of musical, psychological and social factors (Cohen 1991: 50) and as such can be read as an accumulation of popular cultural capital (Fiske 1992). For professional musicians, the quantity or quality of collected instruments is a means of distinguishing themselves from 'lesser' musicians as, for instance, fellow professionals or amateurs. For hobbyists, collecting can be compensation for anything missing, be it professional success, recognition or whatever is lacking in life (Belk 1995b: 486). Collecting instruments is an opportunity to gain mastery and accomplishments denied elsewhere (Belk et al. 1991). Thrill, excitement and anticipation are positive emotions connected to collecting, and success in competition with others brings prestige and status (Storr 1983).

4.3   Obsessive Collecting and Hoarding

The competitive nature of collecting practice underlines the inseparable links between collecting and social status. How collectors react to this competition is determined by their general dispositions. There are the ones not having a strong need to raise their social status in general, or their hobby is not so important to them that it defines who they are. At the opposite end, there are those defining themselves through the symbolic value of their collection and the resulting social standing in collector groups. Such collectors are more likely to develop obsessive behaviours.

The literature on compulsive collecting does not paint a coherent picture. According to Belk (1995b: 480), collectors 'often refer to themselves, only half in jest, as suffering from mania, a madness, an addiction, a compulsion, or an obsession'. As he argues, self-presentation can be jocular because collecting is a socially accepted activity that is not stigmatised like other addictions, such as compulsive gambling. Often, collectors even use medical vocabulary to justify their self-indulgence in collecting (Belk 2001a: 80). Other researchers treat obsessive collecting much more seriously. For Clifford (1985: 238), collecting is an organised acquisitive obsession, 'an excessive, sometimes even rapacious need to have [transformed] into rule governed meaningful desire'. That suggests both an uncontrolled, compulsive urge and a systematic goal system as components of collecting. Goldberg and Lewis's (1978: 94f) assessment is even more severe. They state that

> Obsessed collectors ... are driven ... Their obsession overrules every other aspect of their lives and they devote every waking minute to thinking and planning how to obtain the next object for their collection or how to display it. Objects ultimately become more important than people, and fanatic collectors progressively alienate themselves from friends and family, occasionally even becoming suspicious that others will take away their prized possessions. They tend to withdraw from inter-personal relationships and often do not concern themselves with everyday prob-lems like paying bills or getting the car serviced.

This statement points to a pathological condition. It is currently unknown how com-mon it is in musicians and other music practices such as record production. Psycho-logical studies indicate that such extreme conditions mainly result from childhood insecurities (Muesterberger 1994), the desire for self-expression, sociability, a sense of personal continuity through meaningful objects (Formanek 1991) and the inten-tion to expand the sense of self (Belk et al. 1991). Because of the seriousness col-lecting can take, Belk (1995b: 479f) believes that it is motivated by multiple motives.

These observations do not yet reflect all motives for obsessive collecting; many others lie in various psychological needs. In extreme cases, collecting can be

> experienced as a self-transcendent passion in which the collected objects become more important than their health, wealth, or inner being. Collecting ... becomes a religion for such collectors, and they envision themselves playing the role of savior of society by preserving all that is noble and good for future generations. (Belk 1995b: 481)

A religious component is also found in another associated motivation, the pursuit of immortality (Behrman 1952; Rigby & Rigby 1944). Some people overcome anxie-ties of death symbolically through culturally valued activities (McIntosh & Schmeichel 2004: 87). They believe that collections, just like monuments, will guar-antee them symbolic immortality in the sense of heritage or legacy from which future generations can benefit (Belk et al. 1991). In music, this could take the form of col-lections of records, vintage instruments or instruments formerly owned by famous musicians. If this is the case, a private collection fulfils similar functions to a mu-seum but with limited access. Their owners may believe that they can preserve the instrument and possibly the 'magic' (Belk 1991; Fernandez & Lastovicka 2011) bet-ter than a formal institution.

As McIntosh and Schmeichel's (2004) model of collecting has suggested, the acquisition and collection process is cyclical and potentially never-ending. Their model is consistent with Shuker's (2010: 111) observation of record collection, where acquisition is followed by a new need and a 'return to the chase'. There are several reasons for such a process. For many collectors, extensive research in the form of finding out about items and their meanings brings joy, and it is reinforced by the anticipation of eventually adding them to the collection (Shuker 2010: 109). The prospect of ownership can be a major source of satisfaction for a collector (Belk 1984: 291). The cycle starts again directly after the latest acquisition; in McIntosh and Schmeichel's (2004) model, either in the planning and courtship phase or in the initial phase of defining the collecting goal. This frequent revision of goals contributes to the insatiable nature of collecting because once a broad aim is achieved, the focus may shift to details. Collecting is fundamentally characterised by incompleteness; once an object is obtained, new types or variations can be pursued. Collectors of musical instruments would likely switch their focus to new manufacturers, times of production or amplifiers and effects devices. Even for a single instrument model like the Fender Stratocaster guitar, there are hundreds of different versions for which a collector could find justification if they wished to acquire one.

Earlier, we discussed the concept of 'neophilia' as a fetish-like search for objects that are acquired for the sake of buying. Falk (1994) sees neophilia as the underlying mechanism that drives all consumption and collecting and considers it the main reason for the 'insatiability of the collector's urge' (Straw 2000: 167). In Straw's (2000: 165ff) reading of neophilia, collecting is characterised by a 'succession of fetishes'. For him, collecting is far less systematic than for other authors (McIntosh & Schmeichel 2004; Shuker 2010); instead, it is an arbitrary process marked by a desperate and irrational desire that in its unending ease is only temporarily satisfied by impulsive purchases. This view coincides with 'hunting' metaphors in connection with obsessive collecting practices (Shuker 2010: 27, 42ff). In a guide for record collectors, Semeonoff (1949: 2) writes, '[o]ne never knows when something one has been looking for months or even years, is going to turn up. There is, too, the chance of finding records one did not know even existed'. This quote supports Straw's claim that acquisitions are unsystematic. Besides, once a potentially meaningful item has been identified and a seller been found, a person prone to obsessive collecting must deal with the uncertainty of acquisition. Unlike standard items, such as a current musical instrument model, which can be purchased in any music store and bought any time the budget permits, most collectors buy rare objects as soon as they become available. Their 'fear that if a unique object is not acquired immediately it will be gone forever' (Belk 1995b: 483) contributes to the obsession and leads to difficult budgetary decisions. Fernandez and Lastovicka (2011) report about a guitar player who, in his desire to buy the Beatles' original instruments, regularly flies from the USA to Europe to visit dealers who might sell such rare instruments. Since success cannot be guaranteed, the instruments must be acquired as soon as they are discovered. As the authors describe, success is not easy to achieve, and so the collector 'has settled for a vintage instrument that plausibly could have been played by a member of the Beatles' (Fernandez & Lastovicka 2011: 283). The collecting behaviour shows a progression; first replicas of Beatles' gear, then vintage equipment that the Beatles might have played, and finally certified original instruments. This quest has already cost him several hundred thousand dollars. The more ambitious the collection targets become over time, the higher the demand on time and money. Such practice has profound consequences for the collector's social and family life since for everyone but the wealthiest, the money spent on collectables is missing in the household (Belk 1995b: 482). Family members may come to regard a collection as a 'rival' because of the time and affection devoted to it (Belk 1995b: 483).

Studies on collecting seem to be at odds over the degree of compulsive, irrational obsession and the more rational, systematic planning and realisation of collections. While some sociologists (Falk 2004), anthropologists (Clifford 1985), cultural studies scholars (Straw 2000) and some psychologists (Goldberg & Lewis 1978) emphasise the irrational, social psychologists (McIntosh & Schmeichel 2004), the rational nature of collecting is highlighted by some sociologists (Danet & Katriel 1989). There seems to be no disciplinary correlation for the degree of rationality. Shuker (2010: 46) avoids this problem by distinguishing between accumulation and collection; accumulation he views as being characterised by unselected buying and collecting as involving more systematic and selective acquisition. Consequently, collecting would be more rational than the obsessive nature of accumulation. One can safely conclude from the various forms and motives that collecting is too diverse and complex to favour either side. Collecting is probably systematic in principle, but the emotional involvement and the strong connection to a collector's self-perception and identity create desires. Whether or not these can be controlled depends on the individual.

Some further insights into the characteristics of obsessive collecting can be derived from psychiatric research that has compared collecting with hoarding. Hoarding Disorder (HD) is a standardised psychiatric diagnose that has replaced Obsessive Compulsive Disorder (Pertusa et al. 2010) and Obsessive Compulsive Personality Disorder (Mataix-Cols et al. 2010). Hoarding Disorder is characterised by six criteria: 1) difficulty in discarding possessions regardless of their value, 2) distress associated with discarding possessions, 3) cluttered living areas, 4) distress with the social environment, 5) deviation from other medical conditions, 6) symptoms that cannot be explained by any other form of mental disorder (American Psychiatric Association 2013). Collecting, by contrast, is defined as a methodical pursuit with an attempt at completion and an above-average interest in a topic, which is accompanied by the reading of literature and other information-seeking activities, and it is carried out passionately and becoming persistent over time (Subkowski 2006).

In an overview article, Nordsletten et al. (2013) systematically compare normative collecting and hoarding disorder. As far as object content is concerned, collecting is focused on a cohesive theme, while hoarding lacks cohesion and focus. The acquisition process of collectors is structured by stages such as planning, hunting and organising, which is missing in hoarders. By comparison, excessive acquisition is widespread amongst hoarders but not among collectors. Collections are organised and displayed as defining part of the collecting process, whereas hoarders clutter up their possessions. Collectors are rarely distressed about their behaviour, while hoarders do worry about their obsession. Consequently, collectors hardly suffer from social impairment, yet hoarders do. As can be seen from these differences, hoarders rarely part with possessions but collectors frequently trade, as they see it as an opportunity to update and improve their collections (Pearce 1998a, 1998b). However, other research suggests that parting with items is difficult for serious collectors, who will only consider it if they own an item more than once (Long & Schiffmann 1997). Therefore, Nordsletten and Mataix-Cols (2012) distinguish between average and 'extreme' collectors. While both groups have difficulty discarding and feel distressed, extreme collectors tend to clutter, acquire excessively and are more unreflective than regular collectors. Likely there is a spectrum between collecting and hoarding that defies definite clinical diagnosis. Nordsletten and Mataix-Cols (2012: 174) conclude that 'on a majority of core features, collectors—be they typical or extreme—are overlapping with their hoarding counterparts. Indeed, of the six core criteria, the collecting literature indicates that as many as four may potentially be endorsed by the average collector'. While Nordsletten and Mataix-Cols (2012: 174) see no psychiatric problems in most regular collectors, they are concerned about 'extreme collectors' because they are akin to hoarders, as they are prone to distress and social impairment. Regarding the prevalence in the population, the authors estimate 30% as typical collectors and 2-5% as hoarders. The rate of extreme collectors is unknown. Assuming that musicians do not deviate from the general public, the literature suggests that about a third tends to collect or may even be 'extreme collectors'.

4.4   Collecting and GAS

This chapter aims to get a better understanding of the overlaps and differences between GAS and gear collection. According to Belk (1995a: 67), a characteristic of collecting is that acquired objects are removed from everyday use. Hence it is perhaps not so much the object but the way it is used that determines whether a person identifies as a collector. An ardent musician may have accumulated as much gear over time as a collector but is likely to make frequent use of their equipment in contrast to a collector who may not play instruments often or at all to preserve them. Just as for Shuker (2010: 8) a person owning a record collection is not necessarily a record collector, neither is a person having many instruments an instrument collector. Another criterion of collecting is keeping acquired objects (Belk 1995b: 479). Musicians are likely to sell or trade instruments when their preferences change, while most collectors need to accumulate more equipment over time. Belk (2001a: 66) stresses that acquisition makes the difference between owning a collection and being a collector. According to that, collecting requires regularity of additions, whereas a musician is more likely to acquire new equipment only when the perceived or actual need arises.

As we have seen, there is some disagreement in the literature about the systematic versus irrational nature of collecting. By our initial definition, GAS has compulsive features, while collecting has a rational and strategic side, whether for the sake of social capital, cultural heritage or transcendence. However, collectors' emotional reactions and motivations make it problematic to consider the spectrum of rationality as the main distinguishing factor between GAS and collecting. Both exhibit additional commonalities that show in information-seeking activities, excitement in the 'hunt', flow states, and satisfaction and relief in the event of success. Furthermore, each is a long-term disposition that follows cyclic processes from inspiration and desire to planning and acquisition.

These are not yet all differences between collecting and GAS. Collecting is often a rather serious practice because of the collector's strong tie to self-definition, which becomes apparent from the literature on obsessive collecting. By contrast, the discourse on GAS usually emphasises compulsion in a humoristic manner. Collecting has a stronger sense of purpose, indicating energy and time are deliberately spent on it, contrary to the urge triggered by coincidence when GAS-affected musicians encounter new gear or hear other musicians discuss experiences with their equipment, be it online or in local music scenes. Similarly, the greater purposefulness requires collectors to become experts in gear, while musicians are usually more interested in its benefits for their playing. GAS-affected musicians can, of course, have specialised knowledge of technical details. Another difference concerns the role of exhibiting and cataloguing, which is an integral part of collecting but not decisive for GAS. Collectors often write in fanzines, magazines and on the Internet to get feedback on their collection or gratification. Musicians affected by GAS may proudly present photos and lists of their gear on message boards or on stage, but this is perhaps less motivated by the hope of social advancement than by marking equipment a part of their musical identity. After all, it could be argued that gear acquisition for musicians is motivated by musical necessities, be they real or imagined, whereas collecting is usually more strategic, possibly without any practical musical use. For most collectors, collecting is a social practice, while playing music does not necessarily require other people. Many musicians are not in a band but play their instrument mainly at home, which, however, does not exclude them from being interested in gear and expanding their rig. It is not always for reasons of collecting if musicians do not sell older instruments when they buy something new; the old ones could become useful again in the future, with changing preferences or when needing it for a particular musical project. Also, selling equipment usually involves financial losses unless they are valuable vintage instruments, so musicians may decide to keep them and, over time, build up a 'collection' without strategic deliberations or social motives. Alternatively, they may keep the instrument for nostalgic reasons, especially given the low resale value. Perhaps it is the strategic intention alongside the use-value that distinguishes collecting the most from GAS. Collecting is often motivated by social reputation, whereas GAS is motivated by the benefits musicians likely presume in terms of their playing and musical identity, which by no means suggests that one group spends less money on their customs than the other.

5   Consumption

In the previous chapter, collecting was described as a practice related to but also distinct from GAS. We demonstrated socio-cultural aspects associated with collecting habits, such as social standing and gender differences. We further showed psychological processes which corresponded with procedural assumptions described in blogs on GAS. Pronounced interest in musical gear characterises GAS, the middle letter standing for 'acquisition' defining it as a fundamental aspect of the phenomenon. Consequently, it is linked with consumption, even if the urge to acquire new gear is resisted. Consumption research can help us understand relevant processes from the cause that triggers interest in a product up to the eventual acquisition.

This chapter begins with positioning consumption research in the context of cultural studies rather than critical theory. Consumption is not limited to purchasing a commodity but necessarily includes the steps leading to an acquisition and the way the item is used once it has been acquired. A useful first perspective in our research of consumption is 'serious leisure' (Stebbins 2009), which provides a sociological framework for theorising GAS amongst ambitious amateur musicians. We then expand the already established close relationship between gear and identity with valuable theories and empirical studies from consumption research. Belk's (1988) concept of the 'extended self' is central to understanding why instruments are important to many musicians. This concept is extended by empirically derived frameworks on desire and necessity that examine the impulsive and compulsive buying behaviours documented in Wright's (2006) interviews with guitarists. Other relevant concepts like 'prosumption' and 'craft consumption' are explored to theorise DIY practices such as fabrication, modification and combination of music equipment. Finally, we investigate online practices, as these have become commonplace for many musicians. What can be expected to spark GAS is 'eBaying' and exchanges on message boards that, for example, establish 'taste regimes' (Arsel & Bean 2013), which standardise practices and define must-have items.

5.1   Consumption Research

Consumption research is an interdisciplinary field of research that deals with the explanation of consumers, their consumption behaviours and the production, distribution and purchase of goods (Stebbins 2009: 1). According to Clarke et al. (2003: 3ff), consumption has traditionally been studied from three perspectives. Economics and marketing explore the financial aspects surrounding production, and history and geography look at consumptive practices in time and space. These two approaches are less relevant to the study of GAS but not irrelevant. The third perspective on

consumption is from anthropology, sociology and cultural studies. Such research examines the social and cultural aspects of consumption, making it a useful lens for
studying musical practices around equipment.

As it is beyond the scope of this book to summarise the history of consumption
research comprehensively, we limit our discussion to the most relevant work in the
context of GAS.[24] When considering consumption, it is tempting to focus on the
increasing commodification of society, on the power it has given to manufacturers,
and on the related effects such as citizens becoming passive victims of advertisers,
which concurs with critical theory scholars like Adorno and Horkheimer (Graeber
2011: 489). This traditional view was shaken by cultural studies scholars like Dick
Hebdige (1979), who saw consumers in a more active and self-determined role. Mac-
Kay (1997: 3) summarises this new way of thinking:

> rather than being passive and easily manipulated . . . young consumers were active,
> creative and critical in their appropriation and transformation of material artifacts.
> In a process of bricolage, they appropriated, reaccented, rearticulated or transcoded
> the material of mass culture to their own ends, through a range of everyday creative
> and symbolic practices. Through such processes of appropriation, identities are
> constructed.

Due to the consumer's greater power, the relationship between consumption and
production is now understood as reciprocal. Social and economic forces determine
demand, which can be subject to manipulation (Appadurai 1986). Manufacturers respond to the requests of their customers and customers to some degree to offers and
marketing campaigns. As Miège (1979: 300) puts it:

> The cultural industry is not in the end a responsive pre-existing demand. Rather,
> basing itself on the dominant conceptions of culture, it must as a first stage, at the
> same time as it puts new products onto the market ..., create a social demand, give
> it a consistency, in other words lead certain social groups selected as commercial
> targets to prepare themselves to respond to the producers' offer.

Within popular music, Frith (2001: 27) argues that the popular music industry does
not determine popular music culture. Although the industry influences culture, it is
forced to react to culture continually. This view must be considered in the context of
musical equipment because instrument manufacturers need to know the musicians'
attitudes and preferences in order to sell. At the same time, GAS is likely to be related
to marketing strategies that fuel the desire for new musical objects. This balance in
power is important because it allows for musicians the practices of consumption,

---

[24] For a summary of influential works by Karl Marx, Georg Simmel, Henri Lefevbre, Jean
Baudrillard, Michel de Certeau and Pierre Bourdieu, see Stebbins 2009, pp. 56–81. For an
introduction to consumption research, see Graeber 2011.

'prosumption' and 'craft consumption' when customising their instruments and us-ing them in ways not intended by the manufacturer. As Belk (2007: 737) points out, consumption is not only defined by the activities leading to an acquisition but also by the activities that follow from the acquisition. Holbrook and Hirschman (1982) hold a similar view, claiming that consumption goes beyond buying because time, experiences and feelings are involved as well. In other words, consumption does not end at the time of purchase but includes the use of the acquired product. This defini-tion makes consumption research valuable for the theoretical consideration of GAS as musical practice.

There is some research proposing consumer types. Stone (1954) was the first to create a typology of orientations towards shopping. The 'economic shopper' pays attention to price and quality, while the 'personalising shopper' sees the shopping activity as an opportunity for social interaction. The 'ethical shopper' bases their decision on moral principles, the 'apathic shopper' buys out of necessity. Transfer-ring this thinking to musical practices suggests that the economical shopper is likely to be widespread amongst musicians. The right balance between price and quality is one of the primary criteria for musicians when considering a purchase (Wright 2006: 28), as is the temptation of a good deal (Wright 2006: 38, 40). The personalising shopper can be found in music stores. Often musicians stop at a store to meet up with other musicians or staff and have a chat, or they travel to a store with bandmates as a social event. Online discussion boards serve a similar function. It is unclear how widespread the apathic shopper is, but GAS-related blog posts indicate that some musicians give their music precedence over buying and spending much time con-templating equipment. Ethical shoppers may exist, but they are probably a minority. Moral aspects of music equipment could be related to the working conditions of mu-sic instruments factories or the use of rare material. For example, guitar manufacturer Gibson has been fined for using illegal timber from Madagascar for its instruments. They admitted having violated the Lacey Act, which aims to protect Madagascan wildlife by stopping deforestation (Black 2012).[25]

Stone's (1954) study was based on an all-female sample, which raises the ques-tion of gender differences like those discussed in connection to collecting. Campbell (1997) argues that women see shopping as a leisure activity more than men. As per Campbell, there are some exceptions, especially regarding technology items like cars, computers and DIY equipment. Musical instruments are also likely to fall into this category, which coincides with Danziger (2004: 161), who finds that men are more inclined to buy musical instruments than women. She further concludes that the two genders do not differ in their discretionary purchases when pursuing a hobby

---

[25] Chris Gibson (2019) discusses how the ecological crisis affects musical instrument manu-facture and traces guitars back to the tree, focusing on three 'more-than-musical' themes: materiality, corporeality and volatility (see also Gibson & Warren 2016).

and that persons below 44 years of age are more prone to such buying behaviours (Danziger 2004: 84). Another variable is the household type; persons with children are more active buyers, regardless of gender (Danziger 2004: 161).

Danziger (2004: 6f) defines four kinds of purchases. A 'utilitarian purchase' describes an acquisition of an item that is not essential but does fulfil a practical function. An 'indulgence' is a luxury item that is not too expensive to make one feel guilty about the cost and provides emotional satisfaction in everyday life. 'Lifestyle luxuries' are objects that are not needed but still useful, such as a watch or a car. 'Aspirational luxuries' are purchases made without functional reasons, of which collectors are prone. Such motivation, as per Danziger (2004: 84), derives from the joy of ownership and the thrill of the hunt, which indicates that pursuing a hobby and the corresponding buying is often more satisfying than completing a collection. All these reasons and psychological processes are similar to those described in connection with collecting. What is more, the four types of purchases also apply to musicians. 'Utilitarian purchases' as small accessories or wearing items could be equivalent to guitar strings or drumsticks. How the three other kinds of purchases can be compared depends on musical justification. 'Lifestyle luxuries' and 'indulgences' could be an effects pedal that is nice to have but not essential, and 'aspirational luxuries' could be anything from a T-shirt of a favourite instrument manufacturer to expensive vintage instruments that complement a collection.

Campbell (2005: 23f) summarises four consumer images that dominate the literature on consumption. Following the previously highlighted school of critical theory, critics of mass society see the consumer as a passive individuum easily manipulable. In contrast, economic theory commonly regards the consumer as an active and rational actor whose purchases are limited by budgetary requirements. More recent views see the consumer as a 'self-conscious manipulator of the symbolic meanings that are attached to products, someone who selects goods with the specific intention of using them to create or maintain a given impression, identity or lifestyle' (Campbell 2005: 24). This view is much more consistent with the musical practices described in the earlier chapters. Campbell (2005: 23f) sees a fourth, more recent type in the craft consumer. Such a person combines common goods to create something original and unique, which goes beyond mere personalisation. Since most musical practices require careful selection and combination of gear, musicians are expected to be prone to craft consumption.

5.2   Leisure Studies

Making music and collecting musical instruments are activities that cover a wide range of intentions, from purely recreational without ambitions to dedicated semi-professional or professional work. Most of these intentions fall into the area of leisure. Stebbins (2009: 10) defines leisure as an 'uncoerced activity undertaken during free time. Uncoerced activity is a positive activity that, using their abilities and re-sources, people both want to do and can do at either a personally satisfying or a deeper fulfilling level'. This definition does not include professional activities (Stebbins 2009: 17f) though it should, as leisure time is more than just recreation because the motivation derives from a purpose or desired goal (Stebbins 2009: 10). Musical aims span learning and mastering an instrument, becoming familiar with new styles, joining a band, playing live, recording albums and progressing as a musician, thus gaining musical expertise, even if the player does not intend to turn their leisure activity into a profession. Striving for a goal can be an important feature of leisure, and it likely plays a role in the context of GAS, which is motivated by a certain sense of development and purpose.

Stebbins's extensive work on 'serious leisure' is closely related to consumption because most leisure activities require special equipment. We draw on this useful perspective to distinguish leisure from consumption:

> In their essence the two processes are clearly different. That is the end of consump-tion is to *have* something, to possess it, whereas the end of leisure is to *do* some-thing, to engage in a positive activity. Nonetheless exceptions to this generalization exist, for there are times when consumption and leisure are so closely aligned as to make it impossible to distinguish the two in this way. Consider the hobbyist coin collector who travels abroad in search of a rare piece. (Stebbins 2009: ix)

For Stebbins (2009: 3), the motive for purchase is decisive in this context. If the batteries for an effects pedal were to run out, buying new batteries would be seen as a nuisance, whereas buying batteries to use a new effects pedal for the first time is about leisure because it is likely to be exciting. Consequently, the motivation and emotional attitude determine whether a purchase is to be considered an obligatory or leisure-related consumption (Stebbins 2009: 82).

Stebbins distinguishes between three kinds of leisure engagement: casual, pro-ject-based and serious leisure. 'Casual leisure' is defined as an 'immediately intrin-sically rewarding, relatively short-lived pleasurable activity requiring little or no spe-cial training to enjoy it. It is fundamentally hedonic, pursued for its significant level of pure enjoyment, or pleasure' (Stebbins 2009: 22f). Since most music-making re-quires a minimum of dedication and practice, hardly any musical activity can be classed as casual leisure, except perhaps playful music apps. 'Project-based leisure' is more committed. It is a 'short-term, reasonably complicated, one-off or occasional, through infrequent, creative undertaking carried out in free time, or time free of dis-agreeable obligation. Such leisure requires considerable planning, effort, and some-times skill or knowledge' (Stebbins 2009: 24). Many more musical activities fall into this category, for example, a musical side project, preparation for an open stage or other forms of one-off performances, such as learning another instrument to help an ensemble out with a particular gig. While 'casual leisure' is motivated by the pure enjoyment of the activity, 'project-based leisure' can be pleasurable or fulfilling.

Most of the musical activities related to GAS fall into the third category, 'serious leisure', the form of leisure that requires considerable effort and investment but also offers personal fulfilment (Stebbins 2009: 16). Stebbins (2009: 14) defines serious leisure as the 'systematic pursuit of an amateur, hobbyist, or volunteer activity sufficiently substantial, interesting, and fulfilling for the participant to find a (leisure) career there acquiring and expressing a combination of its special skills, knowledge, and experience'. The wording is noteworthy because a 'career' seems to contradict the definition of leisure as a non-professional activity. Strong identification with a hobby defines serious leisure and, as such, is associated with qualities like earnestness, sincerity and importance (Stebbins 2009: 14). These qualities can be found in six distinctive characteristics of serious leisure (Stebbins 2009: 17ff). A serious leisure enthusiast requires significant personal 'effort' to develop specialist knowledge and skills, which takes 'perseverance' to acquire. It is the prerequisite for pursuing a 'leisure career'. Such a career is motivated by several individual and social aspects. The efforts invested in the leisure activity are motivated by the hope of 'durable benefits', the positive outcomes that lead to 'self-actualization, self-enrichment, self-expression, regeneration or renewal of self, feelings of accomplishment, enhancement of self-image, social interaction and sense of belonging, and lasting physical products of the activity' (Stebbins 2009: 18f). Consequently, serious leisure activity is for many the basis for a 'distinctive identity', an identity lived in a community that shares attitudes, practices, values, beliefs and goals. Such communities are often online, where new serious leisure activists learn about the common 'ethos'.

The nature of serious leisure implies a prolonged, possibly lifelong activity that may require substantial effort and investment before it bears fruit. The motivation for this activity stems from a continuous search for rewards, which Stebbins (2009: 20) divides into personal and social rewards. Personal rewards entail enrichment and self-actualisation as well as developing skills, abilities and knowledge. Self-expression is another personal reward related to the expression of already developed skills, abilities and knowledge. Serious leisure activities after a day of work also encourage other personal rewards such as self-gratification and recreation or regeneration, something that can lead to joy and deep fulfilment. If skills are sufficiently developed and become of interest to others, the activity can yield a financial return. So could profound knowledge of musical instrument technologies and practical skills help a serious leisure pursuer repair, maintain or modify instruments for other musicians for money. Such help is likely to improve self-image. In terms of social rewards, Stebbins emphasises social attraction, such as the association with other serious leisure participants or group accomplishments, which in music could be any activity that involves a band. Because of the high level of engagement, serious leisure activity can lead to tensions with other commitments such as work or family (Stebbins 2009: 20). With the three types of leisure and the typology of rewards, the serious leisure perspective 'offers a classification and explanation of all leisure activities and experiences, as these two are framed in the social, psychological, social, cultural, and historical conditions in which each activity and accompanying experience take place' (Stebbins 2009: 13f).

Previously, we have highlighted the close connection between leisure and consumption. A serious leisure enthusiast in music will most likely need to invest in instruments before they can start learning. As skills develop and preferred styles become clearer, other specialised gear may be required. According to Stebbins (2009: 115), such continued investment can 'perhaps even [be] seen as an indispensable part' of being a musician and 'enable their buyers to perform better'. About violin players, Stebbins (2009: 127) notes that there 'seems to be an almost universal desire to upgrade'. He further states:

> Amateurs and hobbyists, in particular, must occasionally buy goods, the purchase of which can be most pleasant. A horn player sets out to find a new and better horn … The immediate outcome is the prospect, made possible by the purchase, of better and more fulfilling execution of the hobbyist or amateur passion. Furthermore, the process of purchase itself commonly proceeds from a background of considerable knowledge and experience relative to the best products and their strengths and weaknesses. Such knowledge is central to the development of a positive sense of self, which Prus and Dawson (1991) argued can emerge from some kinds of shopping done for leisure. (Stebbins 2009: 93)

This line of thinking corresponds to what practitioners say about GAS in blogs and what we found in Wright's (2006) book. The motivation to upgrade the material objects used in a serious leisure activity has been described as 'facilitation' in consumption research (Hartmann 2016; Warde 2005). According to Hartmann (2016: 12), 'facilitation provides an infrastructure for doings—how to assist objects as carriers of productive moments; and objects—an appropriate material arrangement'. The gear played is significant to the musician not only because of musical characteristics such as playability and sound but also because of the beliefs and connotations associated with it. These beliefs are equally important for the performance as for the material properties of the instrument itself (Hartmann 2016: 12f). Because of this strong symbolic value that co-exists with the object's features, updating gear offers many serious leisure enthusiasts like musicians an opportunity to advance their leisure career, if only symbolically in terms of social rewards (Prus & Dawson 1991) or meaningfully in terms of personal rewards. These reward systems are only partly related to the impact that a new instrument may or may not have on the musician's development because many of the rewards are connected to enjoyment, self-actualisation, re-creation and social attraction, which do not require improvement of musical abilities.

Beyond Serious Leisure: GAS from an Expert Performance Perspective

If one extends the focus beyond leisure activities, the occupation with music equipment, especially in popular music, can also be regarded as part of the process of professionalisation. In the influential 'expert performance' approach in expertise research, it is assumed that, depending on the required physical constitution, anyone can become an expert in the field of their choice with about ten thousand hours of 'deliberate practice'. By definition, deliberate practice 'includes activities that have been specially designed to improve the current level of performance' (Ericsson et al. 1993: 368). As such, these activities have been individually developed by a mentor to improve performance in the best possible way. In this process, the results are monitored and discussed with the practitioner. Studying violinists and pianists of different performance levels, Ericsson and his colleagues were able to show a connection between the extent of deliberate practice and the actual performance level. From this observation, they deduced that excellent performance is not the consequence of innate talent but a direct result of significant amounts of deliberate practice.

While there is common consensus on the considerable amount of practice being required to become an expert on an instrument, the importance of deliberate practice has been disputed ever since the study was published in the early 1990s. Recent research has included critical reviews, meta-analyses and replications of expert performance studies (Hambrick et al. 2016; Macnamara & Maitra 2019). It was found that the suggested amount of ten thousand hours of deliberate practice was often overestimated and that '[f]orms of domain-relevant experience other than deliberate practice (for example, work) positively and meaningfully predict expertise' (Hambrick et al. 2016: 45).

A fundamental conceptual problem in their findings regarding musical expertise lies in the fact that the research conducted by Ericsson and his colleagues exclusively focussed on the prerequisites of European classical music and did not consider other forms of musical expression (Menze & Gembris 2018). As studies on musical learning (for example, Creech et al. 2008; Green 2002; Menze & Gembris 2018, 2019) demonstrate, there are decisive differences between classical music and popular music in terms of deliberate practice, practice strategies and domain-related knowledge. Further differences can be observed regarding the respective understanding of musical giftedness and talent (Gembris 2014). It strongly depends on the conventions within the respective genre and the sociocultural and historical context what is considered an expert performance. Consequently, when studying processes of professionalisation in popular music, a specific concept of musical expertise is required that should not only consider the flawless reproduction of an existing piece, personal interpretation and expression but also a variety of aspects, such as innovative style, improvisation, and maybe even stage performance.

Given the importance of tone in popular music, the ability to create an individual or appropriate sound for musical expression with the selected equipment can be interpreted as a relevant part of musical performance and hence of musical expertise (see Creech et al. 2008; Papageorgi et al. 2010). Furthermore, being able to select and combine the 'right' type of gear and adding the 'right' effects is a precondition for the realisation of individual sound ideas and the creative dealing with genre conventions. Considering that processes of learning and professionalisation in popular music commonly take place in informal learning settings (Green 2002; Längler et al. 2018) and how GAS-related practices are carried out in communicative interaction among peers and like-minded musicians, it is reasonable to understand such processes as a way to acquire domain-relevant experience (Hambrick et al. 2016: 45) and thus a specific form of popular music expertise that is not captured by the conventional concept of deliberate practice. Experience in handling musical equipment may also be seen as a by-product of years of instrumental practice, and its relevance in terms of expert performance could be questioned. We, on the other hand, argue that the explicit and implicit knowledge ('tacit knowledge', see Schmidt-Horning 2004) gained in GAS-related practices can contribute to musical creativity, the versatility of musical expression and aesthetic innovations and therefore must be understood as a relevant factor of expertise in popular music. This presupposes that the time invested in dealing with equipment does not distract from practising and playing the instrument, as critics of GAS have pointed out (Becker 1996; Kwisses 2015).

5.3   Gear and Identity

The previous chapters have shown that for many musicians, their equipment is more than just a tool for making music; it is part of their self-image as musicians and thus part of their musical identity (Hargreaves et al. 2012, 2016, 2017; North & Hargreaves 1999). As mentioned earlier, musical instruments mark a 'loaded symbolic terrain' (Théberge 1993: 166). When sound production is showcased, as in any public musical performance, instruments and equipment come into the spotlight, framing the perception of the performance and adding a further symbolic layer to the musical meaning. Closely related to musical forms of expression, traditions and genres, musical instruments inevitably impact the musicians' artistic expression and perception. By determining their performance, image and cultural localisation, instruments are inseparably linked to the musicians' musical identity.

GAS, by definition, is related to an increased interest in musical equipment, which commonly shapes the musicians' (self-)perception and their self-presentation in the wider music community and beyond. It must be understood as a cultural praxis in which 'people can co-construct each other's musical, social, and personal identities' (Hargreaves et al. 2017: 5). This entails musical instruments blurring the typical division between identities in music (IIM) and music in identities (MII), as per Hargreaves et al. (2017: 4). On the one hand, the status as a musician is always connected to the instrument used or artificially staged, for example, to comply with conventions or to fulfil endorsement requirements. It is therefore part of the musicians' identities in music (IIM), which are defined by 'established cultural roles and categories' and linked to social influences. In a socio-cultural reading, the relationship to the instrument could be interpreted as an interaction with a cultural object influencing the musicians' individual development and accompanying them in becoming their artistic selves (Hargreaves et al. 2012: 126). Besides, instrument and gear choice provide information such as cultural contexts, aesthetic preferences or the musician's role in a band. So, gear is for them presumably the most visible manifestation of a 'badge of identity', predicting 'several other aspects of lifestyle and attitude' (North & Hargreaves 1999: 75). On the other hand, the importance attributed to music equipment and the passion implied in GAS suggest that both are also linked with the concept of music in identities (MII), understood as 'the extent to which music is important in our self-definitions as masculine-feminine, old-young, able-disabled, extravert-introvert, and so on' (Hargreaves et al. 2017: 4). Whether in the context of collecting or through the overt coding of certain instruments as the embodiment of male or female character traits, from the display of an extraverted design and lifestyle, or in the celebration of certain forms of musical expression attributed as loud and rebellious: musical instruments offer a wide range of readings that contribute to the negotiation of the musician's self-perception. For all its personal and cultural implications, GAS is closely related to the musician's musical identity, which in turn is seen as 'an essential part of the explanation of their musical development' (Hargreaves et al. 2012: 125).

Looking beyond the musical context, social science research has been committed to understanding identity not as essentialist but within the framework of poststructural theory (Bauman 2001; Foucault 1982). It is generally accepted that identity is not fixed but dynamic and changing in response to the environment. Accordingly, identity is a process and a practice that is situation-specific and develops in the course of a person's life (Giddens 1991). In today's postmodern culture, people actively construct, maintain and communicate their identity through the symbolic meaning of leisure as a way to progress and avoid existential crises (Elliott & Wattanasuwan 1998). As we have discussed earlier, leisure activities usually require consumption in order to start, maintain and advance a serious leisure career. Building on this idea, we will now focus on research from the perspective of consumption studies to gain a deeper understanding of the relationship between gear and identity and how this relationship may motivate GAS-related behaviours and attitudes.

Several studies show that possessions symbolise identity (Belk 1988; Csikszentmihalyi & Rochberg-Halton 1981; Dittmar 1992), and as identities develop throughout a lifetime, new objects are acquired, and others discarded to reflect this develop-ment (Shankar et al. 2009: 76f). The close relationship between musicians and their material possessions can be explained by the concept of 'extended self' introduced by Belk (1988), which in principle claims that people regard their possessions as part of themselves (Belk 1988: 139). Tuan (1980: 472) argues that '[o]ur fragile sense of self needs support, and this we get by having and possessing things because, to a large degree, we are what we have and possess'. Therefore, possessions help create, reinforce and preserve a sense of identity, and they remind a person who they are and who they have been (Belk 1988: 150). McClelland (1951) argues that all objects can fulfil this function and become part of the self if the person is capable of exer-cising power or control over them. Besides, Belk (1988: 140, 145) builds on McClel-land when he suggests that objects that can be used as tools or instruments are par-ticularly effective in the construction and development of the self because these items enable the person to be different from what they would be without them. For Furby (1978), the power an item gives to its owner is also an important reason for becoming part of the 'extended self'. This power can be either 'instrumental' or 'sen-timental'. Instrumental power relates to any usefulness, whereas 'sentimental' power enables the owner to maintain a sense of self, even when the self-identity inevitably changes throughout a lifetime. All these functions are evident in the case of musical instruments. One can hardly be a musician without owning an instrument or at least having access to one. Possessing even a single instrument or small gear collection may be sufficient to master the instrument, join a band, and to perform live or record music. Consequently, the possession of musical gear enables a person to see them-selves as a musician and experience the lifestyle associated with it in the various subcultures of music, for example, 'sex, drugs and rock & roll' (Fernandez & Lastov-icka 2011: 284f). An example of the sentimental power is 'reflective nostalgia' (Boym 2001) for instruments owned in the past and memories attached to it.

Identities change during life, and material possessions reflect this development. Although such development is directed towards the future, possessions are material reminders of the past, as they are a 'convenient means of storing the memories and feelings' (Belk 1988: 148). Here we see a substantial similarity between Boym's (2001) concept of 'reflective nostalgia' and views on possessions in consumption research. As Davis (1979: 31) reminds us, the purpose of nostalgia is not only to reminisce but, above all, to provide a 'readily accessible psychological lens for the never ending work of constructing, maintaining, and reconstructing our identities'. Therefore, remembering the past, reflecting on the development and thinking about future goals are supported by material possessions. Musical instruments are effective in this function because of the strong emotions that their players often associate with them as reminders of memorable experiences such as playing in a band and the joy of performing on stage.

Next to the 'extended self', the 'humanisation' of objects described in consumption research is noteworthy in the context of GAS. People sometimes see the human in non-human forms, a process described as 'anthropomorphising' (Epley et al. 2007; Guthrie 1993). Consequently, they ascribe human features, beliefs and emotions to objects, which takes form in practices such as naming objects (Aggarwal & McGill 2007: 468). Fernandez and Lastovicka (2011: 289) observe in their study on fetishes amongst electric guitar players that many of their respondents tend to personify their instruments through 'social roles such as confidant, companion, collaborator, wife, or muse'. Previously, we already reported on Joey, a former successful guitarist, who attributed his fame to his guitar 'Goldie'. The companionship to the guitar is clear in his statement:

> it did become a companion. I actually had it in every hotel room I'd go in [when the band was on tour]. It'd never stay with the equipment. I actually slept with it a couple of nights—that was the safest place [for the guitar]. I'd be writing a song and I'd fall asleep and it was right next to me. So we, we're companions, and we became very close. (Fernandez & Lastovicka 2011: 289)

This high degree of intimacy and emotional attachment with even sexual undertones coincide with interviews that Wright (2006: 34, 36) conducted with numerous guitarists. In the case of the guitar, this anthropomorphisation seems relatively natural given that instrument parts are named according to the physiological nomenclature of the human being: head, neck, body and waist (Fernandez & Lastovicka 2011: 288). Anthropomorphisation often leads to the next step, 'personification', when the guitar is perceived to have a unique personality, something expressed by name and gender (Fernandez & Lastovicka 2011: 288; Wright 2006: 34ff). In its most developed form, an instrument has a 'soul', and its owner collects cherished memories, stories and associations made with it, much like a 'human' friend or partner. In his autobiography, singer and songwriter Frank Turner (2016: 72f) describes the persistent loss he experienced when his acoustic guitar was stolen from the van at a tour stop in Finland in 2007:

> In the ten minutes that we'd been inside the venue, someone had come along, jimmied open the back door and taken my instrument—my friend … I've never seen the guitar since, much to my sadness … So I guess my old faithful axe got sold in some Muscovite car-boot sale and who knows where she ended up. I still think about her every now and again and hope that at least someone's playing her … As much as I try not to be materialistic about things—after all, we take nothing with us when we die—it's still pretty hard, as a musician, losing your old friend.

A similar emotional attachment to his instruments becomes apparent from another statement by Joey:

> Each guitar has a soul. Why do I have 117 guitars? … Every guitar brings out a mood in me. Not only a different sound but a different mood. The story behind the

guitar—you don't usually know the story behind it but you know *your* own story—
guitars that have been with you for 40 years, they all have a *story* ... they all take
on a soul. So, the stories behind my own guitars give them a characteristic—of
course we're still doing 30 or 35 shows a year, [and] I'll remember, that's the guitar
I played with the Turtles or Chubby Checker and that was a great show and the
memories ... I'm making new stories. (Fernandez & Lastovicka 2011: 292f)

The guitar's tonal qualities are equally human-like, as it is often described as 'singing', and The Beatles song 'While My Guitar Gently Weeps' (1968) lends it even
more human emotions. How this anthropomorphisation and personification takes
shape in other instruments has not yet been investigated. The bass has a similar shape
to a guitar, so the physiological connotations are probably perceived the same way.
However, the 'singing' and 'weeping' qualities may be less pronounced because the
bass is rarely used as a melodic lead instrument. That may also be the case with
keyboard instruments. As Moore (2001: 157) points out, rock fans have traditionally
been sceptical about keyboard instruments because there is no direct connection between sound production and result, whereas the guitar directly translates actions such
as string bending or picking into expression. Wind and brass instruments are even
more closely connected to their players; the breath as 'engine' makes playing more
personal and unique than a guitarist's hands and fingers. For this reason, humanisation can be expected for wind instruments. In contrast, drummers may find it difficult
to see their instrument as a human agent because drums link directly between physical gestures and the resulting sound, so the rhythmic, as opposed to melodic, nature
of the instrument is emphasised. Besides, the kit's physical form bears no resemblance to human physiology. Drummers still name and value their kit but for principles other than those for the guitar. These differences in humanisation are relevant
because, as the quote from guitarist Joey has shown, different perceived personalities
can encourage a player to acquire more instruments, not so much for their physical
characteristics but emotional reasons.

'Contamination' is another process related to the 'extended self' that affects the
relationship and emotional connection with a possession (Belk 1988). A newly acquired instrument is not yet part of the extended self. For many new owners, this
happens through 'possession rituals' (McCracken 1988: 85ff), which reduce the initially unaccustomed feeling of a purchased item and give it personal meaning. This
is all the more important if the item is second-hand. In this case, it needs to be 'de-
contaminated' of the previous owner's self and 'recontaminated'. Fernandez and
Lastovicka (2011: 289) describe an example of this process based on the experience
of player Joey:

You have to make every guitar your own ... So I go through a ritual ... You strip
it all down—you take off the strings, you take off the knobs, you take out the wax,
and you just start buffing that thing. Getting all the last life off, and putting your

life on it. After I buy a guitar it will probably be the only guitar I play for the next few months. I'm making it my own; it's kind of a process of making it your own.

The process of decontamination and recontamination overhauls an instrument and ensures full functionality and unrestricted attachment. The only exception to this fundamental requirement is when the previous owner was an esteemed celebrity (Fernandez & Lastovicka 2011: 289). Hoping for inspiration by the aura and magic of the valued artist (Belk 1991, 1996, 2001a), the contamination will likely be preserved. Contamination is significant concerning GAS and gear collecting because, once an instrument has become part of the extended self, the owner may be more reluctant to part with it, which can lead to a constantly growing collection of gear.

Special Case: Digital Goods

So far, we have limited our discussion to 'real' physical instruments. In connection with the guitar, we have seen that digital amplification technologies in hardware devices such as modelling amplifiers have often been perceived as inferior to valve amplifiers, and even transistor-based devices are not equal to valve gear. This suggests, at least for guitarists, that the more advanced electronic and digital technology is, the less valuable the device seems to be (Herbst 2019a, b). Similarly, electronic drum kits are often perceived as a practical alternative to loud and large acoustic sets (Andertons n.d.; Bache n.d.), and for keyboard instruments, analogue devices are still popular and often expensive (Pinch & Reinecke 2009; Pinch & Trocco 2002: 317ff). With the expansion of computational power and the development of digital audio workstations, digital instruments have increasingly become an alternative to hardware devices. Software synthesisers are not limited by physical designs and allow the free combination of sound-generating elements. For guitars and basses, there are now many virtual amplifier simulations based on different technologies that computationally emulate the physical behaviour of components or use 'acoustic fingerprints' in the form of impulse responses of loudspeakers recorded with specific microphones (Eichas & Zölzer 2018). For drums, there are more and more sophisticated forms of drum computers that contain groove templates from real drummers, but none support musicians in the same way as synthesisers and guitar or bass amplifiers do because computers replace humans in their performance. However, commercial drum sample packs with multiple samples and velocities can expand the sound capabilities and quality of an electronic drum kit. In this context, it is interesting to discuss how digital objects may be compared with traditional music equipment in terms of identity and popularity and how they relate to GAS.

Little is generally known about the perceived value of immaterial digital items. One exception is music collecting, where digital collections are less tangible and more prone to loss than physical collections (Fox 2004; Giles et al. 2007; McCourt 2005; Sklar 2008; Styvén 2010). According to Denegri-Knott and Molesworth

(2010), digital items are located in a liminal space between the material and the imaginary world and are therefore less suitable for extending the self and showcasing possession. Others like Lehdonvirta (2012: 22), however, argue 'there is no such thing as completely immaterial consumption', and so virtual goods can satisfy desires, but in different or more limited ways than with material goods. Despite their limitations, digital goods can feel real to their owners (Lehdonvirta 2012) and extend their perceived self (Cushing 2011, 2012). Similarly, it has been found that motivations for digital purchases equal material goods in terms of status (Wang et al. 2009), increasing social attractiveness (Martin 2008) and expression of identity (Bryant & Akerman 2009). Accordingly, consumers can become attached to virtual goods (Belk 2013) just as to material goods, and possession rituals are used to make them their own (Denegri-Knott et al. 2012). As Belk (2013: 479) argues, digital goods can stimulate desire, evoking daydreams and fantasies. All these findings suggest that musicians might develop strong connections to digital music tools and thus experience desires typical of GAS. Siddiqui and Turley (2006), however, note that musicians consider digital instruments less authentic than their material counterparts, which is due to the lesser physical presence, the lack of tactile qualities (Belk 2006) or the 'aura' (Belk 2013; Benjamin 1968) that manifests itself in the identical replication of the item, as opposed to the small and inevitable differences in any material production. Belk (2013: 481) therefore concludes that digital possessions can become part of the extended self but are unlikely to be as effective as material possessions and that they have a lower symbolic value. In the context of GAS, this could mean that digital music tools have the potential to be desirable but less so than 'real' physical instruments. Since hardware instruments need space and are usually more expensive, it can be expected that especially musicians who have limited space for storing physical instruments or those with small budgets are prone to develop a stronger interest in virtual instruments.

5.4   Desire and Necessitation

At the heart of GAS is the question of which gear is genuinely needed for musical purposes and which devices are only desired for the sake of consumption and possession. The latter is for GAS opponents one of the fundamental concerns because they wish to be perceived as reasonable players, not as owners of equipment (Wright 2006: 63).

In the context of collecting, we have looked at McIntosh and Schmeichel's (2004) seven-phase model of the collecting process, which repeats indefinitely and makes collecting a lifelong activity. Consumption research offers further empirically tested theoretical frameworks for understanding the urge, desire and necessity associated with GAS.

Desire

Material desire is at the centre of consumption, especially those consumptive behaviours associated with leisure activities, such as making music or collecting musical gear. Desire has been theorised in many ways. As Graeber (2011: 493) stresses, most reasoning has identified a feeling of absence or lack as the root of desire. However, Graeber refers to Spinoza (2000), who argues that desire is not caused by the longing for a perceived lack but by self-preservation, the desire to live. Both explanations come from completely different perspectives, but either supports the close relationship between material possessions and identity discussed earlier. Identities change and lead to new acquisitions, which in turn are motivated by the desire to develop an identity. Therefore, the strong will to live and develop is expressed in various desires, one of which is materialistic.

A central element in many definitions of desire is imagination (Graeber 2011: 494). Imagining the objects of longing helps to intensify the feelings and ultimately increases desire further, while at the same time developing hopes for a better life (Belk et al. 2003: 328, 341). The relevance of imagination for desire is supported by Wright's (2006: 22) vivid description of a 'GAS attack': 'Your mind races, as you imagine the rest of your life with this baby in it—how much more skilled, happy, and fulfilled you would be. Then you begin to imagine how incomplete and unfulfilled the rest of your life would be without it'. It is therefore fundamental to GAS to image a better future, which could lie in the hope of becoming a better player (Jones 1992: 91) or gaining social recognition for the equipment played. Graeber (2011: 494) argues that desire is always rooted in imagination and that it 'tends to direct itself toward some kind of social relation, real or imaginary'. This social relation is often motivated by recognition, an underlying motive for constructing and developing the self. Therefore, material desires tend to be nourished by social motives, which may be explained by sociological concepts such as prestige, capital and habitus (Bourdieu 1984, 1991).

There have been numerous studies that position desire in a similar field to impulsive and compulsive consumption. According to the American Psychiatric Association (1985: 234), compulsions are 'repetitive and seemingly purposeful behaviors that are performed according to certain rules or in a stereotyped fashion'. O'Guinn and Faber (1989: 150) speculate that compulsive buyers may have an above-average desire for products and a low level of willpower, but stress that it is fuelled by the motivation to relieve anxiety or tension rather than by the desire for material acquisition (see also Lejoyeux et al. 1996). In other words, it is not the object but the purchasing act that is the characteristic feature. Compulsive buying differs from impulsive buying. While compulsive buyers suffer from a chronic loss of impulse control that becomes a routine with potentially severe consequences for daily life, impulsive buyers tend to focus on the acquisition of specific items (O'Guinn & Faber

1989: 150; Rook 1987). In his book on GAS, Wright shares many interview statements by guitarists who show such impulsive behaviour. One respondent explains, '[m]y first thought is "I want that." Never mind that I have some perfectly good guitars at home that I haven't mastered' (Wright 2006: 32). This quote underlines the irrational character of GAS; the guitarist understands that the guitar is not necessary, yet this hardly diminishes the desire for the instrument. Another guitarist explains that he has learned to satisfy impulsive desires because otherwise, they would hunt him for a long time:

> My favorite GAS purchases are when I pick up a guitar at a dealer or a guitar show, and I cannot seem to put it down. It's as if the guitar has become a part of me, and I sit there playing all kinds of things I normally wouldn't play—like I'm playing out of my head. These moments are rare, but when they happen, I've learned that the best thing to do is to just find some way to buy that guitar right then and there. (Wright 2006: 40)

In such cases, he would be prepared to beg his wife for money or take a loan if he could not afford the instrument immediately. If he did not buy it, he would be sorry later. Since he knows from experience that all the impulsively bought instruments would be played, there would be no reason to feel bad about these purchases. Another guitarist suggests that impulsive acquisitions are useful as a self-reward and thus act as emotional regulators:

> I had a very good Fernandes Sustainer type black Strat with gold hardware. I had some truobles[26] with my work, and the problems put me down, and GAS arrived! I had to give myself something as a gift! So I decided to change my guitar with a more caracteristic, indivudual sounding instrument. Went into a shop, and had my eyes on a Legacy. It was so unknown for me that I took it in my hand, plugged in, and knew immediately that I found HER! (Wright 2006: 29)

Like the previously discussed player, this guitarist stresses that he still plays the guitar every day and does not regret the impulsive acquisition.

Most of the statements Wright (2006) collected demonstrate impulsive rather than compulsive tendencies. Signs of compulsion are found in a habitual frequency, for example, in this guitarist's confession: 'I suffer from acute GAS periodically. When my GAS kicks in, there is only one solution and that is to buy the gear that preoccupies my every waking moment. Scouring the internet, searching eBay, trolling for that special instrument, when will it end?' (Wright 2006: 35). Other interviewed musicians state that although GAS hits without an 'incubation period', they are aware of the emotional processes or stages of GAS and know that if they refrain from the acquisition long enough, 'anywhere from an hour up until a few

---

[26] Here and in the following chapters, we do not correct grammatical errors of interview statements in Wright's book. Neither do we mark the errors with 'sic!'.

days', the urge will eventually pass (Wright 2006: 33). In other cases, something needs to be bought to ease the compulsive urge:

> And GAS always leaves a mark. Every attack builds on the other, forming a pyramid of unfulfilled wishes. Eventually, this will be too much, and I'll have to buy a guitar. Sometimes I buy something cheap, but fun, just to ease the pain. Basically, anything guitar-related will do, such as a stomp box or a nice new cord. This minute, I could easily name twelve guitars, make, model, colour, modifications and year I'd like to own. And, strangely enough, that really does make me feel better. (Wright 2006: 33)

The compulsive nature shows in the fact that any purchase will suffice. It is not so much a desire for a particular object as the urge for acquisition per se, which characterises compulsive buying behaviours (O'Guinn & Faber 1989; Rook 1987).

GAS is sometimes accompanied by feelings of guilt, shame, regret and despair over the purchase and a lack of self-control, indicating that GAS-affected consumption has more traits of impulsive than compulsive behaviour (Faber & O'Guinn 1989; Faber & Vohs, 2004; Garcia 2007; Lo & Harvey 2011, 2012; McElroy et al. 1991, 1994). For compulsive buyers, the acquisition usually takes place without the presence of friends or family (Elliott 1994; Schlosser et al. 1994), so it involves social withdrawal and isolation (Kellett & Bolton 2009: 90). Such indicators of compulsive buying are rare, at least for the musicians interviewed by Wright (2006) and those observed in sociological studies on online message boards (Cole 2018; Hartmann 2016). But then, it must be considered that people affected by compulsive GAS would probably neither talk nor openly express their feelings of guilt and shame in such special-interest forums, especially since GAS is commonly celebrated there (Cole 2018). In contrast, musicians who tend towards impulsive buying behaviour are less ashamed and therefore more vocal about their tendencies, as quotes from musicians in this chapter suggest. Furthermore, Rook and Fisher (1995: 306) define impulsive buying as a 'consumer's tendency to buy spontaneously, unreflectively, immediately, and kinetically. Highly impulsive buyers are more likely to experience spontaneous buying stimuli; their shopping lists are more "open" and receptive to sudden, unexpected buying ideas'. This definition is much more consistent with the characteristics of GAS described in blogs, Wright's (2006) book and other GAS-related studies (Cole 2018; Hartmann 2016). Moreover, in contrast to compulsive consumption, the buying impulse does not need to be suppressed (Rook & Fisher 1995: 306). Impulsive buying is not pathological, and almost everyone can be affected at times. In most cases, however, the impulse is controllable (Vohs & Faber 2007: 538), and the buyer usually feels no guilt or remorse (Atalay & Meloy 2011). The impulsive buying urge is triggered by the mood in a potential buying situation. People prone to impulsive buying behaviour can get the urge either from positive excitement (Rook & Gardner 1993) or from negative moods in the hope of being cheered up (Mick & Demoss 1990). No matter which of the two urges triggers consumption, such purchases are harmless or even beneficial for mental health (Hausman 2000; Thompson et al. 1990), yet possibly at the expense of financial detriment (Fenton-O'Creevy et al. 2018). Both the moods and effects following an acquisition can be reasonably assumed in the context of musical gear. As the examples and GAS-related quotes in this book suggest, many musicians weigh up the positive psychological effects against the negative consequences on their economic situation, and while they are tempted, their rational control and willpower usually win. According to Hoch and Loewenstein (1991), most people reflect on their economic position, time pressure, social visibility and impulse in a potential buying situation and take a reasonable decision.

It is difficult to determine how closely GAS and compulsive buying are related. Compulsive buyers are likely the extreme, pathological end of the GAS continuum. Their total share has not yet been explored, so we must rely on research suggesting that between 2% and 16% of the US and UK population are affected by compulsive buying.[27] Considering the high emotional value that musical instruments and related gear have for musicians, we can safely assume that they are at least on par with the general population. However, compulsive buyers do not seem to be the main group amongst GAS-affected musicians. Impulsive buying appears to be much more closely related to GAS since spontaneous acquisition impulses are common amongst groups with a pronounced interest in practices based on a material core. Besides, impulsive buying is a natural, non-pathological habit because it is usually controllable. Relatively little is known about how widespread impulsive buying is in the overall population. According to the DDB Needham Annual Lifestyle Survey (1974–1993), 38% of the US population identified themselves as impulsive buyers during that time span. Given the ever-increasing capitalisation of Western societies and the ease of shopping online, impulsive buying must have seen a rise since then.

Baudrillard (1983: 127) suggests that 'everything is reversed if we turn to thinking about the object. Here, it is no longer the subject who desires but the object that seduces'. Seduction is a significant factor of GAS, and it is central to the feeling of desire. Seduction contrasts rationality in that it implies a lack of control, which is why modern societies sometimes reject it. Voices against GAS reflect this rejection when they stress the importance of remaining in control and resisting the urge (Becker 1996; Kwisses 2015). However, although people are seduced to consume by marketers, consumers are often complicit in their seduction (Deighton & Grayson 1995; Reekie 1993). Humans 'do want to be enchanted by desire' (Belk et al. 2003: 327), and so Belk et al. (2003: 342ff) argue that people 'desire to desire' and fear

---

[27] Black (1996): 1.8–8.1%; Iervolino et al. 2009, Mueller et al. 2009, Samuels et al. 2008: 2–5%; Koran et al. (2006): 5.8%; Dittmar (2005): 13.5%; Magee (1994): 16%.

being without desire.[28] For this reason, Baudrillard (1979: 134f) sees self-seduction as an essential part of the motivating power of desire. According to Belk et al. (2003: 345), people want to be controlled by their desires but, as this is a hidden process, they are usually not aware of it. Instead, people 'externalize the power of desire as residing in the object itself' (Belk et al. 2003: 345) and therefore justify their desire with the attractiveness of the object used to externalise the underlying desire (Falk 1994). Concerning GAS, this implies that the desired object itself might not be the primary or sole motivator for longing and the intended purchase. Instead, it might reflect the inner psychological world. Likely, many of the other factors discussed, such as nostalgia, neophilia, role models and musical motives, also play a role, supporting the notion that GAS is a complex, multi-faceted phenomenon.

Some of the guitarists Wright (2006) interviewed show signs of self-seduction. One player explains:

> Most of the time I see an ad, and I start wondering if I really need another one [guitar]. Sometimes I go to a city and stumble into a guitar shop. I simply cannot go past it; I get grumpy if I don't go in. Then it starts ... justifying. I don't have that particular model. I need something cheap for carrying around (won't mind it being stolen), I need something special, because ... well, because. I need something that's missing in my sound. My collection isn't complete without it. This is such a good value for money. I would like to look and sound like ____, and he has that model. It's a really, really nice guitar to look at. (Wright 2006: 31)

Although this statement does not confirm the unconscious self-seduction that Belk et al. (2003: 345) describe, it does show that GAS-inclined musicians visit places voluntarily even if they know that this will awaken the desire for items they do not need. In line with this, another guitarist visits music stores, browses the Internet and watches videos, well knowing that this will spark GAS:

> The seed is always a guitar store window or a manufacturer's website. Germination transpires in the twisted mind of a frustrated picker: 'That shiny new critter is exactly what I need to thrash the dickens out of 'Sweet Home Alabama.' Firey GAS emerges when your favorite axe-slasher is featured (on stage or in a music video) laying down an impossible riff with the same make, model, and color of dream-machine you've been salivating over for the last twelve weeks. (Wright 2006: 37)

Consequently, this desire to desire seems to be strong in musicians who are inclined to GAS.

The difference between wanting, needing and desiring is useful to consider in this context. Belk et al. (2003: 328) do not see a close connection between wanting

---

[28] There is an intricate relationship between desire and collecting in this context. Collections are motivated by desire, but the chance of completing a collection is a great cause for concern because it may also end the desire that a collector most likely wishes to keep (Benjamin 1968; Denegri-Knott & Molesworth 2010).

and desiring because wanting is too controlled and rational to cover the passionate aspects of desire. Need is more revealing when it is contrasted with desire. For Freund (1971), everything can become an object of desire, but need is based on the lack of an object. In a musical context, there can be the need to replace a broken drum cymbal. From a purely functional point of view, any cymbal would suffice. Desire, in contrast, is concerned with a specific cymbal, not just any cymbal. It could be a cymbal line or a specially manufactured model, such as an earth-toned or soil-aged cymbal buried in the ground for several months to give it a darker and warmer tone.[29] These cymbals are usually handmade, unique and expensive and therefore ideal as an object of desire.

Research on desire (Baudrillard 1972; Belk et al. 2003) is consistent with sociological work (for example, Bourdieu 1984, 1991; Foucault 1980) in that it is rooted in social motives and involving a complex interaction with the individual's bodily passions and mental reflections. Within this relational structure, Belk et al. (2003) empirically identify various elements of desire. One major element of desire is *embodied passion*. Desire is experienced 'as an intense and usually highly positive emotional state best characterized as passion' (Belk et al. 2003: 333). Their interviewed respondents used expressions such as lust, hunger, thirst and dreamlike fantasies. Sexual metaphors were common. In comparison to 'wanting', the authors find that desire is probably more intense, unintentional and illogical, shown in expressions such as 'cannot live without'. Many guitarists in Wright's (2006) book show this passionate trait, and often they explicitly mention desire: 'GAS is basically about desire. I have a strong desire to acquire a lot of guitars' (Wright 2006: 32). Another player emphasises the 'cannot live without' character:

> GAS? It's a deep desire followed by dreams of getting the tone that makes you cry. A strange feeling that something is missing in life, followed by flashes of playing the guitar that you still do not own. This continues for long periods. Thoughts that develop are 'Can I live without this?'—'I need it now.'—'Why is life so unfair that other people can enjoy these things and own them and I cannot?' (Wright 2006: 30)

It is the distance to the unattainable object that characterises this passionate if unfulfilled desire. Hence it is not surprising that many GAS-inclined musicians compare their passionate desire with romantic relationships.

> I think it is the same feeling that comes up when you are falling in love. I mean with a woman, of course, but also with a car or a Telecaster: butterflies in the abdomen, the ultimate craving—I must have her/it. You could also call it the libido, which makes life worthwhile and exciting. (Wright 2006: 34)

---

[29] https://www.instructables.com/id/Earth-toning-soil-aging-cymbals-to-get-a-darke; accessed 30 May 2020.

My heart starts to pound, my eyes water, my knees get weak, my focus goes totally
to that instrument and whammo, it's a full-fledged case of GAS!. There is nothing
in the world like it, other than falling in love. If that word's too strong, falling in
lust. I get all tingly. It's an exciting feeling for sure. (Wright 2006: 34)

These two quotes suggest that GAS-induced desires can be as strong as the love
between two people and that there may be similarities between the development of
an interpersonal relationship and the process of longing for, buying and using the
desired instrument. As many of the statements indicate, male musicians are visually
attracted to an instrument (Wright 2006: 28), which they need get to know better to
determine if there is something deeper beyond physical attraction. Descriptions are
used such as: 'feel won't come until attractiveness has drawn me first' (Wright 2006:
28) and '[w]ith certain items ... the combination of physical characteristics and eye-
holding beauty will, when they are together in just the right (magical) way, form a
bond between me and what I am beholding. This is certainly more emotional than
rational, but that's the core of beauty, anyway' (Wright 2006: 28). There is a similarity between GAS and love, from initial attraction to close attachment, which is
associated with positive feelings and likely why musicians want to experience it
again and again. For many players, such feelings must not necessarily be satisfied
by an actual acquisition; for the development of attraction and passionate desire,
longing may be enough.

Belk et al. (2003: 335f) identify another element of desire, *desire for sociality*,
which has several components. As with the social motives described in the context
of collecting, the desire for material objects often arises through the hope of facilitating social relations, which either can be access to a social group or the fulfilment
of conditions for staying in it. For example, specific musical gear is required to join
a band. As the band advances and prepares to play more professional gigs or record
an album, equipment investments may be required. A member might be forced to
invest in better gear to adjust to the others or face problems staying in the band. In
the context of desire, this requirement is not necessarily punitive—although it can
be (Belk et al. 2003: 337)—because it may just as well mean dreaming of a particular
piece of equipment to replace or extend the current set of tools. A second component
of the desire for sociality is mimesis. Girard (1977) described 'mimetic desire' with
attributes that could be transferred to GAS. Here, desire is initiated by observing
other musicians who acquire or have acquired new gear. This form of desire means
that the 'objects of desire are sought in order to be and feel like one of the others, not
for the object per se' (Belk et al. 2003: 337). Some guitarists in Wright's (2006: 41)
book describe a feeling of 'gear envy': 'I am in a constant state of "gear envy". It's
not that I don't love my guitars or my amps, but when I find a pedal, a guitar, or
something unique, I really have to fight my gut on purchasing it right there'. Constant
comparison of one's gear with that of other musicians probably leads to GAS, or it

can be a habit rooted in GAS. The social context of GAS is even more evident in another quote:

> One visits shops that treat you badly, eBay ... They also start to get the need to enjoy and, in turn, fuel your desire. This whole process develops into a group of addicts who enable each other by using the internet to share and educate where to find the best places to get a fix. This passes a point of no return where GAS is a pleasure that can only be experienced to be appreciated. (Wright 2006: 30)

Like collectors, GAS-affected musicians have discussion forums that fuel GAS-behaviour. Such behaviour could generally be problematic because it affirms consumption. The quote above, however, suggests that participation in such communities is motivated by pure pleasure, allowing musicians to indulge in their desires together.

Another element of desire relevant to GAS is the relationship between desire, *inaccessibility* and, relatedly, *hope* (Belk et al. 2003: 340, 343; Denegri-Knott & Molesworth 2010: 69). If an object is readily available, no strong feeling of desire is likely to develop. Certainty does not spark desire. At the other end of the spectrum is the unattainable goal. Without the possibility to acquire the item at some point, desire will not last. Although hope is not the same as desire, it is a fundamental component of desire because '[w]ithout the hope of obtaining the focal object, desires dissolve into mere wishes or impossible fantasies' (Belk et al. 2003: 343). Hope is thus the perceived possibility of achieving desire, while desire is the emotional attraction to the object itself. Just as desire is pleasurable, so is hope (Belk et al. 2003: 343).

In line with other models we discussed (for example, McIntosh & Schmeichel 2004), Belk et al. (2003) claim that desire is ultimately infinite and repeats in cycles. They argue that 'desire is seen as involving self-seductive imagination and active cultivation of desire. Desire is cultivated and kept alive until the object is acquired or until it becomes clear that it is beyond hope, that it will never be acquired' (Belk et al. 2003: 340). Once a desire has been realised, it ceases. An object that is owned cannot be desired anymore because desire must be nourished by lack as a fundamental requirement. Obtaining the desired item is sometimes accompanied by negative feelings, mainly due to the illogical and emotionally intense character of desire. Belk et al. (2003: 337ff) highlight that for some of their respondents, desire is negatively connotated with the experience of being out of control, which is frequently accompanied by feelings of guilt and sin and, in extreme cases, by addiction and intense cravings. A guitar player's statement reflects such strong emotions:

> GAS often is nearly overpowered by buyer's remorse at times, even when the deal is sweet ... All the sounds of the music store seem far away, and you drift to a place where desire, anticipation, and apprehension orbit each other in an interaction that can only end the way asking a girl to dance does: exhilaration or agony. Usually it is agony for any number of reasons. She says no (it's overpriced). She says yes, but has bad breath (the finish is great, but the neck feels like a ball bat sawed in half).

> Her voice is shrill (the pickups are as dead as disco). When everything is right,
> however, it is as smooth and satisfying as your favorite beverage on a hot summer
> day. But alas, just like that beverage, it can only satisfy for a short time before you
> need another. While you may always cherish that girl, that drink, that guitar, you
> will always have a wandering eye. (Wright 2006: 35)

Not only 'risks' and remorse are connected with desire because one of the main
problems is, as the quote highlights, that it cannot be permanently fulfilled. At some
point, a new desire arises. Despite the destructive capacities involved, Belk et al.
(2003: 348) do not regard this unending cycle negatively but as a constructive and
creative process that can be pleasurable, life-affirming and support personal and social development. Their assertion accords with Campbell (1987: 86), who states that
'desiring mode constitutes a state of enjoyable discomfort, and that wanting rather
than having is the main focus of pleasure-seeking'. As Campbell reasons, the main
pleasure of desire is longing and indulging in the 'discomforts of desire' rather than
enjoying the object finally purchased. Hence GAS-related desires can be pleasurable
experiences with the potential for personal growth and musical development. However, healthy desire should not become compulsive, and musicians must avoid becoming what Baudrillard (1970) identifies as 'hyperconsumers', which are consumers tempted to buy more than they need, pay more than the goods are worth, and
spend more money than they can afford (see also Ritzer 2012).

Despite the often humorous statements about GAS, there have been attempts to
find remedies or even cures for it. Becker (1996), Cole (2018) and Kwisses (2015)
emphasise the use-value of instruments and recommend focusing on playing instead
of dealing with equipment, while Wright (2006) sees the solution in external forces
such as the significant other. Since the turn of the millennium, a new line of research
on anti-consumption has developed within consumption research (for example,
Chatzidakis & Lee 2013; Lee et al. 2009; Yuksel 2013). It generally advocates three
strategies: reject, restrict and reclaim (Black & Cherrier 2010; Lee et al. 2011). Rejection involves the refusal to buy certain brands or types of items; restriction aims
to limit the number of purchases, and reclaiming is based on recycling or reusing
items owned. Another more recent strategy targets the source of consumption, desire
(Dholakia et al. 2018), which must be controlled by the consumer's willpower to
stop or prevent excessive consumption (Hoch & Loewenstein 1991; Montoya &
Scott 2013; Siemens & Kopp 2011). Willpower was the focus of earlier studies
(Carver & Scheier 2001; Koenigstorfer et al. 2014), and only more recently has the
attention shifted to desire as the root of excessive consumption (Dholakia 2015;
Myrseth et al. 2009; Redden & Haws 2013). Dholakia et al. (2018) argue that consumptive desire is limited and can be depleted. The underlying mechanism they see
is 'satiation', which is the reduced desire and enjoyment that follows a series of acquisitions (Coombs & Avrunin 1977; McAlister 1982; Redden 2008). As they argue,
for satiation to occur, a person does not need to purchase items; reflecting on past

consumptions will have the same effect (Dholakia et al. 2018: 262). Similar to the use-value approach (Cole 2018),

> reflecting on the recent use of one's possessions through a structured thought list-ing-based intervention will arouse the individual's consumption-related desire for items on this list. As a result of this arousal, … consumption desire will be used up and depleted, leaving less of it available in a subsequent task … This, in turn, will lessen the consumer's interest in buying when a subsequent task provides such an opportunity. (Dholakia et al. 2018: 262)

This principle has proven to be efficient in eating and food choice (Galak et al. 2014). The strategy's effectiveness is also confirmed by the results of Dholakia et al.'s (2018) study. Participants who reflected on their previous purchases and the use of their possessions had better control over themselves in resisting the desire to buy new items. Concerning GAS, this could take different forms. Musicians may in-crease their level of reflexivity as a natural consequence of their maturity and expe-rience in their area of interest. Social activities could be another cause for reflection. When thoughts are exchanged and mirrored through conversations with other peo-ple, be it family, friends or professional therapists, reflection is generally more ef-fective. Talking to other people promotes reflection and, with it, a decreasing desire. Whether or not such interaction reduces the desire for new gear mainly depends on the conversation partner. As the case might be, GAS could be sparked as well.

Necessitation

While desire mainly derives from a combination of sociological and psychological factors, necessitation is more strongly related to a tangible need. Braun et al. (2016) have studied the process of an object becoming a necessity based on interviews with consumers about products without which they said they could not live. Although necessitation intuitively focuses on practical factors, the findings suggest that it might be a suitable theoretical framework for understanding some traits of irrational GAS behaviour. Braun et al. argue that it is essential to acknowledge that no product all of a sudden becomes a necessity. It arises from an experience or a series of expe-riences, which is changing how a person feels about an object (Braun et al. 2016: 209). Accordingly, the authors coin the term 'necessitation' for the perceptual shift of an object from a non-necessity to a necessity. This concept of necessity must be understood in a broader context. Following a social constructivist approach, the study of necessities requires consideration of societal and historical contexts that in-fluence consumer desires and behaviours, as well as personally relevant historical or biographical developments.

The study finds that necessitation goes through five stages: 1) familiarisation, 2) transformation in the form of redemption or contamination, 3) memorialisation, 4) (re)integration and reconstruction, 5) solidification. In the *familiarisation* stage, a person is introduced to a product. Similar to Rogers's (2003) theory of innovation, losing strangeness of the novel item must come first. Braun et al. (2016: 213) suggest that it takes three different forms: 'existential (the presence of a product in a consumer's environment), functional (the range of capabilities or modes of usage supported by a product), or symbolic (the role a product plays in a consumer's self-perception and identity negotiation)'. In this initial phase, no ownership or usage of the item is required to allow familiarisation; exposure through media or conversations with members of the social environment is sufficient. Concerning GAS, familiarisation with new musical equipment can take place in music stores or by watching videos, browsing trade magazines and catalogues, reading blogs and participating in message boards. These encounters serve to introduce and familiarise with diverse kinds of gear.

In the second stage, *transformation*, the product is not yet a necessity but is about to become one. For the product to become a necessity, there must be a critical event that changes consumers' attitudes towards it (Braun et al. 2016: 215). This event does not require the presence of the object itself; instead, the person makes an emotionally positive or unpleasant experience that is in some way related to the object and motivates the potential consumer to become more actively involved with the product. The sequence can either be 'contamination', a movement from a negative scene to a positive experience, or the opposite, 'redemption'. The authors do not offer musical examples, yet transformative sequences can happen regarding equipment and GAS. For example, an amplifier malfunctioning right before or during a gig would turn the otherwise pleasant situation of performing live into a bad experience due to the stress caused by the failure. Such an experience may strengthen the desire to buy a new, more reliable amplifier and to keep the old one as a backup. The transformation takes place through contamination. However, it would be different if the guitarist had encountered an amplifier of higher quality. Taking the example of a failing amplifier on stage again, the guitarist may be invited to play one of a fellow player. That device might give him a pleasurable experience at the gig, as it may offer more control over different tones with its larger number of channels switchable by foot, convincing the player of better functionality and wider tonal spectrum. Such an unexpectedly positive experience in an otherwise negative situation has a high potential to foster future engagement with the amplifier. Developing a positive attitude towards an object would be 'redemption'. Redemption is often associated with a positive outcome, such as higher quality, better functionality or a rise in social standing. The latter could occur, for example, when exclusion from a social group changes to acceptance. The unexpected success with the borrowed amplifier might provoke fellow musicians to see the player in a new light, which could lead to future collaboration or invitations to perform at other events. Experiences in connection with an item the musician does not possess facilitate further engagement. While this is a fictive example of a potential consumer using a borrowed product, there are other possible scenarios. A transformative experience can be triggered when a musician is involved in a project or merely reading about an object on a message board, which would not even require the object to be present.

The relatively short third stage of *memorialisation* involves a recollection of the previous experience that leads to a decision (Braun et al. 2016: 217). This decision-making process requires the potential consumer to develop a positive opinion about the product, regardless of whether it has been shaped by contamination or redemption. Engagement and research on the object mark this phase and lead, similar again to Rogers's (2003) theory, to a deeper understanding of the functions and meanings. Memorialisation can also include moments of imagination of the object's future use, combining the concept of necessitation with desire (Graeber 2011).

In the fourth, *(re)integration and reconstruction* stage, the product becomes more meaningful to the potential consumer, as they discover more benefits than those apparent in the transformative phase (Braun et al. 2016: 217f). To continue the example of a failed guitar amplifier that led to an appreciation of another device with more foot-switchable channels, the player may realise that they like other types of valves. If their amplifier had EL34 valves, which are typical of a 'British sound', playing an amplifier with 6L6 valves that produce an 'American sound' (Stent 2019) could lead to an interest in learning a new style such as US southern rock or country. Alternatively, the player may find a greater appreciation for a more (or less) distorted sound and the favourable consequences it may have on expression (Herbst 2017c). Such experiences can drastically shape the way a player regards areas of practice, whether in their playing or in general.

The final stage is *solidification*; here, the person 'conclusively perceives the product as a necessity—a product he or she cannot live without' (Braun et al. 2016: 218). At this point, affected persons see products 'as indispensable requirements for their well-being' (Braun et al. 2016: 219). The authors argue that a product, which has become a necessity, has obtained 'a permanent presence mentally and/or physically' (Braun et al. 2016: 218). Although they do not explicitly state that the necessary object must be or is bought during the solidification stage, the qualitative examples provided suggest it. They further highlight that products do not have to go through all stages and that some may be repeated (Braun et al. 2016: 219). That is interesting regarding GAS because it is characterised more by the urge to buy—the process of necessitation—than by the value a player places on an item already owned. Hence GAS is likely to happen in the first four stages, from familiarisation to (re)integration and reconstruction. Here the object is gradually seen as a necessity, which creates the urge to acquire it. If it is eventually possessed, the experience probably confirms the purchase to be the 'right choice', but it would end the GAS cycle for the item or group of items, at least for a while. Solidification must accordingly be understood as the time from purchase to the beginning of a new necessitation process. Therefore, Braun et al.'s (2016) theoretical framework on necessitation serves as a useful empirically tested model to help understand the process of a 'GAS attack'.

5.5 Prosumption and Craft Consumption

Prosumption

At the beginning of this chapter, we noted the trend in research to attribute more power to the consumer, who is considered to have a more active and self-determined role. In social sciences and cultural studies, the focus shifted from one extreme to the other. Social theorists in the classical period of social sciences such as Adam Smith (1776) and Karl Marx (1867) placed a clear emphasis on production, while later scholars like Baudrillard (1970), Bell (1976) and Galbraith (1958) concentrated on consumption. In his development from Marxist writing to a more consumption-sided perspective, Baudrillard finally concluded that the distinction between production and consumption is an 'artificial disjuncture' (Baudrillard 1976: 112). He began to think along the line of what has more recently been described as 'prosumption', based on the postmodern understanding that all production requires consumption and vice versa (Pietrykowski 2007; Ritzer 2015; Ritzer & Jurgenson 2010).

The term 'prosumption' was introduced in 1980 in Toffler's futurist writing. Toffler observes that in pre-industrial societies, production and consumption were inseparably linked. The Industrial Revolution artificially, though never wholly, separated this process, but Toffler (1980: 265f) theorised that postmodern societies brought back the 'prosumer'. Since the turn of the millennium, mainly fuelled by Web 2.0 (Ritzer & Jurgenson 2010: 14), research has paid increasing attention to prosumption.[30] It must be understood as an analytical term because it is impossible not to use the terms production and consumption together (Ritzer 2015: 413f). Both terms must be understood as subtypes of prosumption that mark the extremes. These extremes are a theoretical possibility but an empirical impossibility because there can never be production without consumption (Ritzer 2015: 415f).

Modern societies are characterised by prosumer capitalism (Ritzer 2015: 422). Examples are found in all kinds of self-service operations such as gasoline stations, fast-food restaurants, self-checkouts at supermarkets, DIY (Ritzer 2015: 426; Ritzer & Jurgenson 2010: 18f), as well as in most activities on the web, including social media, YouTube, Amazon or Yelp! (Ritzer 2015: 426; Ritzer & Jurgenson 2010: 18f). There, the user is doing work that creates content, which otherwise would require paid work (Ritzer & Jurgenson 2010: 30). Prosumers usually perform such work free of charge, sometimes in return for bargains or just for pleasure (Ritzer & Jurgenson 2010: 25).

---

[30] For an overview, see Ritzer et al. 2012.

There is relatively little research on prosumption in music. Focussing on the arts, Nakajima (2012) identifies three forms of simultaneous involvement in production and consumption. Firstly, any production of artworks requires the consumption of tools and materials such as brushes, paints and canvases. Similarly, making music is a productive activity that, in most cases, requires instruments and other gear. Secondly, artists have always built on ideas and techniques of other artists, which is a form of consumption. It is much the same in music, not only regarding role models but also regarding composition, technology and playing styles and techniques. Thirdly, in contemporary art, the boundaries of producing artists and consuming audiences are much more blurred. Analogously, the rapid growth, availability and affordability of musical instruments in most parts of the world have led to a large number of amateur musicians who play at home, in cover bands or create original music. Nakajima (2012) further discusses 'readymade' as another practice that enables amateurs to produce art. Prosumption in music-making has become common not only in the creation of artworks but also in terms of musical gear, as musicians with no expertise in electronics or engineering can choose from an ever-expanding range of DIY kits to build instruments, effects pedals and amplifiers.[31] Although these kits allow customisation at best, they are a good example of prosumption in music technology.

Another area of prosumption concerns the generation of knowledge (Ritzer et al. 2012: 382), most visible on websites like Wikipedia, online blogs or social media. Concerning music technology, companies benefit from the involvement of prosumers. For example, the online forum of the innovative guitar amplifier company Kemper has a subforum 'Feature requests'. It can be regarded as a kind of customer service for users of this technology, yet these musicians are unpaid 'co-producers', contributing to research and enterprise work for free by suggesting modifications or enhancements to the technology (Arvidsson 2006: 70). Moreover, marketing research has recognised that brand communities cannot be imposed on potential customers but require consumer participation (Muniz & O'Guinn, 2001). Involving users through online message boards or 'user corners', which on the Kemper website present videos of guitar players demonstrating the amplifier, is thus an effective strategy for empowering prosumers to engage themselves in brand development. Modern brand management

> is not about imposing ways of using goods, or behaving or thinking as a consumer. Rather, it is about proposing branded goods as tools, or building blocks whereby consumers can create their own meanings. What people pay for ... is not so much the brand itself as what they can produce with it: what they can *become* with it ... Customers are thus expected to add more or less personal dimensions to the brand,

---

[31] For example, see https://www.modkitsdiy.com for guitar effects pedals or https://buildyourownclone.com for amplifiers.

to accommodate it in their life-world, to produce something—a feeling, a personal relation, an experience—with it. (Arvidsson 2006: 68)

Accordingly, the more musicians can 'work' with their equipment and customise it, the more likely it is that they will develop strong bonds to it, as can be seen from the value players attach to certain brands or instrument models. An example of strong bonds to a manufacturer is given by a guitarist in Wright's (2006: 37) book:

> My GAS reaction only occurs when I look at guitars made by Leo Fender. My gut reaction is I immediately feel inspired to play! I want to pick the guitar up, feel the neck in my hand, how that particular guitar balances, and how it contours to my body. I don't know why that is, but it does not occur with any other guitar; not Gibson, not PRS, not Ibanez, not Rickenbacker. I'm only truly inspired to play a made-by-Leo guitar.

Emotional investment in a brand helps to forge and extend the bond to a manufacturer or an instrument series, which not only benefits the brand but possibly also the prosumer because they feel more passionately about their owned instruments.

Marketing can easily give the impression of manipulation, but in another view 'prosumption could be seen as combining the best of production (the power associated with being a producer) and consumption (the joys of being a consumer) and as being free of external control and not being subject to alienation and exploitation' (Ritzer et al. 2012: 387). Prosumption has numerous advantages for its users; they gain emotionally but also materialistically through access to tools or through earning money by making music, even if not in a professional capacity. In other words, prosumption involves an exchange of unpaid labour for access to tools, emotional gratification and indirect economic gain resulting from a serious leisure career.

Few developments other than Web 2.0 have made prosumption more a part of modern life. The creation of online content shifted the focus away from companies like Yahoo towards ordinary Internet users. One area of particular interest in the context of GAS is online auctions such as eBay, which give musicians access to rare gear and promise opportunities for bargains. Some research has focused on prosumption (Denegri-Knott & Zwick 2012) and desire (Denegri-Knott & Molesworth 2010) in eBay practices that provide a useful framework for understanding GAS-related behaviours on the platform. eBay is a perfect example of prosumption because the work, ranging from offering the items and bidding to shipment and reviewing, is mostly done by its users. Denegri-Knott and Molesworth (2010) argue that the vast choice on eBay creates a crisis amongst users, which is processed by flânerie and daydreaming. Both seduce the user to consume by stimulating desire and allow for experimentation with different consumer identities in the home's comfort.

In the previous subchapter, we discussed the willingness of people to self-seduction. Going to music stores, visiting websites of instrument manufacturers and auction sites like eBay are remarkably similar to window shopping that Benjamin

(1968, 1997) described as characteristic of the urban flâneur. Others have observed flâneur behaviour as one of the consumers' positive experiences (Clarke 2003; Featherstone 1991, 1998). For Featherstone (1998: 921), online window shopping is 'enhanced flânerie' because the user is not limited to physical or spatial restrictions.

According to Denegri-Knott and Molesworth (2010: 63), eBay is a powerful source for imagination and desire that can lead to daydreaming. They argue that 'eBay is not only a resource for the acquisition of needed goods but also an aid to consumption that takes place in the imagination as the construction and maintenance of a daydream rich in the possibility of an ideal state of being' (Denegri-Knott & Molesworth 2010: 67). Here again, we see the strong link between material possessions and identity and, more importantly, material acquisitions as a means to a happier life. Such happiness often becomes evident from expressions about GAS, for example, the already quoted description of a GAS attack by Wright (2006: 22): 'Your mind races, as you imagine the rest of your life with this baby in it—how much more skilled, happy, and fulfilled you would be'. Like desire, where it must be challenging but still possible to acquire the desired object, daydreams require a certain distance and must appear achievable (Denegri-Knott & Molesworth 2010: 60). For McCracken (1988: 110), daydreams are by-products of the mismatch between reality and ideals that signify an idealised state of existence, exemplified by Wright's vivid illustration of the GAS attack. Daydreams are not limited to objects, but the fact that items can be bought makes the dreams more tangible. As has been shown, specialist magazines work effectively to simulate desire, particularly for items like instruments (Belk 1997, 2001b), and Théberge (1993: 159ff) and Jones (1992: 89) find a positive relationship between magazines for musical instruments and interest in gear. eBay, according to Denegri-Knott and Molesworth (2010: 68f), fulfils a similar role. Firstly, it introduces people to objects they did not even know existed. That is visible in a guitarist's statement: 'When I stumble across that rare instrument I thought would never surface and it's for sale—look out' (Wright 2006: 35). eBay, 'full of surprises, dangers, opportunities and promises allowing consumers to craft pleasurable daydreams' (Denegri-Knott & Molesworth 2010: 59), provides never-ending triggers for GAS. Secondly, and perhaps more importantly, websites like eBay offer users the opportunity to acquire the desired object at the touch of a button, which may lead to greater emotional involvement. Ariely and Simonson (2003: 116) find that eBayers may be 'particularly susceptible to escalation of commitment because participation in an online auction can often trigger an intense emotional response'. Other studies suggest that bidding in auctions is motivated by hedonic benefit (Standifird et al. 2005), and with its specific format, it produces winners and losers, thus enhancing emotional excitement (Ariely & Simonson 2003). This heightened level of emotional stimulation makes eBay a 'pleasure dome where consumers engage with novel, elusive and potentially desirable glimpsed objects to create a meaningful act of consumption' (Denegri-Knott & Molesworth 2010: 66).

Websites like eBay provide diverse kinds of pleasure. Monitoring the value of items can be enjoyable, either to strike a bargain when the chance arises or purely to know its price. Denegri-Knott and Molesworth (2010: 65) report about a respondent who drew pleasure from knowing 'how much vinyl records were going for'. Similarly, it can also be enjoyable for collectors of music equipment and 'regular' musicians to study how the value of esteemed instruments develop. Another pleasure on eBay is what Turner (1982) describes as 'liminoid' or a state 'in-between', which for Denegri-Knott and Molesworth (2010: 60) is characteristic of digital consumption. A purchase made on the Internet or remotely by phone creates a temporary situation; the item is owned but not yet in physical possession, which could be either, a negative situation or a pleasurable experience, as a guitarist suggests:

> If those feelings of desire and anticipation aren't enough, I can also buy a guitar over the phone or online. Procuring a guitar in this manner, the GAS takes on an added measure of agony over whether the guitar will match its description in the advertisement or on the website. Needless to say, the level of agony grows considerably if one has ever received a guitar damaged during shipment. Nearly fifteen years ago, a brand new $700 Gibson Firebird arrived at my doorstep with a broken headstock. In spite of not having received another damaged guitar since, the ensuing two-month fight over the loss affects my GAS symptoms to this day. (Wright 2006: 39)

While this quote stresses the disadvantages, waiting for the delivery can be enjoyable because it combines the pleasant emotions of desire with the anticipation and certainty of possession anytime soon.

With auction websites like eBay, this liminoid state is even more pronounced because of the 'roulette' game, in the words of an eBay user (Denegri-Knott & Molesworth 2010: 69). As soon as someone bids on an item, they simultaneously own and do not own it when the auction is still active. In such circumstances, 'ownership is only partially actualized, and the individual can then still focus on the desire of ownership and perhaps also enjoy the pleasures of anticipating winning (or losing) the auction' (Denegri-Knott & Molesworth 2010: 69). The simultaneous agony and pleasure of this liminoid state is apparent in a statement by a guitar player:

> A real twist to GAS and collecting guitars has been the phenomenon known as 'eBay'. While the website offers collectors an unprecedented quantity and variety of used guitars, the purchase of a guitar on eBay is often not the instantaneous 'saw it, thought about it, bought it' process typical with a retail or even an online guitar sale. Instead, because the actual price is unknown until an auction closes, there's a drawn-out waiting period of up to ten days. In the case of a guitar I'm really GAS-ing for, this can seem like an eternity. Thus, a new emotion is inserted into the mix: suspense. This feeling increases exponentially as bidding apparently stalls at a low price, and the auction closing time looms near. The mind races: 'Jeez, does any-

body else realize what's for sale here? Who am I kidding? Two bidders with psy-
chotic tendencies and deep pockets will probably bury me in the last ten seconds.
Maybe the seller's gonna panic at the low price and end the auction early. Man,
only four minutes, twenty-nine seconds left to go!' It's this added unknown, and
the feeling of continuously mounting tension coloring my GAS that makes my
palms grow sweatier and my heart beat faster than in any guitar store. As a matter
of cruel irony, achieving a victory on eBay subsequently mandates enduring the
delivery—related anxieties mentioned earlier. (Wright 2006: 39)

The liminoid state of an auction creates suspense that exceeds most other retail situations. Competitiveness is an integral part of generating urges that go beyond the
rational need, as another player reveals: 'I get nervous at the end of an online auction,
because by then I can't live without the guitar—fully aware that I don't need it'
(Wright 2006: 31). Even if the offer includes a 'buy now' function, this is not a real
cure. As the player further explains, the fact that someone else can buy the item at
any time creates a discomfort that only ends with acquiring the instrument, or else
the person may suffer through the loss of an item that was never owned. Such a loss
can take traumatic forms, leading to a sustained search to get hold of the item after
all. Denegri-Knott and Molesworth (2010) discuss a different case, that of a once
owned object. It is the journey of science fiction writer William Gibson (1999), who
had sold an inherited Rolex watch that he later tried to find and get back via eBay.
Similarly, there are accounts from guitarists who speak of guitars that 'got away':

Then there are ones that got away. In the summer of 1972, I had a summer job to
pay for college. I skimmed $200 from the college fund to get a used Gibson SG.
The next week I found a used Gibson non-reverse Firebird for $200. I wanted that
guitar; I wanted it bad. Alas, I didn't have $200 more to skim. A few years after
that I saw a two-pickup Gibson Melody Maker for sale at a gas station for $40! I
hesitated—$40 was a lot to me. I went back to buy it later, and it was gone. (Wright
2006: 32)

Even if this case does not involve auctions, it still explains why musicians longing
for a specific instrument turn to eBay in the hope of finding and acquiring the long-
desired object.

As the previous deliberations show, eBay can be a source of GAS. However,
interest in eBay is unlikely to last for long, as a study by Denegri-Knott and Zwick
(2012) suggests. In their two-stage model, the first stage of desire and enchantment
is followed by disenchantment. The user's affective and cognitive investment in their
hope of emotional stimulation and pleasure characterises the first stage (Denegri-
Knott & Zwick 2012: 446). New users must learn how to operate the auction system
and become enthusiastic about discovered strategies that can lead to bargains or even
entrepreneurship (Denegri-Knott & Zwick 2012: 447), for example, when music
equipment is bought at a low price and sold at a profit. eBay thus fulfils several
functions, from a mere time-filler in moments of boredom to exciting bargains and

economic activities. Money earned by buying and selling musical instruments can, for instance, be reinvested in other economic projects and ultimately finance a new instrument for the eBay user. Here prosumption is obvious; an eBayer always produces, even if consumption is their primary purpose. It is the 'acquisition and deployment of competencies that make eBay a site of active and enchanted prosumption, rather than passive and disenchanted consumption' (Denegri-Knott & Zwick 2012: 448). However, users eventually enter the second stage, that of 'disenchantment'. It is characterised by a high degree of rationality, efficiency and routine, which 'spells the gradual end to the enchanted experience of early eBaying, when the prosumptive process was still fueled by the magic of the technology, the endless promise of new discoveries, and the possibility to fantasize and daydream' (Denegri-Knott & Zwick 2012: 446). Activities and prospects that once seemed exciting and magical become boring and tedious, mainly because of the activities' repetitive nature. Finally, the desires created by the prospects of auctions, such as bargains or access to rare or vintage instruments, are overshadowed by the routine tasks of the system. According to Campbell (2004: 37), 'we need regular exposure to fresh stimuli if boredom is to be avoided'. This stimulus is not provided by the system and can only be achieved through new user practices. If this does not happen, disenchantment may follow. As far as GAS is concerned, only musicians with a strong inclination to use auction websites like eBay may maintain interest and make it an integral part of their musical practice. For many others, auction or trading websites more likely spark only occasional interest. It can occur when a specific project is coming up or looking for a particular piece of gear. From theory, it cannot be assessed what relevance eBay and similar services have for GAS-affected musicians, so it will require further evaluation in our empirical investigations.

Craft Consumption

The growing understanding of prosumption reflects a change in social and cultural studies that gives the consumer more power without ignoring structures of production. As the previous considerations have shown, prosumption still has some of the traits of Marxism in that prosumers are exploited for free labour, despite the benefits it brings—emotional, social or sometimes economic. In postmodern societies and thinking, consumers are increasingly understood as liberated subjects with agency (Firat & Venkatesh 1995). Bricolage (Featherstone 1991; Lévi-Strauss 1962) is an important concept in cultural studies that enables consumers to use products in ways not intended by manufacturers. Another concept that places a strong emphasis on empowering practices is 'craft consumption', which avoids many of the exploitative elements still existing in views on prosumption. Craft consumption depends on craftsmanship that Campbell (2005: 27) defines as an activity in which individuals not merely exercise control over the consumption process, but also bring skill, knowledge, judgement, love and passion to their consuming in much the same way that it has always been assumed that traditional craftsmen and craftswomen approach their work.

Here we see an overlap with prosumption because every production requires consumption, just as every consumption contains an element of production. From the viewpoint of craft consumption, it is the same person who carries out the production and exercises control over the entire production process, from selecting materials to completing the product, on their own or at least with oversight of outsourced specialist activities. Consequently, the created product is characterised by its maker's personality (Campbell 2005: 27). It is typical for the craft consumer to take mass-produced items as raw material for the creation of a new product, which is usually intended for personal use. This practice goes beyond mere personalisation or customisation of the product because it requires a high degree of personal investment in terms of knowledge and expertise, judgement and evaluation of materials and work, commitment and dedication (Campbell 2005: 31). These are the pillars that define craftsmanship (Sennett 2008).

Craft consumption can take many forms, be it assembling choices from marketplace resources or manufacturing originally designed items from mass-produced commodities (Campbell 2005). The definition suggests that to some degree, most musicians are craft consumers because they select and combine equipment to create their sound. In this respect, instruments are likely to differ, as guitarists, bassists, drummers and keyboardists may have more options for selecting and modifying their kit than, for example, wind instrumentalists. Given the wide range of tone-shaping devices for the guitar, from the instrument and amplifier to various effects in the signal chain, it is not surprising that the few studies on craft consumption in music have concentrated on this instrument (Cole 2018; Hartmann 2016).

Hartmann (2016: 12) stresses the importance of selecting the right combination of items in a craft consumption process, which in the case of the guitar means that the product is the player's sound. As he explains, the sound is

an integral part of the guitar playing performance, achieved through combining 'inputs' (guitar, amp and other gear) in combination to each other (the arrangement). Guitar players devote a notable amount of energy and thought to this process, paying careful attention to crafting sounds. The selection and combination of a range of objects—along with the guitarists' judgements regarding the objects' contribution and role in the creation of sound—help facilitate the acting of guitar gear in terms of producing sound, and through this, the overall performance of guitar playing. (Hartmann 2016: 12)

This quote demonstrates that creating a guitar sound requires careful selection of its 'ingredients', which includes the three pillars of craftsmanship, knowledge, judgment and commitment (Sennett 2008). It is important to note that no traditional craftsmanship skills such as woodworking or electronic engineering are needed to create a unique guitar rig; assembling commodified parts into a 'unique ensemble' is sufficient for achieving a signature sound (Cole 2018: 1056f).

Cole (2018: 1065) argues that by emphasising the 'use-value' in musical practice, craft consumption is a way to overcome the over-commodification of musical practice. Studying online communities of musicians, he finds that guitar setups not created for 'use' are perceived as overly commodified and are therefore criticised or ridiculed. He observes that 'although virtual communities may foster GAS (anomic consumption), they also establish the collective norms and values that can lead individuals to change their commodity consumption' (Cole 2018: 1065). In other words, emphasising 'use-value' could be a way to counteract GAS, even in a social context such as online message boards that are prone to spark the desire for gear. This discussion inevitably concerns the two groups of 'purists' and 'gear heads' (Cole 2018; Hartmann 2016), which differ in their posting behaviour and motivation. Purists will ask for advice in terms of a specific need, whilst gear heads tend to start polls and discussions about the best equipment for a particular purpose to get input for their GAS-inflicted behaviour (Cole 2018: 1059f). Rather 'than the user's specific needs or the product's usefulness for producing music, members attempt to define "best" outside any context of use as if this quality somehow inheres within the commodity itself' (Cole 2018: 1060). For gear heads, the use-value for their playing is often only secondary compared to other qualities inherent to the object, such as its physical attributes, symbolic meanings or social values that make it a fetish (Fernandez & Lastovicka 2011). Cole (2018: 1060f) observes a strong sense of GAS amongst such gear heads and musicians' general tendency to 'feel consumptive exhaustion and fatigue' despite the pleasures they get from 'endless commodity discussion and product announcements' in connection with their quest for improved tone. The advice often given to gear heads on message boards can be summarised as follows: making music rather than consuming equipment is the cure for GAS (Cole 2018: 1062). Furthermore, if the interest in gear exceeds the interest in making music, forum users perceive the rig as over-commodified. A way out is to play more music and make it more original through craft consumption, which should be guided by the intention to improve playability and expression instead of adding new or expensive pieces of gear. However, there is one problem that craft consumption and a focus on 'use-value' does not solve; replacing one element in the sound production chain may require changing other elements. A player buying a custom-made guitar might need, for instance, a different amplifier to do justice to the tone of the guitar (see also Hartmann 2016: 12).

Just as craft consumption involves a potentially endless chain of improvements and adjustments for enjoyment, many musicians want to prolong the process of consumption and advancement, which entails less desire for 'finished products' (Hartmann 2016: 8). That also applies to the practice of building instruments. A guitarist regards fabricating instruments as a strategy to detract from GAS: 'Building a guitar is one way of dealing with GAS, and it keeps me from buying one for a long time' (Wright 2006: 31). Another one elucidates:

> I also like to build guitars and am setting up a shop in order to help manage my GAS better. There are two good ways that my home made guitars help me with GAS control. First is that the activity of working on them helps to keep me out of stores and away from the computer. The other thing is that I don't sell them, which means that less storage space is available. (Wright 2006: 40)

The two statements suggest that building gear helps reducing GAS. However, it takes another form of GAS-related behaviour because the focus shifts from commodified goods to parts. Instead of buying readymade products, the craft consumer, who is inclined to build their own equipment, buys components, modifies them and gradually improves the gear created. This form of consumption may ultimately require similar investments to buying readymade gear. Walter Becker already recognised the problem in 1996 when he pointed to the danger of the 'Guitar Modification Syndrome'. Ultimately, the process of looking up websites of mass-produced music gear is merely replaced by other cognitive investments, such as searching and reading construction manuals and finding the necessary parts for production.

5.6   Virtual Communities

There is probably no other place where music equipment is discussed in more detail than on the Internet. Walter Becker (1996) coined the term in a print magazine, but most musicians will have learned about GAS in online message boards, social media or blogs. For Cole (2018) and Hartmann (2016), such discussions are not merely 'idle fetishized chatter' facilitated by Web 2.0, nor are they completely new because musicians have always 'talked gear' (Cole 2018: 1056).

Virtual communities such as special-interest message boards have been defined by Rheingold (1993: 5) as 'social aggregations that emerge from the net when enough people carry on … public discussions long enough, with sufficient human feeling, to form webs of personal relationships in cyberspace'. People in online communities 'exchange pleasantries and argue, engage in intellectual discourse, conduct commerce, exchange knowledge, share emotional support, make plans, brainstorm, gossip, feud … find friends and lose them … and a lot of idle talk' (Rheingold 1993: 3). Such exchange existed long before the Internet, but Web 2.0 has helped connect special-interest groups, build communities and connect people from distant places (Belk 2013: 484). Online meeting places are what Oldenburg (1999) describes as 'third spaces', which are neither home (first place) nor work (second space) but offer people the opportunity to meet and share ideas about their hobbies (Belk 2013: 486; Steinkuehler & Williams 2006). These spaces can be regarded as imagined communities, not strictly in the sense of Benedict Anderson (1983), but as special-interest communities, whose members usually know each other only by their pseudonyms and not in person (Born 2011). Nevertheless, these communities replicate social phenomena like status and prestige (for example, Bourdieu 1984, 1991; Foucault 1980) and are a rich source of information and help. Professional retailers of musical instruments and other experts stress the value of online communities for the novice collector of musical equipment:

> Read history and specifics, regarding your target brand, model, or instrument type. Share questions and thoughts with specifically directed internet forums. There is a gold mine of experience and knowledge there. Do not purchase instruments without either experience about the purchase technique or a more experienced and trusted collector. (Wright 2006: 111)

> I've done a ton of reading and talking before going out and buying. Online discussion pages are a great place to get advice and feedback. I'm a lot more confident now that I know more about what I'll be looking for. (Wright 2006: 112)

Similarly, Pinch and Reinecke (2009: 162) observe that the Internet is invaluable for vintage equipment enthusiasts, 'modders' and regular players who exchange information about gear and how it can be used to improve their playing. Especially with equipment that is difficult to operate, as is the case with complex electronic instruments like synthesisers, the exchange of advice is motivated by the interest in musical expression. Despite the anonymity, the realness of these communities is evident in the way knowledge is used as power and how language marks hierarchy. Foucault (1980) popularised the idea that knowledge is power, and Bourdieu (1984, 1991) declared taste and habitus to be fundamental markers of a person's social status. Some research has examined the relationship of knowledge, power and reputation on the Internet in the context of home recording and music production (Carvalho 2012; Cole 2011; Crowdy 2013; O'Grady 2019). In an empirical study of sound engineering students, Porcello (2004: 734f) finds that

> the process of learning to be a sound engineer must be thought of in great part as a process in learning to speak like one; an important part of becoming a professionalized 'expert' is gaining the ability (and the sanction) to speak authoritatively as an expert. Learning how to speak about sound positions one as an 'insider', and is therefore fundamentally implicated in the matrix of social and technological practices that constitute the profession.

Sound engineer students learn the principles of sound and sound processing next to a complex technical discourse. That is not only required to communicate aesthetic ideas to different groups of people, from audio expert colleagues to more intuitive musicians, but also to develop a professional identity that is expressed through the ability to speak authoritatively (Porcello 2004: 738). This is not limited to the way a professional sound engineer speaks. The words and terminology used provide clues that help distinguish between 'professionals' and 'novices' (O'Grady 2019: 127).

Furthermore, the students must be capable of distinguishing nuances of sound on a much more subtle level than ambitious amateurs. These expert evaluations sometimes highlight tonal subtleties, which in Crowdy's (2013: 150f) opinion is a proxy for other values and means for social differentiation. Studying message boards for home recording enthusiasts, Carvalho (2012) observes that ambitious amateurs must master the language of professionals and be familiar with a variety of professional gear, their functions and specifications, even if the original is unaffordable and only available as a digital emulation (Kaiser 2017).

Cole (2011) builds on Porcello's (2004) findings, showing how cultural capital in the form of material possessions, knowledge and language shapes the online discourse of those interested in audio recording. He defines the prosumer not by the degree to which an actor sits between production and consumption but by combining the level of professionalism and consumptive behaviours. For him, 'the term "prosumer" also denotes a *pro*-fessional con-*sumer*', which refers both to the users and their technology (Cole 2011: 451). As the analysis of message boards for those interested in audio recording shows, prosumers in Cole's sense tend to use their 'vague knowledge' of professional gear and acoustic science to distinguish themselves from mere hobbyists. Again, those are easily spotted by true professionals who immediately recognise superficial knowledge from less credible sources such as message board discussions or amateur blogs. Prosumers become vulnerable by exposing their 'not quite an expert status' in the attempt to place themselves above the less ambitious recordists. Often the professionals in the community take the opportunity to 'ridicule and diminish the prosumer's expertise, judgement, and "ears"' (Cole 2011: 455). Here, knowledge and language mark social hierarchy in the field of music production, occupied by amateurs, serious leisure enthusiasts and professionals alike.

The other area of distinction related to message boards concerns the ownership of equipment. A 'professional consumer' cannot achieve this status through knowledge alone; they must have appropriate equipment as a prerequisite for producing music and as evidence of their status. Cole (2011: 453) notes that while prosumers require such technological capital to distinguish themselves from hobbyists, 'traditional professionals feel they are "above" the pursuit of technological capital and exhibit the "natural confidence" that accompanies a belief that social hierarchies are justified'. Similar to the belittlement of the prosumer's knowledge and skills, recording professionals often degrade the prosumers' gear by comparing it to 'the "base" tastes of the uneducated masses' (Cole 2011: 454) and by making it clear that prosumer gear does not meet professional demands.

Research on gear discussions in the context of music production is useful for the consideration of GAS. Not only is GAS prevalent amongst recording enthusiasts (Bourbon 2019; O'Grady 2019), but the discourse also suggests that investing in more professional music equipment is a crucial element of a serious leisure career.

Consequently, it is not enough for a dedicated musician to buy a specific piece of gear to last a lifetime, but quite the contrary, continuous investment is required. Two practices are relevant in this respect, the standardisation of practices through taste regimes and the facilitation of consumption, which we shall explore next.

Arsel and Bean (2013), inspired by Foucault's (1991) concept of 'regime of practice', consider 'taste regimes' central for the standardisation of practices that can take the form of expected equipment amongst musicians for specific purposes or different levels of professionalism. The authors define taste regimes as a 'discursively constructed normative system that orchestrates the aesthetics of practice in a culture of consumption. A taste regime may be articulated by a singular, centralized authority such as an influential magazine or blog' (Arsel & Bean 2013: 899f). For them, taste is not an attribute or characteristic of a person or thing but an activity because everything that has to do with taste, such as listening to music or appreciating food, requires an action. Therefore, tastes are developed and modified through practices (Hennion 2007: 101), which means they are never static (Shove 2003) but actively and continuously achieved through actions in socio-cultural contexts (Arsel & Bean 2013: 900). Studying 'Apartment Therapy', an online discourse on interior design, Arsel and Bean (2013) observe four phases in which new objects are introduced and discussed in virtual communities. In the first phase, an object is *discovered* by an individual who presents it to the community, often after some research, to discuss its use-value or symbolic meaning. Subsequently, the object found is *problematised* by the collective who discuss how it aligns with the community's core values and tastes. The discussion entails questions about how the object can be combined with other items and for what it can be used. Many problems are discovered and discussed, and these problems are not limited to the object itself. Rather, the object serves as a mirror for more abstract and overarching meanings, values and intentions. In the third phase of *ritualisation*, some consensus emerges from the joint discussions about how users should use the object and how this use fits the community's core meanings and values. This phase usually involves routines (Rook 1985) like keeping up to date with the discourse through frequent participation in the forum, reading other sources such as specialist magazines or using the object. Eventually, these activities lead to *instrumentalisation*, through which 'materialism and aesthetic consumption are transformed from a problematic obsession or affliction into a deliberate mode of goal fulfilment in the way that an athlete exercises or an artist does study for a painting' (Arsel & Bean 2013: 909). In other words, 'how to' guides are increasingly created, which eventually standardise the way the object is used and thought about. Ultimately, practices and tastes are standardised, as are the objects considered essential to any serious participant of the community.

In the context of a musicians' board, the discovery could be a new tool that is presented to the community where its implications are discussed as part of the problematisation phase. The tool might eventually be accepted if it aligns with core values or at least offers enough practical benefits to tempt musicians to ignore mismatches with their underlying convictions. After a while, standardised practices in the use of this equipment develop. An excellent example of this process is the previously discussed profiling technology for guitar and bass amplifiers, which confronted musicians with the dilemma that it is a digital technology, the diametral opposite of valve amplification. But it is also tempting because it produces authentic valve sounds with the additional benefits of digital devices like an extensive repertoire of easily selectable sounds. As relevant studies show (Herbst 2019a, 2021; Herbst et al. 2018), the technology was introduced through discussions on musicians' boards and magazine reviews, and it was problematised for years, including pseudo-scientific tests comparing different amplification technologies, until there was sufficient consensus that the technology did not break with the community's core values. Eventually, forum users began to write 'how to' guides and published videos with tips and tricks. In retrospect, discussing taste in such online communities, extended by traditional print magazines, helped establish the technology and make it acceptable to the broader community of amateur and semi-professional users. Nevertheless, it led to standardisation because the adopters of this technology either played user-generated profiles or commercial 'rig packs', or when creating individual profiles, they followed standardised methods in their efforts. Campbell (2004: 28ff) believes that modern societies and the socio-historic weakening of groups in a shift towards a greater emphasis on the individual resulted in 'unrestricted individualism' where 'no one but you is in a position to decide what it is that you want'. We, however, agree with Cole (2018) and Arsel and Bean (2013) that taste regimes and peer pressure still have a significant influence on consumptive practices. This expectation of owning standard tools for music-making may not necessarily trigger GAS because there are fewer emotions involved than from purchases motivated by desires. Using standard tools, though, introduces new devices to musicians that keep them occupied over a longer period of time, which may eventually lead to an acquisition.

In many respects, the Internet does not promote fundamentally different practices and social systems from those that exist offline. Musicians have always exchanged ideas about their equipment (Cole 2018: 1056), and magazines have sparked interest in instruments amongst musicians (Jones 1992: 89; Théberge 1993: 159ff) and influenced taste (see also Shuker 2010: 103, 134). Web 2.0 has given its users manifold possibilities to converse. For instance, record collectors have new opportunities to present their collection on message boards, websites or blogs, which are often 'part shrine, part ego preening' (Shuker 2010: 134). However, the Internet has drastically changed marketing and consumption. Marketers have realised that online users do not passively absorb messages and that success is achieved by providing users with systems that promote consumer interaction (Arvidsson 2006: 101). It is much less about direct transactions than about dialogue and relationships (Ind & Rondino 2001: 14f). Consequently, the Internet has become a place closely linked to consumption activities (Kozinets 1999), even if not always obvious. Any place where people interact can potentially promote consumption. Discussions on message boards do not directly lead to purchases, but they create wants and desires that may result in acquisitions elsewhere online or traditional offline environments. Kozinets (1999: 254) defines 'virtual communities of consumption' as a 'specific subgroup of virtual communities that explicitly center upon consumption-related interests. They can be defined as "affiliative groups" whose online interactions are based upon shared enthusiasm for, and knowledge of, a specific consumption activity or related group of activities'. Although few message board operators or their users would probably consider these places 'virtual communities of consumption', they may indeed be such if the shared leisure activity is based on a material core. What makes these communities receptive to consumption is that discussions about products or reports on acquisitions create 'consumption knowledge' that is 'learned alongside knowledge of the online group's cultural norms, specialized language and concepts, and the identities of experts and other group members' (Kozinets 1999: 254). Kozinets (1999: 254f) identifies four types of message board users concerning consumptive activities. There is the *tourist* who visits or participates in the message board only occasionally and therefore has a superficial or passing interest in the consumption activities experienced in these places. The next type, not wholly different, is the *mingler*, who is similarly unaffected by the consumptive activities observed and only differs from the tourist in that they have stronger social ties to the community. *Devotees* have a great enthusiasm for consumption activities with only a weak social bond with the community, while the *insider* has both strong social and consumptive interests. As Kozinets (1999: 255) notes, there is a progression amongst message board users from visitor to insider, provided the community fits a person's interest well.

Previously we discussed taste regimes on message boards. For these regimes to work, there must be some form of social hierarchy. According to Kozinets (1999: 257), devotees and insiders set the standards of the virtual community and are usually the authoritative voice when new items are discovered, problematised, ritualised and finally instrumentalised (Arsel & Bean 2013). The opinions of devotees and insiders, as experts and persons with an identity, however anonymous, tend to have more influence on purchase decisions than professional marketing campaigns (Kozinets 1999: 259). That is why members of online communities value transparency regarding potentially hidden motives, for example, when a fellow user is affiliated with a specific brand.

Online communities can have a strong impact on a serious leisure enthusiast who is a frequent participant. These communities 'hold the potential to foster an anomic, insatiable, and uncontrolled, form of consumption and commodity desire;

for these reasons, consumption can potentially take on its secondary meaning of a "pathology"' (Cole 2018: 1059). Although it would be difficult to find clear evidence, we can expect that GAS has become more common and possibly more pronounced with the advent and popularity of online message boards and other social media for interest groups such as musicians. A guitarist describes that 'GAS is more prevalent now than it has been in the past, thanks to multiple stimuli—especially the internet' (Wright 2006: 15). Cole (2018: 1059ff) concludes in his analysis of musicians' boards that online discussions can 'spin out of control' in manifold ways. Buying items and selling them unused soon after the purchase, only to order something else, is such an example. This practice is known as 'flipping' and can be observed in threads labelled 'What do you have in the mail?' or 'What is the best X'. The latter kind of threads encourages discussion of goods regardless of any needs or purposes for specific applications or contexts, which separates the use-value from the item's inherent properties, thus leading to a fetishization. Another practice Cole (2018: 1059ff) describes is members posting photographs of their gear in photo essays, usually not during use but when 'unboxing', which is often documented in video form and uploaded to websites like YouTube. Cole (2018: 1059ff) shares our impression that such commonplace practices on online boards promote GAS. He concludes that many 'respondents blame GAS on internet "hype" and the groups' ceaseless commodity discussion and display. Thus, although members find their "tone quests" pleasurable, endless commodity discussion and product announcements ... can also lead members to feel consumptive exhaustion and fatigue'. Similarly, Hartmann (2016: 14) finds that experiencing how other players devote their time, energy and money in their quest for tone inspires message board users to do the same, as it helps to build commitment and maintain motivation in times of doubt or crisis.

6   Interviews and Survey of Musicians

GAS is a phenomenon about which little is formally known apart from Wright's (2006) book and some blog posts. A theoretical understanding of GAS was gradually developed in the previous chapters based on relevant empirical data, especially on the electric guitar and the analogue and digital divide in record production. Nearly all these investigations are qualitative designs, either interview studies or analyses of online practices. As there is a lack of quantitative research in all relevant areas, we designed an online survey to study musicians and their dealings with gear.

Theoretical and qualitative research aims to achieve a better understanding of a phenomenon under investigation. Unless a systematic evaluation is taken with larger populations, the gained knowledge remains preliminary. Surveys are a recognised form of examining behaviours, practices and attitudes in the social sciences to derive descriptive data, systematic relationships and differences between groups. Usually, such surveys are designed to test hypotheses deduced from theoretical assumptions. For this survey, we have chosen a more explorative goal because our assumptions are based on a working theory of GAS. In other words, while we had specific hypotheses that were to be challenged, the survey's overarching objective was to gain a better understanding of GAS based on data from a large and diverse population of musicians. As surveys 'permit reliable and generalizable portraits of populations … concerning cultural consumption and social exclusion' (DeNora 2004: 45), they are well suited for studying purchasing and usage behaviours around musical instruments. Carrying out such surveys online makes it possible to target 'specialist populations' (Paier 2010: 99) worldwide, which leads to larger population sizes (Bortz & Döring 2015: 260f). The Internet's perceived anonymity is also believed to capture more honest answers (Hug & Poscheschnik 2010: 123). However, despite access to specialist populations near and far, online surveys can systematically exclude groups of people (Diekmann 2009: 525–528), for example, those who do not have access to online message boards, where surveys are advertised, or those who have no interest in these communities.

The previous chapters suggested that practices and attitudes vary between players of different instruments, either because of specific affordances of the instrument or because of underlying beliefs and attitudes, such as those towards vintage gear or interest in technological innovation. This impression is consistent with previous research suggesting that there are differences in personality traits between musicians of various instruments (Bell & Cresswell 1984; Cameron et al. 2015; see also Rötter & Steinberg 2018). Therefore, the survey's main aim was to examine what roles different instrument types play concerning GAS. Another factor to consider is genre since it determines the instrument's requirements and is closely linked to its player's musical identity. Against this backdrop, the survey was guided by the following questions:

- Which sociodemographic variables and other personal, social and musical motives play a role in instrument consumption?

- Do players of various instrument types and genres differ in their buying and collecting behaviour?

- Do musicians of electric or electronic instruments show a greater tendency towards GAS than those of acoustic instruments?

- What criteria are decisive for musicians when choosing gear?

These questions systematically address many of the previously described music- and technology-related aspects of GAS, which will provide GAS-specific insights into the collection and consumption patterns discussed before. The study's dual objective is to both test our working assumptions and develop our theory of GAS further. We do this by combining survey data with interviews conducted in preparation for the survey and open comments collected in the survey. Through such a triangulation design, 'it should be possible to increase knowledge in principle, for example, to gain knowledge at different levels, which thus goes further than would be possible with one approach' (Flick 2011: 12; our translation). According to Denzin (1978: 300), integrating different methods serves to compensate for their respective short-comings. The chosen triangulation design does not pursue Denzin's postulate of greater validity. It rather understands triangulation as a strategy to substantiate find-ings by gaining further insights (Flick 2010: 311) and as a supplement to perspec-tives that enable a comprehensive coverage, description and explanation of the topic area (Kelle & Erzberger 2010: 304). Due to the combination of quantitative and qual-itative data, this is a 'between-method triangulation', which seeks to mutually vali-date the insights gained with the applied methods (Flick 2010: 314). The qualitative evaluation serves as an aid to the interpretation and a source of supplementary infor-mation (Bryman 1992).

6.1 Interviews in Music Store

Gathering insights into the practices, opinions and attitudes of musicians in their handling of gear is crucial for gaining a better understanding of GAS. These practices can take different forms in offline and online communities. In the next chapter, online practices are covered in detail. Given the vast number of online communities, it is easy to overlook the traditional places where musicians seek advice on instru-ment purchases, try out gear and network with local musicians—music stores. From a methodological viewpoint, conducting interviews in a music store, unlike text-based online communication, offers advantages such as capturing more natural and spontaneous reactions to GAS face-to-face, allowing field observations and addressing female musicians, an underrepresented group in earlier research (Herbst 2017a; Wright 2006). Our interviews were based on a semi-structured schedule that covered musical, emotional and social aspects. Twenty-four interviews with an average length of 4.35 minutes (*SD* = 2.72) were conducted on 25 February 2017 in one of Germany's largest music stores. The interviews were held in German and English, as some visitors came from other European countries, mainly from the Netherlands.[32]

Many musicians are drawn to music stores. After work and on weekends, they flock to music retailers for a variety of reasons. Buying a pack of strings or drumsticks serves as an excuse to see 'what's new', try out gear and have a chat with other musicians and salespersons. On weekends, befriended musicians may travel to bigger music stores to enjoy a wider range of goods and the atmosphere. This social element becomes evident from the structural design of larger stores, which have lounge areas, cafés and food huts. Many well-run music stores are not designed to serve a purely musical function but act as a social hub that allows musicians to exchange experiences with gear (Cole 2018: 1056), talk about favourite artists, discuss the live scene and network with other musicians, which can lead to the formation of groups and side projects (Sargent 2009: 669). Physical message boards are a clear sign of the communicative and networking incentives of music stores. For less experienced musicians, music stores are an opportunity to get advice on the best gear for their ambitions, and more experienced and extraverted players sometimes use the store as a stage to show off their skills (Sargent 2009). Interactions of such kinds occasionally culminate in performance competitions amongst local musicians or other events such as masterclasses. Altogether, music stores are an exciting microcosmos in which many phenomena take place that encompass broader music practice. As Sargent (2009: 665) puts it, '[m]usical instrument shops are social spaces in which both shoppers and workers construct identities as serious rock musicians and insiders to rock culture'. Music stores are concerned with both the instruments they sell and the fantasies and lifestyles associated with them (Sargent 2009: 668).

In-depth knowledge about how music stores are operated is given by a small but outdated number of short essays like 'How to Choose a Music Store' (The Choral Journal 1980). These give career advice for music store managers and future salespersons (Burchuk 1977) and outline strategies for music educators to cooperate with music stores (Rejino 2002). Studies on instrumental lessons undertaken in music stores are even scarcer (Guest-Scott 2008). From a technological perspective, Pinch (2001) analyses the challenges innovative synthesiser inventors and manufacturers

---

[32] Of course, the brevity of the interviews did not allow for an in-depth discussion of the musicians' dealings with gear, but they still contributed to our understanding by supporting or detailing our working theory of GAS. Furthermore, both interviewers being white men was not optimal for exploring the gendered nature of music stores.

like Robert Moog faced when they tried to persuade music stores to add synthesisers to their piano collection in the 1960s and 1970s. Most of the still limited literature on music stores relates to gender. Berkers and Schaap (2018) cover music stores in their interview study of metal musicians in passing. They suggest there is still a gender-specific treatment in which female musicians are frequently seen as girlfriends or family. Carson et al. (2004) dedicate a short section in their book *Girls Rock! Fifty Years of Women Making Music* on music stores, in which they discuss whether music stores were 'friend or foe'. While the authors give many first-hand examples of sexist and belittling practices of male salespeople and male musicians towards women in these spaces, they also report on female musicians successfully competing with men due to their confidence as musical performers. To our knowledge, Sargent's (2009) work is the only study that focuses specifically on music stores. She observes worker and customer interactions in several music instruments stores in the USA, focusing on language and space to analyse the gendered styles of such intercommunications, which proves to be consistent with the notion of gender discrimination prevalent in these stores.

On our field trip to a music store one Saturday morning, gender stereotypes became apparent. While not observing discrimination against women among the predominantly male sales staff and customers (Berkers & Schaap 2018; Sargent 2009), we did perceive the women there (Butler 1988) corresponding to gender stereotypes. Despite aiming for a balanced sample and thus deliberately addressing female customers, they were underrepresented in quantitative terms; only four out of 24 (17%) interviewees were female, which corresponds to Sargent's (2009) interview sample of three women of ten participants. Concerning instrument choice and gender, the picture was less clear; one played the trumpet, one flute and guitar (acoustic and electric), one drums and the last one bass. The interviews suggest that they approach their gear with little ambition, which is in line with research reasoning that women are less serious and competitive in collecting (Olmstedt 1991; Webley et al. 2001) and less likely to buy musical instruments (Danziger 2004: 161). The trumpet player (33 years) visited the store out of sheer 'instrumental necessity' (Belk 1988; Furby 1978). She explained that her trumpet was borrowed from the church and that she had to return it. The only criteria for purchasing her first trumpet were durability, easy playability and 'a good sound' without specifying the desired sound any further. The reason for her visit to the store instead of going online to order the instrument was that she wanted to try it out without possibly having to return it to an online retailer, something she stated she did not know how to do. Another female bass player (22 years) visited the store with a clear purchase intention. She stressed that she did not play very actively and considered it only a hobby. After she had started taking lessons and progressed in her 'serious leisure career' (Stebbins 2009), she was motivated to acquire a second instrument. One criterion for the new bass was a shorter scale length because the neck of her current instrument was too long, which is a common problem among female guitar and bass players (Carson et al. 2004: 12). Colour was the other criterion; one that was considered by just one of the many male participants in Wright's (2006: 29) study. The shape and model of the instrument made little difference to her, nor did the sound. Since she only played at home, sound nuances were not of particular interest either. Still, she would invest in a proper amplifier and effects pedals should she join a band one day and progress further in her serious leisure career (Stebbins 2009). Another female drummer (27 years) travelled with her partner from far and wide to buy sticks and took the opportunity to explore various types of instruments and drum sets.[33] When she tried electronic drum kits for the first time, she discovered their usefulness, especially since she was forced to sell her acoustic drum kit because of the noise it produced. However, she did at the time not own a drum set or other instruments and did not think she would be able to afford one soon. Her drum playing depended on occasional access to a kit in her school. The flute and guitar player (16 years) exhibited a less purposeful visiting behaviour. While her original intention was to buy a music stand, we met her in the guitar area of the store, where she stressed that she did not need a new guitar because she already owned a cheap acoustic and electric guitar and a ukulele. She also made it clear that she had no intention of spending her free time learning more about equipment and that one flute was enough for her. Overall, the interviews were largely in line with gender stereotypes, but due to the limited number of experiences captured, the short interview durations and the random sample, general statements cannot be made.

Many of the male visitors exhibited a strong interest in gear and associated GAS tendencies. From the interviewed musicians, one keyboard player (52 years) explained his visit to the music store with 'actually, I just want to see if there's anything new'. Several others regularly visited music stores to test instruments, preparing to make an informed acquisition as soon as their budget would allow it. A Dutch guitarist (24 years) travelled to Germany to check out gear. As he stated, 'maybe you see some cool guitar stuff that you don't even know' about. This motivation is not based on necessity but neophilia (Falk 1994): 'I think my tone is complete, but maybe there is something new or ... But it's just for fun, just to look around, and all these guitars on the wall, hahaha. Yeah, that's just [a] good feeling'. He would only buy something if he got a bargain, but his primary intention was to find out about gear, test it and do further research at home. He stressed that he always deliberated on a potential purchase for a week before deciding and declared that this systematic routine was almost like a ritual to him. The behaviour of these two musicians fits the concepts of 'desire' (Belk et al. 2003) and 'necessitation' (Braun et al. 2016). Al-

---

[33] The fact that a female musician took her male partner with her to a music store is worth mentioning, as literature usually reports the opposite (Bayton 1998; Berkers & Schaap 2018; Sargent 2009).

though the visits do not suggest any impulsive tendencies, they clearly show an element of 'self-seduction' for the pleasure that discovering and contemplating potential purchases can give (Baudrillard 1983; Belk et al. 2003).

The notion of necessity is worth mentioning in the context of music stores. As the interviews suggest, many musicians spontaneously create a necessity when confronted with an unknown but exciting piece of equipment or a bargain. Ideally, gear is selected based on musical needs, but in the minds of musicians prone to GAS, new equipment sometimes motivates new artistic projects to justify gear purchases. The gear determines what music to make. As one male customer (53 years) explained, '[t]here are always a few gadgets that you don't really need, but still buy'. In line with technologically deterministic thinking, one bassist (24 years) pointed out that the more gear a musician had, the more creative they could be. In the pursuit of creativity, several musicians stated that they browse print and online instrument catalogues, watch videos and search the Internet to find inspiration for new purchases (see also Wright 2006: 35, 37). The interviews suggest that the musicians deliberately create a desire that triggers the beginning of a 'necessitation' cycle (Braun et al. 2016). Through this perceptual process, an object changes from insignificant to essential. First, musicians try to discover items that could be 'useful'. If the desire is strengthened by the chance of a bargain, those prone to impulsive behaviour may already buy the item without extensive testing or further research. People with a higher degree of awareness and reflexivity question the usefulness of new equipment (Braun et al. 2016; Rogers 2003) and probably only buy it if the quality exceeds that of the already owned gear or extends it in other ways. Whether the item is genuinely 'needed' seems less relevant. Yet, it may not be needed for the current playing, but because of its 'instrumental power' (Furby 1978; McClelland 1951), it might facilitate exploring new styles or sounds. Thus, it could become a need in the future when the musician joins a band or extends their stylistic repertoire. This way of thinking, consciously or unconsciously, may help the musician improve, which is consistent with consumption research that regards the purchase of objects crucial for the development of the self (Belk 1988; Belk et al. 2003; McClelland 1951; Shankar et al. 2009).

One of the more musically motivated reasons for visiting a music store is to upgrade gear to adjust it to developing skills, preferences or musical projects like a band, reflecting progress in a serious leisure career (Stebbins 2009). An interview with a guitar player (19 years) showed these motivations in his acquisition history and plans for the future:

> The first one I bought was a Jackson. It was in the lower price range, about 300 euros. This is just a beginner's guitar. After that, I got myself a Fender, to play something quieter in a better price range, which can be played better. Now I want something better to play metal on. Also, because of the band, to have a better playing feeling live, on stage, I would also go one price range higher, about 1,000 euros.

The times between upgrades may be quite long and likely vary between different instrument types. One drummer explained that with 21 years, he reached the point where the kit he got when he started at 14 had to be upgraded. Drums above the entry range are comparatively expensive, and neither can they easily be collected due to their size. A bassist (51 years) treated himself with upgrading his amplifier as a Christmas gift (see also Wright 2006: 29), and only two months later felt the need to acquire a matching bass. That is a clear case of the 'unending ease' that Straw (2000: 166) sees as characteristic of neophilia. Guitarists seem to be similarly prone to frequent purchases (Herbst 2017a). For players of wind instruments, using varying types can have significant effects on their playing. A saxophonist (51 years) explained that when he got an alto in addition to his tenor, he had difficulty with both, often missing the G-sharp because the alto had the older valve arrangement of instruments from the 1950s. Therefore, he sold the alto and limited himself to the tenor, which improved his playing.

One of the primary motivations for new gear was related to playing in a band. We met a newly formed metal band that visited the music store together to try out new instruments. Their guitarist stated not to have paid much attention to his equipment before joining, but now, he had to upgrade from a small practice amplifier to an adequate amplifier head and cabinet. This motivation was probably based on both sound and visual expectations in the metal genre. The band explained that they could use equipment at the youth centre where they were rehearsing, but with the prospect of live shows, they had to buy their own equipment, including extras like effects pedals, which were not essential for playing in a rehearsal room. Thus, aspirations and progress seem a driving force to invest in material continuously. Even though they appeared to be strategic about their future investments, the members' responses suggested otherwise, having different desires, some individual, focusing on gear they cherished personally. Yet, the band as a collective showed a 'desire for sociality' (Belk et al. 2003: 335f), with some pressure on each band member to invest in better gear to keep up with the band's overall progress and its aspirations or risk exclusion.

In connection with the decisive factor of bands for purchases by individual members, we met another metal band in their late thirties. That band showed a different practice of buying instruments, one that is currently not reported in any journalistic blogs on GAS, namely that of democratic decision-making on purchases within the band. Visiting the store was motivated by 'seeing what's on the market' and comparing what others are playing. However, this behaviour was not 'mimetic desire' (Girard 1977) or 'gear envy' (Wright 2006: 41), but instead formed the basis for a carefully thought-out financing plan. The band stressed they were a team, like a football team, and therefore each musician had to make compromises to contribute to the group's benefit. Their guitar player explained that although he liked instruments in the shape of a Flying V, the other band members preferred rounder shapes, so he would not buy his favourite guitar for the band but perhaps for himself to play at home. Consequently, he would invest in more gear than was 'necessary', some for the band and some for playing at home. Using different equipment for different purposes resembles Wright's (2006: 31, 40) finding that some guitarists play their precious instruments at home and cheaper alternatives on stage.

Changing musical preferences as a 'bedroom musician' or as a member of various ensembles also have an impact on gear requirements (Pinch & Reinecke 2009; Wright 2006: 158). As one guitar player (19 years) highlighted, 'then there's another genre you want to play, and then you get another guitar for it'. This statement corresponds to reasons frequently given in GAS-related literature (Kwisses 2015; Leonhardt 2015). Another guitarist (38 years) explained that in the course of a musician's life, an instrument collection is likely to grow:

> I am an amateur, not a professional, but in my amateur career, I have been in many different bands with different music. Metal, but I also had a pop band and a punk band. The equipment goes along with the music style. Ibanez is more of a pop-rock guitar, in the Joe Satriani sound style. And when you get to metal, I have a Jackson metal guitar. For pop, a Gibson Les Paul … I'm not a collector. The twelve guitars have come through the whole career. You switch between styles. I played pop for three years. Lately, I've been looking for something else because it was boring. Then I switched to metal. Ibanez? Okay. Buy a Jackson; it's kind of heavy.

We also met musicians who saw this very differently. A guitarist (49 years) who played for 31 years deliberately owned just one guitar. He started with a Gibson Deluxe that, when it turned out not to be flexible enough for him, was replaced by a more versatile Ibanez Prestige guitar with three pickups and five pickup combinations, which he played through a Line 6 Helix digital simulation amplifier. This setup, he emphasised, allowed him to play any style of his choice.

Other musicians stick to one genre, which not necessarily means that less investment is 'necessary'. For a bassist (26 years), his musical career was marked by the fandom of Metallica, similar to what Fernandez and Lastovicka (2011) observed for guitar players. He started with a regular four-string bass, added a five-string and then bought a custom model dedicated to Metallica's *And Justice For All* record, which has the album artwork and lyrics printed on it. Metallica's late Clive Burton is a cherished role model for him (see also Wright 2006: 37), which is reflected in his equipment. It consists of a tribute wah-wah pedal and other gear Burton used in the 1980s, such as a bass Tube Screamer and a compressor from Boss, all of which were 'basically the three main pedals that Clive Burton used in the eighties. And I am really happy with my sound'. This sound is only partly his own because he wants to come as close as possible to his idol, motivated by his role as the bass player in a Metallica tribute band. But this bassist still intends to create a somewhat unique sound (see also Wright 2006: 30f) that differs from the original:

I like the sound of Clive Burton. So, I adapted it to my own. When you hear me playing, you will notice it's not exactly like Clive's sound because I can never reach that because he used equipment from a different era. The newer stuff is not as rough as it used to be. It's much more refined. I just tweak the sound a little bit so that it sounds like Clive, but it is my own sound.

If money were not an issue, he would buy precisely the same instruments as Burton or even the original. The closest would be a signature bass guitar by Aria at the cost of about €6,000, designed posthumously in collaboration with Burton's father. The interviewee stressed that this bass was a long-term goal, although not being sure whether he could ever afford it. His desire is nourished by 'hope'; the instrument is difficult to acquire, but it is possible (Belk et al. 2003: 340, 343; Denegri-Knott & Molesworth 2010: 69).

Regarding GAS and collecting, the interviewed musicians covered a broad spectrum from purists to collectors. Many musicians enjoyed musical gear and acquiring items but still considered it a hobby (Wright 206: 81). A bassist (49 years) stressed: 'It's supposed to be fun. And if there are new items, it's always nice. Then I also have the possibility to look forward to something new for a long time. That is always totally great. It's like a new addition to the family'. It would be boring if he could buy any instrument he liked, as this would devalue equipment for him. He favoured the prospect of eventually adding a new piece of gear in the future. Another guitar player (49 years) shared the joy of equipment, but more so from an interest in technology, characterising him as a 'technophile' (Coulthard & Keller 2012): 'I love the technology behind everything … I am amazed by what you can put in a box like this, it's like a whole studio twenty years ago. That's fantastic. It's just fun to know what's around to see'. Such high interest in innovative technologies rather than vintage gear is rare amongst guitarists (Herbst 2019a, 2021).

Others had no problem stressing their fondness for gear and referred to themselves as 'gear nerds' (see also Cole 2018). A guitarist (19 years) stated, 'I don't have a lot of other things on my mind. You can't get enough and think of nothing else', and the drummer (19 years) of his band added, 'it's such a big part of life'. Age is worth mentioning in this context. One bassist (49 years) stopped playing for 25 years when he started a family, and a drummer (49 years) added in a similar vein that although he continued to make music, he did not have the money for many acquisitions because of his three children. Furthermore, the bassist's wife pointed out that he was not supposed to spend too much money on his hobby, and the wife of a 65-year-old drummer was concerned about the limited space in the basement. These exclamations are consistent with Wright's (2006: 102ff, 174) observation that significant others, by whom he means girlfriends and wives, limit spending money on musical equipment.

As discussed previously, a collection does not make its owner a collector (Belk 2001a: 66; Shuker 2010: 8). A guitarist (38 years) stressed that while he had twelve guitars, some of them even of the same model, he owned them because of musical necessities and thus refused to be considered a 'collector'. The simple reason for his growing collection was that he never sold or traded an instrument. For the same reason, another guitarist, despite his young age of 24 years, already owned ten guitars. Only running out of space for all his gear would prompt him to sell instruments. Yet another guitarist (46 years) emphasised that guitarists can never have enough guitars, and he was not even sure how many he possessed. Still, he did not regard himself as a collector. Only once he sold an instrument, and he regrets it to this day, so he keeps accumulating gear. Others reasoned mainly from a financial perspective. As a multi-instrumentalist (46 years) explained, gear accumulated over time because its value decreases immediately after the purchase, and therefore it made little sense to sell it. According to his argumentation, all musicians are collectors out of pure economic necessity. However, collecting did not necessarily exclude selling instruments, as another guitar player (19 years) stated. He saw himself as a collector but only kept the instruments he would actually play. This statement contradicts Wright (2006: 63) in his distinction between musicians and collectors, claiming that collectors do not or only rarely play their instruments. All these different views suggest that practices overlap, making it difficult to distinguish a collector from a non-collector. For Wright, the kind of motivation is decisive. While agreeing with this assessment, we are convinced that it as well depends on each musician's self-image. Among musicians who behave the same way, some see themselves as collectors, while others do not. As per Wright (2006: 63), most players 'don't like the idea of "closet queens"' and thus prefer smaller instrument collections, whereas our interviewees claimed to gradually expand their gear collection for musical purposes without classifying themselves as collectors. Théberge (1997: 244) proposes that the average size of instrument collections has grown over time, and our respondents support this claim. After all, the size of a musician's instrument collection may contribute to their reputation (Cohen 1991: 50) and, especially if they are not professionals, to their 'serious leisure' career (Stebbins 2009).

The criteria for choosing gear were as varied as the opinions and purposes described before. Some participants highlighted low prices and bargains, mainly offered by specialised musical instruments markets (McIntosh & Schmeichel 2004: 91; Wright 2006: 38, 40). Others were willing to pay more for an instrument if it was of appropriate quality (Wright 2006: 28). Yet others stressed that price would not equal quality. Durability, high-quality craftsmanship, playability and sound quality were other criteria at the top of the list.

In summary, despite serving mainly as a pre-study in preparation for the survey, the ethnographic field trip to a music store provided insights valuable in themselves. Practices not covered in academic (Herbst 2017a) and non-academic (Kwisses 2015; Leonhardt 2015; Power & Parker 2015; Robair 2015; Wright 2006) sources became apparent from the interviews. For example, some bands make joint democratic deci-sions on gear purchases, which confirms the occasional conflicts between the ra-tional mind and the irrational contemplations and daydreams that are highlighted in most journalistic texts on GAS. Some of the issues discussed could not be observed. None of the musicians saw acquisitions as an investment (Wright 2006: 79) but in-stead as a loss of money. This belief can be explained by the product offer in most regular music stores, predominantly selling new products. Only rare equipment like vintage instruments, limited editions or gear formerly owned by renowned players retain or even increase in value. As such items are not commonly sold in music stores, the visitors were neither expecting any rarities (Wright 2006: 35) nor were they on the 'hunt' (Wright 2006: 31, 39). Instead, the visitors saw the store as an occasion to learn about new products in the musical instruments industry, exchange ideas, compare themselves with other players and bands, and try out instruments to determine if new acquisitions could help them in their artistic development.

6.2   Method of the Online Survey

Procedure and Sample

Following the field trip to the music store, we created a survey that was hosted on an online platform (SoSci Survey), which facilitated gathering attitudes towards gear from a much larger and international sample. The survey was advertised in fifteen English-language musicians' forums (Appendix A) and on carefully selected musi-cians' websites and Facebook pages, such as Musikmesse Frankfurt, the world's big-gest musical instruments convention. For a more balanced distribution across all in-struments, music students from the University of Huddersfield ($N = 20$) were asked to participate in the survey. Otherwise, no purposive sampling was carried out.

In our introductory text, we described the survey as a research project on the attitudes and practices of instrumentalists concerning their musical equipment. To not influence the response behaviour, we avoided the term 'Gear Acquisition Syn-drome' and its abbreviation 'GAS'. We pointed out that the project was motivated by research interests from music sociology, cultural studies and music technology and that the data would not be used for marketing purposes. The message boards were regulated by administrators as gatekeepers, which resulted in access to one of the largest drummer forums being denied because the admin feared that users would reject surveys from third parties.

The survey was active from 30 June to 16 November 2017. Participation was voluntary. Out of 940 participants, 668 (71%) completed the survey and are included in the evaluation. 94% of the sample were male, only 28 (4%) female. The partici-pants had the option of choosing a non-binary gender or not answering at all. About 2% selected a non-binary gender ($n = 3$) or preferred not to answer ($n = 9$). The av-erage age was 46.39 years ($SD = 15.52$, min. = 14, max. = 82). Concerning the main instruments, the largest groups were guitar (N = 204, 31%) and bass players (N = 200, 30%), followed by saxophonists (N = 95, 14%), trumpet players (N = 76, 11%), drummers (N = 59, 9%) and keyboardists (N = 34, 5%). Among guitarists, 55% preferred the electric over the acoustic guitar. Most participants were hobby musicians (53%). The others listed music as an additional (30%) or professional (17%) occupation. The average playing experience was 26.43 years (SD = 15.94, min. = 1, max. = 66). About two-thirds of the sample played in bands (68%), and those who did, played in 2.49 groups (SD = 1.86). Most played in cover bands (51%) or bands with mainly original compositions (47%), but also in big bands (23%), orchestras (17%), tribute (9%) and top 40 bands (6%). Three quarters played live gigs (74%), an average of 29.59 (SD = 39.27, min. = 0, max. = 300) gigs in the twelve months before the survey. The most frequently played genre (Figure 1) was jazz (15%), followed by classic / hard / surf rock (12%) and blues / soul (11%).

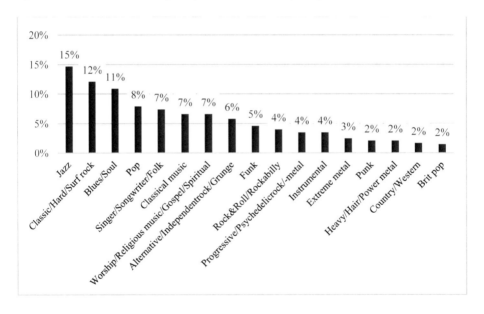

Fig. 1. Genres Played Most Frequently (Number One Choice; Considering only Genres with n > 5; N = 605)

Since these samples were too small for evaluation, the various genres were combined into five groups informed by factor analysis (Table 6), taking aesthetic criteria into account: classical / worship / instrumental (n = 101), jazz / blues / soul / funk (n = 187), pop / folk / rock & roll (n = 127), rock / alternative / punk (n = 130) and metal / progressive / hardcore (n = 56). Hip hop / rap and electronic music formed a separate factor but with only four respondents, this group was excluded from further genre analysis.

The majority of the sample was in a relationship, either married (59%) or unmarried with a partner (22%). 19% were single, divorced or widowed. Consequently, 81% lived with a partner or family, 12% alone and 7% lived in another cohabitation form. Most of the sample population came from Europe (52%), North America (38%) and Australia (9%). Asia (0.8%), South America (0.5%) and Africa (0.2%) formed a marginal group within the sample. Due to this uneven distribution, the location could not be considered in the analysis.

Instrument

The survey consisted of three parts. In the first part, data on sociodemographic background and musical activities were collected: main instrument, size of the instrument collection including accessories (for example, effects pedals or mouthpieces), relationship status, living situation, musical education and professional status as well as experiences on the instrument and in bands. The second part included top-three rankings of multiple choices for the genres most frequently played on the instrument, purchase criteria for equipment and multiple selections for the type of band. The third part consisted of item batteries with 7-point Likert scales to measure attitudes. Only the anchors were labelled, signing (1) as complete disagreement and (7) as complete agreement. For questions on sociodemographic data and most of the items, participants could choose not to answer. Open answer fields allowed to comment on answers or highlight topics that were felt relevant to the study. In total, 30% of the participants (202 of 668) commented, which corresponded to approximately 8,000 words.[34] Such valuable qualitative data not only extends the quantitative data but also shows how seriously many participants took the survey.

Ninety items were assigned to latent dimensions based on theory and reliability analyses. The scales were optimised by stepwise exclusion. This procedure was accompanied by factor analyses, which led to combining two initially distinct dimensions, *General GAS* and *Psychic Effects*, into a comprehensive *General GAS* scale. In the end, theoretical considerations played the determining role in scale construction. 72 items were finally used to create fourteen scales with acceptable to excellent consistencies (Table 1). While most scales have between four and eight items, the *General GAS* scale stands out with seventeen items and the *Collectors* scale and *Democratic Purchases in Bands* with two items each. The latter cannot claim to represent the concept comprehensively, which goes without question. Yet in the service of exploratory research interest, it still provides meaningful insights.[35] Besides, most scales correlate with each other due to scale construction based on averages. That

---

[34] The open comments are presented with all the grammatical and typographical errors their contributors made.

[35] Applying the Spearman-Brown coefficient to the two-item scales led to satisfactory results: *Collectors*: $r_s = .75$, *Democratic Purchases in Bands:* $r_s = .77$.

does not come as a surprise, given the theoretical premise that all scales should help explain GAS. However, it is an indication that they do not describe completely distinct phenomena. A full correlation matrix is given in Appendix D.

Tab. 1. Scales Capturing Different Attitudes Towards Musical Gear

Scale	*N*	Cronbach's α	*M*	min.	max.	*SD*	Items
General GAS	613	.89	4.55	1.00	7.00	1.05	17
Personal Motives							
Collectors	667	.75	2.81	1.00	7.00	1.65	2
Technophilia	661	.74	3.61	1.00	6.60	1.10	5
Vintage	658	.79	3.52	1.00	7.00	1.27	5
Nostalgia	655	.70	4.21	1.00	7.00	1.43	4
Modification and Fabrication	664	.81	3.10	1.00	7.00	1.39	4
Social motives							
Relationships	507	.76	3.44	1.00	7.00	1.45	4
Band as GAS Motivator	449	.88	3.35	1.00	7.00	1.51	5
Democratic Purchases in Bands	457	.74	2.23	1.00	7.00	1.36	2
Musical motives							
Role Models	664	.68	2.34	1.00	6.00	1.08	4
Genre Requirements	665	.73	3.72	1.00	7.00	1.28	4
Expressiveness	660	.91	4.40	1.00	7.00	1.35	8
Experimentation	663	.79	4.01	1.00	7.00	1.29	5
Sound Exploring	665	.74	4.41	1.00	7.00	1.39	3

As this survey pioneered quantitative research on GAS, the instrument and scale properties are included in Appendix C for future studies. To help understand the analysis, we briefly summarise all scales.

The most important scale is *General GAS*. With an excellent internal consistency, it includes items related to the habit of thinking about equipment and researching gear online or in magazines, testing equipment in music stores, looking for deals, desiring to buy instruments, wishing for variety in one's gear collection and valuing music equipment generally. The scale *Collectors* captures views on collecting and buying gear because it is rare or unique. *Modification and Fabrication* measures interest in these practices and the attitude that most ready-made gear benefits from modification. The *Relationship* scale is only available to participants in a relationship and records the partner's influence on buying behaviour. *Vintage* not only captures a fondness for vintage gear, old-worn looks and authentic rebuilds but also gathers opinions on whether older gear sounds better and is not outdated by technological innovations. In contrast, *Technophilia* measures interest in the latest music technology for reasons of being up-to-date, better sound or improved functionality. *Nostalgia* gathers personal memories and the appreciation of instruments the musician played in the past ('reflective nostalgia'). *Band as GAS Motivator* consists of items that address the increased likelihood of buying more gear when playing in a band because the equipment or behaviour of band members affects the desire to extend one's instrument collection. *Democratic Purchases in Bands* captures the willingness to negotiate instrument purchases with fellow band members. The *Band as GAS Motivator* and *Democratic Purchases in Bands* scales are only available to respondents who state that they currently play in one or more groups (bands/orchestras). *Role Models* tracks the musician's fondness for signature models or their favourite musicians' gear. Similarly, *Genre Requirements* measures whether genres require specific instruments, based on the assumption that musicians who play several styles could benefit from a larger instrument collection. *Expressiveness* gathers to what extent new gear helps overcome limitations and inspires. *Experimentation* is about the importance of a personal or innovative sound in connection with an instrumental technology or its unconventional use. *Sound Exploring* is the increased form of experimentalism and measures the importance of trying out and combining sounds. It also includes a comprehensive understanding of the equipment to tweak the sound according to the musician's visions.

Data analysis was conducted using univariate analyses of variance and conservative Scheffé post-hoc tests to examine differences between instruments and genres. The evaluation of the influence of personal factors and attitudes was carried out using correlation analyses, stepwise categorical regression models and *t*-tests, for which the effect size is indicated by the unbiased Hedge's *g*. For all scales, the variation between instruments, groups of genres and types of ensembles was tested. If no results are reported, there were no significant differences at the .05 level.

6.3   Survey Results

Gear Collection

By definition, GAS implies an inclination to buy musical gear, so that a natural consequence is the accumulation of musical instruments if purchases are not offset by selling equipment. Table 2 gives an overview of the average instrument collection.

Tab. 2. Overview of Average Instrument Collection

Drums (*n* = 58)	Range	*M*	*SD*	*Mdn*
Acoustic drum kits	0 – 10	2.05	1.77	2.00
Electronic drum kits	0 – 5	0.47	0.84	0.00
Cymbals	0 – 60	11.60	11.31	8.00
Add. snares	0 – 42	2.84	6.24	1.00
Add. toms & bass drums	0 – 9	0.88	1.56	0.00
Add. kick pedals	0 – 9	1.33	1.53	1.00
Pieces of percussion	0 – 60	5.17	9.36	3.00
Add. sampling pads	0 – 3	0.28	0.72	0.00
Bass guitar (*n* = 200)	Range	*M*	*SD*	*Mdn*
Acoustic bass guitars	0 – 4	0.44	0.70	0.00
Electric bass guitars	0 – 60	5.53	5.73	4.00
Combo amplifiers	0 – 5	1.04	0.95	1.00
Amplifier heads	0 – 8	1.75	1.34	2.00
Speaker cabinets	0 – 8	2.03	1.49	2.00
Pedals and effects	0 – 75	5.63	7.27	4.00
Guitar (*n* = 204)	Range	*M*	*SD*	*Mdn*
Acoustic guitars	0 – 27	3.40	3.53	2.00
Electric guitars	0 – 100	5.25	9.53	3.00
Combo amplifiers	0 – 15	2.02	2.04	2.00
Amplifier heads	0 – 35	0.90	2.99	0.00
Speaker cabinets	0 – 14	0.97	1.83	0.00
Pedals and effects	0 – 200	10.75	23.74	4.00
Keyboard (*n* = 34)	Range	*M*	*SD*	*Mdn*
Keyboards	0 – 12	2.50	2.76	2.00
MIDI master keyboards and pads	0 – 6	1.24	1.33	1.00
Hardware synthesisers	0 – 12	2.59	3.01	1.50
Stage pianos	0 – 3	0.44	0.66	0.00
Electric organs	0 – 1	0.32	0.48	0.00
Grand or upright pianos	0 – 1	0.32	0.48	0.00
Digital pianos	0 – 2	0.18	0.46	0.00
Keyboard amplifiers	0 – 4	0.56	0.86	0.00
Pedals and effects	0 – 12	1.38	2.51	0.00
Software applications regularly used when playing the keys	0 – 100	14.26	27.99	3.50
Saxophone (*n* = 95)	Range	*M*	*SD*	*Mdn*
Soprano saxophones	0 – 5	0.96	0.96	1.00
Alto saxophones	0 – 10	1.86	1.59	1.00
Tenor saxophones	0 – 12	2.01	2.05	1.00
Baritone saxophones	0 – 3	0.55	0.74	0.00
Bass saxophones	0 – 1	0.03	0.18	0.00

	Range	M	SD	Mdn
Other types	0 – 5	0.26	0.75	0.00
Add. necks	0 – 12	0.55	1.42	0.00
Add. mouthpieces	0 – 50	10.21	10.03	6.00
Trumpet (*n* = 76)	**Range**	***M***	***SD***	***Mdn***
Classical trumpets (with rotary valves)	0 – 5	0.53	1.03	0.00
Jazz trumpets (with piston valves)	0 – 45	6.21	8.58	4.00
Piccolo trumpets	0 – 6	0.83	1.03	1.00
Pocket trumpets	0 – 2	0.33	0.55	0.00
Bass trumpets	0 – 1	0.01	0.12	0.00
Other types	0 – 11	1.08	1.78	0.50
Mouthpieces	1 – 450	34.08	59.01	20.00
Mutes	0 – 300	16.79	35.06	9.50

Herbst (2017a) documents guitarists owning five electric instruments plus three amplifiers on average, and Wright (2006: 47) claims that his study's participants consider four to ten guitars the ideal size for their collection. The results of this study confirm the literature; the average guitarist owns five electric guitars and three amplifiers. Comparing the types of instruments and leaving aside amplifiers, effects and other extras, trumpet players possess the most instruments, followed by bass and guitar players, then keyboardists, drummers and saxophonists. The abbreviation GAS originally stood for '*Guitar* Acquisition Syndrome' (Becker 1996). That is why special-interest books show a different emphasis on technology for the types of instruments, with electric guitarists and synthesiser players being most 'technophile' (Coulthard & Keller 2012). It was therefore our underlying expectation that guitar players would be most prone to GAS, while players of wind instruments would be least affected. Measured by the number of instruments the participants gave, trumpet players unexpectedly surpass all other instruments. Economically, trumpet placers benefit from the fact that other than guitarists and bassists, they are not required to buy amplifiers and so can spend more money on instruments. However, this does not explain the considerable differences between trumpet and saxophone players. It may well be that several trumpets are needed for their many tunings, while saxophonists tend to stick to one or two favourite voices, for example, soprano and alto. In the open comments, some brass players noted that the survey did not cover all tunings and trumpet types and that some of the categorisations were confusing, especially the classification of 'classical trumpets' as trumpets with rotary valves and 'jazz trumpets' as trumpets with piston valves. Several respondents point out stylistic differences of the respective type between Europe and other parts of the world. Nevertheless, it should have been possible to assign any instrument to one of the two construction types. That also applies to instruments with different tunings for which no separate categories had been created. Additional uncertainty regards the classification of flugelhorns and cornets, which according to the German classification, usually belong to the family of horns. It cannot be ruled out that these instruments have been entered in the field 'other types' or that the listing has been omitted. At this point, the survey instruments may not have allowed for fully valid results and thus need further clarification in future studies. However, the wide variety of different types of instruments and tunings within the trumpet family may explain why trumpeters own so many instruments.

Based on theoretical deliberations, another expectation was that musicians playing electronic instruments possess more equipment than musicians playing acoustic instruments. As Frith (1986) and Théberge (1997: 244f) argue, electronic instruments quickly become outdated when new sounds come into fashion, sound quality improves or functionality increases. That mainly applies to those benefitting from more modern sounds such as electronic keyboards (Weissberg 2010: 91) but probably less so to guitar and bass (Théberge 1993: 166–177; Uimonen 2016). On the other hand, vintage synthesisers are popular, too (Théberge 1997: 119), which illustrates the issue's complexity. Furthermore, different sounds and playing feels of acoustic instruments may require more instruments than playing a digital simulation. Unlike acoustic instruments such as the piano, electronic devices, at least in the case of keyboard instruments, are significantly more owned, presumably because of their affordability and portability. Requiring less space is also an advantage, given the high average number of instruments. Several practical, musical and individual reasons must therefore be considered. In line with these theoretical considerations, the results support the assumption that musicians own more electric and electronic instruments, but not as clearly as we had expected. Musicians have more electric guitars and basses than their acoustic counterparts. Likewise, keyboards and hardware synthesisers dominate the instrument collection compared to acoustic keyboard instruments. Drummers, on the other hand, possess more acoustic than electronic kits. Among the brass instruments[36], the jazz trumpet is the favourite. Woodwind players prefer tenor and alto saxophones over soprano and baritone models; bass saxophones are uncommon.

Apart from the average collection size of the different instruments, it is useful to consider the standard deviation and median, as they provide further insight into distribution and different practices within an instrument group. Although guitarists own fewer instruments than trumpet and bass players on average, their collections

---

[36] Electronic wind instruments based on sampling and synthesis technology, such as the 'Roland AE-10 Aerophone Digital Wind Instrument' and the 'Akai EWI 5000 Electronic Wind Instrument', were not included in the questionnaire because acoustic instruments seem to be much more common among saxophone and trumpet players.

show the highest variance. The largest instrument collections belong to electric guitar players. For all other instruments except the electric bass and jazz trumpet, the maximum number of instruments and standard deviations are lower.

Overall, the median indicates moderate instrument collections with sometimes even 0.00, meaning that only a minority possesses the equipment within the instrument group. In most cases, the median is slightly below the mean, suggesting a right-skewed distribution. Slightly above the average it is only for guitar amplifier heads ($M = 1.75$, $Mdn = 2.00$), soprano saxophones ($M = 0.96$, $Mdn = 1.00$) and piccolo trumpets ($M = 0.83$, $Mdn = 1.00$). Between mean and median, the greatest deviations exist for smaller and more affordable items, such as guitar pedals and effects ($M = 10.75$, $Mdn = 4.00$), software applications used when playing the keys ($M = 14.26$, $Mdn = 3.50$), mouthpieces for saxophones ($M = 10.21$, $Mdn = 6.00$) and trumpets ($M = 34.08$, $Mdn = 20.00$) as well as mutes for trumpets ($M = 16.79$, $Mdn = 9.50$). This additional gear is popular with all instrumentalists. The highest numbers are mouthpieces for all wind instruments and mutes for trumpets. As a saxophonist notes in the open comments, given that he 'hardly ever need[s] amplification or other electronics, the gear that [he] acquire[s] is limited to new instruments and accessories to instruments'. Since wind players do not require many essential items, they can concentrate on modifying their instruments with new mouthpieces. More generally, pedals and effects are also popular, although more so for the guitar than for bass. Compared to instruments and effects, far fewer amplifiers are owned. For a group of keyboardists, software applications are an essential part of their setup; in contrast, pedals, hardware effects and amplifiers are less relevant. Drummers invest mainly in cymbals and percussion (for example, cowbell and mallets). Additional snare drums are less common, but the maximum number and high standard deviation demonstrate a large variance in this respect. Acquiring extra gear may have musical reasons to personalise or extend the sonic repertoire (Jones 1992: 91; Théberge 1993: 278). Yet such additional equipment is also an affordable alternative to most instruments and therefore suitable as 'discretionary purchase' (Danziger 2004: 6f) to satisfy the 'GAS attack' (Wright 2006: 22) in the short term. Such accessories can be understood as 'indulgences', as small luxury items that provide emotional satisfaction but are not so costly that one feels bad about the expense. It can give the buyer a 'strong emotional gratification that consumers gain from their discretionary purchases [which] is the reward that reinforces continued purchases of things desired, but not needed' (Danziger 2004: 22). Moreover, as is often the case with hobbies, the act of researching and buying objects can be just as fulfilling as their actual use (Danziger 2004: 84).

Absolute figures on the ownership of different pieces of gear are limited in their explanatory power, as these items cannot be easily compared with each other due to their distinct sizes, prices and characteristics. In other words, how many guitar effect pedals are worth an additional bass drum? To enable cross-instrument comparisons, we use z-scores, which bring instrument ownership to a comparable scale. When transforming the ownership of items into z-scores, the average value for each item is set to zero (for example, 2.01 tenor saxophones), and a new scale is adapted on which one scale point corresponds to one standard deviation (for example, 2.05 tenor saxophones). By calculating the means of each instrumentalist's collection on this new score, we can determine how equipment ownership is distributed in the sample concerning above-average or below-average instrument collections.

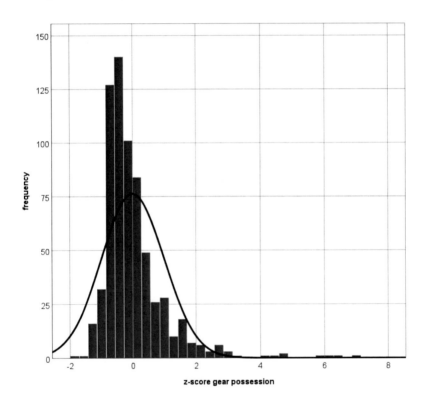

Fig. 2. Z-Standardised Gear Possession Across All Instruments (N = 667)

Categorising all instrument collections after z-standardisation in up to average (≤ 0) and above average (> 0) shows that both groups are not sized equally. About one third (37%) has an above-average number of instruments. Also, the standardised size of the instrument collections does not follow a normal distribution. Regardless of the instrument type, a small group has significantly more gear, resulting in a right-skewed distribution (Figure 2) with scores up to almost seven times the standard deviation. That indicates a substantially higher number of instruments or pieces of gear, considering that one standard deviation represents about ten guitars or two drum kits. The high standard deviations and the distributions suggest two fundamentally different approaches to dealing with gear. The instruments owned by the majority of participants correspond closely to the standardised average, yet not with a normal distribution but with a tendency towards a smaller collection. It remains open whether this main group can be further differentiated. The second group has considerably more instruments, differing from the average by four to seven times the standard deviation.

When testing the standardised number of items for explanatory factors, there are no significant differences between the various genres, relationship statuses and living situations. Consistent with common stereotypes, male respondents ($M = 0.02$, $SD = 1.01$) show higher values and a much higher variance than female respondents ($M = -0.45$, $SD = 0.49$), $t(38.31) = -4.68$, $p < .001$, Hedges' $g = 0.47$.[37] Regarding the different types of bands, musicians playing in cover or top 40 bands own significantly more equipment ($M = 0.17$, $SD = 1.02$) than those who do not ($M = -0.03$, $SD = 0.97$), $t(455) = -2.12$, $p < .05$, Hedges' $g = 0.20$. The same applies to players in tribute bands ($M = 0.46$, $SD = 1.34$) compared to the others ($M = 0.03$, $SD = 0.95$), $t(45.26) = -2.02$, $p < .05$, Hedges' $g = 0.43$. Hobby musicians ($M = -0.11$, $SD = 0.95$) have significantly less musical equipment than professionals ($M = 0.19$, $SD = 1.07$), $F(2, 664) = 5.34$, $p < .01$, $\eta^2 = .02$, although with a small effect.

A regression analysis taking into account sociodemographic data, factors related to musical practice as well as musical and personal motives reveals medium to strong effects, $F(5, 600) = 32.57$, $p < .001$, adj. $R^2 = .21$. Older participants and men appear to have significantly more equipment when the two variables are tested in a separate model. However, these differences are no longer significant in the overall regression model when taking all variables above into account. Since age and playing experience correlate strongly ($r = .654$), it is not surprising that only one variable contributes to the explanation of variance. The findings still suggest that playing experience ($\beta = .14$, $p < .01$) is a suitable predictor for a large instrument collection, which is consistent with Herbst's (2017a) study, according to which the acquisition of gear is a side-effect of an extensive playing history.

Regarding personal and musical motives, the only significant predictors are *Collecting* musical gear ($\beta = .38$, $p < .001$) and *Nostalgia* ($\beta = .11$, $p < .01$). The distinction between collectors and players supports Wright (2006: 63) in that in *Nostalgia* and *Collecting*, we have two scales with personal motives giving the best predictive power for a large instrument collection and showing that musical motives play no

---

[37] Despite deviating from the normal distribution, parametric test procedures are chosen here and in the following with ANOVA and *t*-test. Due to the large sample size, they are considered robust to a violation of the normal distribution (Glass et al. 1972; Rasch et al. 2006: 102).

central role. Unlike restorative *nostalgia* acknowledging heroes of the past, the reflective form (Boym 2001: 10) describing the musicians' appreciation of their previously owned instruments can be observed here. Due to different subsamples, social attitudes were not included in the regression analyses. Anyhow, there were no correlations with the standardised number of items.

Having children does not significantly impact gear collections as might have been expected; households with children generally show a higher number of purchases (Danziger 2004: 161), but seemingly not on musical instruments. There are smaller and more manageable instruments for children that require, in the course of young musicians' developments, new models that correspond to their abilities and body characteristics. It is not clear from the data whether participants included their children's instruments in their answers. Although the accumulated gear size increases, nothing indicates a peak in the 30s and 40s, which is the time frame most players have children learning an instrument. The data neither give clear evidence that parenthood limits the time, motivation and money for musical activities. As to that, some of the open comments are revealing because they suggest that musicians take breaks from their hobby due to family or work commitments, sometimes for several decades. One participant expresses:

> I like many musicians have taken time out during our lives to get 'real jobs' and
> have come back to playing after raising families. That put me like many others is a
> very different taste and economic grouping than when I was younger and trying to
> make it. I feel that this differentiation between musicians who have never stopped,
> i.e. consistent players over many years and those who have stopped have very dif-
> ferent gear buying habits.

Statistically, however, the data do not provide sufficient evidence that children significantly affect instrument collection size.

Criteria for Choosing and Buying Instruments

The participants ranked the three most important criteria when buying instruments. Regardless of any personal variables, three criteria stand out (Figure 3). By far, 'sound quality' is considered the most important feature of an instrument, followed by 'playability and feel' and 'workmanship'. Price and appearance are only relevant if the main criteria are met.

This result indicates that musical aspects and the instrument's quality are most influential on the purchase decision and that extra-musical factors do not play a decisive role. Other factors like role models, authenticity and trends are negligible, as is the suitability for individual genres. The result supports neither Théberge's (1993: 166) notion of musical instruments as a 'loaded symbolic terrain' with 'romantic notions of authenticity and personal expression' nor the theory of restorative nostalgia, which is concerned with glorified instruments and their famous players (Boym

2001: 10; Uimonen 2016). Nor can Cohen's (1991: 135) claim be confirmed that musicians value instruments because of their visual qualities and brand. Furthermore, neither reviews nor price (Jones 1992: 89) plays a significant role. The results, however, are consistent with Wright's (2006: 46) finding that the price of an instrument is not the decisive factor in a purchase decision if it is worth its money. It can be concluded that musical motives are the ultimately determining ones, even though social or personal factors may influence the motivation for dealing with musical instruments and acquiring gear.

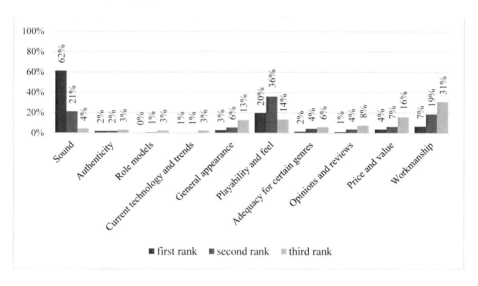

Fig. 3. Criteria when Choosing Instruments (N = 668)

The open comments deepen our understanding of the quantitative data. Participants name several reasons for and against buying, which extend some of the key criteria and the personal, social and musical motives discussed below, and reveal varying opinions and practices. Despite the relatively low importance of the price of gear, several participants stress that exclusive deals (Wright 2006: 40) tempt them to acquire gear that they might not need. Some indicate that they buy equipment when it 'is too good a deal to pass up', either because it is a catch or because they are curious about the item. Other participants work part-time or as a side-line to have money for instruments. Some work at a music store, which 'entices' them to buy gear because of staff discounts and being surrounded by instruments. Much of the money they earn is immediately spent on music equipment. Likewise, money earned from gigs and repairing fellow musicians' gear is spent on an instrument collection.

The open comments are also informative as to why musicians refrain from spending money on new acquisitions. Apart from obvious financial constraints, partly related to the responsibility of providing for a family, some musicians prefer trading gear to change it without having to invest. Similarly, some only buy if a device is broken or outdated (Théberge 1997: 244). Others explain that their living and storage space limits the size of their equipment collection. A minimal number of musicians point out that the lack of music stores within commuting distance makes it difficult for them to try out gear, which prevents them from buying. Online stores would be an alternative, but these are not mentioned in the comments. Other reasons for the reluctance to buy are more musically motivated. Several participants highlight to have found the perfect equipment after substantial experimenting with gear, buying, selling and trading it, so nothing new will be needed. In other words, they obtained the setup that provides the best 'use-value' for their needs (Cole 2018). Others explain it similarly by stressing that they value versatile equipment that can cover all their stylistic needs. A prerequisite for such instruments meeting all musical needs for many years is high quality and durability, as several musicians point out in their comments: 'I've had the same gear for over 30 years. Still going because I bought quality in the first place'. Finding such equipment requires research, testing and comparing instruments, as a trumpeter suggests:

> I am extremely selective in choosing the Instruments and Accessories that I purchase, doing much advance research and play testing many of the same Brands and Models in order to make the best purchase possible. This often, but not always results in purchasing the very high end of the Instrument and/or Accessory. I try to be considerate of the need and longevity of the need. My oldest Trumpet was the first new Professional Trumpet that I bought in 1972 with the assistance of my College Trumpet Teacher. I still perform with this horn from time to time, depending on the type of situation. My other horns range from 1976 (2), 1984 (1), 2016 (1). I also own a pocket Trumpet of unknown Vintage (at least 60 years old). All of my Trumpets were made to fit specific needs and are regularly played in a performance of some type.

The help of more experienced players in finding the best gear that fits a personal style is in line with Gay (1998), who examined the learning processes of New York rock musicians in terms of playing and gear.

Gear Acquisition Syndrome

The size of gear collection and the buying criteria only provide clues to the attitudes and motives underlying musical gear consumption. These factors were captured by a series of scales, where the participants rated their personal, social and musical motives. A more comprehensive Gear Acquisition Syndrome scale was applied to determine how susceptible the individual instrument groups are to this phenomenon.

Tab. 3. Differences Between Instruments

Scale	M scale (SD)	Instruments						ANOVA		
		Drums	Bass	Guitar	Keys	Sax	Trpt	F	p	η2
General GAS	4.55 (1.05)	4.39	4.54	4.77[1]	4.65	4.11[1]	4.54	5.11	<.001	.04
Personal motives										
Collectors	2.81 (1.65)	2.60	2.82	2.90	2.90	2.39	3.17	2.30	<.05	.02
Technophilia	3.61 (1.10)	3.82	3.56	3.49[1]	4.18[1,2]	3.36[2,3]	3.94[3]	5.35	<.001	.04
Vintage	3.52 (1.27)	3.44	3.47	3.63	3.40	3.47	3.51		n.s.	
Nostalgia	4.21 (1.43)	4.30	4.00[1]	4.52[1]	4.44	3.99	4.02	3.74	<.01	.03
Modification and Fabrication	3.10 (1.39)	3.05	3.17[1]	3.36[2]	2.76	2.56[1,2]	3.12	4.97	<.001	.04
Social motives										
Relationships	3.44 (1.45)	3.41	3.51	3.52	3.26	3.42	3.19		n.s.	
Band as GAS Motivator	3.35 (1.51)	3.50[1]	3.63[2,3]	3.94[4,5]	3.33	2.51[1,2,4]	2.85[3,5]	11.45	<.001	.11
Democratic Purchases in Bands	2.23 (1.36)	2.27	2.12	2.69[1]	2.30	1.90[1]	2.19	3.40	<.01	.04
Musical motives										
Role Models	2.34 (1.08)	2.43	2.26	2.54[1]	2.32	2.09[1]	2.26	2.86	<.05	.02
Genre Requirements	3.72 (1.28)	3.78	3.59	3.91[1]	4.28[2]	3.16[1,2,3]	3.97[3]	7.11	<.001	.05
Expressiveness	4.40 (1.35)	4.28	4.21[1]	4.89[1,2,3]	4.81[4]	3.89[2,4]	4.13[3]	10.61	<.001	.08
Experimentation	4.01 (1.29)	3.93	3.89	4.20	4.39	3.86	3.91	2.23	<.05	.02
Sound Exploring	4.41 (1.39)	4.56	4.33	4.56	4.87	4.16	4.21	2.41	<.05	.02

Note: Measured on 7-point Likert scales (1–7); [1,2,...]: significant differences between instruments (Scheffé post-hoc test, $p < .05$)

157

The results show that GAS is not an unknown phenomenon for most participants because the *General GAS* scale received the highest agreement of all fourteen scales (Table 3). That is confirmed by the open comments where the term 'GAS' is widely used, often accompanied by statements such as 'GAS is great' or 'gear is great'. Consistent with Belk's (1988) concept of the 'extended self', several musicians point out that their equipment is part of them and that they would hesitate to sell it. There were also comments demonstrating a strong sense of 'neophilia' (Falk 1994). One guitarist highlights being 'good for a new guitar, bass, amp etc. once a year' and another explains that being unmarried and in a well-paid job allows him to buy instruments whenever he 'fancies' a purchase. Yet other musicians see GAS or collecting gear critically. Some emphasise that they regularly 'clear out' and sell or trade items due to lack of use. Their motives are either to invest in less but higher quality equipment or to reduce the collection size. As one player puts it, 'I recently came to realize that too much gear might stress me. Why not just have a minimum gear and practice with it? I am considering to reduce my gear significantly'. That too much equipment can create stress is hardly covered in the literature on GAS or collecting; on the contrary, most texts focus on the emotional trouble caused by the urge to acquire frequently.[38] Nevertheless, the fact that the scale *General GAS* (Table 3) finds the highest agreement of all scales suggests that it is the label that some reject rather than the practices and interest in gear it represents.

Similar to the differences between the gear collection sizes of the various types of instruments discussed earlier, we expected that instrumentalists would systematically differ in their attitudes towards GAS. The data (Table 3) confirm only minimal but significant differences between two instruments. Among saxophone players, the tendency towards GAS is significantly less pronounced than among guitar players. It confirms our expectation that guitarists are most prone to GAS, ranking highest on the *General GAS* scale, followed by keyboardists, bassists and trumpet players. Drummers and saxophone players have the lowest values. An unexpected result is that trumpeters have a higher GAS score than drummers. Still, it is consistent with the result of trumpet players having the largest instrument collection of all instrumentalists.

Comparing the grouped genres (Table 4) shows that musicians from the metal / progressive / hardcore genres have the highest values and differ significantly from those of the jazz / blues / soul / funk and pop / folk / rock & roll genres. This result is likely due to the typical metal band line-up with often two guitarists and one keyboard player, with both instruments exhibiting the highest values on the *General GAS* scale among the instrumentalists (Table 3).

---

[38] Distress is a common phenomenon amongst hoarders (Nordsletten et al. 2013). It is not known how widespread hoarding is amongst musicians, especially given the high price tags of music equipment that usually do not allow spontaneous compulsive purchases.

Tab. 4. Differences Between Genres

Scale	M scale (SD)	Classical	Jazz	Pop	Rock	Metal	ANOVA		
							F	p	η2
General GAS	4.57 (1.03)	4.68	4.39[1]	4.36[2]	4.70	5.09[1,2]	6.84	<.001	.05
Personal motives									
Collectors	2.80 (1.65)	2.96	2.77	2.54	2.94	2.91		n.s.	
Technophilia	3.61 (1.09)	3.95[1,2]	3.55	3.47[1]	3.45[2]	3.84	4.48	<.01	.03
Vintage	3.56 (1.27)	3.39	3.50	3.56	3.86	3.38	2.66	<.05	.02
Nostalgia	4.25 (1.42)	4.21	4.12	4.05	4.55	4.49	2.89	<.05	.02
Modification and Fabrication	3.10 (1.37)	3.17	2.93	2.99	3.20	3.52	2.48	<.05	.02
Social motives									
Relationships	3.44 (1.43)	3.57	3.48	3.21	3.51	3.45		n.s.	
Band as GAS Motivator	3.37 (1.52)	3.22[1]	2.80[2,3,4]	3.44[2,5]	3.87[3]	4.58[1,4,5]	14.30	<.001	.13
Democratic Purchases in Bands	2.25 (1.36)	2.44	1.94[1]	2.24	2.30	2.89[1]	4.35	<.01	.04
Musical motives									
Role Models	2.36 (1.07)	2.36	2.13[1]	2.34[2]	2.48	2.88[1,2]	6.03	<.001	.04
Genre Requirements	3.73 (1.27)	3.86	3.66	3.57	3.71	4.08		n.s.	
Expressiveness	4.41 (1.34)	4.62[1]	4.09[1,2]	4.34[3]	4.40[4]	5.23[2,3,4]	9.16	<.001	.06
Experimentation	3.98 (1.23)	4.15[1]	3.96[2]	3.59[1,3]	3.93[4]	4.74[2,3,4]	9.63	<.001	.06
Sound Exploring	4.40 (1.35)	4.50[1]	4.16[2]	4.30[3]	4.37[4]	5.28[1,2,3,4]	7.95	<.001	.05

The "Genres groups" span covers the Classical, Jazz, Pop, Rock, and Metal columns.

Note: Measured on 7-point Likert scales (1–7); [1,2,3...] significant differences between instruments (Scheffé post-hoc test, $p < .05$)

No significant variation exists between the two genders, level of professionalism, musical education and living situations. The relationship status makes a significant difference. Participants without a partner (M = 4.80, SD = 1.07) show a greater tendency towards GAS than participants with partner (M = 4.51, SD = 1.02), $t(587)$ = 2.71, p < .01, Hedges' g = 0.28.

Comparing the *General GAS* scale with the possession of music equipment reveals an interesting result: a largely opposing development in GAS and collection size across the lifespan. On average, older and more experienced players own more gear but are psychologically least prone to GAS. However, while GAS decreases with age, the instrument collection grows until reaching its peak in the fifties, after which it begins to decline again (Figure 4).

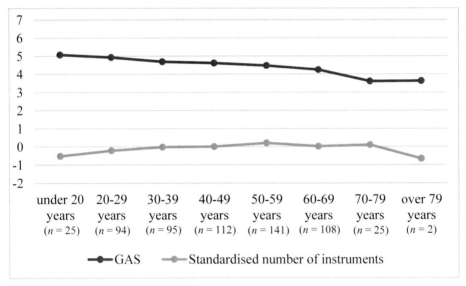

Fig. 4. Development of GAS and Ownership over Lifetime

Since the survey was designed as a cross-sectional study, insights into developmental processes are limited. In the open comments, some participants mention that their answers were based on their current practices. Yet their responses would have been different in earlier phases of their lives, which accords with consumption research arguing that material purchases and possessions reflect developments in life (Belk 1988; Belk et al. 2003; McClelland 1951; Shankar et al. 2009). The data indicate that the urge to buy new gear decreases as the collection increases. These results convey a more differentiated understanding than what Wright (2006: 45) suggests:

> With no glaring differences in the average responses of each group, the differences
> are not likely a function of age ... The younger guys are out there trying to start a
> family and keep the bills paid. The thirty-somethings have their families started,
> but the bills stack up as the kids get older ... The forty-somethings are dealing with
> other major life and career changes and are so disgusted with work that they focus

on early retirements and days of nothing but guitar playing. My group of old gee-zers may have empty nests and paid-up mortgages, but we're also living on fixed incomes. So, I suppose, about all of us are in the same boat, finance-wise and GAS-wise.

Several explanations can be given. Once the personally relevant models are in pos-session, there may be little need for further instruments or to buy the same model again (Straw 2000: 156f). In a musical context, the question remains how different a potential new instrument would have to be to justify its acquisition. Another expla-nation as to why experienced players are psychologically less affected by GAS is natural saturation. Older and more experienced players likely buy equipment based on a conscious decision, less driven by the feeling that this piece of gear is crucial for their musical development and success (Kwisses 2015; Leonhardt 2015). Some open comments support this explanation. Experienced musicians may have come to realise that changing equipment does not contribute much to progress as a player (Kwisses 2015; Leonhardt 2015). Younger musicians, on the other hand, may ex-plore various gear more extensively and change it frequently until they have found what works best for them, or they keep hoping that new gear will make the differ-ence. Especially in later phases of life, living conditions may require downsizing equipment or replacing instruments to account for ageing processes. In this context, the open comments indicate different and even contradictory practices. One guitar player states, 'as I grow older I tend to buy smaller, louder, lighter amps and cabs due to back and shoulder problems'. In a similar vein, another musician stresses to 'replace heavy old gear with lighter, more compact equipment'. Several more sea-soned musicians are reflecting that gear becomes less desirable with increasing age:

> I'm less interested in gear as I get older—it's not as exciting as when your younger, technology is new and changing all the time. Things have stabilised a lot more now, so there is a lot of 'more of the same' gear about, nice though some of it is. It's only gear though, and ultimately, it's not as important as your process, and the enjoyment and music you make from it.

This comment suggests that even though equipment and the latest technology is ex-citing for developing musicians, it is less important than making music. Another participant, a former professional musician about to retire, stresses that he will not buy any more equipment. Although he will continue to play, he will 'use much less of the gear and concentrate more on the music'. Nevertheless, he emphasises that he was interested in learning about gear in the past, which had inspired him in his com-positions. But other musicians of older age have taken a very different approach to gear in their practice. Many have stopped making music or reduced it in certain phases of their lives but enjoy it again later on in retirement. For example, a bassist notes that in the 1980s, he was content with just two instruments, but today he likes to experiment with gear, explaining: 'I'm getting older and don't know how long

I've got left in terms of playing. Better try out some different stuff'. However, he stresses that he does not want to buy new gear and finances his exploration through regular trading and gigs.

A regression analysis reveals clear predictors for GAS, $F(9, 524) = 40.50$, $p <$ .001, adj. $R^2 = .40$. The *General GAS* scale is closely linked to five of the attitudinal scales relating to personal and musical motives, which suggests that they are characteristic of the phenomenon: *Collectors* ($\beta = .31$, $p < .001$), *Expressiveness* ($\beta = .25$, $p < .001$), *Technophilia* ($\beta = .12$, $p < .001$), *Nostalgia* ($\beta = .12$, $p < .01$) and *Role Models* ($\beta = .12$, $p < .01$). Concurring with the challenges of separating GAS from collecting, a strong inclination to *Collecting* is the most important predictor, despite several comments indicating that participants who enjoy gear do not wish to be seen as collectors. *Expressiveness* shows the second-strongest correlation with the *General GAS* scale in the regression model. Also significant are *Technophilia* and *Role Models*, which emphasises that GAS is closely linked to various personal and musical motives and therefore may not be reduced to the mere accumulation of instruments or the pursuit of completeness of a collection. As with the z-standardised instrument ownership, there is a significant connection with the *Nostalgia* scale, but it is relatively weak. Regarding musical practice, the urge to acquire extra gear decreases with increasing playing experience ($\beta = -.16$, $p < .001$). From a sociodemographic perspective, the connections are not entirely clear: with increasing age, GAS is likely to decrease, men seem to be more affected than women, and musicians playing acoustic instruments seem less affected. Again, all these predictors do not load significantly if factors related to musical practice and personal and musical motivations are considered.

Unsurprisingly, all scales measuring attitudes related to musical equipment correlate with the *General GAS* scale. Most correlations are of low or medium strength (Appendix B). The strongest correlations exist with the *Band as GAS Motivator* ($r = .51$, $p < .001$) and the *Expressiveness* ($r = .49$, $p < .001$) scale, the weakest with *Democratic Purchases in Bands* ($r = .21$, $p < .001$). These results indicate that the player's personal development as a musician is a strong motivation for an interest in gear and that this interest is likely to be amplified when the musician plays in a band. The scale capturing the importance of the *Band as GAS Motivator* stems from the interviews conducted in a music store. Most of the musicians who visited the store with their bandmates either planned to buy gear that day or discussed what they wanted to acquire in the future. The survey results show that this practice is significantly less pronounced amongst wind players than drummers, bassists and guitarists. An explanation is that in a smaller band formation of drums, bass, guitars and possibly keyboards, each member's individual contribution to the overall sound of the group is more substantial so that negotiating personal tones makes sense. This interpretation is supported by the results of the *Democratic Purchases in Bands* scale. Although this practice finds hardly any agreement, guitarists differ from saxophone players (Table 3). It can be assumed that in guitar-oriented bands with at least two guitarists, the instruments and amplifiers of each player are discussed to ensure complementary sounds (Herbst 2017b).

The kind of band or ensemble the interviewees play in needs to be considered too. Musicians in a band playing mainly original compositions are significantly more affected by GAS ($M = 4.61$, $SD = 1.07$) than those who only play in other types of ensembles ($M = 4.39$, $SD = 1.03$), $t(421) = -2.09$, $p < .05$, Hedges' $g = 0.20$ (multiple answers were possible). The same applies to musicians who play in tribute bands ($M = 4.85$, $SD = 0.98$) compared to those in other types of ensembles ($M = 4.46$, $SD = 1.06$), $t(421) = -2.19$, $p < .05$, Hedges' $g = 0.37$, which corresponds to them owning a significant higher number of instruments and gear. Interestingly, there are no significant differences in terms of membership in big bands or orchestras. The results suggest that membership in various types of ensembles is associated with different attitudes towards acquiring musical equipment. Such aspects of buying musical gear will be explored in more detail in the following sections on personal, social and musical motives.

Personal Motives

As the predictors for GAS suggest, varying personal motivations might influence the handling of instruments (Table 3). The results confirm our assumption that GAS is not the same as collecting. Despite the strong agreement on practices characteristic of GAS, most participants do not consider themselves *Collectors*. Whereas the analysis of variance indicates significant differences, the conservative post-hoc test does not do so between instruments nor between the groups of genres or various types of bands. Some musicians do not wish to be associated with GAS, yet the connotations of collecting are even more negative. This view is reflected in the fact that this scale is rated by far the lowest among the personal motives. A musician explains accordingly: 'Despite owning a lot of stuff I don't consider myself a collector in the traditional sense and rarely feel like I have GAS or I absolutely have to have something. I never feel like I need to have a piece of gear because it is "the newest" or it is trendy'. Another professional guitarist expresses: 'I have an assortment of instruments, but do not consider myself to be a collector. Though I have participated in an online guitar forum for 15 years, and have learned a great deal about both production and custom instruments, I do not think I have ever had G.(uitar) A.(cquisition) S.(yndrom)'. He emphasises that all purchases were musically necessary because the equipment helped him to develop as a player and served the specific purpose for which the instrument was purchased. Both the quantitative results and comments suggest that GAS and collecting are distinct practices of which musicians have a different understanding, deeply intertwined with the values they associate with them. While the label 'GAS head' divides the musicians, with some rejecting it and others consciously defining themselves as such, collecting has predominantly negative connotations.

The open comments show that many musicians have a well-thought-out view about their use of gear. They acknowledge that there 'is no correlation between the amount of gear one owns and the quality of their gear to how well they play'. Although these musicians reject the notion of being affected by GAS, they stress that they enjoy acquiring new gear. This finding concurs with relevant research (Belk et al. 2003; Campbell 1987), claiming consumption to have life-affirming and pleasurable effects. Consequently, the quantitative data demonstrate that interest in the latest technological innovations and instruments (*Technophilia*) is relatively common. Keyboardists are significantly more interested in newer technologies than guitarists and saxophonists. Surprisingly, saxophonists differ significantly from trumpeters, with the latter having a greater affinity for new technologies. A plausible reason lies in the trumpeters' ideal of persistently playing in high registers, which can be observed in both the playing literature and in terms of musical role models (Haas 2011). When the playing technique reaches its limits, the instrument becomes a decisive factor. Hence the interest in technological innovation in the construction of instruments could be explained by the desired sound ideal and the high technical demands on playing. With trumpets, mouthpieces above all represent the haptic interface between the physical feeling of playing and musical expression, which corresponds to the high average number of mouthpieces reported by trumpeters in the survey (Table 2) and the comment of one trumpeter: 'I'm NEVER satisfied with a mouthpiece and am CONSTANTLY experimenting'. However, there must be more to the trumpeters' pronounced interest in instrument technology than this hypothetical explanation suggests. In order to clarify their affinity for technology, further qualitative research is necessary.

Bassists do not differ from players of other instruments regarding *Technophilia*, and their agreement with the scale is similar to that of guitarists. Both instruments are amongst those for which there is a generally keen interest in vintage equipment. Surprising is that keyboard players also value analogue synthesisers, as we expected them to be more open to technological innovation. The results confirm our assumption, at least for the guitar and synthesiser. Only very few comments explicitly reject technological innovation but stress they are 'not interested in trends'. In rock / alternative / punk as well as pop / folk / rock & roll, musicians score lowest on *Technophilia* and differ significantly from the ones playing classical / worship / instrumental music (Table 4). Regarding types of ensembles, musicians in orchestras rank significantly higher ($M = 3.95$, $SD = 1.10$) than the others ($M = 3.58$, $SD = 1.07$), $t(450) = -2.72$, $p < .01$, Hedges' $g = 0.34$. These two results may come as a surprise but can be explained by the high number of trumpeters in the subsamples. The *Vintage* scale captures the opposite of *Technophilia*. The results of both scales are not entirely conclusive (Table 3). Keyboardists and guitarists correspond to the assumption that they differ in their interest in technological innovation, but on the other hand, they have the same attitudes towards vintage equipment. Statistically speaking, none of the instruments differs in their preference for or against vintage instruments. Several reasons can account for this, for example, personal attitudes independent of the played instrument type or influence of musical preferences. Each instrument has evolved, and there are likely to be proponents of both older and newer technologies and the music traditionally played on them.

Many musicians tend to share a *nostalgic* view of the gear they once played (Boym 2001; Davis 1979) with little difference between instrument types, as the high average rating of the respective scale suggests (Table 3). Why guitarists are significantly more nostalgic than bass players is unclear, especially since their ratings of all scales in the 'personal motives' category are remarkably similar. The open comments are neither conclusive in this respect. One drummer stresses that he wants to keep his first kit for symbolic reasons, while a trumpeter explains just to have inquired about the same kind of instrument he played 26 years ago when he was an instrumentalist and ensemble leader in the US Navy. These reasons correspond to the relevance of 'reflective nostalgia' (Boym 2001: 49f) for musicians when dealing with instruments.

Modifying and fabricating instruments, practices that Walter Becker (1996) described in his introductory of the Gear Acquisition Syndrome as even more 'dangerous' than acquisition, are not too popular amongst the musicians in this study (Table 3). Statistically, the differences between the instruments are rather small. Guitar players modify their gear the most, followed by bass players, which can be explained by the broad consumer market for replacement pickups and assembly kits. Guitarists likely differ from bassists because their motivations for modifications (Herbst 2017c, 2019b) concern instruments rather than amplifiers. Many guitars in the lower and middle price range contain relatively cheap pickups that are not well suited for distorted sounds (Herbst 2016: 86ff). The saxophone, on the other hand, differs significantly from the guitar and bass, with much fewer modification options on the instrument.

The practice of modifying and fabricating is difficult to distinguish. In their open comments, some guitar and bass players state that they build their instruments either from scratch or with special assembly kits. For these instruments, there are also kits for building amplifiers and effects pedals. Modifying or building other instruments such as keyboards, drums and wind instruments is much more challenging if not impossible. A drummer points out that modifying 'the electronic parts of a set [is] far easier and doable than modifications of the drumset or hardware and the wearing parts (drumsticks, drum heads, cymbals, drum hoops) [and that they] get treated differently than more permanent parts. But they are equally important to the sound'. This statement indicates that analogue and electric gear is different when it comes to modifications. Interpreting the results requires taking into account what might be understood as a modification for individual instruments. As the same drummer high-lights, dampening the drumheads or changing the drum hoops could be regarded as modifications or just maintenance and minor adjustment. Again, the options to re-furbish and modify vary for each of the instruments examined in this study.

The differences in personal motives regarding genre are not significant (Table 4), whereas they are for musicians playing in a band with mainly original composi-tions compared to all other kinds of bands. These differences derive from: an interest in *Vintage* instruments ($M = 3.81$, $SD = 1.32$ vs $M = 3.34$, $SD = 1.25$, $t(449) = -3.94$, $p < .001$, Hedges' $g = 0.37$), *Nostalgia* ($M = 4.36$, $SD = 1.36$ vs $M = 4.05$, $SD = 1.46$, $t(449) = -2.30$, $p < .05$, Hedges' $g = 0.22$) and *Modification and Fabrication* ($M = 3.39$, $SD = 1.45$ vs $M = 2.86$, $SD = 1.34$, $t(452) = -4.08$, $p < .001$, Hedges' $g = 0.38$). A possible explanation is that players in bands with original compositions do not need to have overly versatile equipment and therefore can specialise, as, for instance, modifying their instruments for a specific aesthetic or using less flexible vintage gear. Furthermore, members of tribute bands show a more pronounced interest in *Vintage* instruments ($M = 4.17$, $SD = 1.39$ vs $M = 3.50$, $SD = 1.28$, $t(449) = -3.10$, $p < .01$, Hedges' $g = 0.51$), which may be fostered by valuing a long-established artist.

Social Motives

Pursuing a hobby and spending money on it is always influenced by the social envi-ronment. Being in a relationship and having a family can limit the time and money available for the hobby or serious leisure activity (Stebbins 2009). In connection with age and GAS over a lifetime, some of the open comments already demonstrated that the musician's social life could impact their buying behaviour and playing practices. Of the three scales in the category of social motives (Table 3), *Relationships*, which records the perceived influence of relationships on purchasing behaviour, finds the most agreement. In addition, respondents with a partner have significantly lower scores on the *General GAS* scale than those without. This indicates that being in a relationship and maybe even having a family seems to counteract GAS. However, neither the relationship status nor the agreement with the *Relationship* scale shows a correlation with the standardised number of items possessed. From the comments quoted before, we know that some musicians spend less time on their hobby for sev-eral years or even stop for decades to fulfil their family obligations, which is in line with general findings in music psychology (Gembris 2018: 236f). But this does not seem to be reflected in the amount of equipment possessed either. Hence quantitative and qualitative data do not paint a wholly consistent picture. Since we recruited the participants on online message boards, we can safely assume that the ones partaking in the survey are actively engaged in making music, whereas those taking a break did not participate. Consequently, the quantitative data are distorted and only allow the assumption that relationships and family have a stronger impact on a musician's practices (Wright 2006: 102ff) than the quantitative data suggest.

Journalistic sources on GAS only vaguely cover social factors such as new gear of bandmates or friends triggering a musician's urge to improve their equipment, also known as 'mimetic desire' (Girard 1977) or 'gear envy'. The survey filled some gaps in that it contributed to understanding how social factors may influence the urge to buy equipment. Although *Band as a Motivator for GAS* receives only mixed approval, significant differences exist between the instruments (Table 3), genres (Table 4) and types of groups. Saxophone players are less impacted by their bandmates than drummers, bassists and guitarists are. Similarly, trumpet players are less affected than bassists and guitarists. One possible explanation concerns the types of music and band formations that are characteristic of the respective instruments. For players of the two wind instruments, membership in a band may spark less desire to spend time and money on gear than for drummers, guitarists, bassists and keyboardists. These differences could come from wind instrumentalists who tend to play in larger ensembles in which several musicians play the same voice. It is therefore not to be expected that different wind instruments will affect the sound of the entire ensemble. In contrast, the sound of small four- or five-piece bands in a broadly defined pop formation depends on each player's sonic signature. Usually, only one drummer, one bassist, one keyboardist and one or two guitarists play in such bands, each role thus contributing considerably to the sound. The average agreement on this scale is highest among the guitarists, which may be due to a tendency for guitar players to respond to gear changes of the other guitarist, which can trigger a chain of continuous adjustments. Given this background, it is not surprising that jazz / blues / soul / funk score lowest and differ significantly from all other genres but classical / worship / instrumental. Metal / progressive / hardcore score highest and differ from all other genres, except for rock / alternative / punk, with a medium to strong effect size (Table 4). Significant differences between the types of groups support this assumption. For example, the scale is rated highest for musicians in bands with mainly original compositions ($M = 3.69$, $SD = 1.51$ vs $M = 3.05$, $SD = 1.45$, $t(447) = -4.57$, $p < .001$, Hedges' $g = 0.43$), which are probably bands consisting of guitar, bass, drums and keyboards rather than wind-focused ensembles. Lower ratings received members in big bands ($M = 2.77$, $SD = 1.45$ vs $M = 3.52$, $SD = 1.49$, $t(447) = 4.51$, $p < .001$, Hedges' $g = 0.51$) and orchestras ($M = 3.04$, $SD = 1.55$ vs $M = 3.42$, $SD = 1.50$, $t(447) = 1.99$, $p < .05$, Hedges' $g = 0.25$). Another indication for this interpretation of differences between the standard 'pop instruments' and the wind instruments is given by the scale *Democratic Purchases in Bands*. Even though the respective scale finds the least agreement of all, guitar and saxophone players differ significantly (Table 3). Guitar players are more likely to give other band members a say. Consequently, musicians playing metal / progressive / hardcore score significantly higher than those playing jazz / blues / soul / funk. However, there are exceptions to this line of reasoning. A tenor saxophone player points out that he changed his preferred mouthpiece for the first time in thirty years because otherwise, he would overpower the lead alto saxophone in his jazz group. In his previous ensembles, there was no such problem, suggesting that even within a larger ensemble, individual playing styles may require fellow bandmates to adjust their equipment. In general, however, *Democratic Purchases* play a more significant role in bands with mainly original compositions ($M = 2.46$, $SD = 1.48$ vs $M = 2.03$, $SD = 1.21$, $t(415.47) = -3.38$, $p <$ .001, Hedges' $g = 0.32$). Musicians playing in cover or top 40 bands seem to be less affected than those in other types of groups ($M = 2.09$, $SD = 1.25$ vs $M = 2.38$, $SD = 1.45$, $t(435.83) = 2.29$, $p < .05$, Hedges' $g = 0.22$), as cover artists most likely need highly versatile equipment.

At first sight, the survey results seem to contradict the open comments somewhat. While the quantitative results show a rather unexpected low influence of bands on the musicians' gear behaviours, many open comments suggest the opposite. An in-depth analysis of the open comments indicates that many respondents disagree with the assumption underlying the *Band as GAS Motivator* scale that bands create an urge to buy new equipment. These comments suggest that belonging to a band may indeed lead to purchases which, however, are motivated by an actual need to maintain or advance their (leisure) career (Stebbins 2009) rather than by 'gear envy' (Belk et al. 2003; Girard 1977). One drummer highlights that he invests in gear to make his setup work during live performances: 'Most new equipment I purchase is to keep my kit sounding good for gigs (new heads, sticks) to replace broken items (cymbals etc.) or to make gigging easier (memory locks, hardware, drum rug and trolley)'. Another musician points out that the stylistic diversity of the bands he plays in requires him to have a variety of equipment:

> Generally I buy gear when I need a specific piece for a job. I do a lot of live work as well as studio and pit bands, so I need to have gear to cover a multitude of styles/sounds. There are some gigs which allow me the flexibility to use whatever gear I want (e.g. church music director), while others require specific sounds (e.g. pit bands & studio work).

This line of reasoning can be found in several comments. Some musicians stress not only to buy gear according to their band's requirements but also to modify it.

When buying gear in connection to bands, another consideration concerns whether it will be played live or in the studio. As one participant explains:

> for example my live gear is completely separate from my practice gear. This is so that I can have my practice gear always set up and my live gear is always in the same place ready to load in the car. It's about time saving and ease of use as well as the comfort of never arriving at a [gig] finding you forget to pack something because it is still set up in the practice room.

One of the guitarists highlights having different amplifiers for various types of venues, which has nothing to do with the acoustics (Bennett 2017: 175ff) but access to the stage. If access is easy, he uses the better sounding valve amplifier and otherwise, he settles for a lighter but sonically worse transistor option.

Musical Motives

In addition to personal and social factors, we expected musical motives to foster an interest in gear. With their considerable importance for musicians at all career stages (Green 2002), role models can indirectly influence the kind of gear a musician chooses, or unique signature models can get them closer to the valued artist's sound and music. This interest in gear is reflected in books like *Rolling Stones Gear: All the Stones' Instruments from Stage to Studio* (Babiuk & Prevost 2014), *Beatles Gear: All the Fab Four's Instruments from Stage to Studio* (Babiuk 2016) and *Grateful Dead Gear: All the Band's Instruments, Sound Systems and Recording Sessions From 1965-1995* (Jackson 2006), all of which glorify the gear of rock bands from the 1960s and 1970s. According to the blurbs, such books promise to reveal the 'origins and secrets of the Grateful Dead's magical sound', created by 'cutting edge of technological innovation and experimentation' (Jackson 2006). Babiuk (2016) claims to accurately document the development of the Fab Four 'from cheap early instruments to the pick of 1960s technology' in 'an easy-to-read narrative, fully illustrated with many previously unseen photographs, a cache of rare memorabilia, and a unique collection of specially photographed instruments used by the Beatles'. Similarly, Babiuk and Prevost (2014) aim to provide an alternative band story of the Rolling Stones 'but with a new twist: their history as told through what instruments were used during their recording sessions and tour dates' by studying '[e]very song recorded by the band, including all demos and outtakes … with input from people who were involved with the band throughout their career'.

Although research and special-interest books clearly indicate that musicians are affected by *Role Models* when choosing gear, the survey results do not at all support such an assumption. The respective scale is rated second lowest of all (Table 3), and it neither proves relevant across all instruments and genres. Once more, guitar and saxophone players differ significantly from each other, with guitarists showing more interest in the gear of their idols. While the overall low relevance of role models is surprising, the result that guitarists are interested in the sounds of renowned artists corresponds with special-interest books. In *Gear Secrets of the Guitar Legends: How to Sound Like Your Favorite Players*, Prown and Sharken (2003) teach guitarists 'what equipment their favourite players use, and more importantly, how to sound just like them' by drawing on artist interviews and 'featuring rig diagrams, amplifier settings, and sound tips', making the book the 'bible for rock guitar tone'. Similarly, in *100 Great Guitarists and the Gear That Made Them Famous*, Rubin (2018) focuses on revealing the 'magic behind the masters'. These two books show the deterministic belief in the connection between the gear of 'legendary' artists and their playing, which newer players wish to adapt. There are even several books dedicated to just one player. In *Jimi Hendrix Gear: The Guitars, Amps and Effects That Revolutionized Rock 'n' Roll*, Heatley and Shapiro (2009) examine

> all of Hendrix's equipment, providing a nuts-and-bolts analysis of each of his guitars (including serial number, history, provenance), choice of amps, and his singular use of revolutionary effects, from wah-wahs to overdrives to bizzar-o pedals like the Fuzzface. A practical reference book like no other, this volume gives the proper guidance and tools to any guitarist who wants to emulate and learn from the greatest guitar player of all time.

This book is not only a useful resource for those who want to emulate their role model but also for collectors, as little-known facts like serial numbers are disclosed. In *Zappa's Gear: The Unique Guitars, Amplifiers, Effects Units, Keyboards and Studio Equipment*, Ekers (2020) 'offers an unprecedented inside look at the machinery behind the legendary music' of Frank Zappa, primarily focusing on his guitar equipment. What is striking about these books is the role gear plays in connection with musical legacy. In *Paul Kossoff: All Right Now: The Guitars, the Gear, the Music*, in which James (2017) honours the late founding guitarist of the rock band Free, Kossoff, whose equipment is covered in more detail than the music or his life. The gear's relevance is reflected in the title. About the other instruments considered in this study, few special-interest books, if any at all, exist devoting entirely or predominantly to a renowned player's equipment, which supports the results that guitarists seem to have a closer connection to esteemed players and their gear than other musicians. The open comments reflect that; every single one writing about being influenced by role models is a guitarist.

Two further criteria, genre and type of band, have only a weak impact. Metal / progressive / hardcore score highest, differing significantly from pop / folk / rock & roll and rock / alternative / punk (Table 4). Musicians playing in bands with mainly original compositions ($M = 2.54$, $SD = 1.09$) show a much stronger orientation towards *Role Models* ($M = 2.09$, $SD = 0.98$, $t(429.10) = -4.53$, $p < .001$, Hedges' $g = 0.43$). Interestingly, musicians playing in tribute bands do not differ from those playing in other types of ensembles. It might be that these musicians ignored the two related items on the scale, 1) a change in the equipment due to shifting music preferences and 2) a change in the equipment of the role model. In many cases, tribute bands are characterised by an enduring passion for particular musicians or bands. If role models were active in past times, there are no current changes in the equipment used.

Contrary to the generally low importance of role models for most musicians, other musical motives such as *Expressiveness* are more prevalent amongst the survey participants (Table 3). The scale ranks third among all scales, showing that many participants see their gear choice closely linked to expressiveness. They expect that deliberate acquisition of equipment helps them to overcome limitations, improve their sound and inspire their playing, also known as 'facilitation' (Hartmann 2016).

Two instruments are particularly prone to this facilitating effect, the guitar and the keyboard, both of which vary significantly from the saxophone. In this respect, the guitar also differs from the bass and trumpet. This result confirms the expectation that keyboard and guitar players rely heavily on the right sound of their instrument and benefit from its positive effects on playability and expression.

However, despite the high average approval of the *Expressiveness* scale, the open comments present fundamentally different opinions amongst the participants. For some musicians, gear and new acquisitions are deeply linked to their musical development. As a guitarist explains:

> Sometimes if you are lucky, a new guitar, if it is of sufficient quality, will 'teach' you how to play it. I've learned an enormous amount from a particular guitar. It almost insists that it be played in certain ways. All instruments do this for one reason or another. Some are just better teachers with more musically profound lessons to learn.

This quote suggests that instruments can fulfil functions like teachers or more experienced mentors. Unfortunately, the guitarist does not explain the reasoning behind this theory, but it likely concerns the fact that instruments or other gear can expose problems in playing technique. For example, distortion masks sloppy synchronisation between the guitarist's fretting and picking hand and reduces the dynamic range, making playing easier but less expressive (Herbst 2017c, 2019b). That is the reason why with increasing skill, many electric guitarists gradually 'purify' their amplification chain by replacing digital or transistor-based practice amps with valve amplifiers. For keyboardists, new instruments may motivate their players to experiment with sound design or expressive modulation while playing. Drummers may develop more dexterity and control by adding new pieces to their kit. Wind players may benefit from experimenting with mouthpieces or new instruments, which might be models from another period when the music was traditionally played on them. What all instrumentalists have in common is that they benefit from acquisitions that motivate them to learn new styles.

The scale *Expressiveness* captures the assumption of gear to be inspiring, which the high level of agreement supports. Several open comments allow further insight. One guitarist notes:

> The relationship between the artist and the instrument is a complex one and varies a lot from player to player—some just see instruments as tools and others have to have their favourite axe or they just can't play as well... I think for all musicians having a good sound is inspiring and if it doesn't sound good then you probably won't play as well. Some instruments are just special—I've tried a lot of guitars and saxes but only a few of them had that certain 'something'—that indefinable quality that makes it feel almost alive. Some instruments are so good they almost play themselves and you realise the amount of struggle involved in playing lesser

instruments. This is what makes us keep searching for 'the one'. At it's best a musical instrument is the perfect combination of form and function.

Consistent with the guitar as the instrument whose players rate expressiveness highly, surpassed only by keyboardists, it is mostly guitarists who emphasise the instrument's inspirational value in their comments.

> The one thing your survey doesn't tap is a guitarists affection for and fascination with guitars. I really need only one guitar to play everything that I play, but I am interested in how different guitars play and sound. I have ladder braced and x braced guitars because they each have distinct qualities—neither sounds better. Some of my guitars were expensive, some not so much. I have one $300 guitar that has a beautiful quality and I get tremendous pleasure from it partly because it reminds me how price and build don't guarantee anything.

This guitarist brings up the important point that inspirational gear does not need to be expensive. It must be comfortable and functional and support its player's sonic visions and personal styles, which is underlined in several other comments.

In this context, a much larger number of comments stress that the role of gear should not be overemphasised, as it had little influence on music. Some stress that it is the musicians themselves and not their equipment that limits what is possible. A skilled player will always be convincing, as one participant depicts in detail:

> Gear is important, but not the holy grail. Charlie Parker sounded great on a plastic sax, Jimmy Page rocked on an el-cheapo Danelectro, James Jamerson had an old beat up, warped neck, almost unplayable bass by the standards of the day. To me the gear is third in importance. First: Your musicality and what you do with the gear is most important. The nuances, ornaments, dynamics, phrasing, choice of notes, intonation, timing, fx, etc., and how you use them to create something that is expressive enough to connect with the audience. Second: Technique—it's not an end in itself but it allows you to express what you feel inside. IMO [in my opinion] the music should never serve the technique, but you should use your chops to serve the music. Example: Saxophonist Stan Getz had monster chops, but you rarely hear them, all you hear is music. Third: Gear—the gear has to be decent and capable of doing what you ask of it. But there is a point of diminishing returns where X amount of additional dollars gives you less and less benefit for each X you add. Extra expense for things like signatures, road worn, etc., IMHO [in my humble opinion] are a waste of money. When I bought my last guitar I found a model I liked, and had the factory install the pickups that I wanted. That cost $20 extra. When I bought my last sax, I found a model I liked and had them put nickel plating on it because my hands and brass don't like each other. Neither the guitar nor the sax were top-of-the-line, but they were excellent instruments that got to my point of diminishing returns. I'll probably keep them until they wear out or I can no longer play. I think if people spent as much time working on expression as obsessing about new gear, we'd all be playing better music.

Many comments concur with this belief. It is the music that counts, and equipment is just a means to that end (Cole 2018). From those who pursue music as a hobby, several stress it is the enjoyment of playing that motivates them, not the gear they use.

Before, we discussed the comment of a musician who stated that new gear helped him grow musically. Many other musicians contest this claim, as they do not see a connection between their playing and equipment. One states, 'I place my technique ahead of my gear. That is, I believe my musical expressiveness comes from how I play, not from the bass, amp and effects I use. Rhythm, harmony and listening are what will make me a better musician'. These musicians consider gear less relevant than practising, and yet others see no correlation at all between the quantity of their equipment and the quality of their playing. For those who hold this opinion, making music is all about practising while gear would even bear the risk of hampering musical development (Cole 2018). This opinion is consistent with the views of composers who work with manifestos that limit their resources in the hope of being more creative (Herbert 2005). As the experimental guitar and electronic artist Christian Fennesz (2014) in an interview expresses:

> I think that the main problem with the world today is that we have too many options and I really try to downsize mine as much as I can because otherwise it is just too confusing. I could try out a new plugin every two hours but it doesn'[t] lead me anywhere, so over the years I have got a few tools that work for me and that's it now. I just don'[t] want to use more stuff anymore it's just too much. Many options is the biggest problem with technology today.

Yet, some musicians highlight that if gear is old or unsuitable for the purpose, it can indeed be limiting and hindering musical development and creativity. However, with growing skilfulness, new equipment does not help musician to improve much further. To ensure that gear does not become an obstacle to musical intentions, many players, regardless of instrument, stress to be looking for versatility when acquiring new equipment.

The scale *Sound Exploring* measures how crucial it is to try out and combine sounds and to get a comprehensive understanding of the equipment to tweak the tone according to the musician's vision. It is therefore slightly different from the *Expressiveness* scale, which gathers the extent to which new gear helps to inspire and overcome limitations. The two scales correlate with medium strength ($r = .38$; $p < .001$). Both scales find an equally high level of agreement, irrespective of the type of instrument (Table 3). The general approval shows that most players invest a lot of time to understand how their instrument produces the best possible sound. On the one hand, musicians inspired by their gear could benefit from having a good understanding of their equipment. On the other hand, some musicians may not like to tweak their equipment and would rather change it before getting the most out of it, also known as 'flipping' (Cole 2018: 1059ff). Just as Théberge (1993: 248) observes two types of keyboard players, those who like to customise and those who select ready-made preset sounds, musicians of other instruments may prefer to either tweak their sound or hope to get the sound they want immediately, and if not, they would look for other gear. *Sound Exploring* also corresponds to *Modification and Fabrication of equipment* ($r = .42$; $p < .001$). In this respect, the open comments suggest that there may not be a black and white distinction but that habits depend on a player's expertise. Some musicians explain that they did much exploring of sound settings and combining gear, but less and less so when they found out what combinations of equipment, settings and sounds worked best for them. Therefore, the exploring and tweaking of sounds may be a distinct learning phase that, even though frequently occurring in the life of a musician, would not characterise their behaviour in general.

The scale *Experimentation* deals with a similar intention of musicians, the importance of a personal or innovative sound in connection with an instrumental technology or its unconventional application. In this, it shows a similar conceptualisation to the scales *Expressiveness* and *Sound Exploring* and thus correlates relatively strongly with both (*Expressiveness*: $r = .54$; $p < .001$; *Sound Exploring*: $r = .52$; $p < .001$), though each has an individual focus that refers to distinct artistic practices. The category of musical motives (Table 3) shows the three scales *Experimentation*, *Expressiveness* and *Sound Exploring* ranking highest. Interpreting this result suggests that many musicians need to acquire new gear to experiment and tweak it to find a sound that corresponds to their aesthetic idea and playing style. Compared to the lower approval of the scales *Role Models* and *Genre Requirements*, the results suggest that a personal sound of good quality ranks higher than orientation towards external factors. This supposed attitude seems to be familiar with all instrumentalists because the Scheffé post-hoc test again identified no significant differences between instruments for the two scales *Experimentation* and *Sound Exploring*. That may come as a surprise since some instruments like guitar, bass and keyboards can be tweaked and customised more substantially than the wind instruments. On the other hand, wind instruments make it relatively easy to adjust the sound by replacing mouthpieces, which seems to be a widespread practice, especially among trumpeters.

However, there are differences with medium effect size between the genres. Musicians playing metal / progressive / hardcore score highest, differing significantly not only from all other genres on the scale *Sound Exploring* but also on *Expressiveness* and *Experimentation*, except for classical / worship / instrumental (Table 4). Against our assumptions, musicians playing classical / worship / instrumental music achieve the second highest scores on all three scales, demonstrating an interest in sound and its creative affordances. Here again, the kind of bands plays a significant role with musicians in bands playing mainly original compositions differing from others on all three scales: *Expressiveness* ($M = 4.64$, $SD = 1.32$ vs $M = 4.11$, $SD = 1.34$, $t(451) = -4.27$, $p < .001$, Hedges' $g = 0.40$), *Experimentation* ($M = 4.45$, $SD = 1.21$ vs $M = 3.61$, $SD = 1.18$, $t(451) = -4.47$, $p < .001$, Hedges' $g = 0.70$), *Sound*

Exploring (*M* = 4.78, *SD* = 1.29 vs *M* = 4.12, *SD* = 1.37, *t*(454) = –5.33, *p* < .001, Hedges' *g* = 0.50). In contrast, members of big bands score lower on the *Expressiveness* scale (*M* = 3.99, *SD* = 1.44 vs *M* = 4.47, *SD* = 1.31, *t*(451) = 3.16, *p* < .01, Hedges' *g* = 0.35). Regarding *Experimentation*, members of cover or top 40 bands score lower than members playing in other types of groups (*M* = 3.85, *SD* = 1.21 vs *M* = 4.17, *SD* = 1.30, *t*(451) = 2.71, *p* < .01, Hedges' *g* = 0.26). These results are hardly surprising. While musicians in cover and top 40 bands generally try to get as close as possible to the copied artist, bands who write and perform original music normally want to create something new. Such novelty includes compositions but extends to the sonic domain, where uniqueness is usually viewed positively (Théberge 1997: 191).

Research in popular music studies (Cutler 1995; Herbst 2017a, b; Jones 1992; Théberge 1997) indicates that the right equipment can support playing and that there are gear conventions in genres. A glance at online discussion boards or music magazines confirms that instruments are advertised for specific genres. Even subgenres of the same genre may require different instruments, amplifiers and accessories. However, the results do not fully confirm this. The participants hardly agree that playing specific *Genres* require specialised equipment, which corresponds to the negligible relevance of genre-specific criteria when buying gear. Nevertheless, there are differences between instruments; guitar, keyboard and trumpet players see significantly more need for genre-specific equipment than saxophonists. This discrepancy might result from different instrument models, amplifiers and accessories. Not all instrumentalists may need special equipment to conform to genre conventions to the same extent as guitarists. The open comments support the impression of differences between instruments. A saxophonist points out that 'certain mouthpieces are best for certain genres, but the saxophone itself can be used for any genre'. In this respect, saxophonists would not require specialised equipment for different genres, though stylistically versatile players could benefit from genre-appropriate mouthpieces. Guitarists, however, must consider their choice of instrument and amplification for various genres, as one player hints at: 'I play three different styles, fingerpicking, slide and lap steel, and I have several instruments for each'. Here styles are equated with different instruments, which, although being a rare example, still shows that even electric guitar models can be better suited for specific genres. As to that, a guitarist states:

> For every musician I know the main goal is to achieve the desired sound within the band the gear is bought and modded for. For hardcore with a strong focus on recognizable fastly played riffs for example, the fitting gear becomes a neccecity. A git with a blues focus, bass heavy elements put through a Vox amp won't do even though the sound itself is awesome. So gear is bought for the particular Project, not for the ego enlargement.

However, the quantitative data do not support, as theoretically could be assumed, the highly genre-specific gear requirements. Once more only musicians playing in bands with original compositions ($M = 3.90$, $SD = 1.28$) differ from those playing in other types of groups ($M = 3.63$, $SD = 1.26$, $t(453) = -2.28$, $p < .05$, Hedges' $g = 0.21$). For cover and top 40 bands, the results suggest that equipment with versatile sound possibilities is as important as the instruments that are optimally tailored to sound requirements of specific genres.

Another reason why genre might play a relatively minor role in the participants' eyes is that the aim of having an individual sound may compete with genre conformity. As Théberge (1997: 191) argues, 'a concentration on the "right" sounds for a given musical context can shift the musician's attention away from other, more familiar levels of musical form, such as melody, rhythm, and harmony', hence from the structural conventions of genres. A 'unique and personal "sound"' (Théberge 1997: 191) is valued more highly. The results show that the two scales, *Sound Exploring* and *Expressiveness*, are the two highest-rated scales right after *General GAS*, supporting Théberge's claim. It is a clear indicator against the '*push-and-play* or *plug-and-play*' mentality, according to which 'people … do not want to get very involved in the technical aspect of recording and music making, but … do want to perform or to create music' (Jones 1992: 85f).

All in all, the differences between genres and instruments are smaller than we had expected as per the theoretical considerations we made throughout this book. The respective findings are only partly consistent with previous empirical research suggesting distinct personality traits of musicians of diverse instruments types (Bell & Cresswell 1984; Cameron et al. 2015; see also Rötter & Steinberg 2018). The quantitative data may not be conclusive here, but some open comments give hints that different instruments require different practices. A multi-instrumentalist expressed it this way:

> I play sax and keyboard in a few different bands and situations. Although I said my main instrument was sax, I found I answered the gear questions thinking more about keyboards. I own 5 vintage saxes that I play and I'm not planning on buying more. Keyboards and other electronic gear, on the other hand, are constantly being upgraded.

497 of the 668 participants, almost three quarters (74%) of the sample, play more than one instrument. This number includes vocals and other instruments not considered in the survey. One might assume that multi-instrumentalists differ from mono-instrumentalists in their views and practices, as they are part of different instrumental traditions. However, the only scale with significant differences is *Vintage*. Multi-instrumentalists ($M = 3.58$, $SD = 1.27$) appreciate vintage instruments more than mono-instrumentalists ($M = 3.33$, $SD = 1.25$), $t(656) = -2.22$, $p < .05$, with a small effect, Hedges' $g = 0.20$. There is no discernible theoretical reason as to why this is

the case. Neither do differences exist between mono- and multi-instrumentalists in the number of instruments possessed. Yet it should be noted that the questionnaire only asked for instruments and items of the category to which the respondents committed themselves with their main instrument. Since many respondents state to play and presumably own other instruments, the full extent of the instrument collections likely exceeds the reported number, which makes it even more impressive. Other differences between mono- and multi-instrumentalists did not occur, which indicates that multi-instrumentalists have not blurred the differentiation between the types of instruments. It thus appears that more general, overarching attitudes impact the musicians' views and behaviours that cannot be related directly to the instrument. If anything, it is more likely to involve a preference for acoustic or electric models, with players of the latter being more prone to GAS.

Gender

The survey sample was highly uneven in terms of gender, as only 4% ($n = 28$) were women. This low rate is consistent with Herbst's (2017a) study of guitar players, in which even fewer participants were female (2%). Unfortunately, no statistics are available on the gender distribution in online communities of musicians, leaving it open to speculation as to whether women were not motivated by the topic to participate in the survey or whether this number reflects an accurate representation of women in these communities. Traditionally, the drums and the electric guitar, in particular, have been male-dominated, but this seems to be changing as recent developments point to a slow move towards a more balanced proportion, at least for guitar players. Hence, we expect that the female musicians across all instruments in the sample population are under-represented, not even coming close to the actual ratio. Altogether, the number of women in our sample is too small to test gender differences reliably. However, the regression analyses presented earlier indicate only marginal differences in dealing with equipment between men and women. Further research with a more balanced gender ratio is required.

6.4 Discussion

GAS is an unexplored phenomenon in music and many other fields and professions. The purpose of this survey was to challenge our working theory and to extend it based on various sources of qualitative and quantitative data. The results and findings raise as many new questions as they answer others, which fits the research design.

Chapters 4 and 5 have shown how close a person's identity is connected to collecting and consumption. Our expectation that sociodemographic factors would play a role in terms of equipment use and attitudes towards it was statistically only partially confirmed. The data suggest that professionals and experienced players tend to have more extensive equipment collections. The same could be observed for older musicians and men, but these predictors were not significant in the regression analysis. However, the affinity for *Collecting* and maintaining a *Nostalgic* relationship with music contributes to a higher number of owned equipment as well.

GAS has been measured and put into context in several explicit and implicit ways. The scale capturing GAS found the highest agreement of all fourteen scales, suggesting that most participants are impacted in one way or another. Some musicians seem to regard GAS as part of their musical identity, while others are merely interested in music technology. These technophile musicians refuse to be classified as GAS-afflicted because of negative connotations. They justify their interest in equipment and its acquisition with musical necessity and reject the label GAS because they equate it with interest in gear for gear's sake. Negative connotations are even more ascribed to collecting, so most participants do not want to be regarded as collectors. GAS and collection sizes correlate, but GAS decreases with age, while instrument collections grow until the fifties and only then begin to decline. One possible explanation is that older musicians are more interested in music than in gear, either generally or because they have experimented substantially in their younger years and found out what gear they wish to play. Non-musical career development, retirement and family responsibilities are other reasons for GAS to decline. What contributes to GAS is shown by the statistical analyses: being a *Collector*, the belief that gear helps with musicality (*Expressiveness*), an interest in music technology (*Technophilia*), holding a nostalgic view about instruments (*Nostalgia*), being inspired by a *Role Model*. Factors that lower GAS were extensive playing experience, higher age and a preference for acoustic instruments, the latter two not significant in the regression analysis. These findings are largely consistent with the various blog posts on GAS and the theoretical considerations in chapters 2 and 3.

Concerning gender, a nuanced interpretation is necessary, not least because of the gender imbalance in the sample populations of the pre-study and the survey. The survey suggests that men tend to own more equipment and achieve higher scores on the *General GAS* scale and thus appear to be more susceptible to GAS than women. Some men feel restricted in their buying behaviour when they are in a relationship. Otherwise, male and female musicians did not differ in terms of attitudes and criteria for selecting musical instruments in a buying situation.

In addition to these overarching sociodemographic factors, we were interested in personal, social and musical motives related to gear practices. Personal motives hardly determine a strong interest in music technology for the sake of technology (*Technophilia*) or *Vintage* gear. *Nostalgia* is much more relevant, which is supported and further illustrated by some of the open comments. What we did not anticipate was that social motives are, on the whole, of relatively minor significance. Unreferenced in the literature on GAS but observed in the music store, the practice of *democratically deciding on purchases in bands* seems to be uncommon. Some of the musical motives we expected to be relevant were not. The influence of *Role Models* is minimal, and neither are *Genre Requirements* important. Academic literature and special-interest books suggest that specific genres and styles benefit from certain instruments and gear, and so do the musicians who play them. This expectation has only partially been confirmed. Nearly all musicians rejected the *Genre Requirements* scale, which measured the need to select instruments based on the requirements of specific genres. However, we identified minor but significant differences in attitudes towards music equipment and susceptibility to GAS between different groups of genres. Musicians in particular of the genres metal / progressive / hardcore are more affected by GAS and have higher scores on the scales covering personal, social and musical motives towards music equipment. Except for the scales *Band as GAS Motivator* and musical motives such as *Expressiveness*, *Experimentation* and *Sound Exploring*, the differences turned out to be smaller than expected. Especially musicians of the genres classical / worship / instrumental exhibited higher values on some dimensions than we presumed ahead of the investigation. Because subsamples were too small to allow for further statements at the level of individual genres, the genres were combined into groups. Further studies that specifically focus on selected genres could generate additional insights in this context. The quite low relevance of genre conformity and role models might be explained by the relatively high average age of 46 years and the playing experience of 26 years. People are emotionally attached to music most strongly in adolescence and early adulthood (North & Hargreaves 1999; Schäfer & Sedlmeier 2018). As we have seen in the music store, young metal bands 'lived' the genre with all its expectations and clichés. The older metal bands we observed and interviewed showed no such signs. Another finding was that 82% played four or more genres, while the remaining 18% of the survey population played less than three. Due to this stylistic versatility and openness, which goes hand in hand with older age and higher playing experience, it is unlikely that musicians will want to conform completely to each of the genres they play. We can therefore assume that performing a larger number of styles does not typically lead to a more extensive instrument collection, as we have argued in chapter 2, but when it does, then most likely by younger musicians.

The criteria decisive for choosing an instrument are similarly mature. Essential is, without a doubt, 'sound quality', 'playability and feel' and 'workmanship'. Price and appearance play a minor role, but only if the main criteria are met. In line with previous results, other factors such as role models, genre suitability, authenticity and current trends are quite insignificant.

Our observations, experience as musicians and music lecturers, besides the literature on music technology and popular music, suggest that players of different instruments have diverging attitudes and practices regarding musical equipment. Yet the survey did not give definite answers, thus meeting our expectations only partly.

The size of gear collections is somewhat arbitrary to allow for a thorough comparison between instruments. Neither did the scales provide us with the clear distinctions we had expected. While nine of the fourteen scales showed significant differences between instruments in the post-hoc test, these were often only between two or three of the instruments, and in all cases but one, *Band as GAS Motivator*, had small effect sizes. On the other hand, many open comments supported the notion that the characteristics of each instrument afford different practices and correlate in various ways with the underlying attitudes towards gear.

Further evidence of this differentiation can be found in comments on the survey design. Some multi-instrumentalists emphasised that their answers concerned their primary instrument and would have turned out differently if they had been for another instrument. It is impossible to say whether the size of their gear collection and their attitudes towards them would have been impacted. Comparing the attitudes between mono- and multi-instrumentalists only revealed a minor significant difference regarding interest in *Vintage* instruments. Nevertheless, we must keep in mind that some questions may have been more relevant for a group of instruments than for another. Participants also pointed out that some questions were guitar-related, such as gear settings, which has no direct counterpart in the wind instruments.

Since sampling took place on online message boards for musicians, it can be assumed that the survey captured a specific group of participants. Most were from Europe and North America, predominantly male and likely to have an above-average interest in musical instruments. Many might have sensed that the study was on GAS, preventing them from participating, with the consequence that musicians without pronounced interest in gear might be underrepresented in the sample. Insights into developments over the lifespan are limited due to the cross-sectional design of the study. Another uncertain factor concerns the truthfulness of the answers due to participants anticipating the survey's topic. We do not assume that the respondents deliberately gave wrong answers, but the ambiguous thinking we found in the qualitative interviews and extensive instrument collections could infer *perceived* reality. Furthermore, the sub-samples of the instruments did not equal in size; keyboardists and drummers were less represented than guitarists and bassists. As a final minor limitation, the results may have been influenced by a tendency towards higher alpha errors due to the calculation of several analyses of variance.

7 Online Message Boards

In the previous chapters, we have discussed personal, musical and social motives for musicians to spend time, money and thought on equipment. Many of the personal and musical reasons were partly of social nature. In popular music, it shows in musicians generally performing together with other musicians, so it is to be expected that playing and dealing with instruments reflects social order. This chapter extends the previous survey and the theoretical considerations on GAS by shifting the focus from individual musicians to special-interest communities meeting on online message boards. These forums can be understood as 'Communities of Practice' as introduced by Lave and Wenger (1991) and refined by Wenger (1998). Wenger (1998: 45) explains these communities of practice as follows:

> Being alive as human beings means that we are constantly engaged in the pursuit of enterprises of all kinds … As we define these enterprises and engage in their pursuit together, we interact with each other and with the world and we tune our relations with each other and with the world accordingly. In other words, we learn. Over time, this collective learning results in practices that reflect both the pursuit of our enterprises and the attendant social relations. These practices are thus the property of a kind of community created over time by the sustained pursuit of a shared enterprise.

As per Wenger (1998: 47), any practice is a social practice, characterised by both explicit and tacit elements that are expressed through language, images, symbols, codified procedures, untold rules of thumb and shared world views, most of which are never openly articulated.

Communities of practice are defined by three dimensions (Wenger 1998: 73–83). *Mutual engagement* refers to the nature of the community and the relationship of its participants. Although not everybody needs to know the entire community, a member is expected to understand the group's unwritten rules and knowledge. This does not mean that communities are homogenous; on the contrary, 'conflict and misery can even constitute the core characteristic of a shared practice' (Wenger 1998: 77). Nevertheless, the norms, whether accepted or disputed, are vital for the community. Communities of practice are further established through a *joint enterprise*, the shared practice of its members. In other words, the community results from the collective practices and the negotiation thereof. These practices do not exist in isolation, as they overlap with other communities of practice, and besides, collective practices are situated in broader historical, social, cultural and institutional contexts. *Shared repertoire* is the resources created in collaborative practice that define meaning. Such resources include routines, stories, gestures, practices and symbols that shape the 'discourse by which members create meaningful statements about the world, as well as the styles by which they express their forms of membership and their identities as members' (Wenger 1998: 83). Indicators of communities of practice are engaging in doing things together, sharing information in a rapid flow without any introductory preambles, quickly setting up a problem to be discussed, knowing what others know, local lore, shared stories and inside jokes, jargon and other shortcuts to communication (Wenger 1998: 125f).

The concept of communities of practice was developed based on physical communities but later adapted to online settings commonly referred to as 'Virtual Communities of Practice' (Dubé et al. 2005; Hara et al. 2009; Von Wartburg et al. 2006). In these communities, less experienced members learn from interaction with more experienced members, not only explicit knowledge but also the tacit knowledge that keeps these communities alive. In message boards, the level of expertise is often expressed in 'ranks' depending on the number of posts written and the assumed influence exercised on others. Kozinets (1999) has observed a hierarchy from *tourists*, *minglers*, *devotees* to *insiders*, with devotees and insiders welcoming newcomers, passing on the community norms and shaping the negotiation of meaning.

Online forums for musicians meet all the requirements of offline and online communities of practice because they are organised around the common interests of community members but, as a rule, are not working toward achieving specific performance goals (Ardichvili 2008: 542). The shared practice is to make music. Although the community members do not play together, their discourse acts as a proxy for their music, which is more than just playing and encompasses an entire system of meanings, practices and interests. Two of the main interests are playing and equipment, which is often reflected in subforums dedicated to either. Both interests are usually catered for in musicians' boards, but some of the forums focus explicitly on the material side of music-making, such as 'The Gear Page' or 'Gearslutz', while others like 'Bandmix' promote networking to help musicians to join a band.

Message boards can provide valuable insights into the way GAS is negotiated in a significant community of practice. Though not replacing local communities of musicians, online forums for many players have become a source of information and a fundamental part of their musical identity. Online and offline communities are not identical, but they are similar (Hartmann 2016; Orton-Johnson 2014) and shape each other (Bakardjieva 2003, 2005; Wenger 1998: 79). Experiences from offline communities are often the basis for online discourses, whereby meanings and practices from virtual communities equally influence local practices. For example, not all members of a band need to be part of an online community. Even if only one band member participates online, their online community experience can explicitly and implicitly shape the negotiation of meaning in the local group.

We analyse online communities of practice for two reasons. Firstly, it allows evaluating the previous theoretical deliberations on GAS that were informed by academic sources on music technology and theories from other disciplines such as consumption studies, sociology, psychology and psychiatry. Secondly, since the survey of musicians raised as many questions as it answered, qualitative data from a 'natural' source may help explain some of the remaining questions. Our research interest is therefore to understand the GAS discourse in these communities of practice. How explicitly is GAS discussed in the general negotiation of meaning? What cultural practices are associated with it? What are the affective responses to it? Is GAS a shared practice that defines the community? And if so, to what extent is GAS a 'learned' behaviour resulting from participation in the community?

7.1   Method

The analysis uses Kozinets' (2020) method of 'netnography' as a differentiated set of techniques that allows for a 'cultural focus on understanding the data derived from social media data' (Kozinets 2020: 6f). Netnographic inquiry 'seeks to understand the cultural experiences that encompass and are reflected within the traces, practices, networks and systems of social media' (Kozinets 2020: 14), including message boards. In contrast to other ethnographic methods, netnography is systematic and requires following a defined set of 'moves' (Kozinets 2020: 139ff). In the first move of *initiation*, the research objectives and ethical considerations must be addressed. The second move, *investigation*, narrows down the scope by exploring web sources. The third move of *immersion* involves reading and observing online traces and collecting notes in an 'immersion journal'. The fourth move of *interacting* with online participants is optional. In the fifth move of *integration*, the data are collected, analysed and interpreted in a holistic and hermeneutic manner, reflecting an iterative research process. The final move of *incarnation* consists of a structured presentation of the findings.

Ethics

Despite the popularity of online research, there are still no standard ethical practices (Eynon et al. 2016). Woodfield's (2018) collected edition *The Ethics of Online Research* highlights many challenges but offers little concrete advice or guidance, while Halford (2018) argues that ethical best practice standards are rarely transferrable to online research. She suggests not to rely on established deontological and consequentialist ethical practices but to turn to 'situational ethics' that 'recognizes the importance of moral deliberation throughout the ethics process' (Halford 2018: 21). Eynon et al. (2016) emphasise that the three pillars of ethics—confidentiality, anonymity and informed consent—present a challenge in online research. The Internet's perceived anonymity let people disclose more details and discuss topics or even express extreme opinions that otherwise, in a face-to-face situation, they would not be prepared to reveal (Eynon et al. 2016: 23; Kozinets 2020: 203ff). Another ethical issue often debated is unobtrusive observation, known as 'lurking'. Such a non-re-active approach enables the researcher to collect data in a naturalistic setting because the people under investigation are not aware that they are being studied (Janetzko 2016: 76). There is also a wealth of easily accessible and searchable online discussions (Hewson 2016: 68). However, in contrast to offline settings where the observer is recognisable at least to some extent, the researcher's complete invisibility in online research has been a concern of many scholars (see also Garcia et al. 2009).

For Kozinets (2020: 197ff), the degree of public access determines ethical procedures. Private sites that require registration and login with a password should be treated more confidentially than public sites that anyone can open in a browser, which is the case with most message boards that only require registration to post messages. Still, this is not a free ticket because members may have a reasonable expectation of privacy. Kozinets (2020: 203) suggests focusing on forum users' discussions instead of the users themselves. In certain situations, 'cloaking' may be required, for example, to cite the website, but not the pseudonym, or to subtly alter verbatim quotes to make users difficult to trace (Kozinets 2020: 400f; Markham 2012). Especially when dealing with sensitive topics or a vulnerable population, this precaution is demanded. Cloaking is not required if the data are not sensitive, the population not vulnerable, and pseudonyms are used.

Since our analysis of musicians' boards focuses neither on a sensitive topic nor vulnerable groups, we have not altered verbatim quotes because it would change the original statement and likely alter its meaning (Markham 2012). However, we have not revealed the users' nicknames nor specified the forum unless necessary for the argumentation. Following Kozinets (2020) and Halford (2018), we used our moral discretion to protect forum users wherever possible.

Data Collection and Investigation

Netnography follows a structured approach to search processes and data collection. It is characterised by a 'double funnel' which, in an explorative first step, narrows down the topic or keywords before the actual research begins. This first step is essential, given the vast amount of data available online. The data collection undertakes five distinct 'operations' (Kozinets 2020: 215ff). First, the topic is simplified by determining search terms or keywords, which are explored in a second operation using a search engine. The third operation of 'scouting' serves to get a 'feeling' for the topic, documented in an immersion journal that replaces traditional ethnographic field notes (Kozinets 2020: 136). Fourth, the most relevant data sites are selected; the data need not be comprehensive but must contain high-quality information representative of the phenomenon. Finally, the chosen data, such as forum threads, are stored.

Tab. 5. Analysed Forums and Occurrence of Search Terms

Forum	Number of hits		
	'GAS'	**'Gear Acquisition Syndrome'**	**Combined Boolean search**
https://forum.bandmix.com	154	1	3
https://www.harmonycentral.com/forum	1,720	5	112
https://www.thegearpage.net/board/index.php	57,300	256	273
https://talkbass.com	78,800	495	592
https://basschat.co.uk	12,700	33	78
https://www.guitarscanada.com/forums	1,380	7	9
https://www.ultimate-guitar.com/forums	21,000	172	201
https://www.gearslutz.com/board/so-many-guitars-so-little-time	844	24	40
https://www.drummerworld.com/forums	2,310	61	112
https://www.drumchat.com	1,280	396	335
https://www.drumforum.org	3,070	46	26
https://www.keyboardforums.com	40	13	13
https://forum.saxontheweb.net/forum.php	4,440	144	197
https://cafesaxophone.com	1,120	41	30
https://www.trumpetherald.com/forum	2,390	7	7

Note: Numbers taken on 14 July 2020

As Kozinets (2020: 193) explains, '[i]nvestigative data are not directly created by the researcher's questions or writing but, instead, are created by generally unknown others and selected for various reasons by the netnographic researcher to include in the project'. Participant engagement allows further targeted data collection, but most netnographies only utilise unobtrusive online observation (Kozinets 2020: 194).

Having already engaged with forum users who participated in our survey upon our invitation, we limited our analysis to observing message boards. A practical problem we immediately encountered was that the search functions on message boards generally do not accept short terms such as 'GAS'. This problem can be worked around by searching for '*GAS*', but the results will include all words containing the three letters in that order and other meanings of the word, such as gas as a synonym for fuel. To improve search quality, we used Google and its 'site:' operator, which does not require specific search terms. Google's search engine also automatically included different spellings like 'G.A.S.'. The best results were finally achieved with the Boolean operator 'OR' (Karch 2020) to search for 'GAS' and 'Gear Acquisition Syndrome' in one go: 'site:https://www.drummerworld.com/forums "GAS" OR "Gear Acquisition Syndrome"'. Google's intelligent engine, combined with the Boolean operator, ensured that all results were GAS-related in the right sense. Furthermore, setting the search engine to display 100 hits per page helped to filter out duplicate results. Table 5 shows the forums analysed and the number of hits for the search terms 'GAS', 'Gear Acquisition Syndrome' and the combined Boolean search. Forums for which the search procedure did not work were not considered in the analysis.

All identified threads from the fifteen message boards were scouted manually. Data-thin and redundant threads were excluded when saving the data or gradually removed during the analysis. This process resulted in our final sample of 433 threads. Observations made during the scouting and saving procedure were collected in an immersion journal so that overarching observations beyond the level of individual threads and forums were captured.

Data Analysis and Interpretation

Following Kozinets's (2020: 321ff) suggestion, we used qualitative data analysis software (QDAS) to systematically investigate a large amount of data. Since the data analysis guidelines of netnography are relatively vague apart from collating, coding and optionally triangulating data or methods (Kozinets 2020: 332ff), we applied Mayring's (2014) systematic 'summarising content analysis' method, which is compatible with netnography and gives more structure to the analysis. This form of content analysis aims to 'reduce the material in such a way that the essential contents remain, in order to create through abstraction a comprehensive overview of the base material which is nevertheless still an image of it' (Mayring 2014: 64). The category system is created inductively. Not all material is considered for analysis. According to Mayring (2014: 82), no new categories can be found once ten to fifty per cent of the data has been coded. At this point, the category system will be revised and refined to ensure that the research questions are exactly addressed and that the categories do neither overlap nor are too broad or narrow.

Our analysis started with 'The Gear Page' as the most gear-centred forum with the largest number of threads dedicated exclusively to GAS. Although it represented only ten per cent of the total sample, most categories of the final category system could be derived from this forum alone. The subsequent analysis of the other forums added some details and further examples for different instruments. After approximately fifty per cent of the material, we reached 'theoretical saturation' (Glaser & Strauss 1967: 61; Strauss 1987: 21) so that only potentially useful verbatim quotes were coded. That sped up the coding process considerably, which, however, prevented us from analysing the category system quantitatively. The immersion journal still provided sufficient insights into the quantitative relevance of specific practices. The decision to prioritise a higher number of forums was taken to ensure that all instruments necessary for our investigation are represented. As far as interpretation is concerned, we drew on references to the theories and studies discussed in the previous chapters.

7.2 Findings

7.2.1 Standard Community Practices

GAS as Learned Communal Behaviour

The message boards' analysis confirmed that musical equipment plays a prominent role in community life and is part of its social and discursive conventions, regardless of the forum and type of instrument. Membership in these communities implies an interest not only in playing but also in gear. Introductory threads where new members are welcomed make this evident. These threads can be classified into two kinds, with the first one warning newcomers of the danger of 'infecting' themselves with GAS, which takes forms like:

> Welcome to the home of GAS (gear acquisition syndrome). Proceed at your own risk.

> Beware the dreaded GAS. It lurks here. Daily.

> Beware the dreaded GAS. Gear Acquisition Syndrome will take up residence with you at some point after you've got your first bass and rig. Pretty soon you'll be looking at other basses, amps, cabs and all sorts of geeky stuff with raw lust whilst reaching for a remortgage[39] application form. It's inevitable. Just thought I should warn you.

> You'll have fun here but it can be expensive. So will need to learn about GAS, which is gear acquisition syndrome. After looking at and reading about so much nice gear you will be lusting after much of it.

The last quote is particularly illustrative because, in line with the notion of 'communities of practice', it shows that joining the community requires learning the common discourse and practices (Wenger 1998). For many musicians, this means socialisation with an emphasis on the material requirements and luxuries of playing music.

---

[39] In this chapter, we do not correct grammatical errors in user posts, nor do we mark them with 'sic!'.

The second kind of threads comprises introductions characterised by the new-comers 'outing' themselves as 'GAS addicts'. The following quotes portray some of the most representative examples:

> My name is … i live in northern virginia and i am a long time sufferer of gear acquisition syndrome.

> My name is … and I have GAS!

> I suffer badly from Guitar Acquisition Syndrome, or GAS, and I have a tendency to encourage it in others.

> [I'm] a chronic case of Guitar Acquisition Syndrome. I have a team of specialists from three of the area guitar purveyors working around the clock in an effort to satiate my G.A.S., but things are not looking good. The luthiers are telling me I only have a few weeks before my new bout of severe G.A.S. will surface. It's a tough time, I'm slacking at work and it's difficult to socialize with my girlfriend, but I'll keep fighting the good fight and hopefully I can beat this horrible disease.

With these introductory posts, newcomers likely intend to show commonality with other community members and demonstrate familiarity with the common discourse, which may allow them to start at a higher 'rank', as they are fluent in the social conventions (Kozinets 1999).

The previous discussion of virtual communities concluded that although musi-cians' boards cannot be defined per se as 'virtual communities of consumption', they seem to share characteristics because consumption knowledge is acquired 'alongside knowledge of the online group's cultural norms, specialized language and concepts' (Kozinets 1999: 254). There are several indicators that GAS is expected behaviour, which new members need to learn. As a universally known abbreviation, GAS is omnipresent in pinned threads on forum acronyms on all message boards. Most fo-rums have several 'lingo' threads where terms are continuously added to the com-mon knowledge of language use (Wenger 1998: 125f), and in all of them, GAS is expected. It is therefore not surprising when a user marvels: 'Two pages into a thread about abbreviations on TGP [The Gear Page], and not a single mention of GAS (gear acquisition syndrome)?!?!?'. Similarly, experienced users are expected to know the abbreviation, or else they will be accused of being a forum troll or bot: '1000 posts on TGP and doesn't know what GAS is??? I smell a rat'. However, the attitude is different when new community members genuinely ask what GAS means; such threads are frequent on all the analysed message boards. For example, one user won-ders: 'I've heard the expression Gas which I figure means that you're needing some-thing … anyone able to tell us what it really means?'. In such cases, experienced members are more than willing to illuminate the novice with answers like: 'GAS: Acronym for Gear Acquisition Syndrome. The unavoidable compulsion to spend money one doesn't have, on gear one doesn't need, in the misguided belief that doing so will make one a better player'. As this explanation suggests, the forums differ in their general attitude towards GAS, with some being more critical than others, but generally, it is discussed in all forums. In no one is this more evident but The Gear Page, whose primary purpose is to discuss music equipment in order to accommodate the musicians' mutual interest in lusting for gear. The following statements are examples thereof:

> Welcome to Gear Lust Central! This is where the motto is 'If you ain't got it, You NEED it!' The most profound purveyors of G.A.S. on the interwebs! G.A.S. = Gear Acquisition Syndrome. Where EVERYBODY is waiting for some new toy in the post/FedEx/UPS. Rest assured that simple requests for product guidance will be met with recommendations to buy the biggest, baddest product with ALL the bells and whistles that you won't need or use for a minimum of 5 years (if ever) and that during that time the biggest, baddest, bestest will have changed at least 3 times. No cynicism involved, just a hard look at the reality that is TGP.

> Welcome to The Gear Page and a lifelong struggle with gear acquisition syndrome (GAS).

> TGP has never been about building the house, its about worshipping the hammer.

> I expect my TGP membership to be revoked soon—I realized last week I haven't purchased an amp in 2019.

Communities of practice are not limited to either online or offline groups, and they overlap with other parts of society (Bakardjieva 2003, 2005; Wenger 1998: 79). This fact is proven by the discussion and remembrance of Walter Becker, who coined the term GAS (Becker 1996). Apart from threads in nearly all forums that describe Becker as the 'inventor' of the term, some forums like The Gear Page praise him for his impact on such online communities: 'Did you guys see that Walter Becker died? Aside from all the music, the man created the term Gear Acquisition Syndrome. We owe him, and our creditors, a great debt'. Becker's editorial put him on the map of musicians' online communities of practice. After his passing, the auction of his equipment—an impressive total of 1,085 items, mostly guitars and amplifiers (Julien's Auction 2019)—further strengthened Becker's status as an icon in the gear-fixated musicians' world. As a member of The Gear Page states in awe, '[t]he man had some world class GAS!'.

Another variation of GAS as learned behaviour on these message boards is seen in the tendency of new members to quickly develop the expectation that they should spend time researching and updating their equipment:

> When I first starting playing guitar in mid-2015 (I'm 49 now) I spent so much time on Reverb, eBay, Craigslist, etc. looking and buying gear. I thought that's what all guitarists did, buy as much gear as possible so I joined the party. My homepage at work was Reverb, I was online all day until I fell asleep acquiring stuff. In late 2016 my playing wasn't advancing as fast as I'd liked. Long story short I realized it was because I wasn't playing guitar all that often. Why? I was spending all my

time GAS-ing. On the flip side of that I was chasing tone so hard I would spend
hours dialing amps, pedals, etc. and still not playing all that much.

This post indicates that the new player had gained a false impression by observing
the common discourse, which let him exaggerate the expected material occupation
beyond the average. The illustrated player overemphasised research on gear until he
eventually realised that the ratio between research and playing was off. These threads
are relatively common, suggesting that learning an instrument while participating in
forums can easily lead to a discrepancy between playing and dealing with gear (see
also Cole 2018) that, if the imbalance is realised, can be readjusted during musical
maturation. Nevertheless, the community gives its newer members the impression
that buying and upgrading their musical equipment is expected. The following post
by a 15-year-old novice guitarist makes this quite clear:

> So I made the mistake of walking into a guitar store and checking out the new
> Christmas stock and I felt like a paedophile at Disney land looking at all the expen-
> sive guitars XD I tried a red ESP custom shop and I loved it. It had a beautiful red
> finish and it was equipped with emg 81/85s. I wanted it so bad. The guitar I have
> right now is an ltd ec 331 with emg 81/85s and tbh [to be honest] I probably
> wouldn't be able to tell the difference in tone between the two guitars with my 15
> year old undeveloped ears since they're both mahogany guitars with emgs. But
> seriously I have an obsession now! I've also made the mistake of looking up zakk
> wylde signatures (I'll admit I'm more of a zakk wylde fan boy than I'd like to
> admit) and his Gibson les Paul bullseye is now my dream guitar. Seriously the fact
> that it's gonna be years before I can afford something like that makes me miserable.
> I get this weird notion in my head sometimes that my guitar isn't good enough for
> me to advance on and I honestly don't think that's true and I think I'm just
> overthinking. As I said before my ears probably can't tell the difference between a
> zakk wykde bullseye with emgs and my current ltd. I'm planning on taking up a
> job soon and start saving for new gear such as pedals but I might put it towards a
> new guitar. Have any of you guys suffered from bad gas? How did you get through?

Aware that it is not true, the guitarist nonetheless blames their current equipment's
inadequacy for the slow progress as a player. They may not even be able to distinguish instruments by their sound, but a more expensive guitar, or one played by an
esteemed player, still raises hopes of musical improvement. This insensitivity to musical details matches Crowdy's (2013) observation that musicians tend to make un-
founded claims about equipment based on their attitudes and beliefs and that the
instrument is more important as a proxy for something else than how it actually
sounds. This observation is also consistent with the findings of Fernandez and
Lastovicka's (2011) study, according to which a tribute or signature guitar is expected to channel 'magic' into its player.

The following post shows another form of the expected buying and upgrading
behaviour:

Does every pedal board need a booster? I was going to get one, but I am pretty happy how my board is behaving so far. I placed an overdrive before my distortion pedal and it seems to work great. When should you use a boost/pre-amp?

The guitarist has no need for a boost pedal, but conformity to social conventions makes them ask if they were doing something wrong. Other related threads pose questions such as 'at what point do you upgrade from your first guitar and amp?', 'when is it a time for a guitar upgrade?' or 'how many guitars are enough?'. These threads suggest that it is not the musical needs that dictate buying behaviour but rather the expectation of the community of practice. The 'use-value' (Cole 2018) is replaced by social conformity.

A variation of this phenomenon occurs when users want to adapt to the pressure to buy but feel the need to justify their gear collection by their level of playing:

This probably is a stupid question, and I know you[r] skill doesn't determine how many guitars you can have, but I'm 15 and don't have a lot of cash. I don't wanna buy another guitar and have two if I don't feel like I'm good enough to actually need two. How good should I be to have two guitars? (what songs/techniques should I be able to know/play)

This musician seems to be reflective enough to realise that owning several instruments may only be musically useful if needed for specific playing styles, songs or genres or if the player's abilities are good enough to utilise the potential that another instrument might offer. However, the post points to the idea that an expansion of the gear collection accompanies musical progress. Such threads are commonplace in all forums. Therefore, it is only natural that many threads are asking for inspiration when it comes to the 'problem' of running out of GAS and equipment to buy:

Can anyone relate to the feeling of... I'm done buying drum stuff? I'm there. No desire for anything else since I got a tom tree for my walnut set. I mean where else is there to go? I'm in the promised land already. I worked so hard to get here, why would I want to leave and start over? I got a great guitar amp, 2 Fender guitars, and I am done buying guitar stuff too. It's a good feeling not being distracted by gear. One less distraction to stand between myself and my playing. I never thought I would get to this place. Not sure how long it will last, but right now I feel like it's permanent. To illustrate this, I still have $1,000 of play money from what I got when my Mom passed on. It's my money to do with as I wish. I honestly can't think of anything to spend it on musically, and I've tried. That's how I know. The money is not burning a hole in my pocket. Weird.

This member feels relieved presently not to 'suffer' from GAS, and some others share that they were at this point for a while before they 'relapsed'. Such threads of players reporting on their newly developed mastery over the compulsive urge to buy are relatively rare, though. More common are the ones reading 'What could bring you out of your GAS retirement?', 'Want a new instrument but don't know what' or

'It was Christmas so it's time for new gears'. These threads demonstrate that al-though some users may seriously wish to be free of GAS, most like the desire to buy (see also Belk et al. 2003) irrespective of whether the item is needed for their playing. The inspiration for purchases comes in various forms. Like in the practice of record collectors displaying photos of their collections online (Shuker 2010: 199), there are photo documentary threads (see also Cole 2018) entitled 'My year in GAS' or 'Show me your pedalboard' that help musicians, in the words of a forum member, to 'make mental notes of what you want from that setup' of other players. These are attractive threads that allow musicians to find pleasure in self-seduction (Baudrillard 1983; Deighton & Grayson 1995; Reekie 1993). On a pure content level, they are mean-ingless, as even the threads' creators acknowledge. They are mainly meant to inform the community of gear-related practices in the expectation of receiving positive re-inforcement and potentially gaining status. Another related purpose is to maintain the discourse on equipment that is crucial for the community's social life, which is reflected in three exemplary posts:

> I thought I'd post what gear I bought and sold this year... not that anyone cares, but it might make for an interesting thread for each of us to talk about what we sold and what we bought.

> GAS: Gear Acquisition Syndrome. The constant need for musician to constantly buy and hoarde masses of musical equipment that they probably won't use very much any way. It's been too long since I saw one of these threads and they're al-ways good fun (and surprisingly educational and relevant too.) So post which ever basses, amps, pedals, strings, straps, parts, etc in this thread to let off your mad GAS.

> I know I'm not alone in my perpetual quest to acquire certain pieces of gear. Often this list changes... I find something new I didn't know existed, I try something out that disappoints... Life happens. It would be interesting to see what everyone's cur-rently GASsing over, see what interests we share, hopefully be introduced to new gear I was unaware of.

These posts are further evidence that GAS is prevalent in these communities, which shows in that it is expected of members to learn about equipment and in the frequent discussion of gear-related behaviour. Looking at other musicians' setups and proudly presenting gear they intend to buy or have bought is what gives them pleasure. Like collecting, discussing and presenting gear is a shared social practice (Christ 1965; Formanek 1991; Sherif et al. 1961; Shuker 2010). Although this can be motivated by social hierarchy (Bourdieu 1986), most of the respective threads tend to suggest comradery (Formanek 1991). Gear envy—or 'mimetic desire' (Girard 1977)—is rel-atively uncommon. Users rather delight in receiving kind feedback on their favourite equipment, and they are happy to support others in their gear-related efforts. More-over, in addition to threads in which members report retrospectively on their GAS items at the end of a year, there are dedicated wish list threads in which desired gear for a new year is presented and discussed. These lists contain both realistic acquisitions and dreams of items that are unlikely to be affordable but can still be hoped for, which makes the desire even more pleasurable (Belk et al. 2003: 340ff; Denegri-Knott & Molesworth 2010: 69). Planning and dreaming about gear are standard practices in these forums that serve to bond people. They get to know each other better because the envisioned gear allows the informed musician to draw conclusions about a fellow musician's personality. Such social practice shows a strong resemblance with what Belk et al. (2003: 335f) have described as 'desire for sociality'.

Events are an integral part of online communities. These, however, rarely happen at the same time for the entire community. Instead, events are long-term themes to which every community member can contribute with something worth announcing. A significant 'event' is the day new equipment is bought, celebrated with posts in dedicated threads for the occasion, such as 'New Guitar Day', 'New Amp Day' or 'New Pedal Day' (see also Cole 2018). As with most GAS-related practices, there is some ambivalence because users commonly continue buying and posting pictures of their new gear although recognising the futility of this practice:

> New Guitar Day... has lost its mojo … That's right fellas... today was NGD [New Guitar Day]. I barely even plugged the damn thing in. It was a Hamer Special I bought from a guy here on TGP [The Gear Page]. Nice guitar, but when I did finally get it tuned up and I played a few things, it just sounded like... me. Tone is in the fingers I guess. Need to stop buying **** I don't need... like more guitars.

> I've discovered that I'm getting bigger thrills these days out of discovering and learning new things about music than getting another big rectangular box from UPS again. My hands have morphed into good tone producing tools after being honed over literally thousands of gigs, so new effects, amplifiers, and cabinets aren't of much interest anymore. I do spend some money on Skype lessons these days, which isn't inexpensive when the best instructors are involved … Of course there is no NBD [New Bass Day] glamor attached to any of this, and there are no endorsement deals for players that value knowledge and concepts over hard goods.

The second post is particularly interesting because it highlights the 'glamour' of reporting newly acquired items. Communities work with positive reinforcement (Skinner 1938), and in some forums, it seems that gear-related actions like buying and trading have a higher value than playing it. One reason could be that playing involves a much larger world of preferences and tastes (Bourdieu 1986; Foucault 1991), such as genres, styles or musical role models, making it more challenging to relate to community members from various places in the world. In contrast, an interest in gear is universal, possibly making it easier to find common ground.

As the previous deliberations have shown, it is commendable, if not a mark of excellence, to come out as a 'GAS addict' and to frequently show off purchases. Many threads point to comradery, while others indicate a kind of social order. On several message boards, there are 'Rate my gear' threads, in which more exquisite pieces of equipment show good taste (Arsel & Bean 2013; Foucault 1991), thus identifying their owner belonging to the social group's elite (Bourdieu 1984, 1986; Kozinets 1999). A variation is 'GAS test' threads, from which the community can assess who is affected by the syndrome the most. These tests are manifested in all forums. Often, they are specific to individual instruments, such as this sophisticated test for saxophonists:

> In response to …'s request for a numerical scoring system to quantify saxophone-based Gear Acquisition Syndrome (GAS), I offer the following scale.
> - For every saxophone you own over one each of SATB, give yourself 10 points.
> - For each sax that is the same pitch as another sax, add 5 points.
> - For each sax that hasn't been played in more than six months, add 5 points.
> - For each mouthpiece in excess of the number of playable saxes, add 2 points.
> - For each mouthpiece that hasn't been played in more than six months, add 2 points.
> - For each mouthpiece marked with the words NEW YORK or HOLLYWOOD, add 10 points.
> - For each mouthpiece professionally refaced, add 5 points.
> - For each mouthpiece professionally refaced more than once, add 20 points.
> - For each sax not currently playable, add 5 points.
> - For each sax that has remained unplayable for more than one year, add 10 points.
> - For each sopranino, bass, or sax in a key other than Bb or Eb, add 20 points.
> - If you own or have ever owned more than one bass sax at a time, add 100 points.
> - For each weirdo instrument such as straight alto, typewriter, slide, plastic body, padless, tubax, etc., add 25 points.
> - For each High Pitch, manual octave key, experimental, prototype, or 19th century Franco-Belgian horn with little round blobs instead of roller keys, add 40 points.
> - For a full-size contrabass, add 200 points.
> Classifications:
> 0-9 points: You are relatively free of GAS. Blow in peace, and remember that an artist never blames his tools.
> 10-49 points: You have a roving eye but still put most of your air through the horn. Stay focused!
> 50-99 points: You may have GAS. If you're either spending more time acquiring gear than playing, or acquiring more gear than you'll have time to play, open an eBay store or seek support in SOTW [Sax on the Web] Forum.
> 100-199 points: You have GAS. In addition to the remedies previously discussed, family intervention may be necessary, along with moving to a smaller living space.
> 200-499 points: You have Bipolar-Acquisitive Disorder with GAS ('BAD GAS'). In BAD GAS phase, your living space HAS become smaller. Your family has either intervened or left completely. If you have ever attempted to play more than 3 saxophones at once, or gone more than a year without needing to buy reeds, you definitely have BAD GAS.
> 500 or more points: You are a GAS Hoarder, Obsessive Genus ('GAS HOG'). Why

are you reading this? Go look at The Marketplace. Or eBay. Or netinstruments.com. Or Craigslist. Or the classifieds. Or...?

The following test is aimed at guitarists, yet it is general enough to cover all instruments:

> How can you tell if you have GAS? One way is to answer some of these questions. If you answer 'yes' to any of them, then you probably have GAS.
> 1- Each time you sign on to a Guitar Forum, do you have to check your signature to see if it's still right?
> 2- Have you ever just visited a Guitar Forum for 'fun and information' then all of a sudden you're in your Paypal account hoping to score a new peice of gear?
> 3- Have you ever bought gear and sold the item the day it arrived?
> 4- Have you ever bought an item and sold it before it arrives in the mail?
> 5- Do you see a 'cycle' occuring with your rig? Meaning; you swap guitars for a while, then pedals, then amps looling for the perfect rig and then as soon as you 'cycle through' it all you start all over?

Similarly, this keyboard-specific test could be applied to all electric instruments:

> 1. When the behavior you exhibit when waiting for the UPS guy is as erratic as that of man at the hospital waiting to hear that he just became a father
> 2. When you tell the UPS guy you've been playing all your life, because you're so excited that you don't know a better, more truthful answer, lol
> 3. When you use all the locks to lock that door before you unbox the stuff
> 4. When you get an ungrounded extension power cord
> 5. When you turn on your synth right on the floor, immediately after unboxing it, before first setting it on a stand or table
> 6. When your heart sinks if your synth turns on then immediately turns off on its own
> 7. When the spot for your new baby has already been cleared

Other threads list symptoms for the reader to check their GAS-level or to add to the list of indicators, which include:

- Searching the Internet for videos and demos of something that caught your eye.

- Actually watching unboxing videos is a very strong indication of GAS.

- Downloading PDF manuals.

- Rehearsing the script you 'might' use with your significant other 'if' you were going to buy the gear in question.

- Stopping by a music store on your lunch break to see if they have a demo unit available... just out of curiosity.

- Looking at your creative workspace and considering where the new gear would go if you ever did make the purchase.

- Searching Internet forums and reading every thread relevant to your new obsession. (Note: If you find yourself composing a response to someone's criticism even though the critic's post is weeks or months old then you need to plan and budget for the purchase... it is going to happen.)

- Placing an item in the cart knowing full well you won't or can't buy it. Just to see what it looks like in the cart.

- Placing a low bid on an item you know you won't or can't afford to win, but hey you owned it for an hour or day, until you get outbid and let it go.

- Checking the status of the shipment by using the tracking number online repeatedly, sometimes several times a days... UNTIL the box arrives.

- Your heart sinking when the status says 'OUT FOR DELIVERY', meaning the truck is coming SOON today!!

GAS is widely accepted and so omnipresent that community members find it worthwhile starting threads to discuss gear for which they never had GAS or think they will ever have. This humorous presentation of GAS resembles that of collectors who, according to Belk (1995b: 480, 2001a: 80), often joke about their obsessive behaviour because unlike other addictions, GAS is socially accepted.

There are, however, numerous users who regard GAS-fetishization as problematic and mention 'help groups' like the 'GAS sufferers anonymous support group', 'GASaholics anonymous' or 'Gear Minimalism and GAS Support Group', or urge founding them. We also found confessions that could just as well come from anonymous alcoholics, for example: 'Hi everyone, my name is ... and I have GAS'. Such confessions show that GAS can be on the threshold between joyful pastime and problematic compulsive behaviour (O'Guinn & Faber 1989; Rook 1987), of which this post is an example:

> Oh my God, I'm truely not alone with my addiction, an amp junkie in the worst way. If my nose was any bigger, I'd be snorting amps! There hasn't been any room in my closet for the last 10 years, and it's a big closet. And, I'm on my second story stacking them. F*** the clothes anyway. There's no place left to hide things from my wife. You KNOW you have a problem when you're buying doubles of the same amp! And, it doesn't help when your guitar playing buddies tell you, "'Hey, two of those would make great end tables.' You think to yourself, 'Yea, they would, wouldn't they.'

Support groups for GAS-afflicted musicians host, for example, 'No buying' threads to help the community deal with the problem. Some threads are open all year round, and others appear at the beginning of a year when musicians declare their resolution not to buy any more equipment.

Often, it is not clear how serious members are when they discuss their desires and compulsions. One of the more serious topics seems to be finances, especially when it comes to using credit cards regularly to pay for new equipment. Some musicians argue that it can make sense to buy equipment on credit if it is a good deal and kept long-term because it reduces the need or desire to buy other, possibly inferior, items that may not meet individual requirements. Others point out that 'credit inflates the price of whatever you are buying' and should only be used if 'the gear makes you more money than the monthly payments'. Since only a minority of the community makes substantial money from their music, most musicians agree that 'buying on credit leads to a life fighting uphill' and should be avoided at all costs. If a fellow musician is recognised to be spending more money on gear than they can afford, the humorous tone will usually be abandoned; instead, they will be warned about such risky behaviour.

One of the main questions throughout our investigation has been whether players of different instruments vary in the degree of their propensity to GAS. There are currently no studies that have systematically compared instrument-specific behaviour on message boards. We observed that guitarists are the most vocal about their interest in gear. When playing more than one instrument, they tend to perceive 'guitar GAS' worse than, for example, 'saxophone GAS'. The main reason speculated for GAS being so pronounced amongst guitar players is the instrument's general affordability. Moreover, GAS is considered more common among electric guitar players than acoustic guitarists because more equipment is to buy, particularly devices that are not too costly such as cables, effects and other gadgets. Objectively, however, there is insufficient evidence that one instrument group is significantly more or less affected by GAS than any other, which is consistent with our survey results. Similarly, communal practices and discourses differ marginally at best.

Effects of the Internet

Musicians have always discussed gear (Cole 2018; Hartmann 2016), but only the Internet and particularly Web 2.0 implemented the basis to connect people from distant places, which contributed to form special interest groups and facilitate discussions over long periods of weeks, months or years. The positive correlation between participation in the observed online communities and a pronounced interest in gear is so evident that no verbatim quotes are needed. We will instead examine some of the facilitating effects of the Internet on GAS-related behaviour, which can be divided into two categories: the wealth of information and the bigger and more convenient consumer market.

As far as available information is concerned, the discussions stress how easy it has become to find out about equipment on the Internet, for example, what is generally offered and what is on sale (McIntosh & Schmeichel 2004: 88f). Some older musicians reflect that they had read musicians' magazines and catalogues before Web 2.0, which, however, limited their access to new information because the time between an item was introduced and finally appearing in a magazine or catalogue was then much longer. Gathering information from print sources involved completely different practices, as one guitarist explains:

> I remember when I started with guitar I used to love the sweet water and musicians friends catalog. Used to read them non stop and memorize the specs of all the guitars. There was so much time in between catalogs I came up with a few 'games' to keep them interesting. I would play 'what guitar I would buy on this page, these two pages, or what guitar would I love to have if I didn't have to pay for it.' Internet didn't give me GAS. I already had that. But it did change things. Comparing specs is easier. Information is more abundant. And I don't look through those catalogs any more.

When musicians were interested in a piece of equipment, research was 'labour-intensive and time-consuming', delaying the immediate impulse to buy or stopping the urge altogether. Other musicians stress that music stores were the primary source of information that was passed on by word of mouth. Also, buying and trading were carried out in local scenes so that equipment was exchanged between fellow musicians in close vicinity. The Internet has made information more accessible and, as many players argue, it has awakened desires, made 'gear lust much easier, faster and more frequent' and conditioned the brain in its continuous demand for something new ('neophilia'). Musicians' boards are regarded as particularly influential in this respect, with musicians reflecting that they were rarely ever tempted to trade equipment before joining the community. Internet access alone does not seem sufficient to trigger such urges. However, the Internet is said to have accelerated the GAS cycle (Leonhardt 2015; Power & Parker 2015; Wright 2006) so that by the time an online order arrives, a new object may already be desired (Denegri-Knott & Molesworth 2010). This acceleration is characteristic of increasingly commodified practices (Shuker 2010: 111; Straw 2000: 166). But not only forums, blogs and other websites dedicated to musical equipment are to blame. YouTube also creates desires for many musicians: partly because the desired gear can be seen and heard in contrast to text-based discussions or reviews, and partly because idols can be observed playing or presenting their rig.

The second significant benefit of the Internet is access to a bigger market, together with a much wider range of products in the musical instruments sector (Théberge 1997). Musicians highlight that 'so many more types of guitars are available to buy than there were pre-Internet' and that the increased choice from the larger variety of models has fuelled the desire that only weakly existed before the Internet. Furthermore, the Internet has forced local music instruments retailers to align their prices with national and international standards. Likewise, when shopping online, gear on sale can be purchased from remote retailers, making equipment less expensive to acquire and tempting musicians to buy. 'Bargain hunting', the 'thrill of the hunt' (Belk 1995b; Danet & Katriel 1989; McIntosh & Schmeichel 2004; Shuker 2010), has become a hobby for many musicians, especially on eBay and other trading websites (Denegri-Knott & Molesworth 2010; Denegri-Knott & Zwick 2012). As many musicians admit, good deals have seduced them to buy more gear than they need which, however, would bear little risks of losing money. On the contrary, the practice of 'flipping' gear—buying and selling used equipment—even promises a plus if one knows the market. Increased opportunity and reduced risk seem to be the principal factors, as this musician suggests:

> All the internet did was make it easier to dump gear for enough money to buy something else decent, and make it easier to find other decent gear. To the extent GAS has been enabled, I actually think that's more to do with online sales. Before ebay/etc. it was really hard to get decent prices on used gear. Now we reasonably expect to get a decent return on used gear.

The downside of this stable second-hand market is that it has become increasingly difficult to score deals on eBay, even for lesser-known brands, as most auctioneers have become familiar with a wide variety of gear and its value (Denegri-Knott & Molesworth 2010). Denegri-Knott and Zwick (2012) propose that while eBay is a 'pleasure dome', its users quickly lose interest when bidding in auctions becomes a routine. Their observation is not consistent with our investigation, as we observed quite the opposite in the discussions. Many musicians study the market for years and use the service regularly to buy and sell gear. To minimise the efforts and ease boredom, they set up alerts and create other forms of automatisms that ultimately maximise their 'flipping' efficiency.

In addition to used gear, the increased number and availability of cheap devices manufactured outside the USA and Central Europe made many community members change their consumer behaviour. A guitarist explains the attractiveness of such products as follows, 'I have fun buying cheap pedals direct from China about every month. For the price of dinner for two at Olive Garden I can get a new pedal and test it out'. Conversely, the Internet has allowed access to exclusive boutique devices that are not offered in local music stores:

> The internet was awful for my GAS. I Live in the Midwest and rarely saw anything beyond the basic Fender, Gibson, Ibanez, Martin, Music Man, or Taylor. I'd see exotic guitars and pickups in magazines. Didn't do much for me. I'd hear of various bands, but there wasn't much I could do if my local shops didn't have it in stock.

> The Internet sure opens up the entire world of possibilities. Before 1996, anything I wanted in the way of gear was decided by what I could get in a local music store or order from the Musicians Friend or Mandolin Brothers catalogs. I used to fly from Atlanta to Charlotte on business once a month, and always left room in my suitcase for my Reliable Music shopping sprees! And yes, I would even make a day trip drive to Charlotte on a weekend if the purchase was too big for the plane.

Overall, the Internet provides access to a wealth of inexpensive and exclusive items, and it has facilitated a mass-market for used goods. The globalisation of these markets has minimised the chance of unexpected bargains, which is not much of a downside because standard prices are, in general, already low due to price matching. In line with interview statements of guitarists that Wright (2006) collected, most GAS-affected musicians prefer used gear, as it allows them to acquire items regularly without losing money. 'Flipping' gear appears to be an affordable way to realise 'neophilia' (Falk 1994), the fetish of striving or desiring continuously for something new.

Gendered Discourse

Judging by nicknames and profile photos, most musicians who post in gear-related threads appear to be male, consistent with the sample of our survey and similar studies (Herbst 2016, 2017a). We cannot say with certainty whether the gender ratio varies between the differently themed sub-forums of the message boards. Still, the common notion that GAS, just like record collecting (Bogle 1999; Shuker 2010) and hi-fi audio (Jansson 2010; Schröter & Volmar 2016), is a predominantly male phenomenon (Wright 2006: 26) is reflected in the communities analysed. Several threads are theorising why GAS may be a male behaviour. Some of the statements are outright sexist:

> My theory of G.A.S. is, as follows, after a day's worth of thinking about this idea I got this morning: G.A.S. hits us guys. Women don't just understand. In fact, it is a biological/evolutionary thing for males. How many times have you heard a piece of gear described as 'sexy'? This is the clue. Males want to own all females. They want to, even if they are married, still 'own' any female they deem worthy. And, when they can't do this in modern society, they buy sexy gear. If they don't do it at first, agonizing over a piece of gear, they end up saving and agonizing over it, before they give in and commit.

> My day job happens to be as a researcher and teacher in the field of Evolutionary Psychology, so I can't help but chime in here. There are both good theoretical reasons and tons of empirical data to support the idea that men and women differ, on average, in the characteristics they most value in potential mates. At risk of oversimplification, this boils down to men placing primary value on physical attractiveness in potential mates (i.e., cues of youth and fertility -- i.e. producing babies), and women placing primary value on status and resources (i.e., cues of the ability to provision for those babies). With this in mind, it makes sense than men probably suffer from G.A.S. more than women, the idea being to accumulate impressive stuff (like fancy sports cars, etc.) to advertise their resource-acquisition abilities. In contrast, the things that women 'G.A.S.' for (more broadly defined) tend more toward things that they believe will enhance their physical attractiveness, such as shoes and clothing, jewelry, and so forth.

[GAS is] inherent to our [male] nature because we want to live longer, attract more mates and make more babies. It's biology baby!

Several key concepts of consumption research focusing on desire like seduction, enchantment, lust, and other characteristics of embodied passion (Baudrillard 1983; Belk et al. 2003), clearly apply to these threads. As long as these attractions are limited to goods, they are harmless (Belk et al. 2003: 348; Campbell 1987: 86), but the objectification of women by equating them with equipment is purely sexist. Some musicians argue against such sexist explanation, stressing that the quest for constant improvement is inherent in human nature, regardless of gender. Their view accords with research suggesting that acquisition of possessions is fundamental to human development (Belk 1988; Campbell 1987). Others point out that it is individual interest, although this argumentation is disputed by those who claim, from an 'evolutionary perspective', that interest in (music) technology tends to be male (see also Berkers & Schaap 2018; Comber et al. 1993; Hallam et al. 2008, 2017). Little effort is made to refute this argumentation, which becomes evident from posts hardly ever referring to female musicians having GAS. On the other hand, we found only one female musician in all the analysed forums who 'shouted out' that women can just as well have GAS. Research on collecting in general (Baekeland 1994; Belk 2001a) and record collecting (Shuker 2010) indicates that women are no less ambitious collectors than men, but on the other hand, they neither tend to make their practice public because they feel less comfortable showing off cultural capital in competition. Therefore, it is quite possible that women, even as members of online communities, do not participate in gear contests that shape the GAS discourse.

Against the background that men in the forums outnumber women by far, conclusions about how GAS might differ between genders cannot be drawn from our analysis. Those communities do not take gender diverse or fluid categories into account. The discourse is based on binary gender distinctions that follow traditional role expectations (Ridgeway 2011). Wives and girlfriends are overwhelmingly regarded as obstacles to GAS (Becker 1996; Wright 2006). There are innumerable posts thereof, which can be divided into two categories. The distinct influence the significant other has on a purchase decision—financially or motivationally—is seen either as a factor making GAS-related behaviour more difficult or as a support in controlling irrational acquisitions for the musician's benefit. Whether or not the musician genuinely feels this way cannot be said, but it seems that adhering to this common trope is expected in the community and thus practised continuously, and across all the message boards we have analysed.

Variations and Cycles of GAS

The previous deliberations have discussed to what extent GAS is a defining aspect of communities of practice and how it is structurally embedded in the form of common threads. Now we will take a closer look at how GAS is discussed in the threads dedicated to GAS and in posts in response to more general threads.

One common way to justify or play down the adverse effects of GAS is to compare it with similar behaviour outside music. Relevant hobbies prone to GAS include ceramic and porcelain figurines, basketball shoes, fishing gear and golf clubs. Such comparisons lead to considerations like '[c]ompared to other hobbies, a $1000 Guitar is not that much money' and 'I figure I could spend my money on worse things'. The community members claim that everything can become the focus of GAS and that everyone has 'xAS of some sort'. This formula is found on all message boards and results in specific modifications of the term GAS that are more tailored to the community or special interests within it. Examples of such modifications are: 'Amp Acquisition Syndrome (AAS)', 'Boutique Amp Acquisition Syndrome (BAAS)', 'Pedal Acquisition Syndrome (PAS)', 'Fuzz Acquisition Syndrome (FAS)', 'Pickup Acquisition Syndrome (PAS)', 'Kit Acquisition Syndrome (KAS)', 'Snare Acquisition Syndrome (SAS)', 'Trumpet Acquisition Syndrome (TAS)', 'Saxophone Acquisition Syndrome (SAS)', 'Mouthpiece Acquisition Syndrome (MAS)' and 'Musical Instruments Acquisition Syndrome (MIAS)'. The term can be adapted for practically anything and is not limited to instruments, instrument parts and electronics. The 'Finish Acquisition Syndrome (FAS)' refers to the desire to own instruments in a particular colour or lacquer, and the 'Gadget Acquisition Syndrome (GAS)' concerns relatively inexpensive discretionary purchases (Danziger 2004: 6f). The 'Guitar Repair Syndrome (GRS)' and the 'Tool Acquisition Syndrome (TAS)' are widespread amongst DIY enthusiastic musicians. Technophiles may identify themselves with the 'Firmware Acquisition Syndrome (FAS)' and guitar and bass players with the 'Profile Acquisition Syndrome (PAS)' in conjunction with virtual amplifiers (Herbst 2019a, 2021; Herbst et al. 2018). A synonym for 'Gear Acquisition Syndrome' is the 'Tone Acquisition Syndrome (TAS)', both sharing the same motivation yet TAS being much less commonly used. There is even mention of a 'Skill Acquisition Syndrome (SAS)', which one musician describes as 'much more rewarding long-term than GAS'. However, this expression is very uncommon, consistent with the greater emphasis on gear than playing in these forums. The examples demonstrate that 'gear', representing the first letter of GAS, can be replaced by anything. Moreover, the discourse suggests that such specialisations in niche equipment find an interested audience on these musicians' boards.

One variation of 'xAS' is the 'Tool Acquisition Syndrome (TAS)', which some musicians have additionally or instead of GAS. It is considered as bad, if not worse, as GAS, in line with Walter Becker's (1996) claim that 'Gear Modification Syndrome' is more severe than the acquisition syndrome. As a musician notes:

> Tell you what is worse than GAS... TAS: tool acquisition syndrome. Unfortunately for me, my interest in remodeling and woodworking is greater than my GAS. Suddenly 500 dollar pedals seem downright affordable compared to 700 dollar router tables and 3K cabinet saws.

Some musicians regard frequent maintenance and modification as a side-effect of GAS that costs them time and money. Others believe that building their equipment from scratch or with kits is financially less dangerous because it involves lower expenses, and the building process takes longer than a normal GAS cycle occurring during practising and playing (Wright 2006: 31). In line with research on craft consumption (Cole 2018), the building of instruments and other gear can therefore be an effective way of breaking the over-commodification of the musical instruments industry.

As we have seen, GAS is treated by the community with humour but also as something that affects most of them noticeably. The strong personal interest in gear is expressed in what may be called 'academic considerations'. Occasionally, journalistic and scholarly texts are discussed, for example, Wright's (2006) book on GAS, which a musician discovered reading the article 'Gear Acquisition Syndrome: Lustily Buying More Tools Than You Need' in *Psychology Today* (Sherman 2011). Such discoveries support the community by validating that GAS, in the words of a member, is a 'real thing'. Another article under discussion is 'Urge to Own That Clapton Guitar Is Contagious, Scientists Find', published in *The New York Times* (Tierney 2011), which includes excerpts of Fernandez and Lastovicka's (2011) study and interviews with other academics. The thread discussing scholarly theories shows a high degree of critical thinking. There is the example of the 'mojo', which is supposed to motivate musicians to buy replica instruments, but the threads dismiss it as simplistic. Similarly, the study's explanation for the differences between collectors and musicians who want to improve their gear to enhance their playing experience is felt to lack detail. Overall, the responses suggest scepticism about academic studies on GAS. One user writes:

> I think that they [Fernandez & Lastovicka 2011] have focused on one dynamic fetishization with which they are familiar, and have put all buyers' motivations inside their particular cognitive box. Biased science, to me, in that they are so tied to their deeper social theories that that's all they see.

This rejection of scholarly work does not keep them from discussing GAS themselves in a quasi-academic manner. Similar to the various cycles and processes of collecting and buying we have discussed in the previous chapters (for example, Belk et al. 2003; Braun et al. 2016; McIntosh & Schmeichel 2004) and that are described in blogs on GAS (for example, Power & Parker 2015), the community develops models based on their experience. One user proposes the following model:

1) obsesses for weeks over a piece of gear
2) read every post and watch every YouTube video on that piece of gear
3) try and tell myself I don't need it and don't really want to spend the money
4) forget about it
5) remember it weeks (or months) later and happen upon an unbeatable deal on a used version, which is cheap enough that I can resell and not lose much if need be
6) pull the trigger after much anxiety
7) after a brief period of exhilaration, immediate buyers remorse
8) rewatch all YouTube videos & read every post again to make sure I made the right choice
9) gear arrives in the mail, I play it, it's fine, I forget all about the turmoil

At large, the posts in this thread confirm the model but point out that the cycle is too long. For most users, the 'honeymoon period' lasts about three weeks, after which 'I start finding reasons why what I have isn't quite good enough or why I should use something else. It's so completely stupid. I have various bouts of this throughout the calendar year. In fact, it usually flames up around summer'. The model Power and Parker (2015) propose on a blog (chapter 2.1) is also discussed critically, and revisions are suggested, for example, these three:

1. Opportunity (forum, catalog, ect.)
2. Discovery
3. Research
4. Justification (defining why you need)
5. Sacrifice (deciding what to sell to make the new need a purchase)
6. Trigger pulling
7. Anticipation (shipping, or making time to drive to the store with the cash burning a hole)
8. Acquisition
9. Euphoria (the only thing we can focus on)
10. Regret/return to reality (not always regret, sometimes just acceptance of the item)
11. Relapse

1. Discovery. 'Hmmm cool thing there, what does it do?'
2. Research. 'What cool things does it do?'
3. Study. 'Man if I had this thing, think of all the cool things I could do!'
4. Obsession. 'Must look at every picture I can find! Must start/find threads that justify my usage of this thing! Must start finding things I can sell!'
5. Acceptance. 'I'm buying it today.'

1. Discovery. 'Hmmm cool thing there, what does it do?'
2. Research. 'What cool things does it do?'
3. Study. 'Man if I had this thing, think of all the cool things I could do!'
4. Compare. 'Well, this isn't really as cool as device X, and device Y doesn't have shortcomings A, B, and C, and device Z is just cheaper.'
5. Obsession. 'Must look at every picture I can find! Must start/find threads that justify my usage of this thing! Must start finding things I can sell!'
6. Acceptance. 'I'm buying it today.'
7. Evangelization. Post overwhelmingly positive reviews of the thing you bought within the first few days of buying it, before you've found out about all its faults.
8. Rejection. The item ends up in either the closet, basement, garage, craigslist, or returned to the store where you purchased it.
9. Repetition. Find the next thing to GAS over...

The reasons for GAS and how it can be counteracted are discussed at great length. A frequently cited reason for repeating GAS cycles is that the acquisition of new gear triggers the urge for other updates, which is consistent with the idea of 'craft consumption' (Cole 2018; Hartmann 2016):

I don't know if my amp GAS is made worse by my guitar GAS, or the other way around. But whenever I satisfy one, the other flares up.

My GAS just shifts. Bought a few nice guitars, bass amp, SR5, pedals, now looking for new amps. It never ends.

I have a problem that once I buy something … it makes me buy other stuff to go with it.

It is not clear whether changes to the setup necessitate updating other parts of the gear (Hartmann 2016). It may well be that the desire to acquire depends on the kind of gear. For example, there may be different GAS cycles for instruments, amplifiers and other devices active at the same time but at different points in the cycle. Signs thereof can be seen in the following statement: 'My amp GAS is gone. My guitar GAS has seriously been curbed. Pedal GAS is starting to trail off as well'.

7.2.2 Playing Versus Gear

GAS is concerned with, maybe even defined by, the relationship between gear and its actual use in playing. This determining distinction, as well as the overlap, are reflected in the discussions. Many musicians stress that they simply have an interest in gear. One form this interest can take is the curiosity to try out and compare brands or types of instruments as a form of musical exploration and as part of the development as a player (Pinch & Reinecke 2009). One bassist explains, 'I like to get a new bass, especially if it's a brand I haven't owned before, and figuring out what makes it tick. Each brand has its quirks, its strong points, etc. Some brands sound best with a certain kind of string. I like to find these things out'. These individuals point out that their curiosity does not require a long-term investment or even a purchase. For some, it is enough to play the equipment in a music store or rehearsal room. If the device is rare or brand new, then a purchase might be considered, even if selling is intended after trying it out.

In this context, several discussions emphasise that experimenting with different instruments and doing extensive research on equipment help musicians understand what sounds are available and which ones they prefer. This practice is considered 'reasonable' and should not be classified as GAS, as one musician argues:

> If you don't know what you want, then you should research what's out there so you can make a choice. I think that's different from just buying stuff for the sake of having it, which is what I think GAS is. I've been around drums for so long, that I can kinda guess what piece of gear will give me what I want, and then I make it do so.

In the same vein, another community member stresses that acquiring instruments 'is not GAS if you genuinely believe the gear will help you improve'. The intent is crucial, and as several musicians argue, will the investment benefit musical projects and development, then it is legitimate and should not be dismissed as 'just GAS'.

Like the interest in exploring equipment, an experienced drummer speculates that the way of learning an instrument may have changed. In the past, drummers began learning their instrument on a practice pad or snare before slowly building up their mastery to a full drum kit. Nowadays, newcomers would tend to start with a full kit, and experimenting with equipment has become common. This forum member does not elaborate further, but it may be that technical command has been at least partially replaced by sonic exploration (Théberge 1997). If this is the case, then frequently acquiring and trading equipment must almost inevitably become a routine habit of the modern player and accompany their musical development. Such increasing importance to sonic variety equally applies to instruments other than the drums (Pinch & Reinecke 2009; Théberge 1997).

A large number of posts demonstrate an interest in gear without the urge to buy, for example: 'I like to read about gear but I'm not much interested in getting more stuff'. Such musicians like to browse gear-related websites and catalogues and visit music stores, knowing that they would not buy anything because their current setup has everything they need. Their interest in gear is based partly on an inherent interest and partly on being well informed to be able to participate in the community's common discourse (Wenger 1998). This behaviour accords with research showing that record collectors and avid eBayers find pleasure in knowing for how much vinyl records are going (Denegri-Knott & Molesworth 2010: 65).

In connection with the previous point of genuine interest, many community members stress that gear is part of the fun of their hobby or profession:

> I long ago gave up explaining or defending the GAS thing to those who don't get it. I have played for 40 years, most of those for a living, and will always be obsessed with guitars. Amps, too ... Gear is just part of my fun. I am mostly a cheap guitar guy these days, but I still love buying and selling. I worked in a guitar shop for 20 years and I just can't stop. Don't want to stop.

> I spend far more time looking at gear and watching demos than I do playing, but it's part of the enjoyment of the hobby as well I suppose.

> If the gear itself is what makes you happy and you're happy with your playing standard, there's no harm whatsoever in spending all your time messing around with the gear aspect. You're no inferior to the guy practicing his iambic panta-loonian modes all night ... If the gear is the hobby and you're not getting into debt because you can't stop buying, then embrace it and accept that's what you're into.

Similarly, many musicians openly acknowledge having a greater passion for musical equipment than for playing. This passion for gear coincides with interview statements in Wright's (2006: 29) book that highlight musical purchases as a means of dealing with stress or as a reward for an accomplishment. Gratification is a major motivation for acquisitions, which is why many posts are stating that 'gear makes me happy'. Interest in gear for gear's sake culminates in the expressed fear of finding the perfect instrument or rig, which would make all future research into equipment and subsequent acquisitions pointless. Several threads point to this 'severe' but rare situation:

> I really like trying different gear. And right now I have more than I need already. So just buying more (even though I could easily afford it) just seems silly.

> Well I have been looking at all the new basses and amps and I feel like I have ran out of GAS. I have my bass that I love and I really like my amp, so I do not see the need to get anything else. It's kind of a bummer. Has anyone else ran out of GAS?

> ... that horrible feeling of withdrawal when there's absolutely no need to go to the guitar store for anything...

Other reasons for a pronounced interest in gear have more to do with personal circumstances. Several musicians describe it as a side-effect of boredom, having too much free time or time to bridge between classes or when commuting to work. Occupying oneself with gear and finding out about it on the Internet is much easier than playing when time is scarce. Consequently, GAS-related research is more compatible with family life and a busy work schedule than with practising:

> It's a lot easier to obsess over gear than it is to use it, when you have a wife, children, and full time employment. Those hours spent searching those sites are very rare hours.

Hours of playing time are comprised of blocks of minutes when I'm actually at home with my gear, and my wife and children are busy with other things that don't require my presence. The gear hunt takes place on my phone, usually at work or while watching the idiot box with the family, winding down for bed. I still haven't figured out a way to make more time to play that doesn't require sacrificing my time with my loved ones, so I don't flagellate myself over the GAS too much. It just wouldn't [be] fair to myself.

For many years when I had a day gig that took 50 hours a week and I was exhausted the rest of the time I could only play 30 minutes a day on non gig weekdays. So for me I simply could't practice. I filled that void of not getting any better with buying and selling lots of stuff that made me marginally better or worse. Now, 10 years into retirement where I can spend a couple of hours practicing a day I no longer search actively. I see progress on a regular basis and behold all I've had to buy are lessons. But I know from both as a player and a teacher until you can find the time to actually do something to make your playing better sometimes that new mouth-piece/horn/reed/lig/corkgrease seems like a step toward enjoying playing more. Just how it is.

These quotes show that when the time for practising is limited, the occupation with gear at least keeps the hobby alive without neglecting the family (Belk 1995b: 483; Goldberg & Lewis 1978: 94f; Stebbins 2009: 20).

Several posts express the serious conviction that updating equipment helps one progress as a player, which is in line with Stebbins's (2009: 115) assertion that continued investment is indispensable for musicians pursuing a serious leisure career. We have already discussed the widely held belief that musicians associate better gear with better performance (Kwisses 2015; Leonhardt 2015; Wright 2006). The truth of this belief is easy to dismiss from a musical perspective, but this would also disregard the underlying psychological processes that are worth exploring. One musician reasons:

I think a lot of people like going through gear because it feels like progress. It lights up the parts in the brain that give you a sense of accomplishment. Often, it is really more of a distraction from the work it takes to actually become better. I realize that about myself, so I make a conscious effort to counteract that urge. I constantly remind myself that you can be a great musician on a student horn if it works properly, and what is needed is practice and study (work). But if someone likes the gear and it makes them feel good, and they really don't care that much about becoming a better musician, than that's OK. My main advise is try to make sure you are not lying to yourself. I think it is way too easy to justify new gear by thinking 'this is going to help me better my art form'. It think it is healthy to be brutally honest with yourself. Some of us have probably witnessed the dude at a jam on a beat up Bundy blowing circles around guys with $12,000 of gear hanging from their neck. That is what it's all about.

Especially when there is not much time for practising, musicians understandably turn their attention to their hobby's material side. As the statement indicates, improving the equipment can give a sense of accomplishment and a feeling of progress. Well aware that acquisitions do not make them better players, most musicians nevertheless feel better when they have bought something. However, in many threads, those affected by GAS are accused of their lack of vision or artistic direction. This criticism is commonly related to the unquestioned belief that buying more expensive gear is an improvement regardless of musical needs (Leonhardt 2015). Musicians who join a band often feel the urge to improve their gear, as suggested by these two posts:

> I'm finally putting a band together. While listening to songs we think we wanna cover, we figured out that i will need a couple things for these songs. So instead of finding just what i need, i went a little crazy with the wishlist and, well, I'll let it speak for itself...

> I was eventually gonna get all this anyway, but being in a band now prompted me to take a closer look at my kit. imma be broke by the time this list is all taken care of.

While the first post indicates that there has been some musical exploration and discussion with band members, the second post suggests that the musician feels compelled to upgrade their drum kit without even having tried it out in practice.

Since GAS overlaps with the practice of collecting, we assumed that collecting would be a frequent topic of discussion in online communities. Our assumption was hardly met, consistent with the general rejection of the term collector observed in the survey and Wright's (2006: 63) distinction between GAS and collecting as different practices. The GAS-related discussions suggest that the understanding of a collector has changed over time. A musician reflects that in the 1970s, anyone who owned more than four guitars was called a collector. Another guitarist adds that when he started collecting 35 years ago, such a habit was not called 'collecting' but 'being nuts'. These accounts indicate that collecting instruments was regarded suspiciously and that common perception has gradually become more liberal, accepting larger equipment collections as normal musical behaviour. This interpretation concurs with Shuker's (2010: 199) finding that record collecting has become less stigmatised over time. Another group of musicians argues that collecting and accumulating gear is the defining criterion of GAS. Collecting and accumulating equipment is considered GAS, while frequently 'flipping' gear should not be regarded as such. The opinions are diverse and do not reflect a clear view. Some musicians do not consider themselves collectors despite owning more than fifteen instruments. Others find that collectors do not necessarily own many items because they 'flip' instruments to upgrade instead of accumulating them. Shuker (2010: 46) shares the opinion that collecting involves acquisition but not necessarily accumulation. The diverging views suggest that equipment size may not be the primary criterion distinguishing players from collectors. Instead, criteria for selecting and keeping gear and the purpose for its use may define both practices. Musicians who see themselves as players accumulate gear because they do not like to part with items, arguing that they were all bought for a reason, have a history or remind them of notable events or people, which suggests nostalgic motives (Boym 2001; Davis 1979; Pearce 1995; Shuker 2010). Others keep instruments because of their low re-sale value or because they are reluctant to invest the time and energy required to sell instruments. These motivations are different from collecting, defined by a systematic pursuit (McIntosh & Schmeichel 2004; Nordsletten & Mataix-Cols 2012; Nordsletten et al. 2013).

Most threads and posts joke about the positive effects of new gear, but only a few acknowledge its benefits for playing and creativity seriously. Some musicians believe that gear can inspire creativity in line with the concept of 'facilitation' (Hartmann 2016: 12), according to which objects provide an infrastructure for doings. These musicians point out that when a plateau is reached in terms of playing technique or songwriting, changing the instrument can help to develop further. For instrumentalists who have the choice to switch from an electric to an acoustic instrument or vice versa, the temporary change can be inspiring. As an electric guitarist elucidates: 'I have 32 guitars and 80 have passed my hands over the years. Having many choices is inspiring and can lead to lots of creativity, especially if you branch out to other KINDS of guitars like steel string, flattop, classical, flamenco, archtop acoustic, Gypsy jazz, etc.'. Likewise, switching from one model to another within the same category can provide new impulses. Another guitarist explains: 'Different guitars = more creativity. I find that I play completely different on an Esquire than I do [on] a Les Paul. I tend to try things on one that I would never do on the other. It keeps me interested which helps me be more creative'. For some instruments, the possible variations extend to amplifiers and other devices that afford specific playing styles or give a direction in songwriting (Herbst 2016). The choice of gear 'sets the scene' ('facilitation'), making creativity more likely. However, not only the musical scene is relevant; always having an instrument at hand can also contribute to creativity, as a guitarist points out:

> Being surrounded by guitars in every room of the house is nearly a spiritual thing; potential musical resonance everywhere. Even though I have a few favorites, I can pick up any guitar in any room, at any time and bond with it to make the air in the whole house vibrate in organized and interesting ways.

Another common view is that new equipment helps to maintain motivation to practise and play. One guitarist reveals, 'I really like having different guitars, I usually stick with one for a week or two and then rotate to another, always keeps it fresh'. That may well differ between various types of instruments. While it is easier for guitarists and bassists to switch between instruments and amplifiers because of the relatively small size and affordable price of their equipment, other instrumentalists may find it more challenging to create variations in their gear collection. Regardless of the individual challenges, creating variation through GAS-related behaviour can build up commitment to music as a hobby and motivate regular practising in times of doubt or crisis (Hartmann 2016: 14).

Consistent with blog entries on GAS (Kwisses 2015; Leonhardt 2015; Power & Parker 2015), many musicians believe that they play better on higher quality equipment. One drummer explains in detail the difference between his beginner set and a higher quality kit purchased later. The sound of the shells was not pleasant, and the cymbals sounded 'ear piercingly clangly'. Because of the poor sonic quality and feel of the kit, the drummer played more often on a practice pad than on the kit. When he played on his friend's set, he felt able to be expressive and experiment more. More importantly so, he did not want to stop playing. As he reflects, it took time to become a better player, but with the more pleasant tone and feel he got from playing with better gear, he began to realise his potential. Such joy resulted in improved skills. Purchasing a better drum kit enhanced his motivation and practice routine, which over time made him a better musician. Another drummer similarly stated that by replacing the stock snare of his kit with a better instrument, he realised how sensitive snare drums could be. As he further explains, the 'less mud factor was definitely inspiring and being able to hear ghost notes, made me feel better about my playing'. Furthermore, re-cutting the bearing edges on the drum set and switching from double to single-ply heads reduced the muffled sound and motivated him to improve his double-stroke roll technique. Still another drummer likewise stresses that having 'round, pure, perfectly tuned, unmuffled notes that sing out with nice sustain' affects his playing, arguing that

> The tone of the toms are just as vital as the notes I choose. When I do tom work, I rely on sustain and a note. That's what I'm hearing in my head. I love it, I want it, lots of it, and need it. If I play a kit with no sustain, like the typical done to death dead splat... my tom ideas... don't work at all, so I use the toms as little as possible on a kit that sounds like that.

A player specifies that such positive effects of better gear do not make a musician play better per se, but that it makes them *sound* better. The distinction between better sound and better playing is significant in the context of GAS, as many musicians equate a better sound with better playing. Better gear can indeed sound better, but it requires playing skills, and the better they are, the better the equipment's potential can be utilised. That playing skills are regarded as necessary to utilise an instrument's potential shows in threads asking about the perfect time to upgrade a rig.

Even though new equipment might increase motivation and improve tone, several posts highlight that changing gear can have a detrimental effect on musical development because instruments have 'learning curves'. One keyboardist emphasises that good synthesisers require considerable experimentation before their potential can be harnessed, and the time 'worrying about the mechanics of managing the instrument rather than evaluating if it has quality sounds' may not be spent 'practising'. Similarly, guitarists argue that switching gear 'can actually impair your progress' and therefore recommend sticking with a setup for several years. While they acknowledge that the affordances of gear challenge a player to develop their skills when the setup is changed, the best approach for optimal progress would be to 'own the right guitars/amps at the right time in your growth as a guitarist'. Saxophonists discuss the optimal mouthpiece in detail. Although many players change them frequently due to their affordability, it is stressed that experience and learning success dictate which mouthpiece should be used to match the playing level. Furthermore, saxophone models differ in their degree of difficulty to play, and specific techniques must be acquired or refined to play specific models. This requirement potentially defines the point at which a new instrument should be purchased by linking time to practice and learning success. Other instruments such as guitar, bass or drums tend to facilitate playing techniques or genres, but generally, models do not differ in their level of difficulty to play.

7.2.3 Emotions and Psychological States

Emotions are at the heart of GAS, as they motivate and follow acquisitive behaviour. In the context of collecting and consumption, we discussed pathological behaviours related to the use of musical equipment. The online discussions show that GAS is sometimes considered a common and 'incurable, contagious disease', which 'can result in acute psychosis'.

We have previously highlighted that the tone generally becomes more serious when spending patterns indicate that community members are financing their gear purchases through loans or willingly accept other financial problems to fund their musical practices. Related consequences like withdrawal from personal relationships or not paying everyday bills are symptoms of a pathological condition (Goldberg & Lewis 1978: 94f). This danger is quite real for GAS-afflicted musicians and can quickly turn into a vicious circle, as this example illustrates:

> I've come to the realization lately that GAS isn't really a logical thing. The endless search for tones seems to derive from consumerism and a need for novelty. I know I have everything I need gear-wise. I'd have everything I need with much less gear. But I always end up cruisin' Reverb and eBay, or walking through Guitar Center, GASing for some new thing. Problem is, I can't really afford it most of the time. I have to sell stuff to fund new things, but of course you can't always sell something for what you paid for it, so it's still a steady loss of money when you buy gear. I also end up realizing I want pedals back that I sold. So sometimes I end up buying a pedal again that I sold at a loss before. The truth is, if I had more money, I'd keep all my pedals, and probably have a cool music room with shelves for them. But that's not the case. Fellow broke people, how do you manage GAS?

Typical responses to such posts are these two:

> There is an awful lot of FOMO [fear of missing out] in these purchases and behaviour. I recognise that in myself when I find myself obsessing over a piece of gear. I'm not saying I've never experienced pathological GAS feelings, cos I have, but financially, I've never gone too far. Truth is, you don't NEED any of it. You might like it, love it, want it, use it, value it or be obsessed by it, but you don't NEED any of it. None of it will fill a hole in your life for a meaningful time. You probably need to go cold turkey to realise this … it's actually a serious topic, and some people here really need help. You are sounding like one of those.

> Jesus people. If you have credit card debt you shouldn't be buying anything aside from what you need to live. It's a trap. Make an austere budget, stick to it, get yourself debt free, sort it out, you will have far more money for fun stuff in the future that way. Not being holier than thou, trying to help!

The discussions attempt to identify the reasons for an irrational urge to acquire gear. There is broad consensus that GAS may be a distraction from other problems and a symptom of underlying problems in many cases. Several musicians reflect that GAS could be a scapegoat for other issues, that if it were not GAS, something else would take its place. There are also arguments suggesting that in the hope of happiness (Belk et al. 2003; Wright 2006: 22), material possessions fill a void in life. In most cases, however, acquisitions only give 'you a little dopamine hit and gets you excited for a minute and then you get bored and want something else'. It is a momentary pleasure but not long-lasting satisfaction (Shuker 2010: 111; Stebbins 2009: 21). The psychological complexity becomes visible from this musician's reflection:

> For me, the key was understanding that … GAS wasn't really about gear. It was about escape, distraction, and loneliness. When I feel anxious or depressed, looking at and buying gear provides a little bit of relief by distracting me and giving my mind something to focus on. Also, when I feel lonely, I sometimes feel that if I could have really cool gear, I would be more accepted by people, and I would feel more connected with others. The problem is that looking at and buying gear doesn't resolve any of these issues, and it can be big waste of resources. Understanding this and dealing with the deeper issues directly has allowed me to get better at seeing GAS for what it is, which has given it a lot less power over me.

The post alludes to several potential psychological problems, but the main one concerns social acceptance and company. Extensive engagement in an online community may hint at a lack of offline social networks, and once the newcomer is accepted into the community, a gear-obsessive behaviour is expected, which in turn promotes (superficial) social bonds. This behaviour is reflective of 'desire for sociality' (Belk et al. 2003; Formanek 1991), whereby the desire for material objects is motivated by the hope of facilitating social relations, either to gain access to a social group or to maintain it.

In the context of desire, we have looked at impulsive buying, which appears to be characteristic of medium to strong GAS. The message boards confirm the frequent occurrence of impulsive acquisitions. Several threads are explicitly dedicated to sharing experiences of impulsive buying. In the overwhelming majority, the related posts show regret about the irrational and sudden purchase, which reflects impulsive and compulsive buying (Faber & O'Guinn 1989; Faber & Vohs, 2004; Garcia 2007; Lo & Harvey 2011, 2012; McElroy et al. 1991, 1994). Impulsive acquisitions are generally sold or traded at a loss, or they are kept but not used for many years until they are finally sold. Reasons for spontaneous acquisitions comprise strong, often visual attraction, bargains or the curiosity to try out something new (Wright 2006: 28ff, 38ff). In many cases, the items proved useless in musical practice, or the musicians were so accustomed to their current setup that they did not want to change it. To counteract impulsive behaviour, a musician recommends committing to keep equipment, making one consider acquisitions more carefully. Another board member refrains from new purchases until having played their current gear extensively, which reaffirms to them that it satisfies their needs and does not require any improvements. Apart from this confirmation, the additional waiting time helps to reduce the impulsive urge. Such behaviour is a strategy described in anti-consumption research (Black & Cherrier 2010; Lee et al. 2011). A further musician has made good experiences with 'setting gear goals' and saving towards them, preventing impulsive acquisitions when managing to remain disciplined.

A small number of threads discusses GAS as a form of 'Obsessive Compulsive Disorder' (OCD) without a consensus. Some users speculate that 'chasing tone' is 'chasing dopamine' in disguise and may therefore not be 'much different than compulsive gambling or sex addiction'. A professional therapist challenges this hypothesis, arguing:

> If there is a link I believe it to be quite small. Especially if we are talking true OCD. OCD as it reaches clinical levels tends to reek havoc on creativity. Creative types certainly have their quirks but they generally dont have true OCD. They may have a few traits but a true OCD individual tends to be a concrete thinker and is far too wrapped up in their own world to seek answers through change. If an OCD individual happened to play saxophone the last thing he or she would want to do is change gear. That would be an invitation to chaos. Change=Pain.

Another forum member supports this view, emphasising that OCD is an anxiety disorder. Since affected people do not cope well with change, they do not continuously feel the urge to buy and update their setup. Some musicians see a stronger link between GAS and 'Attention Deficit Hyperactivity Disorder' (ADHD) because impulsiveness and short attention spans favour occupation with gear over long-term and potentially tedious practice. One drummer shares:

often I find myself in the middle of practicing, say, paradiddles around the kit and wondering how another crash or ride would sound, stopping what I'm doing to replace for no need or reason at all. I'm a gear hoarder. And I'm ADHD. And I'm compulsive. It's a bad combination. I need help.

The few posts do not allow further theorisation, and proper investigation would require psychological and psychiatric research into the connections between GAS, OCD and ADHD. However, research describing a neurological link between OCD and ADHD (Brem et al. 2014) indicates that musicians affected by one or both conditions may be more susceptible to GAS.

A small number of posts refer to 'hoarding disorder' (American Psychiatric Association 2013; Nordsletten & Mataix-Cols 2012). Although it is not clear how serious these 'confessions' are, some seem to be genuine. A representative example is this statement:

GAS took me for a ride for a couple years. I just couldn't turn down a deal. I was on CL [Craigslist] 10-20 times a day. I was buying and selling like a madman. I was looking in nearby cities, travelling out of my way, having stuff shipped across the country. It was a problem. I would try something new for a little bit and then the next piece would come along and I would sell the old. It wasn't until I started collecting a bunch of stuff that I was able to really beat it. I had gear all over the house with no place to hide it. I started using amps for furniture and hanging sh!t on the walls as 'art'. Then one day when the family was away, I sat down with my mountain of crap and started really A/Bing stuff with a critical ear. It became very apparent that a lot of stuff that I really liked and thought I would own forever just wasn't as good as some other item. It was tough to let go of some of it because I really believed it was unique and I would never find another. I was 'collecting' stuff for the sake of having it not because I needed it or would ever find time to actually use it.

The post demonstrates a mild case of hoarding that the individual could solve on their own without external help, but it still shows the mental struggles that an obsession with gear involves (Nordsletten & Mataix-Cols 2012; Nordsletten et al. 2013). Other musicians believe that hoarders disguise themselves as collectors and justify their accumulations with a 'purpose'. The posts show varying degrees of compulsion and intentions regarding the accumulation of gear, which supports our previous considerations that a considerable number of GAS-affected musicians are on the spectrum between unproblematic collecting and compulsive hoarding.

Reactions to observed compulsive behaviours are quite different. Some see compulsive patterns but either consider them harmless or justify them with reasonable arguments, for example, by stressing it is an affordable hobby or by outlining the benefits of owning much gear. Others intend to improve their behaviour when they observe compulsive traits because they regard it as comparable to addiction in gambling, shopping or alcohol. Therefore, some threads describe 'going broke' as a positive moment in a musician's life in the long run. One player expresses:

> Late last year, I was blessed to go broke. It didn't seem like a blessing at the time, but it put the brakes on a very unhealthy obsession with gear. In the ensuing time, I've come to realize that GAS is very much like the legend of the lotus-eaters as told in the Odyssey. It's a dangerous addiction that can permanently derail you if you're not careful.

When the money runs out, the musician is forced to reflect and change their behaviour. For some individuals, this external pressure seems to be necessary to break the GAS circle and develop a healthier relationship with their musical practice, one that emphasises playing over equipment.

Another frequent topic in discussions related to GAS is 'unhappiness'. Many musicians feel that too many instruments are a burden because they need to be stored and maintained. Some players feel compelled to upgrade their instruments, which can become a separate hobby; the time is then spent on crafting instead of practising (Becker 1996). Some even find the thought of owning many instruments stressful, feeling it would pressure them to play each one regularly. Not giving each instrument equal attention would lead to feelings of guilt. The dispensable instruments may end up hanging on the walls, which for some would be a daily reminder of the mismatch between their gear and playing, causing psychological stress. That is why a few musicians emphasise that they used to be happier when they did not have so much equipment and instead concentrated on their playing. Others highlight that with a smaller collection, they could have 'richer relationships and experiences' with their equipment. Several musicians report feeling better when 'thinning out the herd'.

7.2.4 Mitigations and Cures for GAS

On music boards, GAS is expected behaviour, but it is still treated ambiguously. This ambiguity is reflected in the discourse, in which about half of the posts encourage GAS-related habits, whereas the other half discuss mitigations for GAS. The exchange is characterised by the assertion that GAS cannot be permanently cured, at least not when music is a primary hobby. Redirecting a serious leisure career (Stebbins 2009) to another discipline is seen as the most promising approach to reduce or stop music-related GAS, which, however, bears the risk of developing a desire for something else. It is obviously not a cure for those who wish to continue being musicians. With another hobby that is not a substitute for music-making, principles and strategies can at least mitigate the effects of GAS. The most common advice is to avoid possible temptations from message boards, social media gear channels, musicians' magazines, music stores, equipment-related videos and websites such as Craigslist and eBay, arguing that 'if you want to cure it, then just stop feeding the beast'. Abstinence reduces temptations and prevents musicians from discovering and becoming familiar with new items, which also effectively prevents these objects from becoming a necessity (Braun et al. 2016). Accordingly, meetings with fellow 'gear heads' in the 'real world' should be limited and instead, contact with musicians focused on playing be sought. Comparing one's gear and tone with other musicians is also to be avoided because the exchange of ideas and photos of personal setups besides gear envy are key motivators for GAS, in line with research on collecting (McIntosh & Schmeichel 2004; Shuker 2010) and consumption (Belk 1988; Belk et al. 2003; Tuan 1980) highlighting social competitiveness and status resulting from the strong connection between possessions and identity. Another recommendation to resist the temptation of buying new gear, or at least to delay it, is to explore the potential of equipment already owned by experimentation and research, such as reading the manual, watching videos and searching for advice on how to use it. Still another strategy to avoid impulsive buying is to write a wish list for gear to be bought in the future in the hope of 'eventually outgrowing' it (Wright 2006: 33) or that 'logic will take over' (Dholakia et al. 2018). Such an approach will not stop the feelings of GAS altogether, but it may lead to a continuous cycle of desires (Belk et al. 2003), which is favourable in that it starts anew before equipment is bought. Acquisitions and their negative consequences are prevented, next to promoting healthy consumer behaviour, characterised by reflecting on the individual economic position and taking a reasoned decision (Hoch & Loewenstein 1991).

Belk et al. (2003: 343) argue that hope is crucial for any desire to develop and be sustained. Some musicians depicted good experiences with deliberately desiring 'impossible purchases' to avoid gear-related spending:

> Without curing it, it's actually fairly easy to abate. All you need to do is make sure that you are gassing for something that you can't possibly afford. Right now, I am longing for either a new Benedetto or a D'Angelico New Yorker [guitar] made by John. It will be a long, long time before I could think of getting one, but focusing on that makes GAS have zero effect.

> Set your GAS to trigger only on unrealistically expensive, 12k+ instruments.

> Now you start GASsing for an Alembic Classic [bass] worth 30k. You spend lots of time listening to samples, watching pics, documentaries, you stalk the builders around, and know you'll never be able to afford one.

All these recommendations focus on controlling the psychological urge by either avoiding temptation or redirecting it to something unattainable, strategies discussed in anti-consumption research (Dholakia 2015; Hoch & Loewenstein 1991; Montoya & Scott 2013; Myrseth et al. 2009; Redden & Haws 2013; Siemens & Kopp 2011).

One of the main problems of GAS is that an 'unreasonable' amount of money is spent on luxury items not needed. The discussions show that many musicians see the solution to this problem in the decision to make purchases only with money earned through music.

> My GAS cure came when I reduced down to two amps and three guitars... then told myself ANY new gear I purchased would be bought with gig money... and ONLY gig money.

> Music has never been my primary source of income, but I have been making at least a modest profit from music every year since 2008. I can't justify gear purchases otherwise.

> So for the part-time musician with a full time job these gigs are not too bad. They have paid for all of my equipment over the years and have allowed me to fuel my Gear Acquisition Syndrome (GAS) with out dipping into my family money. I have a hobby that is self-sustaining.

As the statements demonstrate, observing this principle can alleviate either the adverse financial consequences of GAS or the psychological burden associated with it. Similarly, many musicians have made it a rule to realise their desire for experimentation with new gear through trading ('flipping') or selling owned equipment so that the collection neither grows nor requires substantial investment.

> Personally, I think that experimenting with new gear can be really fun and inspiring, but it's pretty easy to become caught up in it to the point that it becomes compulsive and distracting. I like to change things up once in a while, but I do it by maintaining a constant net investment in gear. That means that if I want to get something new, I first have to sell something that I currently own. Most of what I currently own works well for me, and so I rarely feel motivated enough to go through the hassle of trying to get something new.

> I have a rule that I (mostly) stick to that says if I buy something I have to sell something, so they don't pile up. 90% of what I buy is used as well.

> I justify new GAS by flipping out redundant guitar gear to give way for new or better GAS. I may have disposed gems I may no longer be having or can still have but have to pay way more than how much I got it but my present GAS won't be where it is now if those transactions didn't push through.

Another strand of discussions does not revolve around strategies and principles that can be applied proactively but instead around constraints that inevitably limit the effects of GAS. Some musicians highlight that becoming older entailed lower ambitions and desires for new gear because the urge has waned, or the rational mind has made it hard for them to justify spending money on unneeded equipment. However, this does not seem true for anyone because posts of musicians over 60 or 70 years prove otherwise, still performing on stage several times a month. By their accounts, they reduced their instrument collection, prioritising a few good-sounding and versatile instruments that are easy to transport and set up on stage. There are yet others like a 71-year-old guitarist who has been playing since 1957, arguing that GAS will never disappear. Although having all the instruments he ever wanted and being completely satisfied with his current collection, he reports recently having spent $6,200 on new gear 'just because something new pops up'. Likely, musicians who have always been prone to GAS will keep to their habits when they get older, and those who have always prioritised their playing will do so even more as they age. This ambiguous observation is consistent with research not being able to confirm a clear link between age and financial decision-making, including impulsive buying (Bangma et al. 2017). As they get older, musicians are more likely to prioritise those aspects of their hobby that interest them the most, be it gear or playing.

Another constraint is limited space, even though the discussions do not clarify how effective it is in mitigating GAS. The posts suggest that limited space reduces GAS only temporarily, as it does not change the root of the behaviour. In contrast, financial constraints are much more effective, although also tackling the symptoms only. The lack of disposable income is one of the main involuntary financial constraints that naturally limits GAS-related spending. There are countless posts like these:

> The one and only way to cure GAS is to go completely broke. Works wonders.

> Usually not having money makes it really easy for me to not spend it.

> When I'm poor (which is most of the time) it's easy to manage GAS. If there's no money, there's no way I can buy anything—so BAM! When I have money... that's when it's hard to manage the GAS.

> NO MONEY! That's the only thing that has stopped me. I have seen so many deals lately. I surely would have pulled the trigger on at least one of them. The only thing that has stopped me has been lack of money. So, if you want to finally get rid of your addiction, go broke! Problem solved.

> Being broke only cures the 'Acquisition' part of GAS... it doesn't stop me from GASsing.

As the last post suggests, lack of money, just like lack of space, does not stop GAS but makes indulgent equipment purchases less likely. However, a severe financial crisis like the Covid-19 pandemic seems to reduce GAS significantly, which can be seen in respective discussions about its consequences like furlough and redundancy. Representative statements include: 'Here's something to cure your GAS. Say you get furloughed or let go. The wages stop coming in. Can't eat a bass, can you?', 'Due to the lockdown, my short scale GAS seems to have abated'. These statements highlight that GAS is a luxury problem that most likely affects musicians from affluent societies and the middle and upper classes.

A final kind of remedy, the most effective one as per Becker (1996) and Wright (2006), is being in a serious relationship or marriage. Apart from the partner critically evaluating excess purchases, children are a strong motivation for many musicians not to spend money unnecessarily on music equipment:

> My 'gear acquisition syndrome' has been replaced with the 'getting kids through college headache'.

> Putting two kids through college has pretty much cured my GAS.

> Getting married pretty much ended my GAS ... But seriously, get married to a sensible Women who is good with money ... have 3 kids and you'll never see an expensive bit of guitar gear passing through your door again. Solved—No more GAS!

Belk (1995b: 483) describes that family members may regard collections of obsessive collectors as rivals. The exemplary posts demonstrate that the family is positioned above equipment, suggesting a still healthy dealing with gear. Shifting the focus to a new relationship is seen as another way to avoid GAS, even if this is only a temporary cure.

Another kind of mitigation can be classified as 'realisations'. Some musicians recognise through more experience that most gear sounds relatively similar if one takes the time to examine and compare it properly (Crowdy 2013). Realising that alternative models are essentially quite similar seems to be an effective way for moderately GAS-affected musicians, who justify acquisitions by their musical use or need, to reduce the frequency of purchases. Likewise, many musicians acknowledge that there is no perfect rig or that it would not improve their playing unless it were significantly better than that they currently use. Some players recognise there is no such thing as the 'perfect tone' and state that they would settle for a 'great tone' while others realise that their playing would always sound like them regardless of the equipment played. For electric guitarists, it can be enlightening to study classical guitar, as it 'is all about technique and musicianship between hands and instrument, everything comes from the player—no "gear" involved'. Related to other electric instruments, several musicians report they have realised that simple setups usually sound better than complex ones, which makes sense from a technical viewpoint because extensive processing and unnecessary cable connections easily diminish audio quality (Välimäki & Reiss 2016).

Observing other players can also lead to helpful realisations. Like the previous recommendation to appreciate the current rig's quality, musicians highlight that hearing it played by a fellow musician helps them realise how good it sounds. Likewise, some GAS-minded musicians, who tend to value idols that use complex setups, realise that their GAS can be reduced by listening to other renowned musicians with great tone produced with simple rigs:

> Many pro's gig with boards that are way cheaper and smaller than TGP 'bedroom player' boards... Just sayin'. You don't need a massive board filled with boutique pedals to get great tones. Practice > pedals.

> GAS can be cured by watching and listening to great musicians performing gloriously with totally uncool gear.

> I cure GAS by watching rig rundowns of the biggest players in the industry, playing with 3 boss pedals in a standard direct from the store marshall/fender, and all of a sudden, my 29 pedal board feels ridiculous and i think of selling it all to get a blues driver and a delay and be happy.

> This world of unlimited gear excess is at best a fantasy world for most people. Robin Trower has used fender hotrods and stock Marshalls for ever.

> Besides, didn't I know that Yngwie Malmsteen shreds on a guitar with a medium action, just like mine has? Yngwie Malmsteen has a guitar just like, or perhaps even worse than, mine. But plays like a God. Hence it cannot be the guitar that is holding me back, for otherwise, it would have held Yngwie back too, but that is obviously not the case.

The previous survey of community members found evidence that role models do not influence musicians in their acquisitions much. But what role models usually do is teach the regular musician that playing matters and not the equipment. Likewise, some musicians who perform live have realised that the audience either does not care about the gear they are playing or may not even be able to tell the difference. In this sense, it is also stressed that good songs do not require perfect sound to be appreciated by the audience.

Another set of realisations revolves around 'becoming a better musician'. A common recommendation to counteract GAS is to remember why one started playing in the first place: 'Think about, meditate upon, and reflect on why you wanted to play guitar in the first place. Was it to acquire gear?' The discussions suggest that many musicians follow a similar development. When they started making music, they enjoyed playing and practising on entry-level instruments. Over time, their interest shifted to gear, either as part of their musical exploration or as a consequence of losing the motivation to practise, when the initial enthusiasm for the new hobby has been waning and musical progress slowing down. Shifting the focus to the musical purpose of leisure activity is considered an effective means to limit the urge to buy new gear. Likewise, most musicians agree that playing their current rig is 'the best GAS killer' and that practice will help them utilise its full potential.

> I went through a period of gear obsessiveness about 5 years ago, during which I bought and sold a lot of guitars. As is the usual pattern, I was getting back into the guitar in a serious way after many years of only casual playing. The gear acquisition syndrome did indeed siphon away a lot of time that would have been better spent on the fretboard. But then, after I had some gear I was reasonably happy with, the gear fixation subsided and I started spending a minimum of 4+ hours a day in serious study. Only then did any of the sexy gear bear fruit. For me, gear acquisition without the accompanying practice time is displacement behavior, and I will never allow myself to go there again. My motto is that no more than 5% of my 'guitar

time' can be spent on gear (research, purchase, repair...), forums, etc. And yes, I keep track of it.

I decided long ago that more or better gear would not make me a better player. I downsized all my equipment, Drums, Bass and Guitar to the minimum I need to play, and I spend my time and effort on playing, experimenting with tuning's, and writing some songs for fun, and recording. I now spend no time wishing and looking and hoping for a better drum or guitar, and spend my time getting the maximum out of what I have. I have not even scratched the surface yet.

It is often suggested that taking lessons contributes to musical improvement and spending music-related money on something 'sensible' while reducing GAS: 'I find nothing kills GAS more efficiently than lessons with an inspiring teacher'. Keeping busy with musical projects can help. While bands can be a motivator for GAS, they can also draw attention to songwriting, recording and performing music, thus avoiding occupation with GAS out of boredom.

My cure for gas is to focus on writing, recording and gigging. Leaves me with no time to really go out and buy stuff.

When I play live, I become more satisfied with what I have, focus more on working with it than on replacing it, and understand more that few of the 'upgrades' I've obsessed over have made a damn bit of difference.

The best cure for Gas for me was getting out and playing in a band again! Made me focus on playing the music. Learning and writing new songs. When I spent a few years not getting out and playing with others I spent far to[o] much time compinsating for the real thing by buying material stuff.

The respective threads discuss whether GAS is the most widespread amongst 'bedroom players', yet the conversations do not come to a definite conclusion. It seems that although gigging musicians like to buy new gear, its use is tested in real-world situations until a rig that works best is found, thereby reducing the urge for further acquisitions.

A considerable number of posts from players claiming to have learned to control GAS indicate that they have found their 'perfect rig'. This realisation resembles Cole's (2018: 1060) solution for GAS by focusing on the setup's 'use-value', which is not an inherent property of objects but defined by individual musical needs. The perfect rig can take various forms. Many musicians have noticed that they are most satisfied with a minimalist setup. However, this realisation often requires years of experimentation with instruments to finally determine what gear works best for the musicians' playing styles.

I'm here to honestly say out loud that after almost 10 years of compulsively checking the classifieds, eBay, and Reverb almost every waking hour for the next thing that would get me 'my tone' or 'that sound' that I am finally GAS free and it feels f***ing awesome. It wasn't cheap or easy... pretty painful at points dealing with builds, bad sellers, shipping companies, girls who couldn't believe that pickups and preamps were more interesting than them, etc + all of the other trial(s) by fire along the way. I finally have the bass, board, amp, cables, strings and everything else to get the perfect sounds I've always wanted. Looking forward to spending more time playing than shopping, jonesin' and flipping! For me-the biggest steps were committing to have one bass, one board and one amp setup with a backup bass+amp at most. Using custom cut pain-in-the-butt patch cables forced me to stick to a setup and see it through. Rather than having a studio full of variety I set out to trim the fat and have the best possible rig.

Many posts suggest that one or two high-quality instruments work better than a medium-sized collection. However, it is up to the personal assessment of what setup is suited for one's style or offers the greatest versatility. Either setup can be effective in reducing GAS long-term. Getting to this point, however, requires not only experimentation but also the budget to afford it. It takes years for most musicians to gradually upgrade their equipment by selling gear and buying better equipment with continuous investment, sometimes referred to as 'horse-trading'. This gradual improvement, achieved through learning, reflecting and investing money, is characteristic of a serious leisure career (Stebbins 2009) and may last decades or even a lifetime. Furthermore, several posts suggest that the perfect rig or the opportunity to experiment with all the desired gear during the leisure career can effectively alleviate GAS. A variation of 'perfect rig mitigation' is building the perfect instrument in the act of craft consumption (Campbell 2005; Cole 2018) because it makes stock models uninteresting. The commission of custom-made instruments is discussed much less than DIY, but it serves the same purpose.

The vast majority of those satisfied with their rig still note that GAS will never disappear completely. Notwithstanding rarely having the strong urge to buy, those players' interest in gear does not wane, which is similar to collecting. A collection either is never-ending or, once it is complete, another one will be started (McIntosh & Schmeichel 2004; Shuker 2010; Straw 2000). If musicians suffer from GAS, the most effective strategy for alleviation is a combination of principles and shifts in mindset. Principles help control the financial burden by delaying the immediate impulse to buy, leading to more purposeful acquisitions. A change of mindset shifting the focus from gear to playing appears most promising to reduce GAS effectively and permanently. The ultimate goal is a rig that meets all musical requirements and matches the level of playing. Getting there, however, usually takes years of GAS; one must find out what gear works best and build up the purchasing power to afford the right setup, which will rarely be entry-level equipment. It seems that for many players, GAS is an integral aspect of the learning process and musical expertise, which eventually leads to a more fulfilling serious leisure career and better musical results unless the musical development is hampered by the interest in gear in that it takes away from practising and meaningful musical projects.

7.3   Discussion

The analysis of virtual communities was motivated to extend the survey results by further explanatory insights and to deepen and consolidate the previous interdisciplinary theoretical deliberations on GAS. Following the overarching framework of 'Communities of Practice' (Lave & Wenger 1991; Wenger 1998) proved helpful, and the three dimensions defined by Wenger (1998: 73–83) were met in our investigation. The various message boards shared unwritten rules, knowledge and norms ('mutual engagement'), they referred to other boards and offline practices ('joint enterprise'), and they produced a joint discourse characterised by routines, events, habits, stories, jargon and jokes ('shared repertoire'). Although all three dimensions include GAS, it does not constitute itself in the communities, except for equipment-centred groups like The Gear Page and Gearslutz, where GAS is a central part of the community discourse. As the analysis has shown, knowledge about GAS is expected, and one must adhere by learning and continuously updating one's rig to function effectively in the community. GAS is discussed in dedicated threads and mentioned in non-GAS themed conversations as a 'running gag', and the term is also used to warn members when their obsession with gear shows signs of going too far. Playing an instrument is the overarching hobby that at times is hard to maintain, especially when an excessive interest in gear replaces music-making or when work, family life or other hobbies do not leave enough time to practise. A keen interest in gear is generally viewed positively as long as it is a conscious decision and not an excuse or distraction for those wishing to advance as players.

Irrespective of the relative importance of playing and gear for the individual, musicians may benefit from GAS in their learning process and socialisation in the communities. Most musicians are curious to experiment with equipment and see it as a way to advance musically. Through purchases of new gear or 'flipping' to modify or upgrade the rig, continuous acquisition accompanies musical development. Only when there is a mismatch between playing and GAS or when musicians buy equipment on credit is GAS generally considered a problem. It is usually a shared joke and treated with humour. Having GAS is part of the community identity, and members compete over the level of affliction. A closer look at the discourse, however, reveals a more serious engagement with gear. Many musicians are aware of the risks of unhealthy behaviours and thus monitor their practices. They accept GAS as an integral part of their leisure career, which, on the one side, is linked to musical progress, motivation and practice, and on the other side is due to plain boredom and lacks purpose and direction. Musically, not being involved in meaningful projects can fuel GAS, as the examples of 'bedroom musicians' have shown. Conversely, musical projects can stimulate GAS in the endeavour to maximise the results of the venture. Often, GAS seems to be a symptom of other feelings, motivations or struggles within the leisure career and of the person in general. As such, GAS is a proxy for something else.

The observed practices differ from studies that examined comparable forums for music producers. Both kinds of communities focus on equipment but vary in the degree of importance they attach to its use. The discourse on forums for music producers is characterised by strong competition and social hierarchy. Ownership of analogue devices distinguishes privileged community members, those with more economic or social capital like participants from more affluent societies (Hesmondhalgh 1998) or industry professionals (Carvalho 2012; Cole 2011; Crowdy 2013; Kaiser 2017; O'Grady 2019; A. Williams 2015). Apart from mere ownership, the use of equipment brings about an even greater differentiation within the communities. That is why becoming part of the social elite requires more than ownership and knowledge of privileged equipment. As Cole (2011) highlights, audio professionals often expose hobbyists or semi-professional 'prosumers' (professional consumers) by their inability to utilise the potential afforded by prestigious gear to demonstrate social capital. Such exposure is based on assessment and discussion of user-generated work. Similarly, Porcello (2004) and Carvalho (2012) find that language distinguishes ambitious amateur and semi-professional recording engineers and producers from professionals, for example, when discussing gear and engineering techniques.

The musicians' boards are far less competitive. New acquisitions are celebrated regardless of the musical necessity and status, experience or expertise of the musician. How it is used is not overly important; it is the process of acquisition that matters, for example, the successfully overcome psychological struggle to part with an instrument to make space for the new equipment or to strike a particularly good bargain. The pleasure comes from the acquisition irrespective of whether the level of playing justifies it. In only very few of the observed GAS-related threads, buyers can be seen posting audio or video recordings where they play the new equipment to demonstrate and discuss its musical use.[40] Is musical necessity ever questioned, then usually by the buyers themselves in their self-assessment. The level of professional-

---

[40] Unboxing videos, of which there is a vast amount on YouTube, are rarely posted in GAS-related threads. The reason is not clear; there may be separate communities on other platforms such as YouTube itself or other social media, where the groups are more interactive and focused on photos and audio-visual media.

ism is irrelevant; musicians participate in the community because of the joy of making music or dealing with gear. There are no strong indications of rivalry or belittlement resulting from social hierarchies or attempts to gain status.[41]

Compared to forums for music producers, communities for musicians are collegial. The members enjoy their 'guilty pleasure' together because equipment would be much less enjoyable if the pleasures were not shared with peers. One musician highlights in their introduction to a GAS-related thread that 'these threads are always good fun (and surprisingly educational)'. The two components, fun and education, seem to be at the centre of GAS. Musicians delight in experimenting with gear and sharing their experiences. At the same time, the way of using it is decisive as to whether gear hampers or facilitates musical development since it accompanies growing expertise. For a player of popular music, knowledge of equipment and how to use it best is essential. Equipment will not replace playing skills and musical intuition, but it is a tool that both requires and facilitates musical expression.

---

[41] Although there are no strong indications of a social hierarchy, the communities show a gender imbalance with an overrepresentation of male members. In general, they accept female musicians, but the frequent occurrence of sexist expressions may still discourage non-male musicians, making these communities a mainly male-dominated space.

8   Conclusion: Towards a Theory of GAS

GAS accompanies many musicians throughout their lives, regardless of whether they are familiar with the term or not. As we have shown, it is debated on message boards and online blogs, and it is implicit in special-interest books for musicians. Most of our survey participants identified GAS as the main topic, suggesting that they are aware of the phenomenon and discursive term. Against this backdrop, the distinct lack of research on this cultural practice came as a surprise and let us explore GAS in popular music. Relevant work in popular music studies and music technology was scarce, which is why we chose a multidisciplinary approach that considered cultural and leisure studies, sociology, consumption research, psychology and psychiatry. Such a multifaceted approach not only proved to be valuable but was necessary to study GAS. This concluding chapter brings together the various evidence and theoretical deliberations to work towards a theory of GAS. In the introduction, we preliminarily defined it as a pronounced and prolonged interest in music equipment, combined with an intense desire to acquire and possess certain items of gear, which still holds. Our explorations yet showed that GAS involves far more forms and practices.

A recurrent interest of our study has been the role of personal, social and musical motives in the consumption of musical instruments, some of which shall be highlighted again. There are several musical reasons why musicians in popular music have a pronounced interest in technology and consider acquisition and upgrade essential for their musical development and performance quality. The right rig is required for maximum expressiveness, and specific setups may be necessary for the convincing performance of individual genres. Specialist gear can enhance stylistic versatility and lead to sonically more convincing performances. Consequently, the more varied a musician's stylistic repertoire becomes, as expertise increases, the more specialist gear may be required. Whether or not this 'necessity' is genuinely justified for musical reasons cannot be said with certainty, yet the survey has shown that greater playing experience correlates with a richer instrument collection. Role models were expected to be influential on musicians' gear choices, but the evidence is mixed. Special-interest books suggest that amateur musicians, especially guitarists, are interested in the gear renowned musicians are playing. Further signs that desires of amateurs can be awakened by the gear their idols play came from our interviews with musicians at a music store, some open comments in our survey and several posts on message boards. The survey results, however, do not confirm a significant impact on buying decisions. The main criteria are sound, playability and construction quality when choosing an instrument. The rig is expected to support the musical intentions and, above all, enable a distinctive personal sound. It seems to have become more important to have an individual sound than to follow role models and adhere to expected genre aesthetics. Therefore, customising and modifying stock instruments in the process of craft consumption is popular amongst musicians to tailor the rig to their individual needs and progress towards a unique setup. Similarly, replacing gear with higher quality equipment or gear that better suits one's style is another step on the path to creating an original sound. Different groups of musicians such as players, collectors, gear heads, crafters and purists are discussed in the literature. Although their practices differ, our theoretical deliberations and empirical findings suggest that all groups work towards upgrading their rig or instrument collection, just with varying goals and justifications. The findings indicate that the distinctions are much less clear-cut than the literature has us believe. Crafters and purists are players, and many who identify as collectors also play. Perhaps it is the group of gear heads concerned the most with their rig, with their interest in gear overweighing playing in some cases. Collectors in the true sense seem to be rare on message boards for musicians because hardly anyone, if any, identified themselves as mere collectors, and neither did the survey participants; all those collecting were also playing. The widespread notion of collectors accumulating and curating rare instruments behind a glass window could not be confirmed. Such collectors likely exist, but they probably socialise in different communities of practice than those for musicians.

Personal situations and motivations also influence how musicians deal with gear. By drawing on a multitude of theories and data from consumption, collecting and leisure studies, we found strong evidence that musicians perceive their rig as part of their (extended) self. Not serving a sole instrumental purpose, the rig represents dreams and hopes, characterises lifestyles, and enables the musician to become a member of communities where gear is part of social etiquette, helping them build bonds and determine their position in the social hierarchy. For many musicians, instruments are more than just tools for making music. The findings suggest that players form relationships with their instruments to which they attribute human qualities over time. The fact that instruments are sometimes given a name further demonstrates the degree of personification. Possession rituals make the objects part of the extended self.

Several sociodemographic variables are essential in the context of GAS. Age is one of them. The survey showed that older musicians tend to own more equipment on average. Yet the peak is reached in the fifties, then the values fall again. Generally, the desire to acquire new instruments diminishes with age, although the qualitative findings also present examples of musicians whose interest in gear is as great, if not greater, than in playing. Some players downsize their rigs to make it easier to transport, while others want to enjoy their retirement and find pleasure in buying gear. Musicians with more playing experience also own more equipment, for which may account occasional discretionary purchases, reluctance to sell or lack of effort to trade gear to keep the collection size stable. Professional players, as has also been shown, possess more gear, which likely is due to their endeavour to play various styles for reasons of employability or professional self-image; achieving this status involves extensive experimenting with instruments. The propensity towards nostalgia contributes to an increasing collection size, accompanied by a generally higher interest in gear. While some posts on the analysed message boards suggest that collecting may be based on upgrading instead of accumulating items, collecting leads to higher numbers of objects in possession, according to the survey results. The survey indicates that some musicians see symbolic meaning in instruments they own and therefore do not sell or trade them. However, many message board users tend to trade equipment with little nostalgic hesitation. Besides collecting instruments as one aspect of GAS, specific musical motives play a crucial role for GAS as an overall phenomenon, the musicians' great interest in the expressiveness of their playing and sound. The same applies to musicians with a strong orientation towards specific role models and their gear.

Gender is another crucial sociodemographic variable frequently discussed in research on consumption and collecting. Traditionally, the music instruments industry paid little attention to women as consumers. Likewise, in the common GAS discourse, they were hardly ever considered or otherwise merely seen as restricting their male partner's GAS behaviour. There are signs, though, that the musical instruments industry is changing. Retailers have created more welcoming spaces for non-male customers, and manufacturers increasingly produce instruments optimised for the female anatomy. These are positive signs, but more effort is required to reach parity. As evidenced, the endorsement practice is unbalanced, prioritising men by awarding them with more endorsements and sponsorship of higher-value gear than women. Our findings are inconclusive in terms of gender equality. On the one hand, women and non-binary genders are drastically underrepresented in the survey's sample population and observed online communities, where sexist comments were commonplace. On the other hand, the survey results give no indication of substantial gender differences. Female musicians likely vary in their gear-related practices more gradually than substantially, which would be in line with the theories and empirical studies in collecting and consumption. Probably GAS is similarly pronounced in women as in men but less openly presented. How it differs in detail is difficult to determine with the given data, which is why more research is needed, either with a more balanced gender ratio or specifically targeting female and non-binary musicians.

There are clear indications of social motivations in dealing with gear and the discourse surrounding it. Many musicians visit music stores with fellow players, and purchases are often motivated by group projects and bands. As the findings suggest, bandmates are important points of reference even though musicians prefer them not to interfere in their gear choice because the rig is very personal to a player. Social considerations often affect acquisitions, be it for gear envy or adapting the rig to the overall sound of a band. The evidence is inconclusive as to whether musicians playing in bands or so-called 'bedroom musicians' are more inclined to GAS; many players in both groups have a pronounced interest in gear. While bedroom players are not influenced by bandmates, being members of online communities impacts, through social conformity, their dealing with gear.

A fundamental assumption guiding the research project was that players of various types of instruments would differ in their buying and collecting behaviour, with players of electronic or electric instruments being more susceptible to GAS than those of acoustic instruments. We expected electric guitarists to be affected by GAS the most, given the term GAS roots in 'Guitar Acquisition Syndrome'. Our analysis of special-interest books indeed suggests that the literature on the electric guitar is gear-centric. Books about the electric guitar focus on the rig and sound production much more than books about the acoustic guitar. Likewise, books about the bass guitar, a similar instrument to the electric guitar, hardly cover gear but scales, grooves and signature lines instead. The literature clearly is technologically deterministic for the two instruments, electric guitar and synthesisers, but not for keyboards. For the other instruments, acoustic guitar, bass, drums, saxophone and trumpet, books cover playing techniques, technical exercises, rhythms and grooves, music theory, songs and etudes. In other words, our assumption that players of electric guitar and other electronic instruments would be the ones most concerned with gear and therefore susceptible to GAS has been confirmed by the analysed books. This impression fits well with the theoretical deliberations on the part of the music technology literature, yet our two empirical studies have not found sufficient evidence thereof. The survey results indicate that the overall differences between the instruments are relatively small, apart from a few instrument-specific attitudes and options, such as modifying the instrument, for which there is a developed market for electric guitars. While the size of equipment collections is difficult to compare, the psychological processes associated with GAS allowed comparison between all instrumentalists. Differences between electric and acoustic instruments were tendential, so the results cannot definitively confirm a systematic inclination to GAS for electric musicians. Hardly any differences between mono- and multi-instrumentalists could be found. Furthermore, the survey results are consistent with the findings of the message boards analysis, which demonstrated a comparable discourse and GAS behaviour in all forums, regardless of the type of instrument. An interesting result shows in the discrepancy between the instrument-specific focus of special-interest books and the similarities between the interest in gear and attitude towards GAS across all studied instruments. Even if not representative of the entire musical instruments industry, these books still suggest that 'the industry'—or at least the authors and publishers of such books—have a wrong impression of their target audiences. Only players of the electric guitar and synthesiser are considered gear- and technology-centric. Players of the other instruments are assumed to be predominantly interested in playing. Hence it seems that special-interest literature is relatively backward. Our findings strongly suggest a readership for gear-centred media tailored specifically to drummers, bass players, saxophonists and trumpeters.

From our own participation in virtual message boards emerged the expectation that online practices contribute to a pronounced interest in musical gear that creates and fuels GAS. Prosumptive practices, such as window shopping on eBay and other online platforms for second-hand instruments, raise hopes of finding exciting new pieces of gear or bargains. The pleasure of observing the market, knowing the value of items and bidding is enhanced by daydreaming and competition because every day can be the day an item turns up, or a low bid is unexpectedly successful due to lacking competition. Empirical research in consumption studies finds that the pleasure of such auction and second-hand selling websites is short-lived, yet our findings suggest the opposite; musicians are visiting them frequently, if not daily, for years. As our findings further indicate, interest in gear and acquisitions is only half as pleasurable if the action and success are not socially shared on message boards and other social media. We have observed that GAS is commonplace in discourse and daily exchange. Evidence thereof is the high number of GAS-related threads, ranging from lingo threads in which the term is included, GAS tests, quasi-academic discussions about GAS, to interest in scholarly work. Overall, online discussions provide ample evidence that the Internet has significantly changed musical and equipment-related practices. Besides a wealth of information on equipment and how to improve tone, there is a continuously expanding consumer market that becomes ever more convenient, and new and used instruments are sold and distributed worldwide. The market for used instruments cannot be overstated as both the survey and the forum analysis suggest that most musicians prefer to buy used instruments and 'flip' their gear in order to upgrade their rig and experiment with gear without losing money on selling newly bought equipment.

Studying musicians based on the theoretical concept of communities of practice turned out to be useful because it highlighted the various ways of learning, not only of the instrument but also of the broader musical culture of being a musician. Learning takes many forms, but two stand out: engaging and experimenting with gear. These practices seem to be important for most players' musical development. Besides, becoming part of musicians' communities requires learning the expected behaviours and conventions that have a material anchoring. The findings suggest that GAS is expected behaviour that newcomers in these communities must learn along with the respective discourse. Members are expected to play the 'GAS game', that is, to show interest in gear and practise self-seduction, which is shared socially. However, they must also find the right balance between gear and playing. While community members rarely share video and audio recordings of their playing, they frown upon an excessive preoccupation with gear that drastically outweighs musical use.

At its core, online communities are about making music, yet equipment is an insep-arable part of it. Musicians delight in sharing their 'guilty pleasures' because, after all, acquiring gear as a communal event is enjoyable and even more so when they are commended for it. As threads like 'New Guitar Day' demonstrate, a certain 'glamour' is associated with the proud presentation of a new acquisition. Interest-ingly, the atmosphere and tone in the musicians' boards are encouraging and posi-tive, whereas in similar communities for recording engineers and music producers, the tone is highly competitive. In the musicians' boards, social hierarchies are either flat or implicit, at least in the observed GAS-related threads. Regarding the second way of learning, that of musical maturation, the research suggests that progressing as a player is accompanied by experimenting with different rigs and finding the one that supports the playing best. The requirements change, and instruments and other gear have 'learning curves', so musical abilities are best mapped to suitable equip-ment that neither restricts expression nor overwhelms the player. It follows that growing musical expertise is ideally correlated with gear upgrades until a stable play-ing level is reached. At this point, new equipment may provide new learning incen-tives, or it will be acquired purely out of curiosity. Learning curves, however, take various forms for different instruments. While a mediocre guitarist is only limited in that they cannot fully utilise a too advanced setup, the wrong saxophone with an unsuitable mouthpiece would make it difficult for the player to perform convinc-ingly, if at all.

GAS is as much a psychological as it is a cultural phenomenon. Even journal-istic accounts describe mental processes in step models for the 'GAS attack'. Fun-damental to the urge to acquire gear is the indefinite quest to improve the rig and the (not always earnest) belief that a bigger gear collection or upgraded setup helps the musician to improve as a player. GAS is assumed to occur in never-ending cycles. Empirically derived models in collecting and consumption studies largely agree with the journalistic models created by GAS-affected musicians. They all show that rarely does GAS truly disappear, even when the perfect rig has been acquired. Most musi-cians have a general interest in equipment as part of their hobby or profession, and in times of doubt, stagnation or other situations preventing them from playing or pursuing musical projects, GAS strikes.

The two empirical studies have shown various attitudes towards equipment and GAS and the respective dealings with gear. Generally, most discussions and opinions revolve around the relationship between interest in gear and playing. Our findings further highlight, in line with journalistic accounts, the burden of GAS that lasts on the individual when they possess too much equipment, something that has rarely been documented so clearly before. As it is stressful for many musicians to have too much equipment, they try to avoid this burdensome situation. However, GAS is also considered a distraction and symptom of other problems, or even a consequence of psychiatric conditions such as obsessive-compulsive behaviours or behavioural disorders like ADHD. For most musicians, however, the interest in gear is harmless and, according to the prevailing view in consumption research, life-affirming and potentially beneficial for their development as musicians and their personal growth. As such, our understanding of GAS differs profoundly from the 'disease' described in blogs, books and musicians' communities.

Roy Shuker (2010: 198) concludes his book-length study on record collecting with the insight that due to the diversity of motives and practices, no standard definition of the 'record collector' holds. He suggests acknowledging instead a range of types associated with specific collecting practices, such as 'the record collector as cultural preserver, as accumulator and hoarder, as music industry worker, as adventurous hunter, as connoisseur and as digital explorer'. Neither do the broad range of practices, intentions and opinions observed amongst musicians concerning equipment give us a basis that would allow for a simple definition or theory of GAS. Decisive for musicians' criticism of academic studies on GAS is the over-simplification that a definite theory would necessarily entail. That is why we will refrain from proposing such a theory. For now, we are content with the findings of our empirical studies and theoretical explanations drawn from multiple disciplines. GAS seems to be a popular umbrella term encompassing a variety of practices related to the way musicians think about and handle their equipment. As a generally known term, it is open to modifications to serve the views and attitudes of individuals and interest groups. What the research has clearly shown is that there is no single form of GAS. That is consistent with the over forty 'strains' Jay Wright identified in *GAS. Living with Guitar Acquisition Syndrome*, all bearing a sense of humour, of which this one is an example:

> Porn Pop-up GAS—a somewhat less dangerous form that seems to only attack online store and auction lurkers. Onset apparently starts with the appearance of professional quality images of the victim's brand and finish preferences, causing a virtual assault on the visual senses. These attacks have been known to serves as powerful libido stimulants. (Wright 2006: 55)

Since relating to and being part of music-making, GAS summarises a spectrum of cultural practices. It accompanies musical learning processes, and so, exploring the creative and expressive affordances of gear should be understood as contributing to musical expertise and reflecting it. We took it for granted that GAS-affected musicians would differ significantly from collectors and other groups such as purists and crafters, which, however, proved wrong. The findings revealed only insignificant differences. Music-making is so multifaceted and varies with changing personal circumstances, ambitions and interests that it is challenging to maintain clear classifications. Interest in gear fluctuates throughout a lifetime; it will never diminish completely, at least for musicians with a respective propensity. GAS is a constant companion for many musicians and perhaps an indicator of the great importance that music-making and music-related practices, be it as a hobby or profession, holds for the individual.

References

Aggarwal, P. & McGill, A. L. (2007). 'Is That Car Smiling at Me? Schema Congruity as a Basis for Evaluating Anthropomorphized Products'. *Journal of Consumer Research*, 34, pp. 468–479.

American Psychiatric Association (1985). *Diagnostic and Statistical Manual of Mental Disorders*. Washington: American Psychiatric Association.

American Psychiatric Association (2013). *Diagnostic and Statistical Manual of Mental Disorders* (5. ed.). Arlington: American Psychiatric Association.

Anderson, B. (1983). *Imagined Communities*. London: Verso.

Andertons (n.d.). 'Electric or Acoustic Drum Kits – Which Should I Buy?'. *Andertons*. https://www.andertons.co.uk/should-i-buy-an-electric-or-acoustic-drum-kit; accessed 2 July 2019.

Appadurai, A. (1986). 'Introduction: Commodities and the Politics of Value'. In: A. Appadurai (Ed.). *The Social Life of Things. Commodities in Cultural Perspective*. Cambridge: Cambridge University Press, pp. 3–63.

Ardichvili, A. (2008). 'Learning and Knowledge Sharing in Virtual Communities of Practice: Motivators, Barriers, and Enablers'. *Advances in Developing Human Resources*, 19(4), pp. 541–554.

Arias, Z. (2013). *Photography Q&A: Real Questions. Real Answers*. San Francisco: New Riders.

Ariely, D. & Simonson, I. (2003). 'Buying, Bidding, Playing or Competing: Value Assessment and Evaluation Dynamics in Online Auction'. *Journal of Consumer Psychology*, 13(1/2), pp. 113–124.

Arsel, Z. & Bean, J. (2013). 'Taste Regimes and Market-Mediated Practice'. *Journal of Consumer Research*, 39, pp. 899–917.

Arvidsson, A. (2006). *Brands: Meaning and Value in Media Culture*. London: Routledge.

Atalay, A. S. & Meloy, M. G. (2011). 'Retail Therapy: A Strategic Effort to Improve Mood'. *Psychology & Marketing*, 28(6), pp. 638–659.

Atkinson, M. (2003). *The Unreel Drum Book: Featuring the Music of Randy Waldman and the Drumming of Vinnie Colaiuta*. Van Nuys: Alfred Publishing.

Babiuk, A. (2016). *Beatles Gear: All the Fab Four's Instruments from Stage to Studio*. San Francisco: Backbeat Books.

Babiuk, A. & Prevost, G. (2014). *Rolling Stones Gear: All the Stones' Instruments from Stage to Studio*. San Francisco: Backbeat Books.

Bache, B. (n.d.). 'Acoustic vs Electric Drum Kits'. *Liberty Park Music.* https://www.libertyparkmusic.com/acoustic-vs-electric-drum-kits; accessed 2 July 2019.

Backhaus, A. (2015). 'Sehr weibliche Rundungen'. *Der Spiegel.* https://www.spiegel.de/stil/private-handybilder-eins-aus-tausend-mit-matthias-jabs-a-1023002.html; accessed 31 July 2019.

Bacon, T. (1996). *Rock Hardware. The Instruments, Equipment and Technology of Rock.* Poole: Blandford Press.

Baekeland, F. (1994). 'Psychological Aspects of Art Collecting'. In: S. M. Pearce (Ed.). *Interpreting Objects and Collections.* New York: Routledge, pp. 205–219.

Bakardjieva, M. (2003). 'Virtual Togetherness: An Everyday-Life Perspective'. *Media, Culture & Society*, 25(3), pp. 291–313.

Bakardjieva, M. (2005). *Internet Society. The Internet in Everyday Life.* London: Sage.

Balmer, P. (2018). *The Drum Kit Handbook: How to Buy, Maintain, Set Up, Troubleshoot, and Modify Your Drum Set.* London: Voyageur Press.

Bangma, D. F.; Fuermaier, A. B. M.; Tucha, L.; Tucha, O. & Koerts, J. (2017). 'The Effects of Normal Aging on Multiple Aspects of Financial Decision-Making'. *PLoS ONE,* 12(8): e0182620. https://doi.org/10.1371/journal.pone.0182620

Barlindhaug, G. (2007). 'Analog Sound in the Age of Digital Tools. The Story of the Failure of Digital Technology'. In: R. Skare, N. Windfeld Lund & A. Värheim (Eds.). *A Document (Re)turn. Contributions from a Research Field in Transition.* Frankfurt am Main: Peter Lang, pp. 73–93.

Baudrillard, J. (1970). *The Consumer Society: Myths and Structures.* London: Sage.

Baudrillard, J. (1972). *For a Critique of the Political Economy of the Sign (Pour une critique de l'économie politique du signe).* Paris: Gallimard.

Baudrillard, J. (1976). *Symbolic Exchange and Death.* London: Sage.

Baudrillard, J. (1979). *Seduction (De la seduction).* Paris: Galilée.

Baudrillard, J. (1983). *Fatal Strategies (Les strategies fatales).* Paris: Grasset.

Bauman, Z. (2001). *The Individualized Society.* Cambridge: Polity Press.

Baumeister, R. F. & Leary, M. R. (1995). 'The Need to Belong: Desire for Interpersonal Attachment as a Fundamental Human Motivation'. *Psychological Bulletin*, 17, pp. 497–529.

Bayton, M. (1997). 'Women and the Electric Guitar'. In: S. Whiteley (Ed.). *Sexing the Groove: Popular Music and Gender.* London: Routledge, pp. 37–49.

Bayton, M. (1998). *Frock Rock: Women Performing Popular Music*. Oxford: Oxford University Press.

Beaster-Jones, J. (2016). *Music Commodities, Markets, and Values. Music as Merchandise*. New York: Routledge.

Becker, W. (1996). 'G.A.S'. http://sdarchive.com/gas.html; accessed 31 January 2019.

Behrman, S. N. (1952). *Durveen. The Story of the Most Spectacular Art Dealer of All Time*. New York: Random House.

Belk, R. W. (1984). 'Cultural and Historical Differences in the Concept of Self and Their Effects on Attitudes Toward Having and Giving'. In: T. Kinnear (Ed.). *Advances in Consumer Research*, Vol. 1. Ann Arbor: Association for Consumer Research, pp. 291–297.

Belk, R. W. (1988). 'Possessions and the Extended Self'. *Journal of Consumer Research*, 15, pp. 139–168.

Belk, R. W. (1991). 'The Ineluctable Mysteries of Possessions'. *Journal of Social Behavior and Personality*, 6(6), pp. 17–55.

Belk, R. W. (1995a). *Collecting in a Consumer Society. The Collecting Cultures Series*. London: Routledge.

Belk, R. W. (1995b). 'Collecting as Luxury Consumption: Effects on Individuals and Households'. *Journal of Economic Psychology*, 16, pp. 477–490.

Belk, R. W. (1996). 'On Aura, Illusion, Escape, and Hope in Apocalyptic Consumption: The Apotheosis of Las Vegas'. In: S. Brown, J. Bell & D. Carson (Eds.). *Marketing Apocalypse. Eschatology, Escapology, and the Illusion of the End*. New York: Routledge, pp. 87–132.

Belk, R. W. (1997). 'The Goblin and the Huckster: A Story of Consumer Desire for Sensual Luxury'. In: S. Brown, A. M. Doherty & B. Clarke (Eds.). *Proceedings of the Marketing Illuminations Spectacular*. Belfast: University of Ulster, pp. 290–299.

Belk, R. W. (2001a). *Collecting in a Consumer Society*. New York: Routledge.

Belk, R. W. (2001b). 'Specialty Magazines and Flights of Fancy: Feeding the Desire to Desire'. In: A. Groeppel-Klein & F.-R. Esch (Eds.). *European Advances in Consumer Research*, Vol. 5. Berlin: Association for Consumer Research, pp. 197–202.

Belk, R. W. (2006). 'Remembrances of Things Past: Silent Voices in Collections'. In: K. Ekstrom & H. Brembeck (Eds.). *European Advances in Consumer Research*. Valdosa: Association for Consumer Research, pp. 392–397.

Belk, R. W. (2007). 'Consumption, Mass Consumption, and Consumer Culture'. In: G. Ritzer (Ed.). *The Blackwell Encyclopedia of the Social Sciences*. Cambridge: Blackwell, pp. 737–746.

Belk, R. W. (2013). 'Extended Self in a Digital World'. *Journal of Consumer Research*, 40(3), pp. 477–500.

Belk, R. W.; Ger, G. & Askegaard, S. (2003). 'The Fire of Desire: A Multisited Inquiry into Consumer Passion'. *Journal of Consumer Research*, 30, pp. 326–352.

Belk, R. W.; Wallendorf, J. F. & Holbrook, M. B. (1991). 'Collecting in Consumer Culture'. In: R. W. Belk (Ed.). *Highways and Buyways: Naturalistic Research from The Consumer Behavior Odyssey*. Provo: Association for Consumer Research, pp. 178–215.

Bell, D. (1976). *The Cultural Contradictions of Capitalism*. New York: Basic Books.

Bell, C. R. & Cresswell, A. (1984). 'Personality Differences among Musical Instrumentalists'. *Psychology of Music*, 12, pp. 83–93.

Belz, C. (1969). *The Story of Rock* (2. ed.). New York: Oxford University Press.

Benjamin, W. (1968). 'Unpacking my Library: A Talk about Book Collecting'. In: H. Arendt (Ed.). *Illuminations*. New York: Schocken Books, pp. 59–67.

Benjamin, W. (1997). *Charles Baudelaire: A Lyric Poet in the Era of High Capitalism*. London and New York: Verso.

Bennett, H. S. (1983). 'Notation and Identity in Contemporary Popular Music'. *Popular Music*, 3, pp. 215–234.

Bennett, H. S. (2017). *On Becoming a Musician*. New York: Columbia University Press.

Bennett, S. (2009). 'Revolution Sacrilege! Examining the Technological Divide Among Record Producers in the Late 1980s'. *Journal on the Art of Record Production*, 4. https://www.arpjournal.com/asarpwp/revolution-sacrilege-examining-the-technological-divide-among-record-producers-in-the-late-1980s; accessed 5 August 2020.

Bennett, S. (2012). 'Endless Analogue: Situating Vintage Technologies in the Contemporary Recording & Production Workplace'. *Journal on the Art of Record Production*, 7. https://www.arpjournal.com/asarpwp/endless-analogue-situating-vintage-technologies-in-the-contemporary-recording-production-workplace; accessed 5 August 2020.

Bergamini, J. (2005). *Drum Techniques of Led Zeppelin*. Van Nuys: Alfred Publishing.

Berkers, P. & Schaap, J. (2018). *Gender Inequality in Metal Music Production*. Bingley: Emerald Publishing Limited.

Berlatsky, N. (2015). 'She Shreds: Guitar Magazine Empowers Women to Rip up Stereotypes'. *The Guardian*. https://www.theguardian.com/music/2015/sep/25/she-shreds-women-guitar-magazine-st-vincent; accessed 31 January 2019.

Black, D. W. (1996). 'Compulsive Buying: A Review'. *Journal of Clinical Psychiatry*, 57, pp. 50–55.

Black, I. R. & Cherrier, H. (2010). 'Anti-Consumption as Part of Living a Sustainable Lifestyle: Daily Practices, Contextual Motivations and Subjective Values'. *Journal of Consumer Behaviour*, 9(6), pp. 437–453.

Black, R. (2012). 'Gibson Settles Discord on Timber'. *British Broadcasting Corporation*. https://www.bbc.co.uk/news/science-environment-19153588; accessed 25 May 2020.

Blackett, M. (2019). 'Mark Knopfler: How Gear Can Influence Music'. *Guitar Player*. https://www.guitarplayer.com/players/mark-knopfler-how-gear-can-influence-music; accessed 15 September 2019.

Blickenstaff, J. C. (2005). 'Women and Science Careers: Leaky Pipeline or Gender Filter?'. *Gender and Education*, 17(4), pp. 369–386.

Bogle, V. (1999). *Women Who Collect Records. Graduate Research Paper*. University of Auckland, New Zealand.

Born, G. (2011). 'Music and the Materialization of Identities'. *Journal of Material Culture*, 16(4), pp. 376–388.

Born, G. & Devine, K. (2015). 'Music Technology, Gender, and Class: Digitization, Educational and Social Change in Britain'. *Twentieth-Century Music*, 12(2), pp. 135–172.

Bortz, J. & Döring, N. (2015). *Forschungsmethoden und Evaluation für Human- und Sozialwissenschafter* (4. ed.). Wiesbaden: Springer.

Bourbon, A. (2019). 'Plugging In. Exploring Innovation in Plugin Design and Utilization'. In: R. Hepworth-Sawyer, J. Hodgson, J. Paterson & R. Toulson (Eds.). *Innovation in Music Production*. London: Routledge, pp. 211–225.

Bourdieu, P. (1984). *Distinction: A Social Critique of the Judgement of Taste*. Cambridge: Harvard University Press.

Bourdieu, P. (1986). 'The Production of Belief: Contribution to an Economy of Symbolic Goods'. In: R. Collins, J. Curran, N. Garnham, P. Scannell, P. Schlesinger & C. Sparks (Eds.). *Media, Culture, and Society: A Critical Reader*. London: Sage, pp. 131–163.

Bourdieu, P. (1990a). 'Social Space and Symbolic Power'. In: P. Bourdieu (Ed.). *In Other Words: Essays Towards a Reflexive Sociology*. Cambridge: Polity Press, pp. 123–139.

Bourdieu, P. (1990b). 'The Intellectual Field: A World Apart'. In: P. Bourdieu (Ed.). *In Other Words: Essays Towards a Reflexive Sociology*. Cambridge: Polity Press, pp. 140–149.

Bourdieu P. (1991). *Outline of a Theory of Practice*. Cambridge: Cambridge University Press.

Boym, S. (2001). *The Future of Nostalgia*. New York: Basic Books.

Braun, J.; Zolfagharian, M. & Belk, R. W. (2016). 'How Does a Product Gain the Status of a Necessity? An Analysis of Necessitation Narratives'. *Psychology & Marketing*, 33, pp. 209–222.

Braun-Thürmann, H. (2005). *Innovation*. Bielefeld: transcript.

Brem, S.; Grünblatt, E.; Drechsler, R.; Riederer, P. & Walitza, S. (2014). 'The Neurological Link between OCD and ADHD'. *Attention Deficit and Hyperactivity Disorders*, 6(3), pp. 175–202.

Brennan, M. (2020). *Kick It: A Social History of the Drum Kit*. Oxford: Oxford University Press.

Brewster, D. M. (2003). *Introduction to Guitar Tone & Effects: A Manual for Getting the Best Sounds from Electric Guitars, Amplifiers, Effects Pedals & Processors*. Milwaukee: Hal Leonard.

Brockhaus, I. (2017). *Kultsounds. Die prägendsten Klänge der Popmusik 1960-2014*. Bielefeld: transcript.

Brown, J. (1997). 'Comic Book Fandom and Cultural Capital'. *Journal of Popular Culture*, 30, pp. 13–31.

Bruck, M. (2005). *Guitar World Presents Guitar Gear 411: Guitar Tech to the Stars Answers Your Gear Questions*. Van Nuys: Alfred Publishing.

Bruford, B. (2018). *Uncharted. Creativity and the Expert Drummer*. Ann Arbor: University of Michigan Press.

Bryant, J. A. & Akerman, A. (2009). 'Finding Mii: Virtual Social Identity and the Young Consumer'. In: N. T. Wood & M. R. Solomon (Eds.). *Virtual Social Identity and Consumer Behavior*. Armonk: M. E. Sharpe, pp. 127–1 40.

Bryman, A. (1992). 'Quantitative and Qualitative Research: Further Reflections on their Integration'. In: J. Brannen (Ed.). *Mixing Methods: Quantitative and Qualitative Research*. Aldershot: Ashgate, pp. 57–80.

Burchuk, R. (1977). 'Retail Music Store Manager/Salesperson'. *Music Educators Journal*, 63(7), pp. 124–125.

Butler, J. (1988). 'Performative Acts and Gender Constitution: An Essay in Phenomenology and Feminist Theory'. *Theatre Journal*, 40(4), pp. 519–531.

Cameron, J. E.; Duffy, M. & Glenwright, B. (2015). 'Singers Take Center Stage! Personality Traits and Stereotypes of Popular Musicians'. *Psychology of Music*, 43(6), pp. 818–830.

Campbell, C. (1987). *The Romantic Ethic and the Spirit of Modern Consumerism*. New York: Basil Blackwell.

Campbell, C. (1997). 'Shopping, Pleasure and the Sex War'. In: C. Campbell & P. Falk (Eds.). *Theory, Culture & Society. The Shopping Experience*. London: Sage, pp. 166–176.

Campbell C. (2004). 'I Shop therefore I Know that I Am: The Metaphysical Basis of Modern Consumerism'. In: K. M. Exstrom & H. Brembeck (Eds.). *Elusive Consumption*. New York: Berg, pp. 27–44.

Campbell, C. (2005). 'The Craft Consumer'. *Journal of Consumer Culture*, 5, pp. 23–42.

Cann, S. (2009). *Becoming a Synthesizer Wizard: From Presets to Power User*. Boston: Cengage Learning.

Carson, M.; Lewis, T.; Shaw, S.; Baumgardner, J. & Richards, A. (2004). *Girls Rock! Fifty Years of Women Making Music*. Lexington: University Press of Kentucky.

Carter, N. (2016). *Electric Guitar Gear: A Complete Beginner's Guide to Understanding Guitar Effects and the Gear Used for Electric Guitar Playing & How to Master Your Tone on Guitar*. Scotts Valley: CreateSpace Independent Publishing Platform.

Carvalho, A. T. (2012). 'The Discourse of Home Recording: Authority of "Pros" and the Sovereignty of the Big Studios'. *Journal on the Art of Record Production*, 7. https://www.arpjournal.com/asarpwp/the-discourse-of-home-recording-authority-of-%E2%80%9Cpros%E2%80%9D-and-the-sovereignty-of-the-big-studios; accessed 5 August 2020.

Carver, C. S. & Scheier, M. F. (2001). *On the Self-Regulation of Behavior*. Cambridge: Cambridge University Press.

Cep (2020). *Synthesizer Explained: The Essential Basics of Synthesis You Must Know as a Digital Music Producer*. Screech House.

Chappell, J. (2010). *The Recording Guitarist*. Milwaukee: Hal Leonard.

Chatzidakis, A. & Lee, M. S. W. (2013). 'Anti-Consumption as the Study of Reasons Against'. *Journal of Macromarketing*, 33(3), pp. 190–203.

Chen, J. L. & Chen, A. (2017). *Astronomy for Older Eyes. The Patrick Moore Practical Astronomy Series*. Cham: Springer.

Christ, E. A. (1965). 'The "Retired" Stamp Collector: Economic and Other Functions of a Systematized Leisure Activity'. In: A. M. Rose & W. A. Peterson

(Eds.). *Older People and their Social World: The Subculture of Aging*. Philadelphia: F. A. Davis, pp. 93–112.

Citron, M. (1993). *Gender and the Musical Canon*. Cambridge: Cambridge University Press.

Clarke, D. B. (2003). *The Consumer Society and the Postmodern City*. New York: Routledge.

Clarke, D. B.; Doel, M. A. & Housiaux, M. L. (2003). 'General Introduction'. In: D. B. Clarke, M. A. Doel & M. L. Housiaux (Eds.). *The Consumption Reader*. London: Routledge, pp. 1–23.

Clarke, P. (1983). '"A Magic Science": Rock Music as a Recording Art'. *Popular Music*, 3, pp. 195–213.

Clawson, M. A. (1999a). 'Masculinity and Skill Acquisition in the Adolescent Rock Band'. *Popular Music*, 18(1), pp. 99–114.

Clawson, M. A. (1999b). 'When Women Play the Bass'. *Gender & Society*, 13, pp. 193–210.

Clifford, J. (1985). 'Objects and Selves: An Afterword'. In: G. W. Stocking (Ed.). *History of Anthropology: Vol. 3. Objects and Others: Essays on Museums and Material Culture*. Madison: University of Wisconsin Press, pp. 236–246.

Cohen, S. (1991). *Rock Culture in Liverpool: Popular Music in the Making*. Oxford: Clarendon Press.

Cole, S. J. (2011). 'The Prosumer and the Project Studio. The Battle for Distinction in the Field of Music Recording'. *Sociology*, 45(3), pp. 447–463.

Cole, S. J. (2018). 'Use Value as a Cultural Strategy against Over-Commodification: A Durkheimian Analysis of Craft Consumption within Virtual Communities'. *Sociology*, 52, pp. 1052–1068.

Comber, C.; Hargreaves, D. J. & Colley, A. (1993). 'Girls, Boys and Technology in Music Education'. *British Journal of Music Education*, 10, pp. 123–134.

Coombs, C. H. & Avrunin, G. S. (1977). 'Single-Peaked Functions and the Theory of Preference'. *Psychological Review*, 84(2), p. 216.

Corfield, C. (n.d.). 'Gibson G-Force. Under the Hood'. *Dawson's Music*. https://www.dawsons.co.uk/blog/gibson-g-force-hood; accessed 13 July 2019.

Coulthard, D. & Keller, S. (2012). 'Technophilia, Neo-Luddism, eDependency and the Judgement of Thamus'. *Journal of Information, Communication & Ethics in Society*, 10(4), pp. 262-272.

Creech, A.; Papageorgi, I.; Duffy, C.; Morton, F.; Hadden, E.; Potter, J.; De Bezenac C.; Whyton, T.; Himonides, E. & Welch, G. (2008). 'Investigating Musical Performance: Commonality and Diversity Among Classical and Non-Classical Musicians'. *Music Education Research*, 10(2), pp. 215–234.

Crowdy, D. (2013). 'Chasing an Aesthetic Tail. Latent Technological Imperialism in Mainstream Production'. In: S. Baker, A. Bennett & J. Taylor (Eds.). *Redefining Mainstream Popular Music*. London: Routledge, pp. 150–161.

Csikszentmihalyi, M. (1990). *Flow: The Psychology of Optimal Experience*. New York: Harper and Row.

Csikszentmihalyi, M. & Rochberg-Halton, E. (1981). *The Meaning of Things. Domestic Symbols and the Self*. Cambridge: Cambridge University Press.

Cunningham, M. (1996). *Good Vibrations. A History of Record Production*. Chessington: Castle Communications.

Cushing, A. L. (2011). 'Self Extension and the Desire to Preserve Digital Possessions'. *Proceedings of the American Society for Information Science and Technology*, 48, pp. 1–3.

Cushing, A. L. (2012). *Possessions and Self Extension in Digital Environments: Implications for Maintaining Personal Information*. PhD thesis, Chapel Hill: University of North Carolina.

Cutler, C. (1995). *File Under Popular: Theoretical and Critical Writings on Music*. New York: Autonomedia.

Danet, B. & Katriel, T. (1989). 'No Two Alike: Play and Aesthetics in Collecting'. *Play and Culture*, 2, pp. 253–277.

Danziger, P. (2004). *Why People Buy Things They Don't Need: Understanding and Predicting Consumer Behavior*. Chicago: Dearborn Trade Publishing.

Davis, F. (1979). *Yearning for Yesterday: A Sociology of Nostalgia*. New York: The Free Press.

Dawe, K. (2010). *The New Guitarscape in Critical Theory, Cultural Practice and Musical Performance*. London: Routledge.

DDB Needham Annual Lifestyle Survey (1974-1993). Chicago: DDB Needham Worldwide.

Deighton, J. & Grayson, K. (1995). 'Marketing and Seduction: Managing Exchange Relationships by Managing Social Consensus'. *Journal of Consumer Research*, 21(4), pp. 660–676.

Delzell, J. K. & Leppla, D. A. (1992). 'Gender Association of Musical Instruments and Preferences of Fourth-Grade Students for Selected Instruments'. *Journal of Research in Music Education*, 40(2), pp. 93–103.

Denegri-Knott, J. & Molesworth, M. (2010). '"Love it. Buy it. Sell it." Consumer Desire and the Social Drama of eBay'. *Journal of Consumer Culture*, 10(1), pp. 56–79.

Denegri-Knott, J.; Watkins, R. & Wood, J. (2012). 'Transforming Digital Virtual Goods into Meaningful Possessions'. In: M. Molesworth & J. Denegri-Knott (Eds.). *Digital Virtual Consumption*. London: Routledge, pp. 76–91.

Denegri-Knott, J. & Zwick, D. (2012). 'Tracking Prosumption Work in eBay. Reproduction of Desire and the Challenge of Slow Re-McDonaldization'. *American Behavioral Scientist*, 56(4), pp. 439–458.

DeNora, T. (2004). 'Musical Practice and Social Structure: A Toolkit'. In: E. Clarke & N. Cook (Eds.). *Empirical Musicology: Aims, Methods, Prospects*. Oxford: Oxford University Press, pp. 35–56.

Denzin, N. K. (1978). *The Research Act. A Theoretical Introduction to Sociological Methods* (2. ed.). New York: McGraw Hill.

Dholakia, U. M. (2015). 'Three Senses of Desire in Consumer Research'. In: W. Hofmann & L. F. Nordgren (Eds.). *The Psychology of Desire*. New York: Guilford Press, pp. 407–431.

Dholakia, U; Jung, J. & Chowdhry, N. (2018). 'Should I Buy this When I Have so Much? Reflection on Personal Possessions as an Anticonsumption Strategy'. *Journal of Public Policy & Marketing*, 37(2), pp. 260–273.

Diekmann, A. (2009). *Empirische Sozialforschung. Grundlagen, Methoden, Anwendungen*. Reinbek bei Hamburg: Rowohlt.

Diiorio, S. (2016). 'The GAS documentary: Gear Acquisition Syndrome'. https://www.youtube.com/watch?v=M4yKK7WWja4; accessed 31 January 2019.

Dittmar, H. (1992). *The Social Psychology of Material Possessions: To Have is to Be*. Hemel Hempstead: Harvester Wheatsheaf.

Dittmar, H. (2005). 'A New Look at Compulsive Buying: Self Discrepancies and Materialistic Values as Predictors of Compulsive Buying Tendencies'. *Journal of Social & Clinical Psychology*, 24, pp. 832–859.

Doerschuk, B. (1987). 'Jam & Lewis'. *Keyboard*, May 1987, pp. 74–85.

Doppler, D. (2013). *The Worship Guitar Book: The Goods, the Gear and the Gifting for the Worship Guitarist*. Milwaukee: Hal Leonard.

Dubé, L.; Bourhis, A. & Jacob, R. (2005). 'The Impact of Structuring Characteristics on the Launching of Virtual Communities of Practice'. *Journal of Organizational Change Management*, 18(2), pp. 145–166.

Duffett, M. (2013a). *Understanding Fandom: An Introduction to the Study of Media Fan Culture*. London: Bloomsbury.

Duffett, M. (2013b). *Popular Music Fandom. Identities, Roles and Practices*. London: Routledge.

Duffett, M. (2015). 'Fan Practices'. *Popular Music and Society*, 38(1), pp. 1–6.

Duffy, M. (2018). 'New Research Shows How Playing Music Can Improve Your Life'. *Fender*. https://www.fender.com/articles/play/new-research-shows-mental-physical-and-emotional-benefits-of-playing-music; accessed 8 July 2019.

Eichas, F. & Zölzer, U. (2018). 'Gray-Box Modeling of Guitar Amplifiers'. *Journal of the Audio Engineering Society*, 66, pp. 1006–1115.

Ekers, M. (2020). *Zappa's Gear: The Unique Guitars, Amplifiers, Effects Units, Keyboards and Studio Equipment*. Milwaukee: Hal Leonard.

Elliott, R. (1994). 'Addictive Consumptions: Function and Fragmentation in Post-Modernity'. *Journal of Consumer Policy*, 17, pp. 159–179.

Elliott, R. & Wattanasuwan, K. (1998). 'Brands as Symbolic Resources for the Construction of Identity'. *International Journal of Advertising*, 17, pp. 131–144.

Emiliani, M. (2015). 'Bass Guitar and Small Hands: Don't Let it Stop You from Playing Bass'. http://smartbassguitar.com/bassists-musicians-website/; accessed 10 August 2019.

Epley, N.; Waytz, A. & Cacioppo, J. T. (2007). 'On Seeing Human: A Three-Factor Theory of Anthropomorphism'. *Psychological Review*, 114(4), pp. 864–886.

Ericsson, K. A.; Krampe, R. T. & Tesch-Römer, C. (1993). 'The Role of Deliberate Practice in the Acquisition of Expert Performance'. *Psychological Review*, 100(3), pp. 363–406.

Eynon, R.; Fry, J. & Schroeder, R. (2016). 'The Ethics of Online Research'. In: N. G. Fielding, R. M. Lee & G. Blank (Eds.). *The SAGE Handbook of Online Research Methods* (2. ed.). London: Sage, pp. 19–37.

Faber, R. J. & O'Guinn, T. C. (1989). 'Classifying Compulsive Consumers: Advances in the Development of a Diagnostic Tool'. *Advances in Consumer Research*, 16(1), pp. 738–744.

Faber, R. J. & Vohs, K. D. (2004). 'To Buy or not to Buy? Self-Control and Self-Regulatory Failure in Purchase Behavior'. In: R. F. Baumeister (Ed.). *Handbook of Self-Regulation: Research, Theory, and Application*. New York: Guilford Press, pp. 509–524.

Falk, P. (1994). *The Consuming Body*. London: Sage.

Falzerano, C. (2008). *Gretsch Drums*. Milwaukee: Hal Leonard.

Farrugia, R. (2012). *Beyond the Dance Floor. Female DJs, Technology and Electronic Dance Music Culture*. Bristol: Intellect.

Farrugia, R. & Gobatto, N. (2010). 'Shopping for Legs and Boots. Tori Amos's *Original Bootlegs*, Fandom, and Subcultural Capital'. *Popular Music and Society*, 33(3), pp. 357–375.

Farrugia, R. & Olszanowski, M. (2017). 'Introduction: Women and Electronic Dance Music Culture'. *Dancecult: Journal of Electronic Dance Music Culture*, 9(1), pp. 1–8.

Featherstone, M. (1991). *Consumer Culture and Postmodernism*. London: Sage.

Featherstone, M. (1998). 'The Flâneur, the City and Virtual Public Life'. *Urban Studies*, 35(5–6), pp. 909–925.

Felton, D. (2016). *The Secrets of Dance Music Production*. London: Attack Magazine.

Fender Musical Instruments Corporation (2018). 'Guitar Isn't Dead: Research Shows Learning to Play Helps Us Live Better Lives'. https://www.prnews wire.com/news-releases/guitar-isnt-dead-research-shows-learning-to-play-helps-us-live-better-lives-300731477.html; accessed 15 August 2020.

Fennesz, C. (2014). 'Fennesz Interview by Innerversitysound'. https://www.cyclic defrost.com/2014/04/fenessz-interview-by-innerversitysound; accessed 10 May 2020.

Fenton-O'Creevy, M.; Dibb, S. & Furnham, A. (2018). 'Antecedents and Consequences of Chronic Impulsive Buying: Can Impulsive Buying be Understood as Dysfunctional Self-Regulation?'. *Psychology & Marketing*, 35, pp. 175–188.

Fernandez, K. V. & Lastovicka, J. L. (2011). 'Making Magic: Fetishes in Contemporary Consumption'. *Journal of Consumer Research*, 38, pp. 278–299.

Firat, A. F. & Venkatesh, A. (1995). 'Liberatory Postmodernism and the Reenchantment of Consumption'. *Journal of Consumer Research*, 22(3), pp. 239–267.

Fisher, J. P. (1997). *Cash Tracks: Compose, Produce, and Sell Your Original Soundtrack Music and Jingles*. Emeryville: Mix Books.

Fiske, J. (1992). 'The Cultural Economy of Fandom'. In: L. A. Lewis (Ed.). *The Adoring Audience: Fan Culture and Popular Media*. London: Routledge, pp. 30–49.

Flick, U. (2010). 'Triangulation in der qualitativen Forschung'. In: U. Flick, E. v. Kardorff & I. Steinke (Eds.). *Qualitative Forschung. Ein Handbuch* (8. ed.). Reinbek bei Hamburg: Rowohlt, pp. 309–318.

Flick, U. (2011). *Triangulation. Eine Einführung*. Wiesbaden: VS Verlag für Sozialwissenschaften.

Formanek, R. (1991). 'Why they Collect: Collectors Reveal their Motivations'. *Journal of Social Behaviour and Personality*, 6, pp. 275–286.

Fornadley, C. (2015). *Tone Wizards: Interviews with Top Guitarists and Gear Gurus on the Quest for the Ultimate Sound*. Pennsauken: BookBaby.

Foucault, M. (1980). *Power/Knowledge*. Brighton: Harvester.

Foucault, M. (1982). 'The Subject and Power'. In: H. L. Dreyfus, P. Rabinow & M. Foucault (Eds.). *Michel Foucault: Beyond Structuralism and Hermeneutics.* Brighton: Harvester Press, pp. 208–226.

Foucault, M. (1990). *The History of Sexuality. Volume 1: An Introduction.* New York: Random House.

Foucault, M. (1991). 'Questions of Method'. In: G. Burchell, C. Gordon & P. Miller (Eds.). *The Foucault Effect: Studies in Governmentality.* Hemel Hempstead: Harvester Wheatsheaf, pp. 73–86.

Fox, M. (2004). 'E-Commerce Business Models for the Music Industry'. *Popular Music and Society*, 27(2), pp. 201–220.

Freund, J. (1971). 'Théorie du besoin'. *L'année sociologique*, vol. 21. Paris: Presses Universitaires de France, pp. 13–64.

Frith, S. (1986). 'Art versus Technology: The Strange Case of Popular Music'. *Media Culture Society*, 8, pp. 263–279.

Frith, S. (2001). 'The Popular Music Industry'. In: S. Frith, W. Straw & J. Street (Eds.). *The Cambridge Companion to Pop and Rock.* Cambridge: Cambridge University Press, pp. 26–52.

Furby, L. (1978). 'Possessions in Humans: An Exploratory Study of its Meaning and Motivation'. *Social Behavior and Personality*, 6(1), pp. 49–65.

GAKMusicBlog (2016). 'Top 10 Most Expensive Guitars!'. https://www.gak.co.uk/blog/expensive-guitars/; accessed 7 June 2019.

Galak, J.; Redden, J. P.; Yang, Y. & Kyung, E. J. (2014). 'How Perceptions of Temporal Distance Influence Satiation'. *Journal of Experimental Social Psychology*, 52, pp. 118–123.

Galbraith, J. K. (1958). *The Affluent Society.* New York: Mariner Books.

Gallier, T. d. (2018). 'Woman Tone: Why is the Guitar Industry Sexist?'. *Guitar.* https://guitar.com/features/woman-tone-sexist-industry; accessed 16 July 2019.

Garcia, I. (2007). 'Compulsive Buying: An Irresistible Impulse or a Reflection of Personal Values?'. *Revista de Psicologia Social*, 22(2), p. 125.

Garcia, A. C.; Standlee, A. I.; Bechkoff, J. & Cui, Y. (2009). 'Ethnographic Approaches to the Internet and Computer-Mediated Communication'. *Journal of Contemporary Ethnography*, 38, pp. 52–84.

Gavanas, A. & Reitsamer, R. (2013). 'DJ Technologies, Social Networks and Gendered Trajectories in European DJ Cultures'. In: B. Attias, A. Gavanas & H. Rietveld (Eds.). *DJ Culture in the Mix: Power, Technology and Social Change in Electronic Dance Music.* New York: Bloomsbury, pp. 51–78.

Gay, L. C. (1998). 'Acting up, Talking Tech: New York Rock Musicians and Their Metaphors of Technology'. *Ethnomusicology*, 42(1), pp. 81–98.

Gembris, H. (2014). 'Talent und Begabung in der Musik'. In: M. Stamm (Ed.). *Handbuch Talententwicklung. Theorien, Methoden und Praxis in Psychologie und Pädagogik*. Bern: Huber, pp. 497–512.

Gembris, H. (2018). 'Musikalische Entwicklung: Das Erwachsenenalter'. In: A. C. Lehmann & R. Kopiez (Eds.). *Handbuch Musikpsychologie*. Bern: Hogrefe, pp. 217–246.

Gibson, C. (2019). 'A Sound Track to Ecological Crisis: Tracing Guitars All the Way Back to the Tree'. *Popular Music*, 38(2), pp. 183–203.

Gibson, W. (1999). 'My Obsession: I Thought I was Immune to the Net, then I Got Bitten by eBay'. https://www.wired.com/1999/01/ebay; accessed 31 May 2020.

Gibson, C. & Warren, A. (2016). 'Resource-Sensitive Global Production Networks: Reconfigured Geographies of Timber and Acoustic Guitar Manufacturing'. *Economic Geography*, 92, pp. 430–454.

Giddens, A. (1991). *Modernity and Self-Identity: Self and Society in the Late Modern Age*. Stanford: Stanford University Press.

Gil, V. (2014). *Extended Range Guitars: Cultural Impact, Specifications, and the Context of a Mix*. MA thesis, Los Angeles: California State University.

Giles, D. C.; Pietrzykowski, S. & Clark, K. E. (2007). 'The Psychological Meaning of Personal Record Collections and the Impact on Changing Technological Forms'. *Journal of Economic Psychology*, 28(4), pp. 429–443.

Gilmer, M. (2017). 'Pre CBS Stratocaster'. https://precbsstratocasters.com; accessed 27 June 2019.

Girard, R. (1977). *Violence and the Sacred*. Baltimore: Johns Hopkins University Press.

Glaser, B. G. & Strauss, A. L. (1967). *The Discovery of Grounded Theory: Strategies for Qualitative Research*. New York: Aldine.

Glass, G. V., Peckham, P. D. & Sanders, J. R. (1972). 'Consequences of Failure to Meet Assumptions Underlying the Fixed Effects Analyses of Variance and Co-variance'. *Review of Educational Research*, 42(3), pp. 237–288.

Goldberg, H. & Lewis, R. T. (1978). *Money Madness: The Psychology of Saving, Spending, Loving, and Hating Money*. New York: Morrow.

Gordon, T. (2018). *Bass Player Q&A: Questions and Answers about Listening, Practicing, Teaching, Studying, Gear, Recording, Music Theory, and More*. Scotts Valley: CreateSpace Independent Publishing Platform.

Gracyk, T. (1996). *Rhythm and Noise: An Aesthetics of Rock*. London: Tauris.

Graeber, D. (2011). 'Consumption'. *Current Anthropology*, 52, pp. 489–511.

Graham, A. (2019). *Electronic Drumfax: Vintage Electronic Drum Kits (1970–1990)*. Amazon.

Green, L. (1997). *Music, Gender, Education*. Cambridge: University of Cambridge Press.

Green, L. (2002). *How Popular Musicians Learn: A Way Ahead for Music Education*. Aldershot: Ashgate.

Greenwood, A. & Hembree, G. (2011). '25 Most Valuable Guitars'. http://www.vintageguitar.com/24453/25-most-valuable-guitars; accessed 4 October 2016.

Griswold, P. A. & Chroback, D. A. (1981). 'Gender Role Associations of Music Instruments and Occupations by Gender and Major'. *Journal of Research in Music Education*, 29(1), pp. 57–62.

Guest-Scott, A. (2008). 'Categories in Motion: The Use of Generic Multiplicity in Music Store Guitar Lessons'. *Ethnomusicology*, 52(3), pp. 426–457.

Guthrie, S. (1993). *Faces in the Clouds: A New Theory of Religion*. New York: Oxford.

Haas, A. W. (2011). 'The Art of Playing Trumpet in the Upper Register'. *University of Miami*. https://scholarship.miami.edu/discovery/fulldisplay/alma991031447761602976/01UOML_INST:ResearchRepository; accessed 30 November 2020.

Halford, S. (2018). 'The Ethical Disruptions of Social Media Data: Tales from the Field'. In: K. Woodfield (Ed.). *The Ethics of Online Research*. Bingley: Emerald, pp. 13–25.

Hallam, S.; Rogers, L. & Creech, A. (2008). 'Gender Differences in Musical Instrument Choice'. *International Journal of Music Education*, 26, pp. 7–19.

Hallam, S.; Varvarigou, M.; Creech, A.; Papageorgi, I.; Gomes, T.; Lanipekun, J. & Rinta, T. (2017). 'Are there Gender Differences in Instrumental Music Practice?'. *Psychology of Music*, 45, pp. 116–130.

Hambrick, D. Z.; Macnamara, B. N.; Campitelli, G.; Ullén, F. & Mosing, M. A. (2016). 'Beyond Born versus Made: A New Look at Expertise'. *Psychology of Learning and Motivation*, 64, pp. 1–55.

Hancock, M. (2017). 'Lick My Legacy: Are Women-Identified Spaces Still Needed to Nurture Women-Identified DJs?'. *Dancecult: Journal of Electronic Dance Music Culture*, 9(1), pp. 73–89.

Hara, N.; Shachaf, P. & Stoerger, S. (2009). 'Online Communities of Practice Typology Revisited'. *Journal of Information Science*, 35(6), pp. 740–757.

Hargreaves, D. J.; MacDonald, R. & Miell, D. (2012). 'Musical Identities Mediate Musical Development'. In: G. E. McPherson & G. F. Welch (Eds.). *The Oxford Handbook of Music Education*. Oxford: Oxford University Press, pp. 125–142.

Hargreaves, D. J.; MacDonald, R. & Miell, D. (2016). 'Musical Identities'. In: S. Hallam, I. Cross & M. Thaut (Eds.). *The Oxford Handbook of Music Psychology*. Oxford: Oxford University Press, pp. 759–774.

Hargreaves, D. J.; MacDonald, R. & Miell, D. (2017). 'The Changing Identity of Musical Identities'. In: R. MacDonald, D. J. Hargreaves & D. Miell (Eds.). *Handbook of Musical Identities*. Oxford: Oxford University Press, pp. 3–23.

Hartmann, B. J. (2016). 'Peeking Behind the Mask of the Prosumer: Theorizing the Organization of Consumptive and Productive Practice Moments'. *Marketing Theory*, 16, pp. 3–20.

Hausman, A. (2000). 'A Multi-Method Investigation of Consumer Motivations in Impulse Buying Behavior'. *Journal of Consumer Marketing*, 17(5), pp. 403–419.

Heatley, M. & Shapiro, H. (2009). *Jimi Hendrix Gear: The Guitars, Amps and Effects That Revolutionized Rock'n'Roll*. London: Voyageur Press.

Hebdige, D. (1979). *Subculture. The Meaning of Style*. London: Methuen.

Hennion, A. (2007). 'Those Things that Hold Us Together: Taste and Sociology'. *Cultural Sociology*, 1(1), pp. 97–114.

Herbert, M. (2005). 'Manifesto'. http://matthewherbert.com/about-contact/manifesto; accessed 10 May 2020.

Herbst, J.-P. (2016). *Die Gitarrenverzerrung in der Rockmusik: Studien zu Spielweise und Ästhetik*. Münster: LIT.

Herbst, J.-P. (2017a). '"Gear Acquisition Syndrome" – A Survey of Electric Guitar Players'. In: J. Merrill (Ed.). *Systematische Musikwissenschaft. Popular Music Studies Today: Proceedings of the International Association for the Study of Popular Music 2017*. Wiesbaden: Springer VS, pp. 139–148.

Herbst, J.-P. (2017b). 'Historical Development, Sound Aesthetics and Production Techniques of the Distorted Electric Guitar in Metal Music'. *Metal Music Studies*, 3(1), pp. 23–46.

Herbst, J.-P. (2017c). 'Shredding, Tapping and Sweeping: Effects of Guitar Distortion on Playability and Expressiveness in Rock and Metal Solos'. *Metal Music Studies*, 3(2), pp. 231–250.

Herbst, J.-P. (2019a). 'Old Sounds with New Technologies? Examining the Creative Potential of Guitar "Profiling" Technology and the Future of Metal Music from Producers' Perspectives'. *Metal Music Studies*, 5(1), pp. 53–69.

Herbst, J.-P. (2019b). 'Empirical Explorations of Guitar Players' Attitudes Towards their Equipment and the Role of Distortion in Rock Music'. *Current Musicology*, 105, pp. 75–106.

Herbst, J.-P. (2021). '"It just Is My Inner Refusal": Innovation and Conservatism in Guitar Amplification Technology'. In: A. Moore & G. Bromham (Eds.). *Distortion in Music Production*. London: Routledge *(forthcoming)*.

Herbst, J.-P. & Albrecht, T. (2018). 'The Skillset of Professional Studio Musicians in the German Popular Music Recording Industry'. *Etnomusikologian vuosikirja (The Finnish Yearbook of Ethnomusicology)*, 30, pp. 121–153.

Herbst, J.-P.; Czedik-Eysenberg, I. & Reuter, C. (2018). 'Guitar Profiling Technology in Metal Music Production: Public Reception, Capability, Consequences and Perspectives'. *Metal Music Studies*, 4(3), pp. 481–506.

Herbst, J.-P. & Vallejo, A. P. (2021). *Rock Guitar Virtuosos. Advances in Electric Guitar Playing, Technology and Culture*. Cambridge: Cambridge University Press.

Hepworth-Sawyer, R. (2020). *Gender in Music Production*. London: Routledge.

Hesmondhalgh, D. (1998). 'Globalisation and Cultural Imperialism. A Case Study of the Music Industry'. In: R. Kiely & P. Marfleet (Eds.). *Globalism and the Third World*. London: Routledge, pp. 163–184.

Hewson, C. (2016). 'Research Design and Tools for Online Research'. In: N. G. Fielding, R. M. Lee & G. Blank (Eds.). *The SAGE Handbook of Online Research Methods* (2. ed.). London: Sage, pp. 57–75.

Hills, M. (2002). *Fan Cultures*. Oxon: Routledge.

Hobsbawm, E. & Ranger, T. (Eds.) (1983). *The Invention of Tradition*. Cambridge: Cambridge University Press.

Hoch, S. J. & Loewenstein, G. F. (1991). 'Time-Inconsistent Preferences and Consumer Self-Control'. *Journal of Consumer Research*, 17(4), pp. 492–507.

Holbrook, M. B. & Hirschman, E. C. (1982). 'The Experiential Aspects of Consumption: Consumer Fantasies, Feelings, and Fun'. *Journal of Consumer Research*, 9 (September), pp. 132–140.

Holland, L. (2013). *Guitar Gear FAQ*. Kindle.

Holliday, L. & Weeks, O. (2007). *Ultimate Drum Play-Along: Green Day*. Milwaukee: Hal Leonard.

Hornby, N. (1995). *High Fidelity*. London: Victor Gollancz.

Hug, T. & Poscheschnik, G. (2010). *Empirisch Forschen*. Wien: UTB.

Hurwitz, T. (2013). *The Serious Guitarist. Essential Book of Gear: A Comprehensive Guide to Guitars, Amps, and Effects for the Dedicated Guitarist*. Van Nuys: Alfred Publishing.

Iervolino, A. C.; Perroud, N.; Fullana, M. A.; Guipponi, M.; Cherkas, L.; Collier, D. A. & Mataix-Cols, D. (2009). 'Prevalence and Heritability of Compulsive

Hoarding: A Twin Study'. *American Journal of Psychiatry*, 166(10), pp. 1156–1161.

Ind, N. & Rondino, M. C. (2001). 'Branding the Web: A Real Revolution'. *Journal of Brand Management*, 9(1), pp. 8–19.

Jackson, B. (2006). *Grateful Dead Gear: All the Band's Instruments, Sound Systems and Recording Sessions From 1965–1995*. San Francisco: Backbeat Books.

James, J. P. (2017). *Paul Kossoff: All Right Now: The Guitars, The Gear, The Music*. Leicester: Matador.

Janetzko D. (2016). 'Nonreactive Data Collection Online'. In: N. G. Fielding, R. M. Lee & G. Blank (Eds.). *The SAGE Handbook of Online Research Methods* (2. ed.). London: Sage, pp. 75–91.

Jansson, S. (2010). '"Listen to These Speakers". Swedish Hi-Fi Enthusiasts, Gender, and Listening'. *IASPM Journal*, 1(2), pp. 1–11.

Jauk, W. (2009). *Popmusic + MedienKunst: Der musikalisierte Alltag der digital culture*. Osnabrück: epOs Music.

Jenkins, H. (1992). *Textual Poachers: Television Fans and Participatory Culture*. Oxon: Routledge.

Jenkins, M. (2007). *Analog Synthesizers: Understanding, Performing, Buying – From the Legacy of Moog to Software Synthesis*. London: Focal Press.

Johnson, C. (2004). *Greatest Hits Signature Licks for Bass Guitar: Red Hot Chili Peppers*. Milwaukee: Hal Leonard.

Jones, S. (1992). *Rock Formation: Music, Technology, and Mass Communication*. Newbury Park: Sage.

Jones, S. E. (2006). *Against Technology. From the Luddites to Neo-Luddism*. New York: Routledge.

Julien's Auction (2019). 'Property from the Estate of Walter Becker'. https://www.julienslive.com/m/view-auctions/catalog/id/312; accessed 23 July 2020.

Kaiser, C. (2017). 'Analog Distinction – Music Production Processes and Social Inequality'. *Journal on the Art of Record Production*, 11. https://www.arpjournal.com/asarpwp/analog-distinction-music-production-processes-and-social-inequality; accessed 5 August 2020.

Karas, S. (2014). *50 Syncopated Snare Drum Solos: A Modern Approach for Jazz, Pop, and Rock Drummers*. Milwaukee: Hal Leonard.

Karch, M. (2020). 'How to Do a Boolean Search in Google'. *Lifewire*. https://www.lifewire.com/boolean-search-terms-google-1616810; accessed 14 July 2020.

Keightley, K. (2001). 'Reconsidering Rock'. In: S. Frith, W. Straw & J. Street (Eds.). *The Cambridge Companion to Pop and Rock*. Cambridge: Cambridge University Press, pp. 109–142.

Kelle, U. & Erzberger, C. (2010). 'Qualitative und quantitative Methoden: Kein Gegensatz'. In: U. Flick, E. v. Kardorff & I. Steinke (Eds.). *Qualitative Forschung. Ein Handbuch*. Reinbek bei Hamburg: Rowohlt, pp. 299–309.

Kellett, S. & Bolton, J. V. (2009). 'Compulsive Buying: A Cognitive–Behavioural Model'. *Clinical Psychology and Psychotherapy*, 16, pp. 83–99.

Kim, E. (2012). '10 Tips on How to Cure Yourself of GAS'. http://erickimphoto graphy.com/blog/2012/03/04/10-tips-on-how-to-cure-yourself-of-gas-gear-acquisition-syndrome; accessed 31 January 2019.

Kitts, J. & Tolinski, B. (2002). *The 100 Greatest Guitarists of All Time*. Milwaukee: Hal Leonard.

Koenigstorfer, J.; Groeppel-Klein, A. & Kamm, F. (2014). 'Healthful Food Decision Making in Response to Traffic Light Color-Coded Nutrition Labeling'. *Journal of Public Policy & Marketing*, 33(1), pp. 65–77.

Koran, L. M.; Faber, R. J.; Aboujaoude, E.; Large, M. D. & Serpe, R. T. (2006). 'Estimated Prevalence of Compulsive Buying Behaviour in the United States'. *American Journal of Psychiatry*, 163, pp. 1806–1812.

Kovarsky, J. (2013). *Keyboard for Dummies*. New York: For Dummies.

Kozinets, R. V. (1999). 'E-Tribalized Marketing? The Strategic Implications of Virtual Communities of Consumption'. *European Management Journal*, 17, pp. 252–264.

Kozinets, R. V. (2020). *Netnography. The Essential Guide to Qualitative Social Media Research*. London: Sage.

Kwisses, J. (2015). 'Gear Acquisition Syndrome – How to Get More Tone with Less Gear'. http://www.kwisses.ca/blog/gear-acquisition-syndrome-gas-how-to-get-more-tone-with-less-gear; accessed 31 January 2019.

Langford, S. (2011). *The Remix Manual*. Oxford: Focal Press.

Längler, M.; Nivala, M. & Gruber, H, (2018). 'Peers, Parents and Teachers: A Case Study on How Popular Music Guitarists Perceive Support for Expertise Development from "Persons in the Shadows"'. *Musicae Scientiae*, 22(2), pp. 224-243.

Lave, J. & Wenger, E. (1991). *Situated Learning: Legitimate Peripheral Participation*. Cambridge: Cambridge University Press.

Le Bon, C. (2017). 'Guitars Were Inspired by Female Bodies. Why Are They Uncomfortable for Women to Play?'. *The Guardian*. https://www.theguard ian.com/music/2017/jan/26/cate-le-bon-first-guitar-designed-for-women-st-vin cent; accessed 16 July 2019.

Ledermann, N. (2015). *Absolute Beginners: Electronic Drums*. London: Music Sales.

Lee, M. S. W.; Fernandez, K. V. & Hyman, M. R. (2009). 'Anti-Consumption: An Overview and Research Agenda'. *Journal of Business Research*, 62(2), pp. 145–47.

Lee, M. S. W.; Roux, H. C. D. & Cova, B. (2011). 'Anti-Consumption and Consumer Resistance: Concepts, Concerns, Conflicts, and Convergence'. *European Journal of Marketing*, 45(11/12), pp. 1680–1685.

Legge, C. (2011). 'Why Guitars are a GAS'. *Daily Mail*, 4 March 2011, p. 66.

Lehdonvirta, V. (2012). 'A History of the Digitalization of Consumer Culture'. In: M. Molesworth & J. Denegri-Knott (Eds.). *Digital Virtual Consumption*. London: Routledge, pp. 11–28.

Lejoyeux, M.; Ades, J.; Tassain, V. & Solomon, J. (1996). 'Phenomenology and Psychopathology of Uncontrolled Buying'. *American Journal of Psychiatry*, 153, pp. 1524–1529.

Leonhardt, S. (2015). 'GAS Powered'. http://www.guitarnoise.com/lessons/gas-powered; accessed 31 January 2019.

Lévi-Strauss, C. (1962). *La Pensée sauvage (The Savage Mind)*. Paris: Plon.

Lévi-Strauss, C. (1963). *Totemism*. Boston: Beacon.

Lewitt, D. (2015). *How to Play Rock*. Milwaukee: Hal Leonard.

Leyshon, A. (2009). 'The Software Slump? Digital Music, the Democratisation of Technology, and the Decline of the Recording Studio Sector within the Musical Economy'. *Environment and Planning A*, 49, pp. 1309–1331.

Linville, P. (1987). 'Self-Complexity as a Cognitive Buffer Against Stress-Related Illness and Depression'. *Journal of Personality and Social Psychology*, 52, pp. 663–676.

Lo, H.-Y. & Harvey, N. (2011). 'Shopping without Pain: Compulsive Buying and the Effects of Credit Card Availability in Europe and the Far East'. *Journal of Economic Psychology*, 32(1), pp. 79–92.

Lo, H.-Y. & Harvey, N. (2012). 'Effects of Shopping Addiction on Consumer Decision-Making: Web-Based Studies in Real Time'. *Journal of Behavioral Addictions*, 1(4), pp. 162–170.

Long, M. M. & Schiffman, L. G. (1997). 'Swatch Fever: An Allegory for Understanding the Paradox of Collecting'. *Psychology and Marketing*, 14, pp. 495–509.

Maalsen, S. & McLean, J. (2018). 'Record Collections as Musical Archives: Gender, Record Collecting, and Whose Music is Heard'. *Journal of Material Culture*, 23, pp. 39–57.

MacKay, H. (1997). *Consumption and Everyday Life*. London: Sage.

Macnamara, B. N. & Maitra, M. (2019). 'The Role of Deliberate Practice in Expert Performance: Revisiting Ericsson, Krampe & Tesch-Römer (1993)'. *Royal Society Open Science*, 6: 190327. http://dx.doi.org/10.1098/rsos.190327

Magee, A. (1994). 'Compulsive Buying Tendency as a Predictor of Attitudes and Perceptions'. *Advances in Consumer Research*, 21, pp. 590–594.

Maloof, R. (2004). *Jim Marshall. The Father of Loud. The Story of the Man Behind the World's Most Famous Guitar Amplifiers*. San Francisco: Backbeat Books.

Markham, A. (2012). 'Fabrication as Ethical Practice: Qualitative Inquiry in Ambiguous Internet Contexts'. *Information, Communication and Society*, 5(3), pp. 334–353.

Marrington, M. (2017). 'From DJ to Djent-Step: Technology and the Re-Coding of Metal Music Since the 1980s'. *Metal Music Studies*, 3(2), pp. 251–268.

Marten, N. (2008). 'Jimi Hendrix Week: "I played Jimi's Woodstock Strat"'. *Music Radar*. https://www.musicradar.com/news/guitars/jimi-hendrix-week-i-played-jimis-woodstock-strat-178118; accessed 14 July 2019.

Martin, J. (2008). 'Consumer Code: Use-Value, Exchange-Value, and the Role of Virtual Goods in Second Life'. *Journal of Virtual Worlds Research*, 1(2), pp. 2–21.

Marx, K. (1867). *Capital: A Critique of Political Economy*. Vol. 1. New York: International Publishers.

Mason, R. S. (1981). *Conspicuous Consumption: A Study of Exceptional Consumer Behaviour*. Farnborough: Gower.

Mataix-Cols, D.; Frost, R. O.; Pertusa, A.; Clark, L. A.; Saxena, S.; Leckman, J. F.; Stein, D. J.; Matsunaga, H. & Wilhelm, S. (2010). 'Hoarding Disorder: A New Diagnosis for DSM-V?'. *Depression and Anxiety*, 27(6), pp. 1–17.

Mayring, P. (2014). *Qualitative Content Analysis: Theoretical Foundation, Basic Procedures and Software Solution*. Klagenfurt. http://nbn-resolving.de/urn:nbn:de:0168-ssoar-395173; accessed 5 August 2020.

McAlister, L. (1982). 'A Dynamic Attribute Satiation Model of Variety-Seeking Behavior'. *Journal of Consumer Research*, 9(2), pp. 141–150.

McClelland, D. (1951). *Personality*. New York: Holt, Rinehart & Winston.

McCourt, T. (2005). 'Collecting Music in the Digital Realm'. *Popular Music and Society*, 28(2), pp. 249–252.

McCracken, G. (1986). 'Culture and Consumption: A Theoretical Account of the Structure and Movement of the Cultural Meaning of Consumer Goods'. *Journal of Consumer Research*, 13, pp. 71–84.

McCracken, G. (1988). *Culture and Consumption: New Approaches to the Symbolic Character of Consumer Goods and Activities*. Bloomington: University of Indiana Press.

McElroy, S. L.; Keck, P. E.; Pope, H. G.; Smith, J. M. R. & Strakowski, S. M. (1994). 'Compulsive Buying: A Report of 20 Cases'. *The Journal of Clinical Psychiatry*, 55(6), pp. 242–248.

McElroy, S. L.; Satlin, A.; Pope, H. G.; Keck, P. E. & Hudson, J. (1991). 'Treatment of Compulsive Shopping with Antidepressants: A Report of Three Cases'. *Annals of Clinical Psychiatry*, 3(3), pp. 199–204.

McGuire, S. & Van Der Rest, N. (2015). *The Musical Art of Synthesis*. London: Focal Press.

McIntosh, W. D. & Schmeichel, B. (2004). 'Collectors and Collecting: A Social Psychological Perspective'. *Leisure Sciences*, 26, pp. 85–97.

McMahon, C. (2015). 'Don't Be that Guy: Is Sexism Hurting Guitar Shops?'. https://reverb.com/news/dont-be-that-guy-is-sexism-hurting-guitar-shops; accessed 31 January 2019.

Menze, J. & Gembris, H. (2018). '"Played it till my Fingers Bled": Domain-Related Fields of Practicing and Gaining Expertise in Popular Music'. http://doi.org/10.13140/RG.2.2.28718.77123

Menze, J. & Gembris, H. (2019). 'Expertiseerwerb in der populären Musik: Ergebnisse einer quantitativen Vergleichsstudie'. In: H. Gembris, J. Menze & A. Heye (Eds.). *Jugend musiziert. Musikkulturelle Vielfalt im Diskurs*. Münster: LIT, pp. 165–190.

Merriam-Webster (2019.). 'Syndrome'. https://www.merriam-webster.com/dictionary/syndrome; accessed 24 June 2019.

Mick, D. G. & Demoss, M. (1990). 'Self-Gifts: Phenomenological Insights from Four Contexts'. *Journal of Consumer Research*, 17(3), pp. 322–32.

Middleton, R. (1990). *Studying Popular Music*. Buckingham: Open University Press.

Miège, B. (1979). 'The Cultural Commodity'. *Media, Culture and Society*, 1, pp. 297–311.

Molenda, M. (2017). 'Who Will Save the Guitar?'. https://www.guitarplayer.com/gear/who-will-save-the-guitar; accessed 31 January 2019.

Montoya, D. Y. & Scott, M. L. (2013). 'The Effect of Lifestyle-Based Depletion on Teen Consumer Behavior'. *Journal of Public Policy & Marketing*, 32(1), pp. 82–96.

Moore, A. F. (2001). *Rock the Primary Text: Developing a Musicology of Rock* (2. ed.). Aldershot: Ashgate.

Moore, A. F. (2012). *Song Means: Analysing and Interpreting Recorded Popular Song*. Farnham: Ashgate.

Moore, A. F. & Dockwray, R. (2010). 'The Establishment of the Virtual Performance Space in Rock'. *twentieth-century music*, 5(2), pp. 219–241.

Moorefield, V. (2010). *The Producer as Composer. Shaping the Sounds of Popular Music*. London: MIT Press.

Morton, D. (2000). *Off the Record. The Technology and Culture of Sound Recording in America*. New Brunswick: Rutgers University Press.

Mueller, A.; Mitchell, J. E.; Crosby, E. D.; Glaesmer, H. & de Zwaan, M. (2009). 'The Prevalence of Compulsive Hoarding and Its Association with Compulsive Buying in a German Population-Based Sample'. *Behaviour Research and Therapy*, 47(8), pp. 705–709.

Muesterberger, W. (1994). *Collecting: An Unruly Passion: Psychological Perspectives*. Princeton: Princeton University Press.

Muniz, A. & O'Guinn, T. (2001). 'Brand Community'. *Journal of Consumer Research*, 27(4), pp. 412–432.

Mynett, M. (2011). 'Sound at Source: The Creative Practice of Re-Heading, Dampening and Drum Tuning for the Contemporary Metal Genre'. *Journal on the Art of Record Production*, 5. https://www.arpjournal.com/asarpwp/sound-at-source-the-creative-practice-of-re-heading-dampening-and-drum-tuning-for-the-contemporary-metal-genre; accessed 28 June 2019.

Mynett, M. (2017). *Metal Music Manual. Producing, Engineering, Mixing, and Mastering Contemporary Heavy Music*. Oxon: Routledge.

Myrseth, K. O. R.; Fishbach, A. & Trope, Y. (2009). 'Counteractive Self-Control When Making Temptation Available Makes Temptation Less Tempting'. *Psychological Science*, 20(2), pp. 159–163.

Nakajima, S. (2012). 'Prosumption in Art'. *American Behavioral Scientist*, 56(4), pp. 550–569.

Negus, K. & Pickering, M. (2004). *Creativity, Communication and Cultural Value*. London: Sage.

Nicholls, G. (2008). *The Drum Book: A History of the Rock Drum Kit*. Milwaukee: Hal Leonard.

Nicholls, G. & Nicholls, J. (2004). *The Drum Handbook*. Lanham: Rowman & Littlefield.

Niu, W. & Sternberg, R. (2006). 'The Philosophical Roots of Western and Western Conceptions of Creativity'. *Journal of Theoretical and Philosophical Psychology*, 26, pp. 18–38.

Nordsletten, A. E.; de la Cruz, L. F.; Billotti, D & Mataix-Cols, D. (2013). 'Finders Keepers: The Features Differentiating Hoarding Disorder from Normative Collecting'. *Comprehensive Psychiatry*, 54, pp. 229–237.

Nordsletten, A. E. & Mataix-Cols, D. (2012). 'Hoarding versus Collecting: Where does Pathology Diverge from Play?'. *Clinical Psychology Review*, 32, pp. 165–176.

North, A. C. & Hargreaves, D. J. (1999). 'Music and Adolescent Identity'. *Music Education Research*, 1(1), pp. 75–92.

O'Guinn, T. & Faber, R. (1989). 'Compulsive Buying. A Phenomenological Exploration'. *Journal of Consumer Research*, 16 (September), pp. 147–157.

O'Grady, P. (2019). 'The Politics of Digitizing Analogue Recording Technologies'. In: R. Hepworth-Sawyer, J. Hodgson & M. Marrington (Eds.). *Producing Music*. London: Routledge, pp. 119–133.

O'Shea, K. (2017). *50 Essential Warm-Ups for Drums: Powerful Drum Exercises to Improve Control, Speed and Endurance*. Hove: Fundamental Changes.

Oldenburg, R. (1999). *The Great Good Place*. New York: Marlowe.

Olmsted, A. D. (1991). 'Collecting: Leisure, Investment or Obsession?'. *Journal of Social Behaviour and Personality*, 6, pp. 287–306.

Orton-Johnson, K. (2014). 'Knit, Purl and Upload: New Technologies, Digital Mediations and the Experience of Leisure'. *Leisure Studies*, 33, pp. 305–321.

Paier, D. (2010). *Quantitative Sozialforschung. Eine Einführung*. Wien: Facultas Verlag.

Papageorgi, I.; Creech, A.; Haddon, E.; Morton, F.; de Bezenac, C.; Himonides, E.; Potter, J.; Duffy, C.; Whyton, T. & Welch, G. (2010). 'Perceptions and Predictions of Expertise in Advanced Musical Learners'. *Psychology of Music*, 38(1), pp. 31-61.

Pearce, S. M. (1995). *On Collecting: An Investigation into Collecting in the European Tradition*. London: Routledge.

Pearce, S. M. (1998a). 'Objects in the Contemporary Construction of Personal Culture: Perspectives Relating to Gender and Socio-Economic Class'. *Museum Management and Curatorship*, 17(3), pp. 223–241.

Pearce, S. M. (1998b). *Collecting in Contemporary Practice*. London: SAGE.

Pejrolo, A. & Metcalfe, S. B. (2017). *Creating Sounds from Scratch. A Practical Guide to Music Synthesis for Producers and Composers*. New York: Oxford University Press.

Pertusa, A.; Frost, R. O. & Mataix-Cols, D. (2010). 'When Hoarding is a Symptom of OCD: A Case Series and Implications for DSM-V'. *Behavior Research and Therapy*, 48(10), pp. 1012–1020.

Peters, T. (2013). 'Horsham Cycling Rider Profile. Meet Tim Peters'. https://www.horshamcycling.co.uk/joomla15/files/chainline/ChainLineMar 13.pdf; accessed 24 June 2019.

Pietrykowski, B. (2007). 'Exploring New Directions for Research in the Radical Political Economy of Consumption'. *Review of Radical Political Economics,* 39(2), pp. 257–283.

Pinch, T. (2001). 'Why You Go to a Music Store to Buy a Synthesizer. Path Dependence and the Social Construction of Technology'. In: R. Garud & P. Karnoe (Eds.). *Path Dependence and Creation.* Hove: Psychology Press, pp. 381–399.

Pinch, T. & Reinecke, D. (2009). 'Technostalgia: How Old Gear Lives on in New Music'. In: K. Bijsterveld & J. van Dijck (Eds.). *Sound Souvenirs. Audio Technologies, Memory and Cultural Practices.* Amsterdam: Amsterdam University Press, pp. 152–166.

Pinch, T. J. & Trocco, F. (2002). *Analog Days: The Invention and Impact of the Moog Synthesizer.* Cambridge: Harvard University Press.

Porcello, T. (2004). 'Speaking of Sound: Language and the Professionalization of Sound-Recording Engineers'. *Social Studies of Science,* 34(5), pp. 733–758.

Power, R. & Parker, M. (2015). '7 Stages of Gear Acquisition Syndrome'. http://www.musicradar.com/news/guitars/7-stages-of-gear-acquisition-syndro me-585947; accessed 31 January 2019.

Prown, P. & Sharken, L. (2003). *Gear Secrets of the Guitar Legends. How to Sound Like Your Favorite Players.* San Francisco: Backbeat Books.

PRS Foundation (2017). 'Women Make Music. Evaluation 2011–2016'. http://www.prsformusicfoundation.com/wp-content/uploads/2017/03/PRS-Fou ndation-Women-Make-Music-evaluation-report-2017-FINAL.pdf; accessed 5 August 2020.

Prus, R. & Dawson, L. (1991). 'Shop 'til You Drop: Shopping as Recreational and Laborious Activity'. *Canadian Journal of Sociology,* 16, pp. 145–164.

Rasch, B.; Friese, M.; Hofmann, W. & Naumann, E. (2006). *Quantitative Methoden. Einführung in die Statistik* (2. ed.). Heidelberg: Springer Medizin Verlag.

Redden, J. P. (2008). 'Reducing Satiation: The Role of Categorization Level'. *Journal of Consumer Research,* 34(5), pp. 624–634.

Redden, J. P. & Haws, K. L. (2013). 'Healthy Satiation: The Role of Decreasing Desire in Effective Self-Control'. *Journal of Consumer Research,* 39(5), pp. 1100–1114.

Reekie, G. (1993). *Temptations: Sex, Selling, and the Department Store.* St. Leonards: Allen & Unwin.

Reitsamer, R. (2012). 'Female Pressure: A Translocal Feminist Youth-Oriented Cultural Network'. *Continuum*, 26(3), pp. 399–408.

Rejino, R. (2002). 'In Unison: What's Right with Being Personal?'. *American Music Teacher*, 52(3), pp. 4–6.

Rensen, M. & Stösser, V. (2011). *Guitar Heroes*. Bergkirchen: PPV Medien.

Reskin, B. F. & Roos, P. A. (1990). *Job Queues, Gender Queues. Explaining Women's Inroads into Male Occupations*. Philadelphia: Temple University Press.

Reynolds, S. (2012). *Retromania: Pop Culture's Addiction to its Own Past*. London: Faber and Faber.

Rheingold, H. (1993). *The Virtual Community: Homesteading on the Electronic Frontier*. Cambridge: MIT Press.

Rideout, E.; Fortner, S. & Gallant, M. (Ed.) (2008). *Keyboard Presents the Best of the 80s: The Artists, Instruments, and Techniques of an Era*. San Francisco: Backbeat Books.

Ridgeway, C. L. (2011). *Framed by Gender: How Gender Inequality Persists in the Modern World*. New York: Oxford University Press.

Rigby, D. & Rigby, E. (1944). *Lock, Stock and Barrel: The Story of Collecting*. Philadelphia: J. B. Lippincott.

Riley, J. (2015). *Survival Guide for the Modern Drummer: A Crash Course in All Musical Styles for Drumset*. Van Nuys: Alfred Publishing.

Ritzer, G. (2012). '"Hyperconsumption" and "Hyperdebt": A Hypercritical Analysis'. In: R. Brubaker, R. W. Lawless & C. J. Tabb (Eds.). *A Debtor World. Interdisciplinary Perspectives on Debt*. New York: Oxford University Press, pp. 60–80.

Ritzer, G. (2015). 'Prosumer Capitalism'. *The Sociological Quarterly*, 56, pp. 413–445.

Ritzer, G.; Dean, P. & Jurgenson, N. (2012). 'The Coming of Age of the Prosumer'. *American Behavioral Scientist*, 56, pp. 379–398.

Ritzer, G. & Jurgenson, N. (2010). 'Production, Consumption, Prosumption'. *Journal of Consumer Culture*, 10, pp. 13–36.

Robair, G. (2015). 'Rough Mix: Relieving GAS'. https://www.emusician.com/how-to/rough-mix-relieving-gas; accessed 31 January 2019.

Rogers, E. N. (2003). *Diffusion of Innovations* (5. ed.). New York: Free Press.

Rook, D. W. (1985). 'The Ritual Dimension of Consumer Behavior'. *Journal of Consumer Research*, 12(3), pp. 251–264.

Rook, D. W. (1987). 'The Buying Impulse'. *Journal of Consumer Research*, 14 (September), pp. 189–199.

Rook, D. W. & Fisher, R. J. (1995). 'Normative Influences on Impulsive Buying Behavior'. *Journal of Consumer Research*, 22(3), pp. 305–313.

Rook, D. W. & Gardner, M. P. (1993). 'In the Mood: Impulse Buying's Affective Antecedents'. In: J. Arnold-Costa & E. C. Hirschman (Eds.). *Research in Consumer Behavior*. Greenwich: JAI, pp. 1–28.

Rötter, G. & Steinberg, R. (2018). 'Die Musikerpersönlichkeit'. In: A. C. Lehmann & R. Kopiez (Eds.). *Handbuch Musikpsychologie*. Bern: Hogrefe, pp. 435–460.

Rubin, D. (2018). *100 Great Guitarists and the Gear that Made them Famous*. Milwaukee: Hal Leonard.

Rudess, J. (2009). *Dream Theater Keyboard Experience: Featuring Jordan Rudess*. Van Nuys: Alfred Music.

Russ, M. (2008). *Sound Synthesis and Sampling*. London. Focal Press.

Ryan, J. & Peterson, R. A. (2001). 'The Guitar as Artifact and Icon: Identity Formation in the Babyboom Generation'. In: A. Bennett & K. Dawe (Eds.). *Guitar Cultures*. New York: Berg, pp. 89–116.

Samuels, J. F.; Bienvenu, J. O.; Grados, M. A.; Cullen, B.; Riddle, M. A.; Liang, K.-Y.; Eaton, W. W. & Nestadt, G. (2008). 'Prevalence and Correlates of Hoarding Behavior in a Community-Based Sample'. *Behavior Research and Therapy*, 46(7), pp. 836–844.

Sandvoss, C. (2005). *Fans. Mirror of Consumption*. Cambridge: Polity Press.

Sargent, C. (2009). 'Playing, Shopping, and Working as Rock Musicians: Masculinities in "De-Skilled" and "Re-Skilled" Organizations'. *Gender & Society*, 23, pp. 665–687.

Sarinana, J. (2013). 'The Science of G.A.S'. http://petapixel.com/2013/08/03/the-fear-to-photograph-and-the-gear-acquisition-problem; accessed 31 January 2019.

Scapelitti, C. (2016). 'The Top Five Signature Models of Women Guitarists'. *Guitar World*. https://www.guitarworld.com/gear/top-five-signature-models-women-guitarists; accessed 16 July 2019.

Schäfer, T. & Sedlmeier, P. (2018). 'Musik im Alltag: Wirkungen, Funktionen und Präferenzen'. In: A. C. Lehmann & R. Kopiez (Eds.). *Handbuch Musikpsychologie*. Bern: Hogrefe, pp. 247–271.

Schlosser, S.; Black, D. W.; Repertinger, S. & Freet, D. (1994). 'Compulsive Buying: Demography, Phenomenology, and Comorbidity in 46 Subjects'. *General Hospital Psychiatry*, 16, pp. 205–212.

Schmidt-Horning, S. (2004). 'Engineering the Performance: Recording Engineers, Tacit Knowledge and the Art of Controlling Sound.' *Social Studies of Science*, 34(5), pp. 703–731.

Schmidt-Horning, S. (2013). *Chasing Sound. Technology, Culture & the Art of Studio Recording from Edison to the LP*. Baltimore: John Hopkins University Press.

Schroedl, S. (2003). *Drum Tuning: The Ultimate Guide*. Milwaukee: Hal Leonard.

Schröter, J. & Volmar, A. (2016). 'HiFi hören. HiFi-Praxis für kritische Käufer und Fachhändler: Eine Fallstudie zum Problem der Analyse historischer Medienpraktiken'. In: B. Ochsner & R. Stock (Eds.). *senseAbility - Mediale Praktiken des Sehens und Hörens*. Bielefeld: transcript, pp. 149–168.

Scippa, G. (n.d.). 'St. Vincent Designs the First Electric Guitar for Women'. *Lifegate*. https://www.lifegate.com/people/lifestyle/st-vincent-designs-first-guitar-for-women; accessed 16 July 2019.

Semeonoff, B. (1949). *Record Collecting: A Guide for Beginners*. Chislehurst: Oakwood Press.

Sennett, R. (2008). *The Craftsman*. New Haven: Yale University Press.

Shankar, A.; Elliott, R. & Fitchett, J. A. (2009). 'Identity, Consumption and Narratives of Socialization'. *Marketing Theory*, 9, pp. 75–94.

Sheldon, D. A. & Price, H. E. (2005). 'Gender and Instrumentation Distribution in an International Cross-Section of Wind and Percussion Ensembles'. *Bulletin of the Council for Research in Music Education*, 163, pp. 43–51.

Shepherd, B. K. (2013). *Refining Sound: A Practical Guide to Synthesis and Synthesizers*. Oxford: Oxford University Press.

Sherif, M.; Harvey, O. J.; White, B. J.; Hood, W. & Sherif, C. (1961). *Intergroup Conflict and Cooperation: The Robbers Cave Experiment*. Norman: University of Oklahoma Institute of Intergroup Relations.

Sherman, J. E. (2011). 'Gear Acquisition Syndrome: Lustily Buying More Tools Than You Need'. *Psychology Today*. https://www.psychologytoday.com/gb/blog/ambigamy/201110/gear-acquisition-syndrome-lustily-buying-more-tools-you-need; accessed 28 July 2020.

Shove, E. (2003). *Comfort, Cleanliness and Convenience: The Social Organization of Normality*. New York: Berg.

Shuker, R. (2010). *Wax Trash and Vinyl Treasures: Record Collecting as a Social Practice*. Burlington: Ashgate.

Shuker, R. (2013). 'Record Collecting and Fandom'. In: M. Duffett (Ed.). *Popular Music Fandom. Identities, Roles and Practices*. London: Routledge, pp. 342–381.

Siddiqui, S. & Turley, D. (2006). 'Extending the Self in a Digital World'. In: C. Pechmann & L. Price (Eds.). *Advances in Consumer Research*, Vol. 33. Duluth: Association for Consumer Research, pp. 647–648.

Sidwell, J. & Dickinson J. (2011). *Complete Guitar Manual: The Step-by-Step Guide to Playing Like a Pro*. London: DK.

Siemens, J. C. & Kopp, S. W. (2011). 'The Influence of Online Gambling Environments on Self-Control'. *Journal of Public Policy & Marketing*, 30(2), pp. 279–293.

Skinner, B. F. (1938). *The Behavior of Organisms: An Experimental Analysis*. New York: Appleton-Century.

Sklar, A. (2008). 'I Want My MP3: Music Collecting in the Digital Age'. In: S. Koppelman & A. Franks (Eds.). *Collecting and the Internet: Essays on the Pursuit of Old Passions Through New Technologies*. Jefferson: McFarland, pp. 81–95.

Slutsky, A. & Silverman, C. (1997). *Funkmasters: The Great James Brown Rhythm Sections, 1960–73: For Guitar, Bass and Drums*. Burbank: Warner Bros.

Smith, A. (1776). *An Inquiry into the Nature and Causes of the Wealth of Nations*. London: Strahan & Cadell.

Smith, G. D. (2017). *Sound Advice for Drummers*. Scotts Valley: Create Space Independent Publishing Platform.

Snoman, R. (2009). *Dance Music Manual*. Oxford: Focal Press.

Solie, R. (1995). *Musicology and Difference: Gender and Sexuality in Music Scholarship*. Berkeley: University of California Press.

Speed, B. (2010). *Beginners Guide to Electric Guitar: Gear, Technique, and Tons of Riffs*. Van Nuys: Alfred Publishing.

Spinoza, B. (2000). *Ethics*. Oxford: Oxford University Press.

Standell-Preston, R. (2018). 'Why I Fought the Sexist Gear Community (And Won)'. *Pitchfork*. https://pitchfork.com/thepitch/why-i-fought-the-sexist-gear-community-and-won-braids-raphaelle-standell-preston; accessed 8 July 2019.

Standifird, S. S.; Roelofs, M. R. & Durham, Y. (2005). 'The Impact of eBay's Buy it Now Function on Bidder Behaviour'. *International Journal of Electronic Commerce*, 9(2), pp. 167–76.

Stebbins, R. A. (2009). *Leisure and Consumption: Common Ground/Separate Worlds*. Houndmills: Palgrave Macmillan.

Steinkuehler, C. & Williams, D. (2006). 'Where Everybody Knows Your (Screen) Name: Online Games as "Third Places"'. *Journal of Computer-Mediated Communications*, 11(4), pp. 885–909.

Stent, E. (2019). 'British vs. American Amps – What's the Difference?'. *Andertons*. https://blog.andertons.co.uk/learn/british-vs-american-amps; accessed 27 May 2020.

Stockton, N. (2014). *The Worship Bass Book: Bass, Espresso, and the Art of Groove*. Milwaukee: Hal Leonard.

Stone, G. (1954). 'City Shoppers and Urban Identification: Observation on the Social Psychology of City Life'. *American Journal of Sociology*, 60, pp. 36–45.

Storr, A. (1983). 'The Psychology of Collecting'. *Connoisseur*, 213, pp. 35–38.

Strauss, A. (1987). *Qualitative Analysis for Social Scientists*. Cambridge: Cambridge University Press.

Straw, W. (1997). 'Sizing Up Record Collections. Gender and Connoisseurship in Rock Music Culture'. In: S. Whiteley (Ed.). *Sexing the Groove: Popular Music and Gender*. London: Routledge, pp. 3–16.

Straw, W. (2000). 'Music as Commodity and Material Culture'. *Repercussions*, 7-8, pp. 147–172.

Strong, J. (2012). *Home Recording for Musicians for Dummies*. Hoboken: Wiley.

Styvén, M. (2010). 'The Need to Touch: Exploring the Link between Music Involvement and Tangibility Preference'. *Journal of Business Research*, 63(9–10), pp. 1088–1094.

Subkowski, P. (2006). 'On the Psychodynamics of Collecting'. *The International Journal of Psychoanalysis*, 87, pp. 383–401.

Süer, M. & Alexander, J. (2017). *Rock Drumming for Beginners: How to Play Rock Drums for Beginners. Beats, Grooves and Rudiments*. Hove: Fundamental Changes.

Taylor, T. D. (2001). *Strange Sounds: Music, Technology & Culture*. New York: Routledge.

Théberge, P. (1993). *Consumers of Technology: Musical Instrument Innovations and the Musicians' Market*. PhD thesis, Montreal: Concordia University.

Théberge, P. (1997). *Any Sound You Can Imagine: Making Music/Consuming Technology*. Hanover: Wesleyan University Press.

Théberge, P. (2001). '"Plugged In": Technology and Popular Music'. In: S. Frith, W. Straw & J. Street (Eds.). *The Cambridge Companion to Pop and Rock*. Cambridge: Cambridge University Press, pp. 3–25.

The Choral Journal (1980). 'How to Choose a Music Store'. *The Choral Journal*, 20(8), pp. 49–49.

Thomann (2019). 'Thomann's Gearhead University'. https://www.thomann.de/blog/en/tgu19-summercamp; accessed 26 April 2020.

Thompson, C. J.; Locander, W. B. & Pollio, H. R. (1990). 'The Lived Meaning of Free Choice: An Existential-Phenomenological Description of Everyday Consumer Experiences of Contemporary Married Women'. *Journal of Consumer Research*, 17(3), pp. 346–361.

Tierney, J. (2011). 'Urge to Own that Clapton Guitar is Contagious, Scientists Find'. *The New York Times*. https://www.nytimes.com/2011/03/09/science/09guitar.html; accessed 28 July 2020.

Toffler, A. (1980). *The Third Wave*. New York: William Morrow.

Toscano, J. (2019). *Filling in the Grooves: The Ultimate Guide to Drum Fills*. Van Nuys: Alfred Music.

Tuan, Y.-F. (1980). 'The Significance of the Artifact'. *Geographical Review*, 70, pp. 462–472.

Tuchman, G. & Fortin, N.E. (1984). 'Fame and Misfortune. Edging Women out of the Great Literary Tradition'. *American Journal of Sociology*, 90(1), pp. 72–96.

Turner, F. (2016). *The Road Beneath My Feet*. London: Headline.

Turner, V. (1982). *From Ritual to Theatre*. New York: PAJ Publications.

Uimonen, H. (2016). 'Celebrity Guitars: Musical Instruments as Luxury Items'. *Rock Music Studies*, 4, pp. 117–135.

Vail, M. (1993). *Vintage Synthesizers: Groundbreaking Instruments and Pioneering Designers of Electronic Music Synthesizers*. San Francisco: Miller Freeman Books.

Vail, M. (2014). *The Synthesizer: A Comprehensive Guide to Understanding, Programming, Playing, and Recording the Ultimate Electronic Music Instrument*. Oxford: Oxford University Press.

Välimäki, V. & Reiss, J. D. (2016). 'All About Audio Equalization: Solutions and Frontiers'. *Applied Sciences*, 6(5), pp. 1–46.

Vohs, K. D. & Faber, R. J. (2007). 'Spent Resources: Self-Regulatory Resource Availability Affects Impulse Buying'. *Journal of Consumer Research*, 33(4), pp. 537–47.

Von Wartburg, I.; Rost, K. & Teichert, T. (2006). 'The Creation of Social and Intellectual Capital in Virtual Communities of Practice: Shaping Social Structure in Virtual Communities of Practice'. *International Journal of Learning and Change*, 1(3), pp. 299–316.

Waksman, S. (1999). *Instruments of Desire. The Electric Guitar and the Shaping of Musical Experience*. Cambridge: Harvard University Press.

Waksman, S. (2003). 'Reading the Instrument: An Introduction'. *Popular Music and Society*, 26, pp. 251–261.

Waksman, S. (2004). 'California Noise: Tinkering with Hardcore and Heavy Metal in Southern California'. *Social Studies of Science*, 34(5), pp. 675–702.

Walser, R. (1993). *Running with the Devil. Power, Gender, and Madness in Heavy Metal Music*. Middletown: Wesleyan University Press.

Wang, J.; Zhao, X. & Bamossy. G. J. (2009). 'The Sacred and the Profane in Online Gaming: A Netnographic Inquiry of Chinese Gamers'. In: N. T. Wood & M. R. Solomon (Eds.). *Virtual Social Identity and Consumer Behavior*. Armonk: M. E. Sharpe, pp. 109–124.

Warde, A. (2005). 'Consumption and Theories of Practice'. *Journal of Consumer Culture*, 5, pp. 131–153.

Warner, T. (2003). *Pop Music – Technology and Creativity: Trevor Horn and the Digital Revolution*. Aldershot: Ashgate.

Webley, P.; Burgoyne, C.; Lea, S. & Young, B. (2001). *The Economic Psychology of Everyday Life*. Hove: Psychology Press.

Weissberg, D. (2010). 'Zur Geschichte elektroakustischer Instrumente aus dem Blickwinkel der Körperlichkeit'. In: M. Harenberg & D. Weissberg (Eds.). *Klang (ohne) Körper: Spuren und Potenziale des Körpers in der elektronischen Musik*. Bielefeld: transcript, pp. 91–104.

Wenger, E. (1998). *Communities of Practice: Learning, Meaning, and Identity*. Cambridge: Cambridge University Press.

Wheeler, B. (2000). *More Drum Techniques of Rush: Drum Transcriptions*. Van Nuys: Alfred Publishing.

Williams, A. (2015). 'Technostalgia and the Cry of the Lonely Recordist'. *Journal on the Art of Record Production*, 9. https://www.arpjournal.com/asarpwp/tech nostalgia-and-the-cry-of-the-lonely-recordist; accessed 5 August 2020.

Williams, D. (2015). 'Tracking Timbral Changes in Metal Productions from 1990 to 2013'. *Metal Music Studies*, 1(1), pp. 39–68.

Wolfenden, D. (2016). 'Breaking Down the Marine Aquarium'. *UltraMarine Magazine*, 59, pp. 66–73.

Wolfle, P. (2013). 'Luna Guitars: Not for Women Only'. https://www.guitar-muse.com/luna-guitars-women-8023; accessed 10 August 2019.

Woodfield, K. (Eds.) (2018). *The Ethics of Online Research*. Bingley: Emerald.

Wright, J. (2006). *GAS! Living with Guitar Acquisition Syndrome*. Raleigh: Lulu.

Wych, G. M. F. (2012). 'Gender and Instrument Associations, Stereotypes, and Stratification'. *Update: Applications of Research in Music Education*, 30, pp. 22–31.

Yuksel, U. (2013). 'Non-Participation in Anti-Consumption: Consumer Reluctance to Boycott'. *Journal of Macromarketing*, 33(3), pp. 204–216.

Zagorski-Thomas, S. (2014). *The Musicology of Production*. Cambridge: Cambridge University Press.

Zak, A. (2001). *The Poetics of Rock: Cutting Tracks, Making Records*. Berkeley: University of California Press.

Zalot, M. C. (2013). 'Buying "Time" on eBay: Cybertime, Nostalgia, and Currency in Online Auctions'. *Atlantic Journal of Communication*, 21(1), pp. 17–28.

Zeiner-Henriksen, H. T. (2006). 'A Comparative Study of Changes in Bass Drum Sounds from 70s Disco to Electronic Dance Music of the 1980s and 1990s'. http://folk.uio.no/hanst/Edinburgh/Comparison.htm; accessed 28 June 2019.

Zervoudakes, J. & Tanur, J. M. (1994). 'Gender and Musical Instruments: Winds of Change'. *Journal of Research in Music Education*, 42(1), pp. 58–67.

Zubraski, D. & Jenner, C. (2001). *Fast Forward: Hip-Hop Drum Patterns*. London: Wise Publications.

Appendix

A: List of Musicians' Forums Used in the Acquisition of Participants

- https://forum.bandmix.com
- https://talkbass.com
- https://www.guitarforbeginners.com/forums
- https://cafesaxophone.com
- https://themodernvocalist.com
- https://acousticguitarforums.com/forum
- https://www.ultimate-guitar.com/forums
- https://forum.saxontheweb.net/forum.php
- https://basschat.co.uk
- https://www.trumpetherald.com/forum
- https://www.harmonycentral.com/forum
- https://www.ozbassforum.com
- https://www.drummerworld.com/forums
- https://www.soundonsound.com/forum
- http://guitarplayersforum.boards.net

B: Classification of Genres

Tab. 6. Classification of Genres

Genre	n
Classical/Worship/Instrumental	**101**
Classical music	40
Worship/Religious music/Gospel/Spiritual	40
Instrumental	21
Jazz/Blues/Soul/Funk	**187**
Jazz	89
Blues/Soul	66
Funk	28
World music/Salsa/Latin	3
Reggae/Ska	1
Pop/Folk/Rock&Roll	**127**
Pop	48
Singer/Songwriter/Folk	45
Rock&Roll/Rockabilly	24
Country/Western	10
Rock/Alternative/Punk	**130**
Classic/Hard/Surf rock	73
Alternative/Independent rock/Grunge	35
Punk	13
Brit pop	9
Metal/Progressive/Hardcore	**56**
Progressive/Psychedelic rock/Metal	21
Extreme metal	15
Heavy/Hair/Power metal	13
Hardcore/Grindcore	4
Nu rock/Nu metal	3

C: Item-Scale-Statistics

Tab. 7. Scale Statistics of Quantitative Study

Scale	M	min.	max.	SD
General GAS	4.55	1.00	7.00	1.05
I often think about new musical gear.	5.12	1.00	7.00	1.68
I like to buy new gear just for the variety.	3.83	1.00	7.00	1.88
I sometimes spend more money on musical gear than I intend to.	4.56	1.00	7.00	1.81
I sometimes buy instruments knowing I won't play them frequently.	3.60	1.00	7.00	1.95
After buying, it usually won't take long until I search for another piece of gear.	3.46	1.00	7.00	1.78
You can never have enough gear.	4.04	1.00	7.00	2.07
I like to search for information on musical gear (online, magazines, trade shows).	5.74	1.00	7.00	1.40
I like to visit music stores.	5.12	1.00	7.00	1.66
For me, testing and buying gear is just as appealing as playing.	3.70	1.00	7.00	1.73
I enjoy owning a lot of gear.	4.46	1.00	7.00	1.79
I am willing to save money to buy new gear.	5.33	1.00	7.00	1.51
I often look out for special deals.	4.88	1.00	7.00	1.66
I like the thrill of hunting for gear.	4.39	1.00	7.00	1.79
I sometimes feel the strong urge to own a particular piece of gear.	5.46	1.00	7.00	1.52
I feel euphoric after buying new gear.	4.78	1.00	7.00	1.66
Looking out for new gear distracts me from other tasks.	3.82	1.00	7.00	1.92
My gear is an important part of my life.	4.70	1.00	7.00	1.62
Collectors	2.81	1.00	7.00	1.65
I buy gear because it's rare or unique.	3.18	1.00	7.00	1.93
I consider myself a collector.	2.44	1.00	7.00	1.75
Modification and Fabrication	3.10	1.00	7.00	1.39
I like to modify my gear.	3.66	1.00	7.00	1.87
Most ready-made gear profits from modification.	3.47	1.00	7.00	1.59
I regularly vary with the modifications to my gear.	2.73	1.00	7.00	1.66
I like to fabricate musical gear myself.	2.56	1.00	7.00	1.89
Relationships*	3.44	1.00	7.00	1.45
My partner/family influences my buying decision.	3.28	1.00	7.00	1.99
I try not to spend too much money on gear because of my partner/family.	4.18	1.00	7.00	1.95
I feel the need to justify my buying of instruments to my partner/family.	3.55	1.00	7.00	2.00
My partner/family is annoyed by spotting me buying new gear.	2.77	1.00	7.00	1.81

Vintage	3.52	1.00	7.00	1.27
I like vintage gear.	4.42	1.00	7.00	1.77
I am willing to pay more money for authentic rebuilds or relics.	2.83	1.00	7.00	1.67
I like a road-worn look.	2.98	1.00	7.00	1.82
Older gear sounds better.	3.24	1.00	7.00	1.58
Vintage gear doesn't become outdated by technological innovation.	4.14	1.00	7.00	1.76
Technophilia	3.61	1.00	6.60	1.10
I am interested in the latest music technology.	4.76	1.00	7.00	1.79
I replace gear with more modern pieces.	3.11	1.00	7.00	1.52
One has to keep up with trends in music technology.	3.41	1.00	7.00	1.80
I'm afraid that my gear / sound may become outdated.	1.90	1.00	7.00	1.13
I value the functionality of modern gear.	4.89	1.00	7.00	1.47
Nostalgia	4.21	1.00	7.00	1.43
I keep the instruments I played in my early years.	4.12	1.00	7.00	2.15
I like instruments being played in the past (e.g. 40s swing, 70s rock).	4.27	1.00	7.00	1.78
Some of my instruments remind me of my past.	4.42	1.00	7.00	1.97
Selling instruments feels like giving away a part of myself.	4.06	1.00	7.00	1.97
Band as GAS Motivator**	3.35	1.00	7.00	1.51
I upgrade my gear when joining a group.	2.71	1.00	7.00	1.69
I invest into gear more when playing in a group.	3.77	1.00	7.00	1.94
New instruments of my bandmates inspire me to think about my gear.	3.32	1.00	7.00	1.81
I extend my gear collection when playing in a group.	3.38	1.00	7.00	1.85
The more groups I play in, the more different gear I need.	3.59	1.00	7.00	1.92
Democratic Purchases in Bands**	2.23	1.00	7.00	1.36
I ask my bandmates for their opinion before I buy new gear.	2.67	1.00	7.00	1.74
My bandmates have a say when choosing gear.	1.79	1.00	7.00	1.25
Role Models	2.34	1.00	6.00	1.08
I like to play the same gear as my favourite musician(s).	2.82	1.00	7.00	1.74
I like to buy signature instruments.	2.12	1.00	7.00	1.45
With new music preferences, I am thinking about changing my gear.	2.96	1.00	7.00	1.76
When my favourite musicians change their gear, I am also inclined to do so.	1.45	1.00	7.00	.94

Genre Requirements	3.72	1.00	7.00	1.28
I need particular gear for every style or genre.	2.76	1.00	7.00	1.65
Certain instrument models are characteristic for genres.	4.61	1.00	7.00	1.68
Instruments are connected to sounds of their times (e.g. the 80s).	3.97	1.00	7.00	1.70
You cannot play a specific style with every piece of gear.	3.55	1.00	7.00	1.86
Expressiveness	4.40	1.00	7.00	1.35
New gear helps me overcome my limitations.	3.04	1.00	7.00	1.73
New gear improves my sound.	4.60	1.00	7.00	1.63
New gear extends my tonal variety.	4.86	1.00	7.00	1.57
New gear inspires me.	5.23	1.00	7.00	1.61
New gear affects my compositions.	3.87	1.00	7.00	1.99
New gear enhances my expressiveness.	4.37	1.00	7.00	1.76
New gear helps me get the sound I'm hearing in my head.	4.93	1.00	7.00	1.70
New gear helps me keep my playing vivid.	4.27	1.00	7.00	1.77
Experimentation	4.01	1.00	7.00	1.29
Having a personal sound is important to me.	5.23	1.00	7.00	1.56
Having an innovative sound is important to me.	3.94	1.00	7.00	1.71
I use new gear to develop my personal sound.	4.24	1.00	7.00	1.75
I like to use gear in an unconventional way.	3.16	1.00	7.00	1.83
My development as a musician is linked to experimenting with gear.	3.50	1.00	7.00	1.88
Sound Exploring	4.41	1.00	7.00	1.39
I try to understand every nuance of my gear's sound.	4.95	1.00	7.00	1.68
I am willing to spend time to get to know how the sound of my gear is put together (e.g. sound settings, mechanics).	5.17	1.00	7.00	1.63
Tweaking my rig takes as much time as playing and practicing.	3.11	1.00	7.00	1.80

Note: Measured on a 7-point Likert scale: 1 = "strongly disagree" – 7 = "strongly agree"; * = only considers respondents who state that they live in a partnership; ** = only considers respondents who state that they play in one or more groups (bands/orchestras)

D: Correlation Matrix of Scales

Tab. 8. Correlation Matrix of Scales

	General GAS	Collectors	Technophilia	Vintage	Nostalgia	Modification and Fabrication	Relationships
General GAS		.396**	.290**	.232**	.306**	.302**	.241**
Collectors	.396**		-	.349**	.238**	.264**	-
Technophilia	.290**	-		-.118**	-	.267**	.094*
Vintage	.232**	.349**	-.118**		.433**	.132**	-
Nostalgia	.306**	.238**	-	.433**		.186**	.115*
Modification & Fabrication	.302**	.264**	.267**	.132**	.186**		.130**
Relationships	.241**	-	.094*	-	.115*	.130**	
Band as GAS Motivator	.505**	.184**	.161**	.160**	.248**	.284**	.220**
Democratic Purchases in Bands	.206**	-	-	-	.129**	.207**	.147**
Role Models	.372**	.196**	.243**	.298**	.260**	.237**	.144**
Genre Requirements	.305**	.206**	.215**	.164**	.237**	.221**	-
Expressiveness	.493**	.185**	.344**	.096*	.239**	.335**	.182**
Experimentation	.405**	.287**	.320**	.208**	.206**	.413**	.129**
Sound Exploring	.336**	.172**	.373**	.087*	.154**	.419**	.117**

Note: $* p < .05$; $** p < .01$

	Band as GAS Motivator	Democratic Purchases in Bands	Role Models	Genre Requirements	Expressive-ness	Experimen-tation	Sound Exploring
General GAS	.505**	.206**	.372**	.305**	.493**	.405**	.336**
Collectors	.184**	-	.196**	.206**	.185**	.287**	.172**
Technophilia	.161**	-	.243**	.215**	.344**	.320**	.373**
Vintage	.160**	-	.298**	.164**	.096*	.208**	.087*
Nostalgia	.248**	.129**	.260**	.237**	.239**	.206**	.154**
Modification & Fabrication	.284**	.207**	.237**	.221**	.335**	.413**	.419**
Relationships	.220**	.147**	.144**	-	.182**	.129**	.117**
Band as GAS Motivator		.469**	.376**	.339**	.516**	.326**	.219**
Democratic Purchases in Bands	.469**		.265**	.240**	.277**	.238**	.176**
Role Models	.376**	.265**		.317**	.380**	.319**	.178**
Genre Requirements	.339**	.240**	.317**		.439**	.320**	.249**
Expressiveness	.516**	.277**	.380**	.439**		.542**	.382**
Experimentation	.326**	.238**	.319**	.320**	.542**		.517**
Sound Exploring	.219**	.176**	.178**	.249**	.382**	.517**	

Note: $* p < .05; ** p < .01$

Index